Gabriel García Márquez
in Retrospect

Gabriel García Márquez in Retrospect

A Collection

Edited by
Gene H. Bell-Villada

LEXINGTON BOOKS
Lanham • Boulder • New York • London

Published by Lexington Books
An imprint of The Rowman & Littlefield Publishing Group, Inc.
4501 Forbes Boulevard, Suite 200, Lanham, Maryland 20706
www.rowman.com

Unit A, Whitacre Mews, 26-34 Stannary Street, London SE11 4AB

Copyright © 2016 by Lexington Books

All rights reserved. No part of this book may be reproduced in any form or by any electronic or mechanical means, including information storage and retrieval systems, without written permission from the publisher, except by a reviewer who may quote passages in a review.

British Library Cataloguing in Publication Information Available

Library of Congress Cataloging-in-Publication Data
ISBN: 978-1-4985-3338-6 (cloth : alk. paper)
eISBN: 978-1-4985-3339-3

∞™ The paper used in this publication meets the minimum requirements of American National Standard for Information Sciences—Permanence of Paper for Printed Library Materials, ANSI/NISO Z39.48-1992.

Printed in the United States of America

To all Gabo fans, everywhere

Contents

Acknowledgments	ix
Introduction: García Márquez: His Vast Range, His Varied Legacy *Gene H. Bell-Villada*	xi

PART I: OEUVRE, BACKGROUNDS, LEGACY — 1

1. Gabriel García Márquez: Writer for the World — 3
   Nicholas Birns and Juan E. De Castro

2. Gabriel García Márquez: Politics and Death across His Life of Writing — 21
   Regina Janes

3. Translation and Apprenticeship: Cervantes, Faulkner, and García Márquez — 41
   Edith Grossman

4. García Márquez and *Mamagallismo*: On Fatigued Roosters, Resistance, Sense of Humor, and the Colombian Character — 49
   Marcela Velasco

PART II: RE-READING THE HISTORY OF MACONDO — 65

5. Names and Narrative Pattern in *One Hundred Years of Solitude* — 67
   Gene H. Bell-Villada

6. The Enlightened Blindness of Úrsula Iguarán — 77
   María del Mar López-Cabrales

Contents

7   Satire, Ecocentrism, and Luddite Discourse in *One Hundred Years of Solitude:* Regional Approaches for a Global Environmental Crisis   89
    William Flores

8   Rediscovering Ice: García Márquez, Aira, and Vallejo on Chilling Memories   103
    Héctor Hoyos

PART III: LATER WORKS   **115**

9   After the End: Bolívar in the Labyrinth of History   117
    Michael Wood

10 The Magic of Love, the Horrors of Death, and Other Themes in the Short Stories of Gabriel García Márquez   129
    Rubén Pelayo

11 Gabriel García Márquez: Pilgrimage and Gastronomy   147
    Fernando Valerio-Holguín

12 Reading Illness in Gabriel García Márquez's *Of Love and Other Demons*   165
    Olivia Vázquez-Medina

13 Translation, Unreliable Narrators, and the Comical Use of (Pseudo-)Magical Realism in *Of Love and Other Demons*   183
    Ignacio López-Calvo

PART IV: OTHER GENRES, OTHER MEDIA   **195**

14 Felt History and the Permutations of the Fictional, Real, and Autobiographical "I" in Gabriel García Márquez's *Chronicle of a Death Foretold* and *Living to Tell the Tale*   197
    Robert L. Sims

15 Big-Screen Adaptations of Two Gabriel García Márquez Novels: A Reappraisal   213
    Rudyard J. Alcocer and Haley Osborn

16 Remembering Broadway's *Chronicle of a Death Foretold*   231
    Zhanna Gurvich

Permissions   243

Index   245

About the Contributors   255

Acknowledgments

I wish to express my sincere thanks to Professor María del Mar López-Cabrales and her colleagues at Colorado State University, and to Professor Angela Willis and the executive board of the Southeastern Conference of Latin American Studies (SECOLAS), who, by inviting me to speak at their respective symposia, availed me of the opportunity to craft and present my reflections on Gabriel García Márquez and also to absorb the ideas of others. To them I owe a good portion of the contents of this collection.

I am enormously grateful to Lindsey Porambo, Acquisitions Editor at Lexington Books, who first saw the potential of this project and encouraged me to pursue it. Her ongoing advice and guidance over the past year and a half have proved invaluable in bringing this venture to fruition.

I am indebted to Williams College and its generous sabbatical policy that allowed me a semester's leave to commit to this book full-time through Spring 2016.

Finally, I thank all of my fellow contributors to this volume, whose learned essays have helped shed further light on one of the literary masters of our age, now sadly departed.

¡A todos, mil gracias!

Introduction

García Márquez

His Vast Range, His Varied Legacy

Gene H. Bell-Villada

The great novelist Gabriel García Márquez died in Mexico City on 17 April 2014, at age 87. In the wake of his passing, we are gathering these essays in homage to his total oeuvre, and to some of his later works in particular.

Both in its internal range and its wider, real-world impact, the writing of García Márquez has few equals. To many readers of this volume, what I will be saying about the Colombian master may be well-trod territory. Yet there are truths that bear being told more than once.

With his masterpiece, *Cien años de soledad* (1967; trans. *One Hundred Years of Solitude*, 1970), the thirty-seven year old author-journalist brought off a kind of artistic miracle. To wit, it's a novel that depicts the broadest possible range of human experience, from birth to death, from war to all sorts of peacetime, from life private to life public. A novel that touches upon a widely encompassing gamut of human emotions, from wonder to grief, love and loss, comedy to tragedy, motherliness to ribaldry. A novel that gathers in its pages a teeming variety of human types, from chieftains to bureaucrats, soldiers to holy innocents, syndicalists to hedonists, hustlers, tinkerers, and a scholarly recluse. Beyond all this, the novel integrates within its small-town family saga the vast legacy of high literary Modernism, with lessons learned from Joyce, Faulkner, Virginia Woolf, and Kafka, yet bringing it off so seamlessly that one is scarcely conscious of savoring what one might accurately think of as an "experimental" or even avant-garde work.

Even the origins of the book are nothing short of miraculous. How it got written is in itself a story worth retelling. Between 1961 and 1964, García Márquez was burdened by a terrible writer's block, he really believing he'd never write again. Then, in 1965, as he and his wife and two sons were riding in their white Opel on the Mexico City-Acapulco highway, he suddenly realized he could imagine the novel that he'd been trying to write since 1942.

And so, he did a U-turn and asked his spouse Mercedes to handle the family finances for a few months while he spewed out this novel. For eighteen months, it turned out, he hid in his room, feverishly writing eight hours a day while Mercedes pawned off all their belongings and friends provided emergency loans. A year and a half later there were a ten thousand dollar debt and a thick manuscript called *Cien años de soledad*.

The publishing history of the book adds to the miracle. According to the author himself, both he and its Argentine publisher had expected his novel to go slowly but steadily through its first printing of then thousand copies. Well, the original press run sold out in just one month, mostly at news stands in Buenos Aires subway stations. Soon the volume was taking the continent by storm, with reports of ordinary folks talking about it in buses and readers raving about it in whatever settings books mattered. It became one of the best-selling literary novels ever, with tens of millions sold in Latin America and in forty translations across the globe.

Cien años remains a best-seller today, not just in college courses or among literati, but also among people who simply like to read for pleasure. In my travels in Colombia I've encountered nurses and entrepreneurs, civil servants, traveling salesmen, and high school students, all of whom knew García Márquez's work and expressed pride in it. Moreover, they'd refer to him by his nickname, Gabo, as I too shall now be doing from time to time here. Outside of Colombia I've met Chinese, Russian, Japanese, Italian, French, Turkish, and of course American fans who have read the book in their native tongue and marveled at it. Probably no other late-twentieth-century literary work has achieved such world diffusion and celebrity on artistic grounds alone. The ultimate miracle of this action-packed book was its showing that great literature can be exciting, moving, and sheer fun all at once.

Within literary history, *One Hundred Years of Solitude* represents something new. For the first time, a full-length novel that was neither pure fantasy nor standard-issue science fiction was depicting a series of magical, unreal events as they cropped up in recognizable, palpable, everyday places. Few precedents exist for this sort of thing, among them Nikolai Gogol's short story "The Nose," about a Russian government employee whose nose escapes its owner one morning and is seen strolling around the streets of St. Petersburg, and of course Franz Kafka's "The Metamorphosis," which starts right off with its commercial-traveler protagonist Gregor Samsa, transformed into a bug in his bourgeois apartment. Kafka's novella, it bears mention, had a crucial formative influence on young Gabo, who saw in it a way to get beyond traditional realism in narrative.

"Magical realism" is the term usually invoked in characterizing *Cien años* and Gabo's other fictions of that ilk. And indeed the magic is there, famously so. A priest who is trying to raise funds for a church levitates six inches off the ground, always after sipping some hot chocolate. The funeral of the Buendía family founder is accompanied by a rain of yellow flowers, which need to be removed with picks and shovels the next day. A beautiful young virgin rises to heaven as she hangs up the wash (and she waves good-bye during her ascension). An auto mechanic always arrives surrounded by a swarm of yellow butterflies. At the same time, however, these magical instances go hand in hand with some aspect, or some concrete object, of real life, as we've just seen.

In the equation "magical realism," then, the "realism" portion carries equal weight. García Márquez's everyday world is not some fanciful, mystical, imaginary realm, but rather the ordinary, such quotidian realms as a tropical small town or an anonymous Caribbean republic, in either of which the mundane and the magical mingle freely. Gabo is not J.R.R. Tolkien; nor is he Walt Disney. It's not for nothing that García Márquez always thought of himself as "a realist writer," with the caveat that, in his own words, "Reality is not restricted to the price of tomatoes." Reality to him also comprises the common people's folk beliefs and legends, even their superstitions. What people believe about their reality is also part of that reality.

In addition, García Márquez is one of the great writers on social topics such as civil war, labor struggles and their suppression, political divisions and intrigues, barracks dictatorship, occupation by foreign military troops, the oppression of women via the cult of virginity, and more. Subject matters such as these are the familiar stuff of social and left-wing protest literature, a species of writing that can too easily go out of date. By mixing these events with magic, however, the author succeeds in avoiding any heavy-handed preachiness or didacticism. Hence, when describing the massive repression of the banana-company workers in *One Hundred Years*, Gabo masterfully distracts from the blood and gore by bringing in a number of magical occurrences. There's the fugitive labor leader, José Arcadio Segundo, who is rendered invisible to an army officer's gaze while hiding in the gipsy Melquíades's room. There's the overnight erasure of the memory of the three thousand dead strikers by official government propaganda. And there's the rainstorm that lasts four years, eleven months, and two days, putting an end to future labor talks, and leaving the town of Macondo in ruins.

Similarly, Gabo's second great novel, *El otoño del patriarca* (1975; trans. *The Autumn of the Patriarch*, 1978), depicts a fairly typical Latin American dictator. The continent has seen hundreds of such literary as well as journalist accounts, most of them now languishing in library stacks. Gabo did model his imaginary dictator after real-life tyrants such as Venezuela's Juan Vicente Gómez, the Dominican Republic's Trujillo, and Nicaragua's Somoza clan. But he magically outdoes these rather crude and banal despots via outrageous exaggeration, rendering outsized everything associated with the tinpot tyrant, giving the martinet a reign of possibly two hundred years, and assigning to him uncanny intuitive, even ESP capacities, that facilitate his grip on power. The climax of the novel involves the dictator's outright sale of the Caribbean Sea to the US military occupiers, who put the water into numbered crates and ship it off to the deserts of Arizona, probably the most amazing spoof of American imperialism in literary history.

What helps further enrich and sustain these episodes as well as the entirety of both these books is their humor. Gabo is, quite simply, one of literature's great comic writers, with *One Hundred Years* among the funniest masterworks ever written, and with *Patriarch* not far behind. Many of those magical episodes are in themselves funny—imagine the very notion of an auto mechanic surrounded by yellow butterflies. But there are other brands of drollery, too. For example, there's the far-fetched incongruity of the founder José Arcadio Buendía's scientific researches, his desire to make a magnifying glass into a naval weapon, or his obsession with taking a daguerreotype of God, or his grandiose declaration while at dinner that "The earth is round like an orange." There's cartoon-style farce in the literally earth-shaking return of world navigator José Arcadio and his oft-repeated, laconic, one-word greeting, "Buenas" ("Hello"); in his Indian arm-wrestling with five guys at the barroom and winning; and in the prostitutes who pay *him* for their bodily pleasures. Or there's the relentless eating, imbibing, and fornicating of Aureliano Segundo, one of literature's unforgettable portraits of total dissipation.

Much of the humor in *One Hundred Years* is sexual or scatological, as is the episode in which Pilar Ternera seduces and deflowers an adolescent José Arcadio by first throwing him over her shoulder like a sack of potatoes; or the golden, emblazoned chamber pot in which upper-class snob Fernanda del Carpio does her physical necessities. Many of the countless jokes in Gabo's history of Macondo involve urinating, evacuating, or the sex act, yet without so much as a hint of locker-room sexism or vulgarity. The humor in *Patriarch* is even more outrageous, and brings levity to the horrors inevitably depicted in that novel, but I shall spare readers those details for the time being. On a related note, even the strike scenes in *Cien años* have their dollops of humor, for instance the sextet of company lawyers dressed in frock coats and top hats in the tropical heat, who argue with all sorts of fancy sophistry that, actually, the banana workers do not exist; or the company infirmary that dispenses a copper-colored pill for any conceivable malady; or the little kids who line up to get their hands on those all-purpose medications and then use them as bingo markers.

There's another side of García Márquez that is scarcely recognized: namely, that he is one of the supreme novelists of romantic love. *One Hundred Years of Solitude* comes brim-filled with all manner of love stories, from teen-age crushes and conjugal love to a torrid obsession, a ménage à trois, and an impassioned true love that finalizes in *Liebestod*, in love-death.

And in *The Autumn of the Patriarch*, it is the female object of desire, Leticia Nazareno, who ends up conquering, controlling, and in some ways surpassing the dictator. In later works Gabo thoroughly alters the familiar formulas of the love genre. The short novel *Eréndira* (1972; trans. *Innocent Eréndira and Other Stories*, 1978) spoofs the fairy-tale narrative about courtship and living happily ever after. In *Crónica de una muerte anunciada* (1981; trans. *Chronicle of a Death Foretold*, 1983), the author subverts the expected outcome of a grand public wedding, leading us through an abrupt post-nuptial separation and twists of plot that go on for twenty-three years plus two thousand love letters sent by the rebellious bride to her arrogant groom, who simply accumulates her missives without so much as opening them, and who shows up one day with the letters stuffed in a suitcase and says to her, "Well, here I am."

Not accidentally, two of García Márquez's later novels feature the word "amor" in their respective titles. *El amor en los tiempos del cólera* (1985; trans. *Love in the Time of Cholera*, 1988) tells of a romance between two adolescents that is cut short under orders of the thirteen-year-old girl's social-climbing father. In one of those outcomes that is known to occur in real life but that it took a visionary Gabo to imagine and invent, the amour is re-stoked and indeed consummated only when the twosome are well into their seventies. (The joys and wonders of Eros, in Gabo's magical world, are not exclusively for the young!) Another book, *Del amor y otros demonios* (1994; trans. *Of Love and Other Demons*, 1995), a somewhat neglected yet one of Gabo's most beautiful works, traces the chaste but intense companionship that develops between a thirtyish, scholarly, librarian priest and an ethereal yet vital twelve-year-old girl in eighteenth-century Cartagena. The love interest moreover is placed within a larger context of black slavery, Afro-Hispanic religion, Spanish colonialism, and the intellectual and human ravages of the Holy Inquisition. Gabo's experimentalism as literary pioneer even manifests itself in so well-pedigreed a topic as is male-female romance. In this book, I believe, he comes close to, perhaps surpasses what Vladimir Nabokov did in his *Lolita*, with which Gabo's book shares certain obvious similarities.

The cultural legacy of García Márquez runs deep. He has bequeathed to us an oeuvre that comprises a fair number of genuine book-length masterpieces as well as a couple of dozen highly subtle, formally perfect, and deeply moving short stories. And of course his readership, his fan base, is something world-wide. For a fiction writer of such reach and stature we would have to look back to the nineteenth century, when Charles Dickens and Victor Hugo could spin forth novels that brimmed with issues of social justice, winning the hearts and minds of millions in the process.

García Márquez has also left behind a model allowing free rein to the fictional imagination in the United States and elsewhere. The imprint of Gabo's magical realism and of his everyday ghosts can be seen in Nobel laureate Toni Morrison's richly textured novels of African-American life, notably *Beloved* (1987). Or in William Kennedy's novelized evocations of his native town of Albany, New York, notably *Ironweed* (1983). Or in John Nichols's comic fiction about northern New Mexico, *The Milagro Beanfield War* (1974). Or in Cristina García's lovely evocation of three generations of a Cuban family, both living and deceased yet present in spirits, in her *Dreaming in Cuban* (1992). Or in Robert Coover's extravaganza about the execution of the Rosenbergs, *The Public Burning* (1977). It's worth noting that William Kennedy as well as Robert Coover wrote admiringly about García Márquez back in the 1970s; they also speak fluent Spanish. (On a personal note, I might mention that Kennedy and my mother, Carmen Villada, worked briefly as colleagues at the *Daily Journal*, an English-language newspaper in Puerto Rico, in the 1950s.) In addition, the foregrounded magic in such films as Gregory Nava's *El Norte* (1983), and Alejandro González Iñárritu's *Birdman* (2014) may not have been possible without the originating influence of García Márquez.

The list of Gabo's American readers and admirers stretches even further, and higher. Let me explain. García Márquez never made a secret of his leftist political views and associations. And so, starting in 1961, his name started figuring regularly on the US immigration blacklist, in accordance with legislation dating back to the McCarthy era. From that year on, Gabo could enter the United States on a visa that allowed him visits only under special circumstances and that restricted his movements to a very limited radius. These conditions applied even at a time when his own son Rodrigo was attending Harvard College in the late seventies and early eighties. Well, in an interesting turn of events, the favorite novel of President Bill Clinton happened to be *One Hundred Years of Solitude*. And so, in 1994, Clinton met with Gabo himself, together with fellow novelists Carlos Fuentes and William Styron, on the island of Martha's Vineyard. In the wake of that social and literary encounter, the President went on to lift the immigration ban on this very dangerous individual called Gabriel García Márquez. The decision proved quite helpful when the author contracted lymphoma in 1999 and sought medical treatment at a highly specialized health center in Los Angeles, the city where his son Rodrigo, now a filmmaker, was residing.

Gabo did recover from the cancer and then survived another decade and a half, during which he went on to write his memoirs, *Vivir para contarla* (2002; trans. *Living to Tell the Tale*, 2003), and yet another love novel, *Memoria de mis putas tristes* (2004; trans. *Memories of My Melancholy Whores*, 2005). I cannot say for sure if either the preceding or succeeding Republican presidents, George H. W. Bush or George W. Bush, had ever read *One Hundred Years of Solitude*, or expressed admiration for the novel. However, it does seem as if Bill Clinton's tastes as a reader and his initiative as head of state helped prolong Gabo's life span, and allowed him the opportunity to come up with his last two books.

There are other ways in which García Márquez has made his mark on life outside the literary world. As many readers may know, *One Hundred Years* was a selection for Oprah's Book Club in 2004. (Incidentally, I served as a six-week consultant for that project.) And later, in 2007, the TV hostess chose Gabo's *Love in the Time of Cholera*. Yet another sign of the Colombian author's works having entered a larger domain and broader public consciousness can be found in newspapers, where it's not uncommon to see headlines saying, for instance, "**One Hundred Years of X**" or "**X Years of Solitude**," or "**Love or X in the Time of [whatever]**" or "**Chronicle of [this of that] Foretold**." (In one particularly humorous instance, an anonymous book on dog training entitled *Dogtology* has a subsection called "Love in the Time of Collars" [64].[1]) Such echoes crop up, naturally enough, in Spanish-language publications, and in French ones, too.

The proper noun "Macondo," moreover, has taken on a life of its own. I personally have seen a Macondo bookstore in New York, a Hotel Macondo in Santa Marta and a Farmacia Macondo in Barranquilla, and there is an excellent Latin pop song called "Los cien años de Macondo." Furthermore, in a bizarre irony, the BP oil rig that blew up in the Gulf of Mexico in 2010, killing eleven workers and polluting the sea waters and coastline, chanced to be called the Macondo oil well. I would have liked to know how Gabo felt about the name of his mythological small town becoming associated with a large-scale environmental catastrophe and human tragedy.

On yet another note: Some years ago I got to chatting about *One Hundred Years of Solitude* with a medical doctor from China whom I'd often see at our university's swimming pool. And at one point the good doctor remarked, "Ah, yes. You know, that episode about the massacre of banana workers? Well, it's just like what happened at Tiananmen Square!" He was referring, of course, to the horrendous killing of hundreds of Chinese student demonstrators that occurred on June 4, 1989, and also the official ban on any public discussion or commemoration of the event that followed. Political life, in that case, was imitating literary art and at its most blood-curdling and gruesome.

A couple of other casual if revealing signs of Gabo's presence in the most unexpected places are worth mention. In December 2015, I was visiting a pair of friends in Brussels. One pleasant afternoon we were strolling through a park. And standing on one of its streets was a big, white tourist bus that bore, in big, black letters, the telling inscription "**BUENDÍA TOURS**." An Internet search identified the outfit as a firm specializing in travel for Hispanics in Belgium and Holland.

A couple of weeks later, the syndicated US Latino comic strip *Baldo* featured in its colorful Sunday edition, dated 10 January 2016, an episode in which a schoolboy gives a girl a book. In the final of six frames, the twosome have this exchange: She remarks authoritatively, "The railroad represents the arrival of the modern world in Macondo." And he qualifies her statement, saying, "Yes, but it's also the beginning of the end for the village."[2] The cartoonists, Héctor D, Cantú and Carlos Castellanos, do not even bother to identify their volume by name or by author (www.gocomics.com/baldo/2016/01/10). García Márquez can at times seem ubiquitous.

I wish to add a personal reflection. I came of age as a student in the late 1960s, an era when, among other things, a great narrative literature was emerging from Latin America. *El boom de la novela*. The Boom of the Novel. That is how that cultural moment was known and is still known today. To our amazement and surprise, a region that had existed in world consciousness more as a land of volcanoes and earthquakes, of grinding poverty and vast inequities, of political conflict and military dictatorship, was suddenly coming up with a series of sophisticated, complex, and highly original works that were the equal of and a challenge to the Euro-American canon, bold narrative texts that were joining as well as altering what the French literary critic Pascale Casanova, in a book by that name, has called "the world republic of letters." It was a bit like living at a time when a feudal, peripheral Russia was producing authors on the order of Turgenev, Dostoevsky, Tolstoy, Chekhov, and others.

And amid that already rich harvest along came *Cien años de soledad*. I'll never forget the sheer wonder and boundless enthusiasm that Hispanic readers were expressing when talking about the book. I myself first read it in Spanish in 1969, and from the very start I was caught up in its intricate yet lucid web of words, stories, magic, politics, sex, romance, and humor. And I must confess: when I reached and finished its concluding sentence, in which the last Buendía, his family home, and the town of Macondo are all swept away by a windstorm, I broke down and cried, so moved and so spellbound did I find myself. To this day, I can still get occasional chills up my spine from re-reading that final passage. I knew back then that I would like to write about and teach this novel. Sharing the book with my students (in both Spanish and English) and with fellow readers—as in this volume—has been one of the joys of my life.

Our Section One, "Oeuvre, Backgrounds, Legacy," aims to provide overviews of the García Márquez phenomenon. Nicholas Birns's and Juan E. De Castro's "García Márquez: Writer for the World," after a brief look at the novelist's growth and achievement, gives us a panorama of Gabo's global, writerly presence on all six continents, Australia included. While some of the examples they cite—Edwidge Danticat, Toni Morrison, Salman Rushdie, US Latino authors—should come as no surprise, one is nonetheless astounded to see select British realists and Joyce Carol Oates's *Bellefleur* as yet other instances of "Marquezian" literary art (not to mention their passing reference to basketball coach Phil Jackson). All of these writers, Birns and De Castro point out, have succeeded in imagining and creating "Macondos" of their own. Looking into precedent farther in the past, the two scholars draw an interesting parallel with the sway once held by Walter Scott over nineteenth-century novelistic practitioners. Looking ahead, they offer an initial glimpse at the emerging, anti-Gabo backlash among subsequent fictionists in Latin America (e.g., the "McOndo" movement) who, in their "anxiety of influence," specifically define themselves as *not* belonging to the "magical" camp.

Mutability. Dying. Survivor's grief. These topics are arguably as old as narrative itself. The title of Regina Janes's eloquent meditation, "Gabriel García Márquez: Politics and Death across His Life of Writing," conjoins two salient preoccupations of the Colombian's existence, both as man and artist. As Janes accurately notes, the fact of death (or the imminence or threat thereof) is a near-obsession, a driving force throughout Gabo's oeuvre—from the raw, still-immature juvenilia hastily compiled in *Eyes of a Blue Dog* or the funeral in *Leaf Storm*, on through the two male deaths serving as catalysts in the first chapter of *Love in the Time of Cholera*, on up to the old-age struggle against breathing one's last in his swan song *Memories of My Melancholy Whores*. Although, as a onetime altar boy turned secular leftist, García Márquez presumably disbelieved in the afterlife, via magical realism he could bring back the dead as revenants in his transition tale "The Sea of Lost Time" or in the figures of Prudencio Aguilar and Melquíades in his most famous book. Conversely, politics, the other member of Janes's dyad, brings much death to Macondo and to the amoral Patriarch's fictive nation. The predominant geopolitics during Gabo's adult life, Janes reminds us, were that of decolonization and anti-imperialism, and in his public positions the author defined himself as such. Janes brings an original insight in this regard when she interprets the murder of Santiago Nasar in *Chronicle of a Death Foretold* as a kind of allegory for the tragic death of Socialist President Salvador Allende in Santiago, Chile.

The renowned translator Edith Grossman, in her graceful survey, "Translation and Apprenticeship: Cervantes, Faulkner, and García Márquez," elegantly notes how budding authors will often learn their day-to-day craft and higher art from the study of works made available to them in a tongue other than the one in which it first appeared. (She tellingly cites the instance of young Gabo's discovery of Joyce's *Ulysses*.) In this respect, Grossman traces a four-century legacy that stretches from Cervantes, via divers translators (including Smollett) on through novelists Fielding, Sterne, Flaubert, Twain, and Dostoevsky, and culminates in Faulkner, whose pathetic Southern heroes, like the Knight himself, devote themselves to pining and fighting for an illusory and idealized past. The Mississippian in his prose style retains the Spaniard's love of long, winding sentences, yet imbues them with his own innovative mode of circular, nonsequential narration—an approach then picked up on by his famous disciple from Colombia. García Márquez, along with his Latin American cohorts, in their effort to depict their multilayered societies and intersecting histories, strive to go beyond linearity in their story-telling, attempting to "say several things at once and evoke multiplicity." Grossman draws on an illuminating analogy with music, an art that, via harmony (and counterpoint) creates its own simultaneity—something that Gabo, Fuentes, and Vargas Llosa aim for in the musicality, as it were, of their narrative prose.

Political scientist Marcela Velasco anatomizes an untranslatable Spanish term and its complex, layered jocularity as it underlies Gabo's oeuvre via her seminal essay, "Gabriel García Márquez and *Mamagallismo*: On Fatigued Roosters, Resistance, Sense of Humor, and the Colombian Character." *Mamar gallo; mamador de gallo*: one encounters these notions frequently in Caribbean South America (as I did during my teens in 1950s Caracas). The concept is emblematic as a feature of what she designates "anti-solemn pranksters." In her highly erudite survey, Velasco first delves into the bewilderingly varied semantic subtleties of the phrase, then goes on to trace its oppositional spirit to numerous economic, geographic, and cultural sources—popular vs. élite, coastal vs. highlands, the "carnivalesque." These should come as no surprise for readers who know Colombia. Velasco breaks new ground, however, in demonstrating the influential role played by the indigenous Wayúu (Guajiro) culture and its oral traditions of "sarcasm, irony, and exaggeration." Among the Wayúu's institutions she notes the figure of the *pütchipü'ü*, an antic word-master who gives voice to issues ranging from ordinary drunkenness to broader sorts of conflicts. Significantly, in 2006, "a group of Wayúu word masters offered García Márquez a *guararo*..., a staff that identifies the authority of a *pütchipü'ü*." Velasco caps her illuminating performance with a look at *mamagallismo* in specific works by Gabo, the phrase actually cropping up in "Big Mama's Funeral" and in (of all places) *Chronicle of a Death Foretold* (a fleeting character had thought that the Vicario twins with their death threats were just "*mamando gallo*").

Few modern novels have elicited as much critical commentary as has *One Hundred Years of Solitude*. Yet as with all great works of art, its possibilities for exploration are all but limitless. We are pleased to offer four chapters shedding light on aspects of Gabo's iconic masterpiece.

The bewildering array of oft-repeated first names in the saga of the Buendías inevitably causes confusion for the book's first-time readers, who might even voice occasional frustration at this striking feature. In his essay, "Names and Narrative Pattern in *One Hundred Years of Solitude*," Gene H. Bell-Villada untangles and sets forth the rigorous naming system that underlies the numerous José Arcadios and Aurelianos, the Remedios girls and Amaranta/Úrsula women inhabiting the novel's pages. As Bell-Villada points out, certain personality traits are regularly assigned to one specific series of characters, while contrasting attributes are allotted to otherwise named personages. With the odd exception and seeming divergences scattered here and there, the division is closely adhered to throughout García Márquez's narrative.

María del Mar López-Cabrales's chapter, "The Enlightened Blindness of Úrsula Iguarán," starts out by passing in review a sizable corpus of scholarship that examines characterization in this novel. The "archetypal" nature of its personages is a critical commonplace; some feminist critics see the "virgin-or-whore" and "good-bad" polarity in its women characters; others place them on a continuum with female figures from ancient mythology. For López-Cabrales, Úrsula is the dramatic exception to all these patterns. The author concentrates in particular on her old-age blindness, beginning with the matriarch's initial awareness of vision loss as she raises José Arcadio the Pope-to-be and witnesses Remedios's ascension. Concurrently, Úrsula's other faculties—memory, her sense of smell—become more acute via compensation, she achieving greater insight into the personalities of her offspring and grand-offspring. López-Cabrales signals noteworthy parallels with the novel *Blindness* by José Saramago, the Portuguese Nobel laureate. She concludes with an eloquent comparative observation on the play of light and darkness in Caravaggio's *Conversion of St. Paul* to Úrsula's illumined blindness.

"Ecocriticism" is a growing, indeed exciting new subfield within literary studies, and we are pleased to include an instance thereof in William Flores's "Satire, Ecocentrism, and Luddite Discourse in *One Hundred Years of Solitude*: Regional Approachest for Global Environmental Crisis." The author finds in García Márquez's novel numerous and vivid signs of an "ecological consciousness" that anticipates the rise of the modern environmental movement, with especially striking parallels to the foundational concepts of the philosophy of "Deep Ecology." The Macondians' evolving relationship to nature—the early settlement, the varied treatment of local animals, the development of technology, the arrival of the banana company and its consequences, and more—is explored fruitfully and in detail by Flores in his illuminating analysis.

Reactions to "canonization," along with intergenerational rivalries and politics, are a familiar enough feature throughout literary history. G. B. Shaw, Irish socialist that he was, frankly disliked the English worship of Shakespeare, an informal cult he termed "Bardolatry." In African-American letters, a 24-year-old James Baldwin attacked Richard Wright's *Native Son* as "protest literature." The high artificer Nabokov regularly let fly against social art (and, for that matter, against hundreds of canonical authors).

And Jorge Luis Borges as renowned master had his own younger Argentine detractors, as chronicled by Emir Rodríguez-Monegal and others. In the wake of García Márquez's quasi-mythical status across Latin America, there has been an inevitable generational backlash (cf. the "McOndo" movement spearheaded by Chilean novelist Alberto Fuguet). Héctor Hoyos's thoughtful anti-celebratory essay, "Rediscovering Ice: García Márquez, Aira, and Vallejo on Chilling Memories," gives us a detailed look at various manifestations of "literary parricide" vis-à-vis Gabo, the public ideology of *macondismo*, and the commercialization and sway of magical realism. First, he focuses on Argentine writer César Aira's *How I Became a Nun*, with its initial episode of a boy first tasting a dollop of spoiled strawberry ice cream—a subtle spoof, in Hoyos's view, of the discovery-of-ice scene in *One Hundred Years*.

Second, there is Aira's own parodic *Dictionary of Latin American Authors*, in which the entry for "García Márquez" purposely avoids adulatory language and treats the Nobel laureate and much of his work in deadpan, perfunctory fashion. Third, there is the Colombian novelist Fernando Vallejo's 1997 magazine piece on Gabo that took the latter indirectly to task for his famous countryman's support of Cuba's "homophobic repressive regime" and for his closeness to power. (It is nonetheless worth noting that, since 1979, homosexuality has been legal in Cuba, and that, in 2010, Fidel Castro assumed responsibility for the Revolution's earlier anti-gay policies, which the Cuban leader frankly admitted had been "unjust.") As only expected, the sheer outsized weight of Gabo's oeuvre, and what it stands for, end up spawning ambivalence and even resentment among successor literati.

Much of García Márquez's post-Nobel writing stands in the shadow of his most celebrated works, even though its artistic interest or quality might in some cases be equal or come close to that of the books and stories to which he owed his prior renown. In our Section 3, we examine select instances from Gabo's latter-day phase.

In "After the End: Bolívar in the Labyrinth of History," the distinguished man of letters Michael Wood subtly and gracefully brings out the complex ways in which time and memory, history and myth, are played out and intertwined in *The General in His Labyrinth*. Wood touches on the ambiguities of character Bolívar's final departure from Bogotá, and on the curious fact that we readers never actually witness the moment of his death. Particularly rich is Wood's account of how time operates within the novel, with its double and triple retrospectives (flashbacks-within-flashbacks, as it were). Wood, moreover, latches onto one of Gabo's signature stylistic features—the verb construction "había de" + infinitive ("was to" + infinitive). The phrase (which indeed serves as the main verb in the opening sentence of his most famous work) covers a variegated semantic field, from a plan or a design to a destiny or, simply, to how things turn out. Wood has counted a total of thirty-four uses of the collocation in *The General...* and makes the most of this key discovery. In the end, Wood reflects on the merging of the life and legend of the Liberator; past events and one's own thinking thereof inevitably become one.

The pieces gathered in *Strange Pilgrims* have not garnered as much attention as Gabo's earlier, now-classic stories. Two contributions to our volume help fill this gap. Rubén Pelayo in "The Magic of Love, the Horrors of Death, and Other Themes in the Short Stories of Gabriel García Márquez," after initially noting the presence of Eros vs. Thanatos in Gabo's work, brings out the "pilgrimage" aspect of this his last collection of short narratives, and also sheds light on its autobiographical dimension (even down to the two young children present in three of the narratives). Pelayo's encyclopedic survey places the book within the larger context of Gabo's total short-story oeuvre. Toward the end he brings up some fascinating examples of the Colombian's world-wide presence: a public square in Sardinia named after *One Hundred Years of Solitude*, and a Korean singer song-writer who has based one of her compositions on a García Márquez story!

Fernando Valerio-Holguín provides a specific focus on the same book in "Gabriel García Márquez: Pilgrimage and Gastronomy," bringing a highly novel, "culinary" approach to its narrative contents. Starting with certain parallels (drawn by the Colombian master himself) between writing and cuisine, Valerio-Holguín then goes on to explore the matter of food as personal, social, and cultural marker, as expression and symptom, for the "articulation of meaning." While a published poet himself, Valerio-Holguín as critic is not averse to spicing up, with judiciously chosen smidgens from Freud, Barthes, Claude Fischler, and George Yúdice, the materials he has laid out on the table. Other topics he examines are the sense of smell, the concepts of "paratopia" and of "non-places" (the latter from Marc Augé: airports, hotels, etc.), and the paradoxical character Neruda (in "I Sell My Dreams") as both "gluttonous and refined." Valerio-Holguín caps his general reflections with some close, food-based readings of a quartet of the more culinarily pertinent and striking fictions from *Strange Pilgrims*.

By comparison with Gabo's other mature novels, *Of Love and Other Demons* has arguably suffered some critical neglect. Two of our chapters bring pioneering interpretations of that haunting work. Taking as her point of departure Gadamer's idea of "situated reason" and the corollary of interpretive horizon, Olivia Vázquez-Medina's theoretically sophisticated, richly complex article, "Reading Illness in Gabriel García Márquez's *Of Love and Other Demons*" first notes the presence of infirmity as a fairly common theme in much of the author's total oeuvre. From there she deftly demonstrates how disease in *Of Love...* intersects with larger issues of racial conflict, religious intolerance, and femininity, as well as with techniques of characterization and plot development. The innocent body of protagonist Sierva María becomes "a site of conflicting readings" under the gaze of successive observers. (The instances Vázquez-Medina adduces from the book's various and sundry doctors are vivid and dramatic.) Official diagnoses of the young girl's condition move tragically from rabies to madness to demonic possession. In addition, illness forms part of the fictive, colonial Cartagena's general atmosphere. An enamored Cayetano can subsequently be seen as becoming lovesick from his being bitten by Sierva; erotic desire in the end is adjudged as yet another malady.

The prolific scholar Ignacio López-Calvo undertakes a distinctive, highly original approach to this same work in "Translation, Unreliable Narrators, and the Comical Use of (Pseudo)-Magical Realism in *Of Love and Other Demons*." The author starts from the premise that, inasmuch as the magical-realist mode had become too much expected and predictable, too formulaic, García Márquez in *Of Love...* purposely set out to modify the technique, to give it a different basis, a change of tone. Hence, Gabo now devised what López-Calvo designates "pseudo-magical realism," whereby a seemingly magical event turns out to be the work of an able trickster (e.g., Sierva María's strange voices), or the product of an unreliable, ignorant, or superstitious source (e.g., Catholic doctrine)—or conversely, an ignorant superstition may indeed end up as an actual instance of magical realism itself. López-Calvo, moreover, takes a bold leap in making a case for *Of Love...* as a work of humor, a trait he finds necessary in providing comic relief from the unrelenting sadness of the principal story. In addition, he remarks, magic and humor fuse frequently in the course of the plot. López-Calvo notes obvious instances of superstition spoofed, but also cites some of the numerous one-line jokes emanating from the characters (especially foul-mouthed wife Bernarda's sexual and scatological utterances) as well as from the narrator's own voice. After one peruses López-Calvo's perceptive essay, *Of Love...* stands out as much for its wise and witty satire, its mirth and levity, as for its wrenchingly tragic ending.

Besides writing fiction, García Márquez worked on autobiography (as a youthful columnist and as a seasoned artist) and in theater (cf. his as-yet untranslated play *Diatriba de amor contra un hombre sentado*). For most of his life he was also a first-rate journalist and reporter; at various points he fashioned film scripts, too (notably the half-dozen movie libretti he penned for a Spanish television series in 1988, under the umbrella title *Amores difíciles*). Conversely, several of his works have been adapted for the screen and the stage. Our Section Four provides a much-needed glimpse at the Colombian's active role and his recurring presence in other literary genres.

In a densely theoretical essay, "The Permutations of the Fictional, Real and Autobiographical 'I' in Gabriel García Márquez's *Chronicle of a Death Foretold* and *Living to Tell the Tale*," Robert L. Sims delves into the larger topic of life writing, its multiple issues and implications, as manifested in a spectrum that ranges from autobiographically-based fiction to the confessional genre itself. The various layers of Gabo's narratorial "I" and of the life recalled within those two texts are examined in depth. The complex interplay that exists between Gabo the journalist, the novelist, and the memoirist is ably teased out, as is the "felt history," the master's customary emphasis on *how* things happen rather than on *what* things happen. Within this composite picture, *Chronicle* comes off in part as autobiography, with the teller (who resembles the novelist) reconstructing past events, while the voice in *Living* resembles in turn an unreliable narrator. Sims insightfully compares and contrasts the madeleine episode in Proust's *Swann's Way* with the soup-tasting scene that appears early on in García Márquez's memoirs. That García Márquez regularly mined his own life and background for his art is a truth widely acknowledged; Sims deploys a wide array of technical concepts in demonstrating how this is so.

Rudyard Alcocer and Haley Osborn start out their lucid and informative essay, "Big-Screen Adaptations of Two Gabriel García Márquez Novels: A Reappraisal," with a recounting of the author's multifaceted, evolving, personal association with the cinema, followed by their look at the disappointing quality of films based on the Colombian's work (most of them acceptable at best; others worse than that). In their view, until recently the most successful filmic remake of a Gabo text was a 1964 version of "No Thieves in This Town." Alcocer and Osborn then examine in detail two feature films that brought Gabo novels to the screen. The first is Francesco Rosi's lavish 1987 version of *Chronicle of a Death Foretold*, which, its stellar cast aside, greatly simplifies García Márquez's "concentric" structure into a linear account; omits the epistemological uncertainties and the what-might-have-beens of the original; and totally reverses the author's feminist-inflected re-encounter between Ángela and Bayardo, the latter now a handsome beau who blithely and effortlessly woos back his estranged spouse. The movie is "far inferior to the novel," the two scholars rightly state.

A refreshing contrast is the excellent 2010 adaptation of *Of Love and Other Demons* by Hilda Hidalgo (b. 1970), a Costa Rican cinéaste and onetime student of García Márquez at Cuba's international film school (where in fact he uncharacteristically encouraged her to take on the project). Alcocer and Osborn note the artistic differences between book and movie—the latter's "atmospheric" rather than linear approach, and its more "feminist" vision, with an increased role allotted to feminine agency, to female characters (particularly the slave Dominga) and to their relationships and selves. Hidalgo's movie ably evokes the Spanish-colonial ambiance and the matter of repressive Church power, yet also reduces somewhat the part played by secret dissenter Abrenuncio. A joint Colombian-Costa Rican production, the film earned high critical praise on web-based venues, and our scholarly duo gives it implicit high praise. (Having seen the movie myself, I happily concur.) Unfortunately, owing to meager marketing resources, Hidalgo's fine picture had mostly festival showings and local public exposure, though it is now available on DVD.

Last but hardly least, Zhanna Gurvich, a set designer by profession, offers an engaging inside tour in "Remembering Broadway's *Chronicle of a Death Foretold*," giving us a rare, nuts-and-bolts look at the logistics that went into the musical theater production she worked for in 1994. We read of the efforts at creating physical spaces and artifacts suitable for a staging of Gabo's novel. There is the giant wall with several apertures representing the story's different locations; and there is the fashioning of the necessary props—the Nasar home's fateful front door, the mother's hammock, the opening scene's kitchen table, the butcher shop, the wedding festivities, the bishop's parade, the telltale bloodless sheet, and more. Finding a stylistically and geographically appropriate sculpture of the Virgin Mary, and the daunting difficulties involved in visually representing the thousands of love letters sent by Ángela and left unopened by Bayardo, all make for suspenseful reading. (Unlike Rosi's flawed film, the musical retained García Márquez's nonlinear approach, though also placing the couple's reunion chronologically at the end.) Gurvich's search for a theater venue spatially right for the production shows us the roadwork required by any such enterprise.

Not surprisingly, the novelist was at first reluctant to give the play his blessing; fortunately, director Graciela Daniele's efforts succeeded in convincing the author. Gurvich here duly credits the work's actors/singers/dancers, composers, lyricist, and scriptwriter. Excellent reviews and multiple Tony nominations notwithstanding, the musical's commercial success was limited, owing in part to the competitive Broadway scene that year.

The passing of García Márquez grew into a public event in Latin America. A few days after he had breathed his last, thousands of mourners in Mexico City stood waiting in line to attend a memorial service for him in the Palacio de Bellas Artes, the Fine Arts Palace, a typical sort of cultural center on the Hispanic continent. The stately neo-classical building was festooned with flowers and with images of butterflies, all in yellow. The presidents of both Mexico and Colombia gave solemn speeches in tribute to the novelist. Meanwhile, back in Gabo's original hometown of Aracataca, a funeral procession drew three thousand admirers of all ages. Next day, readings from his works were scheduled at schools and libraries throughout Colombia. All of this collective grieving served as a vivid reminder of just how revered a figure Gabo is and was among those who treasure great literature in the Spanish-speaking world.

And now we are honored to pay our respects to a master storyteller, to honor a visionary mythmaker who has enriched our cultural life, our repertory of narratives and character types, our ideas of magic and reality, even our daily newspaper headlines, comic strips, and books about dogs. We sincerely hope that these reflections on García Márquez and his work will be considered worthy of his stature as an artist and as a person. Writing about Gabo is in some measure a labor of love—love of his work and what it stands for.

NOTES

1. I am indebted to Mary-Anne Vetterling for this canine reference.
2. My thanks to my brother, Kanani Bell, for calling this item to my attention.

WORKS CITED

Anonymous. *Dogtology: Live. Bark. Believe*. Austin, TX: Greenleaf, 2015.
Cantú, Hector, and Castellanos, Carlos. *Baldo*. www.gocomics.com/baldo/2016/01/10
Casanova, Pascale. *The World Republic of Letters*. Trans. from the French by M. B. DeBevoise. Cambridge, MA: Harvard University Press, 2004.

Part I

OEUVRE, BACKGROUNDS, LEGACY

Chapter 1

Gabriel García Márquez
Writer for the World

Nicholas Birns and Juan E. De Castro

The death of Gabriel García Márquez, on April 17, 2014, of pneumonia, probably the consequence of his long struggle with lymphatic cancer, brought a period of Latin American and, perhaps, world literature to an end. García Márquez, the most successful writer of his era, was best known for *One Hundred Years of Solitude* (1967), the work that popularized magical realism—a style characterized by the presentation of fantastic events as if they were ordinary. This novel told the story of the jungle backwater town of Macondo, "a village of twenty adobe houses" and of several generations of the Buendía family, and was redolent of the bizarre, stagnating world in which the writer grew up, one which he loved despite all but which he saw desperately needed to change. He was also the author of other widely admired novels, like *Chronicle of a Death Foretold* (1981), a story of an honor killing told with such intensity that we read on even though the outcome of the story is revealed at the beginning, and *Love in the Time of Cholera* (1985), a moving and dignified story of love regained in old age. *The Autumn of the Patriarch* (1975) was the ultimate "dictator novel," which is both riveting and strangely horrifying, an elegy for a despicable state of political being. *The General in His Labyrinth* (1992) concerned Simón Bolívar, telling the story of the last years of the leader who won independence for much of South America against the Spanish. This was a case of one of the greatest of Latin Americans writing about perhaps the greatest Latin American, and an enlightening overview on what historically, has gone both wrong and right with Latin America. Though García Márquez's portrait of Bolívar was far from heroic, the novel's warts-and-all presentation gave the most compelling representative of the Latin American independence movements in fiction.

Lest one think García Márquez could only work on a large canvas, the novella *Leaf Storm* (1955), also set in Macondo, has all its events transpire in one room. García Márquez was a master of the small as well as the large. His early work in journalism grounded him in reality, while his grasp of the novel's potential for imaginative enlargement allowed him to create worlds of entrancing, mesmerizing, and sometimes horrifying characters, many of whom represented the tragic situation of a Latin America not yet freed from its burdens of history and foreign domination. Though García Márquez's writing contained elements of humor and satire, much of it was colored by a tragic if exuberant pessimism, as seen in the famous final line of his most famous novel, *One Hundred Years of Solitude*, "because races condemned to one hundred years of solitude did not have a second opportunity on earth" (417).

García Márquez, who won nearly every prize of pertinence within the Spanish speaking world, received the Nobel Prize for Literature in 1982: *"for his novels and short stories, in which the fantastic and the realistic are combined in a richly composed world of imagination, reflecting a continent's life and conflicts"* ("Gabriel García Márquez Facts" n. pag.). As evidenced by the Nobel Prize, his work was celebrated by critics and writers as among the most important of the twentieth century. With perhaps some exaggeration, Pulitzer Prize-winning novelist William Kennedy declared *One Hundred Years of Solitude* "the first piece of literature since the Book of Genesis that should be required reading for the entire human race" (qtd. in "The Great Novel of the Americas" 11). The novel was also embraced by readers worldwide. Not only were his major novels bestsellers at the time of their first publication, but also both *One Hundred Years of Solitude*, in January 2004, and *Love in the Time of Cholera*, in October 2007, were included in Oprah's Book Club. García Márquez, with his disciple Isabel Allende, were the only Latin Americans included in the American talk show host's popular canon.

Gabriel García Márquez was perhaps the most successful high-literary writer of his era. Indeed, if one were to list writers who were most influential in the twentieth century, one would have to list his name alongside James Joyce, Franz Kafka, and T. S. Eliot as one of the four most influential writers of the twentieth century. Given that all the others were born in the late nineteenth century, one might say that, alongside Samuel Beckett, García Márquez is the *only* writer born in the twentieth century to have become a household name throughout the world. What is notable indeed is how global this influence has been, in other words hardly restricted to Latin America, where, in recent years, Jorge Luis Borges has become consecrated as the major canonical writer. Salman Rushdie, whose breakthrough book *Midnight's Children* (1981) was nearly an overt homage to García Márquez, would never have had the career he did without García Márquez; nor would the Australian novelist Peter Carey. Many writers working in the last decades of the twentieth century wanted to use the innovative formal techniques of

Modernism yet not lose touch with living subject matter: place, people, and history. García Márquez's techniques, particularly the way he told the story of a place over several generations, allowed writers of the century's second half to give Modernism a local habitation and a name. They also enabled a growing political relevance free of the reductive ideology of naturalism or socialist realism. Finally, even though García Márquez rarely employed fantasy outside his best-known novel, the success of *One Hundred Years of Solitude* opened the door for a wide spectrum of visions that sampled both reality and fantasy, and also encouraged the use of fantasy to depict situations, such as political oppression in Latin America, that seemed beyond the reach of conventional realism, yet urgently demanded imaginative attention.

LIFE AND WORK

García Márquez was born in Aracataca, a small town in the Magdalena department on the Colombian Caribbean coast in 1927. Although he enrolled as a law student—first at the Universidad Nacional de Colombia in Bogotá in 1948, and later, after the institution was closed due to the political violence of the famous *nueve de Abril* at the Universidad de Cartagena—his first profession was that of journalist. Journalism would always be one of García Márquez's main concerns. In 1984, he helped found the important Mexican center-left newspaper *La Jornada* and, in 1991, the Colombian TV news magazine program QAP, which ceased broadcasting in 1997 (Vargas 8; Nullvalue n. pag.).

His early work as a journalist, which included writing film reviews, also helped foster in him a passion for the movies. He even enrolled in 1955 at the Centro Sperimentale di Cinematografia in Rome. In 1965, having moved to Mexico, he wrote, with fellow novelist Carlos Fuentes, the screenplay for *El gallo de oro* (*The Golden Cockerel*). Although he would write several more screenplays and have more than twenty of his novels and stories adapted into movies, his major contribution to the region's film-life was his participation in the founding of the Escuela Internacional de Cine y Televisión in Cuba.

In the 1960s, García Márquez was a central figure of what came to be known as the Boom of the Latin American novel, together with the Argentine Julio Cortázar, the Mexican Fuentes, and the Peruvian Mario Vargas Llosa, the latter the recipient of the Nobel Prize in Literature in 2010. While one can easily argue that there were important novelists writing before the 1960s— Alejo Carpentier published the proto-magical realist *The Kingdom of This World* in 1949; Juan Rulfo's 1955 *Pedro Páramo*, a work that García Márquez claimed as a major influence on his best-known novel; José María Arguedas's *Deep Rivers* in 1958—the Boom brought the Latin American novel to the attention of what has been called "the world republic of letters." In fact, the success of García Márquez's *One Hundred Years of Solitude* frequently led readers and even some critics to mischaracterize the Boom as a whole as magical realism. However, magical realism was never the dominant narrative mode in the region. For instance, Vargas Llosa is a realist; Cortázar, is an experimental writer; and Fuentes, though more of a maverick, only occasionally flirted with magical realism. Moreover, with the obvious exception of *One Hundred Years of Solitude*, García Márquez has mainly written works that are not primarily magical realist, including *Chronicle of a Death Foretold* and *Love in the Time of Cholera*.

It is easy to forget in the midst of the posthumous multitudinous commemorations of García Márquez's life—his death was on the front page of newspapers throughout the world; President Juan Manuel Santos declared him to be "the greatest Colombian of all time;" and he was mourned by figures as varied as British novelist Ian McEwan, Bollywood star Soha Ali Khan, and René Pérez of reggaetón group Calle 13—that one of the defining traits of Latin American narrative during the last twenty years has been the rejection of magical realism ("Reaction to the death of Nobel Laureate" n. pag; Khan n. pag; Pérez n. pag.). For instance, Roberto Bolaño, unquestionably the most influential Latin American writer after the Boom, dared to criticize García Márquez and magical realism: "Who are the official inheritors of García Márquez? Isabel Allende, Laura Restrepo, Luis Sepúlveda, and others. Every day García Márquez seems to me to resemble more and more Santos Chocano or Lugones" ("Entrevista con Roberto Bolaño" n. pag.) This statement links García Márquez to an outmoded, sentimental, faintly genteel tradition, one easily accepted by middlebrow readers as a bland, pseudo-idealistic, and self-consoling anodyne.

Bolaño, who was not beyond contradicting himself, would in other occasions also claim to admire the Colombian master though never his disciples. For many younger Latin American writers, magical realism became a cliché, more applicable to how outsiders imagined Latin America than to what the region actually was. Writers born after 1960, such as the Chileans Alberto Fuguet and Alejandro Zambra, and García Márquez's own countryman Juan Gabriel Vásquez, have eschewed magical realism as a model, even though some of their contemporaries worldwide, such as the Indonesian writer Eka Kurniawan, have continued to revere the Colombian master as a model. Kurniawan said, in a 2015 interview, "As for more modern writers, I admire Garcia Márquez, Knut Hamsun, Faulkner, and of course Kafka" (n. pag.). Magical realism is still a powerful element in an acclaimed younger world writer's literary genealogy. One can add, in an ironic touch that reminds one of García Márquez best known novel, that his country's Ministry of Tourism, Foreign Investment, and Export Promotion is currently promoting tourism to the country with the slogan "Colombia is Magical Realism."¹

Nevertheless, one cannot avoid also seeing a connection between this rejection of magical realism and, to a much lesser degree, of García Márquez and his work, with a generational repudiation of the Nobel Prize winner's unapologetically traditional left-wing politics. The more that neoliberalism in its various avatars became *de rigueur*, the less currency García Márquez's vision came to exercise in the region. Unlike Vargas Llosa and Fuentes, who would distance themselves from the Cuban government in reaction to the "Padilla Affair"—the jailing of Cuban poet Heberto Padilla and some of his associates, and their later being freed after confessing to their anti-revolutionary activities—García Márquez became a close friend and confidant of Fidel Castro. One cannot underestimate the importance of the friendship with Castro in the life of García Márquez. Even his move from his native Colombia to a Mexico that, at the time still under the rule of the old-style PRI, was friendlier to Cuba than most Latin American countries, can be seen as an expression of this closeness. There was clearly something personal as well as political in their friendship: the two most famous Latin Americans of their time, both of whom had come up the hard way. Castro also got something out of the relationship, the allure of a kind of socialist cosmopolitanism, which belied the reality of the Cuban regime's often harsh and intolerant treatment of writers. At a time when Latin American intellectuals saw the right-wing regimes of Augusto Pinochet in Chile and Jorge Rafael Videla in Argentina as far more menacing than Castro's Cuba, García Márquez's friendship with the Cuban leader did not hurt him. Nor did it impair his popularity with the US center-left. As David Jackson noted in his April 18, 2014 article, "Obama, Clinton Praise García Márquez," both President Bill Clinton and President Barack Obama have embraced García Márquez's fiction in a way that positioned it as both imaginatively fruitful and ethically relevant.

Indeed, García Márquez was as much an "official" writer of the US Left in this era as any US-born writer, certainly outstripping US-born candidates such as E. L. Doctorow, with his only serious rival being (as Dane Johnson has pointed out in his 1996 article) Toni Morrison. There was a bit of a sense that García Márquez's enthusiasm for Castro was a justifiable anti-American acting out, explicable in terms of previous US arrogance in the region (particularly relevant to a Colombia that had lost Panama to US economic ambitions). Once world opinion shifted rightward in the 1980s, however, attitudes toward García Márquez's embrace of Fidel became less tolerant. It may be symptomatic of the political changes that have taken place in the region that Mario Vargas Llosa, despite having become the best-known Latin American advocate for the free market, is seen by many younger writers as an example if not a mentor, while García Márquez had long before he died become a classic rather than a living influence.[2] (One must also note that García Márquez's health problems that began with his cancer diagnosis in 1999, and which necessarily led to the diminution of his public activity, also played a role in his loss of influence among younger writers, as he was less able to operate in the role of literary taste-maker and patron).

MAKING LATIN AMERICA VISIBLE TO THE WORLD

García Márquez made Latin America visible to the world. When he first started publishing, Latin America was a backwater, the world's seemingly least interesting and pertinent region. The Cuban Revolution garnered Latin America headlines. But it was the fiction of García Márquez that made the world realize Latin America could produce figures of world cultural eminence and that the stories of the region were worth being told and had talented writers to tell them. Any Latin American writer or artist who has attained world success since the publication of *One Hundred Years of Solitude* owes a good deal of their visibility to García Márquez, as well as does the very possibility of the wide scale study of Latin American literature in the US academy.

To understand how important García Marquez's work is in providing the exposure of Latin American literature to the English-speaking world, one has only to look at the statement by Kent B. Stiles writing in the July 26, 1942 *New York Times*, referred to García Márquez's fellow Colombian, Jorge Isaacs (1837–1895), as "the most famous Spanish American writer," a statement made when, for instance, the Uruguayan Horacio Quiroga and the Argentine Roberto Arlt had written far more challenging works (n. pag.). Although not less than twenty years later Jorge Luis Borges had unquestionably surpassed Isaacs, whereas Isaacs embodied an extreme, almost lurid romanticism, playing into stereotypes of Latin America as passionate and sentimental, Borges's cerebral parables were seen as embodying almost the other extreme, as being fundamentally European in their philosophical orientation and being only accidentally of their region. García Márquez, on the other hand, was both powerfully embedded in his region but also part of an innovative aesthetics stemming from Modernism. He was to become a writer at once exemplary of the region but also, unlike Isaacs, a writer of international importance, who affected the world canon outside his own region. Importantly, it was García Márquez, not Borges, who helped make older innovative writers from Latin America such as Carpentier, Juan Carlos Onetti of Uruguay, Miguel Ángel Asturias of Guatemala, or Rulfo visible in the United States, as well, of course of Boom contemporaries of his such as Fuentes, Vargas Llosa, Chile's José Donoso, and Paraguay's Augusto Roa Bastos.

GARCÍA MÁRQUEZ IN THE COLOSSUS OF THE NORTH

García Márquez's status as a classic is indisputable and his impact in Latin American and world literature undeniable. While he has had direct Latin American disciples, such as Chilean novelist Allende and Mexican Laura Esquivel, who in different ways rewrite *One Hundred Years of Solitude* in a female key, and the late Peruvian Manuel Scorza, who radicalized the politics of magical realism as he fused it with *indigenismo*, it is internationally that his influence has been greater and less problematical. For many US Latino and Latina writers, including Sandra Cisneros, Rudolfo Anaya, Helena María Viramontes, or Cristina García, magical realism has become a marker of identity. Internationally renowned novelists Rushdie, Toni Morrison, Mo Yan, Ben Okri, Eka Kurniawan, and Edwidge Danticat have acknowledged the importance of his influence on their development as authors. Danticat, for instance, has said that, in Haiti, "What people were calling magical realism was so much incorporated into people's daily lives. People create their own mythologies for their lives" ("The Rumpus Interview" n. pag.). If Alejo Carpentier, as Danticat has acknowledged, was her predecessor in seeing the susceptibility of Haitian material to magical realism, it was the example of *One Hundred Years of Solitude*, and, as Danticat noticed in her *New Yorker* obituary of the Colombian writer, short stories of his such as "One Of These Days," that gave her the confidence to use imagination to "depict somewhat common yet unbearable realities" ("Gabriel García Márquez: An Appreciation" n. pag.). In her novel *The Farming of Bones* (1998), Danticat begins chapter 13 with this passage, supremely redolent of García Márquez:

> I dream of the sugar woman. Again.
> As always, she is dressed in a long, three-tiered, ruffled gown, inflated like a balloon. Around her face she wears a shiny silver muzzle, and on her neck there is a collar with a clasped lock dangling from it.
> The sugar woman drags her skirt and skips back and forth around my room. She seems to be wearing a kalanda in a very fast spin, locks arms with the air, and pretends to kiss someone much larger than herself. As she swings and shuffles, the chains on her ankles cymbal a rattled melody. She hops to the sounds of the jingle of her chains, which with her twists grow louder and louder.
> "Is your face underneath this?" I ask. The voice that comes out of my mouth surprises me; it is the voice of the orphaned child, at the stream, the child who from then on would talk only to strange faces. (132)

The sugar woman is a figure in dreams, a figure of social marginality and of magic, of relegation and of power. She is a symptom of the uneven developments of the world of the dreaming character, its divergence from the main narrative of the world, which at once denotes the marginalization of the

Haitian people but also the distinct experience that their writers can provide the world. From his most journalistic pieces to his most imaginative flights, García Márquez was a reporter on the separate development of Colombia, on how it was at once part of the Western world yet had its own rules, its own barriers, its own dreams and its own pathologies.

Danticat is writing about an acknowledged "Third World" context, but US-born writers also emulate García Márquez. Toni Morrison, as with García Márquez, was powerfully influenced by Faulkner, another writer of experimental technique, heterocosmic ambition, and uneven social development; García Márquez's Macondo is routinely compared to Faulkner's Yoknapatawpha as a region that is an entire fictional world, one that, as Melville said of the home of his character Queequeg in *Moby-Dick* "is not on any map. True places never are" (65). Although Morrison might be said have had other "magical realist" influences in the vernacular, African-American tradition, García Márquez was an important reference point for her, as was even more true of white American writers often speaking from a position of comparative privilege. Michael Chabon's *The Amazing Adventures of Kavalier and Clay* (2000), a novel of two Jews, one a refugee from Nazism, who end up creating a successful comic book character in the 1940s, begins with a paragraph detailing how one of the major characters, Sam Klay, remembers his father taking him to see the great magician Houdini, an almost certain intertextual reference to *One Hundred Years of Solitude* beginning with Colonel Aureliano Buendía remembering his father taking him to discover ice. In a conversation with Victoria Ramirez and Patrick Murphy, Chabon attributes his frequent employment of a passage of dialog in which one of the characters changes their mind to techniques used by García Márquez. Chabon listed *Love in the Time of Cholera,* as one of his top ten books, saying

> Márquez takes the love triangle to the limit in this story of an ever hopeful romantic who waits more than fifty years for his first love. When his beloved's husband dies after a long, happy marriage, Florentino Ariza immediately redeclares his passion. After the enraged widow rejects him, he redoubles his efforts. Set on the Caribbean coast of Colombia, this wise, steamy, and playful novel jumps between past and present, encompassing decades of unrest and war, recurring cholera epidemics, and the environmental ravages of development. ("Michael Chabon's Top Ten List" n. pag.)

Notably, Chabon sees García Márquez both as telling a moving story and bearing social witnesses, something Chabon does not just in *Kavalier and Clay,* which dealt with gay issues as well as those of Jews in the era of extermination, but his *Telegraph Avenue* (2012), which in turn deals with the role of music in interracial relations in the United States. Chabon's ability to go between imaginative whimsy and reportage samples many parts of the

Colombian's oeuvre. It is notable in this respect that, as Gene H. Bell-Villada points out, two of García Márquez's first American champions and emulators were Paul Theroux and William Kennedy, both of whom composed nonfiction—Theroux travel writing, and journalism in the case of Kennedy (286–87). Kennedy, indeed, got his start writing about the New York state capital of Albany as a journalist, and then took it as a subject of award-wining fiction, much the same way the Colombian writer did. One might see Faulkner as an enabling influence on Kennedy here, but even after Faulkner, Albany as a subject—provincial, but lacking the historical weight and tragic condition of the South—was not really a viable subject of literary fiction. García Márquez's ability to show how backwaters could register asymmetries in power and justice, though, enabled Albany to register; only through an act of international reading could literary regionalism seem more than provincial. Similarly John Barth, whose 1980 essay "The Literature of Replenishment," presented García Márquez as a step beyond the late-Modernist "Literature of Exhaustion," swerved more toward a Maryland regionalism in his works of the 1980s. Philip Roth adapted his comic and self-interrogating idiom from what the French would call the études introspectives of his pre-1980 work to the more experimental yet also historically and socially minded instances of his later work. In a way that, though not as explicitly influenced by García Márquez as the later Barth, Roth perhaps took inspiration from the wider imaginative warrant that US writers seemed to derive from the Colombian's example. John Updike's *The Coup* (1979) was an odd hybrid, a book set in a fictional African country that owed much in technique to Nabokov, but the very subject of the dictator-novel would not have been possible without *The Autumn of the Patriarch*. Joyce Carol Oates in her *Bellefleur* (1980) presented a tableau of another part of upstate New York that the French critic Marc Chénétier saw as inspired by García Márquez in evading "received readings of history" (142). The many members of the Bellefleur family—manic, inspired, impetuous, corrupt—in the book are highly reminiscent of García Márquez's multiple Buendías, and both names even contain a reference to words that mean "good" or "beautiful," references in both cases meant partially ironically. Similarly, if less effectively, T. Coraghessan Boyle imitated García Márquez's ability to sum up the felt life of an entire community in *World's End* (1987), set in yet another part of upstate New York; Rebecca Singleton told the story of hijinks in New Jersey's Pinelands in *Jersey Blue* (1982); and, a generation later, Jonathan Lethem used Marquezian magical realism to evoke the racial and cultural tensions of growing up in brownstone Brooklyn in the 1970s in *The Fortress of Solitude* (2003), whose very title might refer not just to Superman's Arctic retreat but to *One Hundred Years of Solitude*. What all these books, with their varying levels of tribute to the Colombian, attested to was, first, a sense of reportage, as much in these books was devoted to fairly straightforward, realistic chronicling of a place, and yet on a parallel level these places were always fictional, imagined, and frequently magical. Geographical areas in the United States that might have seemed too prosaic or banal for fiction, in other words were reinvigorated into putative imaginative glory by what García Márquez had done with Macondo.

Moreover García Márquez's oeuvre, despite his radical politics and sympathy with Cuba, became, in its Faulknerian combination of historical consciousness, representational totality, and moral sympathy for the poor, an acceptable literary token for the center-left. US president Bill Clinton routinely cited him as his favorite novelist. This is something remarkable in that one might think a US politician would give a US author as their favorite. One could see Clinton as courting the Latino vote here, but in reality what was most likely happening was a genuine act of readerly recognition, in that Clinton was noting the applicability of the uneven development so noted in the Colombian novelist's work to the situation in his home state of Arkansas and the South in general.[3] In other words, Clinton was seeing García Márquez as Faulkner's successor. García Márquez, along with Toni Morrison, were the two novelists most visibly, despite their manifest radicalism, seen as the consensus novelists of Clinton's center-left brand of progressive politics. García Márquez visited the Clinton White House in 1997.

Another consensus leader of this era, the basketball coach Phil Jackson, who coached the Chicago Bulls and Los Angeles Lakers to multiple championships in the 1990s and 2000s, put a quotation from *One Hundred Years of Solitude* in chapter 9 of his memoir (120) and routinely touted García Márquez's books to his players, among whom were such legendary stars as Michael Jordan and Kobe Bryant. The pop singer Jane Wiedlin, in 1985, released a song called "A Hundred Years of Solitude," that was clearly aware of the novel, although the lyrics concerned a romantic relationship with few social implications.

However watered-down his political message became, García Márquez was thus yet an intimate part of US national life, a household word among even moderately educated Americans. For many readers in the United States, *One Hundred Years of Solitude* was their most beloved book, a symbol for a lifetime dedicated to reading. In December 2015, Black Cat Books, a second-hand bookstore in Shelter Island, New York, had two books in a glass case near the cash register. One was an Italian hardcover of Umberto Eco's *The Name of the Rose*, the other the Harper and Row first edition of *One Hundred Years of Solitude*—a rare sight to US readers so much more familiar with the original Avon paperback. Both books embodied popular appeal, but they also embodied aspirations that were above all intellectual, cosmopolitan, and literary. Even though, in subsequent decades, Americans would gravitate to very different sorts of translated fiction, *One Hundred Years of Solitude* would provide a precedent for such work.

A WRITER FOR THE WORLD

García Márquez, however, was not just a writer for the United States, but for the broader English-speaking world and beyond. García Márquez's ability to mix reality and fantasy helped bring a viable postmodernism into the British novel in the works of Martin Amis, Graham Swift and Julian Barnes, and helped sanction the imbrications of fantasy and the large-scale. Amis's *Einstein's Monsters* (1987) with its reimaging of a post-nuclear world, and Barnes's *A History of the World in 10 ½ Chapters* (1989), both used Marquesian magical realism as a warrant to reintroduce aspects of science fiction and fantasy that had been long déclassé in mainstream British fiction, and also to conjure a broader political level of reference than merely the surface questions of who was in Parliament, what ideologies prevailed among the chattering classes and so on. Graham Swift's *Waterland* (1983) rebaptized the English shire of Norfolk, not previously thought to be a place where particularly evocative fiction was set, into "Waterland," a Macondo, as it were, in Britain, where the viscosity and squishy nature of history was revealed as against those who would pronounce definitively on the past to serve narratives of present-day authority. If, as with many of these American writers, there was an element of the mock-subaltern in place of García Márquez's genuinely subaltern, using the sense of relevance and value García Márquez had generated in order to make these writers' own localities seem more socially urgent than they in fact were, the influence of García Márquez unquestionably broadened the range of possibility of US and British fiction. Equivalent achievements were seen in Canada in Jack Hodgins's *The Invention of the World* (1977), in Australia in Peter Carey's *Illywhacker* (1985) and Rodney Hall's *Just Relations* (1982), and in New Zealand in Maurice Shadbolt's *The Lovelock Version* (1980). García Márquez became a model for any writer from a particular region that had been affected or afflicted by uneven development, that seemed to lag behind the advanced West. It is this association of novelistic technique with uneven social development that has made the example of the Colombian writer relevant even to writers depicting out-of-the-way regions of First World countries like the United States, much less Ghana, Nigeria, and India. Indeed, in writers' zeal to appropriate the felt, almost organic despair-cum-exuberance of García Márquez's Macondo world, they have often pretended to a greater sense of marginality than they have in fact possessed. Odd local alcoves have been elevated to the imaginative pitch of Macondo while lacking that imaginary region's genuine sense of marginalization and relegation. However, this false cultivation of marginality elevated only one of García Marquez's many novels over other possible models in his vast oeuvre—the lyrical pure imagination of *Love in the Time of Cholera* or the scrupulous, if barbed, historical fidelity of *The General in His Labyrinth*, or the psycho-political insight of *The Autumn of the Patriarch*, the latter of which, unlike *One Hundred Years of Solitude*, concentrates on the experience of those in power.

Even more, the tendency of First World writers to use García Márquez's techniques to claim a false afflatus of marginality for themselves made the Colombian writer's techniques seem more on the side of history as a force, more Hegelian in its sense of historical data as eligible for synthesis and positive transformation, than his actual more tragic vision warranted. There is also a simple issue of scale here. Rushdie's *Midnight's Children* was a Mumbai (then Bombay) novel, a novel of India, a novel even, in its latter reaches, of Pakistan; it embodied what Timothy Brennan has called "the national longing for form," the yearning for the great novel to embody the aspirations and contradictions of a nation. Marquesian techniques allowed Rushdie to do this more capaciously than even many nineteenth-century realist novels, but this also meant taking aesthetic risks that were bound to lead to a sense of letdown after the initial thrill of seeing, as it were, "India" and its history between the pages of a book.

It is this history-incarnating avatar of García Márquez that made magical realism, in the 1980s, resemble the vogue enjoyed by the sort of historical fiction popularized by Sir Walter Scott in the 1810s: an infinitely adaptable method (employed by Fenimore Cooper, Balzac, Manzoni, Pérez Galdós, Brazil's José Alencar, Poland's Henryk Sienkiewicz, Australia's Rolf Boldrewood, this list alone representing four continents) by which marginalized regions could claim their own history in fiction all the while imitating established international masters and fitting into what was, in representational terms, a conservative paradigm that combined both primitivism and urbanity, the vitality of the life of the land and the sophistication of the latest metatextual technique. This adaptability helped make García Márquez not just *a* world writer but *the* world writer for roughly twenty years from 1970 to 1990; yet it is also what made his global reputation pall quickly.

The Australian writer Gerald Murnane, for instance began his 2013 novel *A History of Books* by having his narrator denouncing magical realism as a mode of easy exoticism, written by writers who were "followers of fashion and ignorant," "with their works nowadays forgotten" (1). Even a writer like Orhan Pamuk, the Turkish Nobel Laureate, who might have been expected to use techniques similar to *One Hundred Years of Solitude* in depicting the developmental odyssey of modern Turkey, decidedly eschewed such techniques, unlike in the case of Rushdie, not needing them to represent "Istanbul" or "Turkey."

LATIN AMERICA'S TURN FROM MAGICAL REALISM

After 1995, those Latin American writers to whom the world looked were, as the Bolaño quotation mentioned beforehand heralded, precisely those who swerved away from García Márquez. Again, there was a political aspect to this rejection of the old master. His friendship with Fidel, his unabashed leftism, no longer seemed to fit the liberal, if not neoliberal, ideologies and lifestyles that had been adopted by many in the region, especially its young, hip, and obviously talented writers. However, the region's intelligentsia was also reacting against aspects of García Márquez's writing. For many, the worlds denoted and connoted by magical realism seemed foreign to the experience of Latin Americans at the end of the twentieth and beginning of the twenty first centuries. In "I Am not a Magic Realist," an article published in the well-known internet magazine *Salon,* Alberto Fuguet, after complaining about the "folklore and a dash of tropical heat" expected in all *Latino* writing, notes:

> Unlike the ethereal world of García Márquez's imaginary Macondo, my own world is something much closer to what I call McOndo—a world of McDonalds, Mackintoshes, and condos. In a continent that was once ultra-politicized, young apolitical writers like myself are now writing without overt agendas, about their own experiences. Living in cities all over Latin America, hooked on cable tv (CNN en Español), addicted to movies and connected to the net. (n. pag.)

Despite the obvious class dimension found in these words—there are many Latin Americans without cable TV or Macs—Fuguet's rejection of magical realism is based on what he considers the style's refusal to portray the actual reality of the region as experienced by those who live in it, which, instead, it exoticizes. Elsewhere in this essay, he ascribes magical realism's popularity to US market expectations of an exotic Latin America. In this text, he also depicts his experience at the Iowa Writer's Workshop where he discovered "I was Latin American alright—I just wasn't Latino enough" (n. pag.). In his own writings, for instance in *The Movies of My Life* (2003), a novel about growing up in Pinochet's Chile, Fuguet finds magic not in self-exoticization, but in, of all places, Hollywood movies like *The Sound of Music, Close Encounters of the Third Kind,* and even *Airport 79.*

Even if his words seem at first less combative, Juan Gabriel Vásquez, the best-known contemporary Colombian novelist, agrees with Fuguet noting: "In my personal search for models—of methods, as García Márquez calls them—*One Hundred Years of Solitude* was never an option because there is nothing further from the Bogotá of the end of the century" (n. pag.).[4] Vásquez, however, adds a writerly and professional dimension—and perhaps a level of respect for his renowned fellow Colombian—to this rejection of magical realism and its greatest representative. Explicitly referring to Harold Bloom's notion of "the anxiety of influence," he adds:

What I say does not deny the preeminent position of *One Hundred Years of Solitude*. That position, let's be clear, constitutes a clear and present danger; but only for Colombian novelists who, due to lack of talent, ignorance, or simple laziness, have not gone off into the world in search of new tools—in other words of creating their own tradition, of creating their own predecessors—and have been happy with what they had available at home—that is, the territorial tradition where the tree of *One Hundred Years of Solitude* still casts a long shadow. (45)[5]

Perhaps unlike writers from other regions, Latin American and especially Colombian writers have to develop by struggling with the shadow of García Márquez. However, even if they ultimately reject García Márquez's example, the best novelists of Latin America and elsewhere today write with an awareness of the breadth and depth of global subject matter and a sense of the interaction of emotion, time, and history that could not have been achieved without the precedent of the Colombian master.

CONCLUSION

Perhaps it is best to end this brief overview of García Márquez's brilliant literary career and its worldwide influence with a brief quotation from the Colombian writer's Nobel address: "The Solitude of Latin America." One of the most eloquent pieces of writing he ever penned, it expresses with passion and precision the utopian desire that informed all of his writing: "We, the inventors of tales . . . feel entitled to believe that it is not yet too late to engage in the creation of [a] . . . new and sweeping utopia of life, where no one will be able to decide for others how they die, where love will prove true and happiness be possible, and where the races condemned to one hundred years of solitude will have, at last and forever, a second opportunity on earth" (n. pag.).

NOTES

1. According to *El Tiempo*: "The allusion to the works of Gabriel García Márquez is clear. In fact, Proexport, with the help of the [Colombian] Ambassador to Mexico, José Gabriel Ortiz, asked the writer's wife for her opinion about the idea. The project continued with her approval" ["La alusión a la obra de Gabriel García Márquez es clara. De hecho, Proexport, con la ayuda del embajador en México, José Gabriel Ortiz, le consultó a la esposa del escritor su opinión sobre la iniciativa. Luego de la aprobación, el proceso continuo."] (Uribe n. pag.). All translations from the Spanish are by the authors of this article.
2. Santiago Roncagliolo, perhaps the best-known "younger" Peruvian writer wrote about García Márquez and Vargas Llosa: "The two old enemies maintained

opposing trajectories. The end of Gabriel García Márquez coincides with the greatest splendor of Mario Vargas Llosa: the awarding of the Nobel and the foundation of the biennial literary award with his name" ["Los dos viejos enemigos mantuvieron trayectorias opuestas. El fin de Gabriel García Márquez coincide con el máximo esplendor de Mario Vargas Llosa: la recepción del Nobel y la inauguración del premio bienal que lleva su nombre"] (n. pag.).

3. According to García Márquez, Clinton stressed the connections between the US South and the Caribbean in the context of Faulkner's works during a dinner at William Styron's house that also included Carlos Fuentes and, surprisingly, Harvey Weinstein: "Faulkner got us to talking about the affinities between Caribbean writers and the cluster of great Southern novelists in the United States. It made much more sense to us to think of the Caribbean not as a geographical region surrounded by its sea but as a much wider historical and cultural belt stretching from the north of Brazil to the Mississippi Basin. Mark Twain, William Faulkner, John Steinbeck and so many others would then be just as Caribbean as Jorge Amado and Derek Walcott. Clinton, born and raised in Arkansas, a Southern state, applauded the notion and professed himself happy to be a Caribbean" ("The Mysteries of Bill Clinton" n. pag.).

4. "En mi búsqueda personal de modelos—de métodos, como dice García Márquez—*Cien años de soledad* nunca fue una opción, porque no hay nada más alejado que la Bogotá del cambio de siglo." Vásquez (45).

5. "Lo que digo no niega la posición preeminente de *Cien años de soledad.* Esa posición, digámoslo de una vez , es una amenaza clara y presente; pero lo es para aquellos novelistas colombianos que, por falta de talento, por ignorancia o por simple pereza, han sido incapaces de salir al mundo en busca de herramientas nuevas—es decir, de crear su propia tradición, de crear a sus antecesores—, y se han contentado con lo que había en casa—es decir la tradición territorial donde el árbol de *Cien años de soledad* todavía hace sombra." (Vásquez 45).

WORKS CITED

Anonymous. "The Great Novel of the Americas?" In *One Hundred Years of Solitude.* By Gabriel García Márquez. New York: Harper Perennial, 2006. 8–12. Print.
Bell-Villada, Gene H. *Gabriel García Márquez: The Man and His Work.* Second edition. Chapel Hill: University of North Carolina Press, 2010. Print.
Bolaño, Roberto. "Entrevista con Roberto Bolaño." Interview with Luis García Santillán. *Crítica Cl: Revista Latinoamericana de Ensayo.* 4 Apr. 2002. Web. 11 Dec. 2015. http://critica.cl/entrevistas/entrevista-con-roberto-bolano
Brennan, Timothy. "The National Longing for Form." In Homi K. Bhabha, ed. *Nation and Narration,* London: Routledge, 1991. 44–70. Print.
Chabon, Michael. "Michael Chabon's Top Ten List." *TopTenBooks.net.* n. d. Web. 11 Dec. 2015.
Chénetier, Marc. *Beyond Suspicion: New American Fiction Since 1960.* Trans. Elizabeth A. Houlding. Philadelphia: University of Pennsylvania Press, 1996. Print.
Danticat, Edwidge. *The Farming of Bones.* New York: Soho Press, 1998. Print.

———. "Gabriel García Márquez: An Appreciation." *The New Yorker.com.* 18 Apr. 2014. Web. 25 Dec. 2015.

———. "The Rumpus Interview with Edwige Danticat." Interview with Kima Jones. *The Rumpus.net* 1 Jan. 2014. Web. 25 Dec. 2015. http://therumpus.net/2014/01/the-rumpus-interview-with-edwige-danticat/

Fuguet, Alberto. "I Am Not a Magical Realist." *Salon.com.* 11 Jun. 1997. Web. 26 Dec. 2015. http://www.salon.com/1997/06/11/magicalintro/

García Márquez, Gabriel. "Gabriel García Márquez—Facts." *Nobelprize.org.* Nobel Media AB 2014. Web. 12 Dec. 2015. http://www.nobelprize.org/nobel_prizes/literature/laureates/1982/marquez-facts.html

———. "The Mysteries of Bill Clinton." *Salon.com.* Web. 1 Feb. 1999. Web. 11 Jan. 2016. http://www.salon.com/1999/02/01/cov_02news_2/

———. "Nobel Lecture: The Solitude of Latin America." *Nobelprize.org.* Nobel Media AB 2014. Web. 12 Dec. 2015. http://www.nobelprize.org/nobel_prizes/literature/laureates/1982/marquez_lecture.html

———. *One Hundred Years of Solitude.* Trans. Gregory Rabassa. New York: Harper Perennial, 2006. Print.

Jackson, David. "Obama, Clinton Praise García Márquez." *USA Today*, 18 Apr. 2014. Web. 11 Jan. 2016. http://www.usatoday.com/story/theoval/2014/04/18/obama-clinton-gabriel-garcia-marquez/7859947/

Jackson, Phil, with Hugh Delahanty. *Eleven Reigns: The Soul of Success.* New York: Penguin, 2012. Print.

Johnson, Dane. "The Rise of Gabriel García Márquez and Toni Morrison." In William B. Warner and Deidre S. Lynch, eds. *Cultural Institutions of the Novel.* Durham: Duke UP, 1996. 129–55. Print.

Khan, Soha Ali (sakpataudi). "'The scent of bitter almonds always reminded him of the fate of unrequited love.' A favorite author Gabriel García Márquez passed away today." 17 Apr. 2014, 3:04 a.m. Tweet.

Kurniawan, Eka. "Eka Kurniawan: A New Face in World Literature." Interview with Alice Lewinsky. *AlineaTV.com* 20 Aug. 2015. Web. 25 Dec. 2015.

Melville, Herman. *Moby-Dick, Or, The Whale.* New York: Airmont, 1964. Print.

Murnane, Gerald. *A History of Books.* Artarmon, NSW (Australia): Giramondo, 2013. Print.

Nullvalue. "La última emisión de QAP." *El Tiempo* 30 Dec. 1997. Web. 11 Dec. 2015. http://www.eltiempo.com/archivo/documento/MAM-711688

Pérez Joglar, René (Residente). "La muerte nunca nos venció porque todo lo que muere es porque alguna vez nació... QDP Gabriel García Marquez." 17 Apr. 2014, 1:11 p.m. Tweet.

Ramírez, Victoria and Patrick Murphy. "On Comics, Genres, amd Stèles: A Conversation with Michael Chabon." *Conversations with Michael Chabon.* Ed. Brannon Costell. Jackson: UP of Mississippi, 2015. 104–19. Print.

Roncagliolo, Santiago. "Enemigos íntimos." *La República* 4 Apr. 2014. Web. http://larepublica.pe/columnistas/rayos-y-centellas/enemigos-intimos-18-04-2014

Stiles, Kent B. " Colombia Pays Novelist Honor." *The New York Times.* 26 Jul. 1942: D13. Print.

Uribe, Juan. "Así nació la idea de unir turismo y realismo mágico." *El Tiempo* 14 Apr. 2013. Web. 11 Jan. 2016. http://www.eltiempo.com/archivo/documento/CMS-12740926
Vargas, Ángel. "Soy fundador de *La Jornada*." *La Jornada* 18 Apr. 2014: 8. Print.
Vásquez, Juan Gabriel. "Malentendidos alrededor de Garcia Márquez." *Letras Libres* Nov. 2005: 42–45.

Chapter 2

Gabriel García Márquez
Politics and Death across His Life of Writing
Regina Janes

Now that Gabriel José García Márquez is dead, it is time to look at death, dying, saying farewell and returning from the dead in his fictions. We hesitated before then. Although critics had noticed death's persistent infiltration, no one followed it out, infected perhaps with magical thinking. We were afraid, if we talked about death, it would happen. Now we are free to talk, by grace of the commonplace catastrophe.

Across his writing life, Gabriel García Márquez grudged at death, the terminus that gives life urgency and pathos. Death slithers in narcissistic despair through his earliest works, surges in apocalyptic jubilation for the great novels, and subsides to grim, ironic resolution, life gripped, not resigned, toward the end. García Márquez also grudged at Colombian and Latin American politics, except for the Cuban revolution, which, in turn, filled him with enthusiasm, led to a brief period of employment in New York City with Cuba's Prensa Latina, and culminated, after he acquired fame with *One Hundred Years of Solitude*, in an enduring friendship with Fidel Castro and a refusal to engage in public criticism of Cuba. Guillermo Cabrera Infante, trickily dissident Cuban, diagnosed García Márquez with "delirium totalitarium," complicated by "castroentiritis" (Ésteban and Panichelli, 66, 166).

Death and politics would not seem to have much to do with each other, except for politics' killing habit of sending so many people off earlier than anyone expected. Death is eternal, always there and forever; politics is ephemeral, always changing, daughter of mutability. Mutability's ever-whirling wheel sways all mortal things, and as Edmund Spenser knew, the mutable and ephemeral challenge what seems eternal.[1] So a new sense of political possibility enabled García Márquez briefly to raise the dead. Ordinarily death gives the prick to life, rousing libido, stimulating desire; psychologists call the phenomenon "mortality salience," Freud intuited it in "the death wish," and it explains the fondness for tragedy that so puzzled David Hume. In García Márquez's case politics gave death a jolt.

Scholars know a great deal about the Colombian politics found in García Márquez's fictions, from the War of a Thousand Days to *la violencia*. The banana-workers' massacre of *One Hundred Years of Solitude* echoes in history, sociology, and ecological studies by Dan Koeppel, Peter Chapman, Marcelo Bucheli, Catherine C. Legrand, and others. Now fading, however, is the politics from within which García Márquez wrote and that enabled his great fictions' peculiar shape. Briefly put, the Cuban revolution supplied the air breathed by readers and writer alike of *One Hundred Years of Solitude* and *The Autumn of the Patriarch,* while the martyrdom of Chile's Salvador Allende haunts *Chronicle of a Death Foretold.* The Cuban revolution, that somersault of possibility, gave García Márquez his dénouements, the crushing finality of the first two books' endings. That revolution's impetus should not be a new idea. Lucila Mena almost proposed it long ago, and Donald Shaw thinks her proposal "lame" (Mena 218, Shaw 29).[2] So revolutionary an impact is worth returning to, however, now that the history within which García Márquez wrote is dead, buried under the rubble of the Berlin Wall in 1989, a generation ago. Allende's ghost is more contentious—the only Allende in Swanson's *Cambridge Companion to García Márquez* (or Williams's *Companion*) is Isabel. Some will consider this claim a phantom, nonexistent, though the face is familiar.

What were those politics? García Márquez's writing career began within a specific twentieth-century political moment: the decolonization of the Third World after the Second World War, as whole continents ejected European colonial powers, Britain from India and Africa, France from Indochina and Algeria, Belgium from Congo, Portugal from Angola and Mozambique. Japan had led the way, thrusting the west from the east, then losing China and Korea. US foreign policy maneuvered to keep the world's property safe for capitalists and capitalism, and out of the hands of nationalists and reformers and land redistributors, who turned to the Soviet Union for support or declared themselves nonaligned.[3] In Latin America the 1940s and 1950s were decades of US-supported dictators, and in Colombia in particular of political violence. Gerald Martin has counted the dictators in place in the 1950s: Odría in Peru (1948–1956), the Somozas in Nicaragua (1936–1979), Castillo Armas in Guatemala (1954–1957), Trujillo in the Dominican Republic (1930–1961), Batista in Cuba (1952–58), Pérez Jiménez in Venezuela (1952–1958), Rojas Pinilla in Colombia (1953–1957) (*García Márquez*, 195). Martin leaves out Perón in Argentina, Stroessner in Paraguay and the Duvalier family in Haiti. Of 20 national governments from Mexico to Tierra del Fuego, only six, Uruguay and Chile, Bolivia, Ecuador, and Brazil enjoyed democratic governments, with Mexico always its own story.

In the mid-fifties, changes began. In an anecdote García Márquez often retold of the period when "Latin America was paved with dictators," Cuban poet Nicolás Guillén leaned out of his Paris window in 1955 after his morning coffee and shouted, "The man has fallen." Everyone thought it was his own dictator, "Argentinians, Paraguayans, Dominicans, Peruvians ... I heard him too, and thought 'Shit, Rojas Pinilla's gone!'" But "[t]he man" was Perón (Martin, *García Márquez*, 198). Colombia's Rojas Pinilla fell in 1957, replaced by the National Front, the alternation in power of the two political parties of oligarchs who had long controlled—and still do—the politics of Colombia.[4] The next year in Venezuela, García Márquez was present for Pérez Jiménez's toppling by a military junta. Then at the New Year, as 1958 became 1959, the US-supported Fulgencio Batista fled Cuba, ejected by a guerrilla movement led by Fidel Castro and Che Guevara, cheered on by Cabrera Infante. García Márquez also was an enthusiast. In Cuba for the trials of Batista military leaders in February 1959, he went to work for Prensa Latina, a press agency founded to counter US coverage with a Latin perspective on Latin American politics. He worked for Prela first in Bogotá and then January to June 1961 in New York City, just as the United States was arranging the Bay of Pigs invasion, a secret that everyone knew (April 17, 1961; 2016 is the 55th anniversary). "As [he] would later say, 'there never was a war more foretold'" (Martin, *García Márquez*, 264). García Márquez's friends and allies in Prela had their own ideological differences within the revolution, and García Márquez left Prensa Latina in 1961, four years before Cabrera Infante finally abandoned the cause.[5]

The García Márquez family traveled by bus to Mexico, through the US south, Faulkner country, marveling at "whites only" drinking fountains, cardboard cuisine, and signs prohibiting "dogs and Mexicans," until they finally reached Mexico. There they stopped and stayed, García Márquez working for advertising agencies and learning about film's limitations as a medium. His story "No Thieves in This Town" was filmed with cameos of himself, Juan Rulfo, painter Leonora Carrington, and Luis Buñuel—as a priest, delivering a sermon.[6] Through this period, his contacts were not with the revolution but with his fellow enthusiasts for its independence and promise.[7] And then there arrived the moment on the road to Acapulco for a family vacation when he heard the sentence that would begin *One Hundred Years of Solitude*. That was the beginning. He already had a version of the ending.

That the end was already in sight is clear from death's vicissitudes. In the earliest workings of his imagination, García Márquez played dead. In "The Third Resignation" (1947) when the author was only twenty years old, the protagonist dies three times and is buried partly alive, without desire but without resistance. The next year, another protagonist moves to "The Other Side of Death," and four decades later Florentino Ariza still hopes to arrive there, "at the other side of death, in safety" with Fermina Daza in *Love in the Time of Cholera* (259).[8] In "The Third Resignation," "The Other Side of Death," and "Someone Has Been Disarranging These Roses," García Márquez writes death from inside the dead, imagining the self immobilized, silenced, an active mind in a paralyzed body. Those dead never leave the body even as the living also await "the irremediable and final death" and merge consciousness with the dead ("The Other Side of Death," 18, 20).[9]

Still staying close to corpses, García Márquez moved outside them. Writing in the shadows of Colombian political violence, he went beyond solipsistic burial alive (a young man's fantasy) to life in Colombia's present. The paralysis of the community politicizes the earlier condition of his helpless dead, alert but impotent. Grittily, hopelessly defiant tales sketch resistance to the hostility of a town, the indifference of a government, the malign watchfulness of a community that is alert to danger, but never intervenes in *Leaf Storm*, *In Evil Hour*, and *No One Writes to the Colonel*.[10] "Someone Has Been Disarranging These Roses" already points to the living woman, not the dead boy.

Siding with the survivors rather than with the dead bodies or a grandson's soul, García Márquez began arranging other people's funerals. A sad, solitary funeral gives shape to *Leaf Storm*; a mother and daughter find a grave in "Tuesday Siesta"; Montiel's widow buries her husband Chepe, whom the town suspects of playing dead until he is walled in his tomb; Pastor takes the town's music with him to the grave, and Pepe Amador is disappeared in *In Evil Hour*. Then, suddenly a vibrant, raucous funeral erupts in "Big Mama's Funeral." Everybody knows that the Cuban revolution set off Big Mama's obsequies—or everybody should.[11]

Stephen Hart credits Dasso Saldívar with the insight.[12] A power that has endured too long is finally being buried. Big Mama, who collects the rents and owns, among many other things, the subsoil, the rights of man, and the colors of the national flag, is dead at last; the Pope and the presidents have paid tribute, and the last word of her story—at least before the historians get to it—belongs to the one who leans "a stool against the doorway to tell this story … so that not one of the world's disbelievers would be left who did not know the story of Big Mama, because tomorrow, Wednesday, the garbage men will come and will sweep up the garbage from her funeral, forever and ever" (200).[13] Something politico-economic-symbolic has come to an end—forever.

García Márquez was in Havana in February 1959 for the trial of Jesús Sosa Blanco, one of Batista's colonels, and although he signed Sosa's wife's petition for clemency, he considered the execution two days later justified.[14] In August 1959, his newborn son Rodrigo was baptized by the radical priest Camilo Torres, the latter killed in 1966 fighting alongside Colombian guerrilleros.

"Big Mama's Funeral" was written about the time Rodrigo was born, in the first flush of enthusiasm for a dictator overthrown not in a military coup, but in a popular, leftist guerrilla movement. Latin America had clinched independence too early to be "postcolonial" in the post–Second World War postcolonial period,[15] but Cuba's resistance to US hegemony (assumed in 1823's Monroe Doctrine, compounded by US occupations 1898–1902, 1906–1909[16]) reinserted Latin America in the postcolonial matrix as a guiding (or blinding) light, a single Caribbean star. What García Márquez had found in "Big Mama's Funeral" was the hyperbolic, apocalyptic finality that ends *One Hundred Years of Solitude* and *The Autumn of the Patriarch*.

A characteristic break with the past marks the structure of "Big Mama's Funeral," *One Hundred Years of Solitude* and *The Autumn of the Patriarch*. Imagining such a break would not have been possible without the concomitant hope of political transformation. The Cuban revolution proposed a terminus, an end point, a death, that finished off an old way of being. What lay beyond was not yet clear, what afterlife would emerge, but the old could be thrown away. The ending of "Big Mama's Funeral" promises that the "garbage" is going to be swept up and away forever and ever, this Wednesday. The "garbage" is the existing social, political, economic order with all its ownership, exploitation, oppression, and profits. That world could finally be imagined as ending, not as proceeding forever in a dialectical crab-walk to more of the same. For García Márquez, believing in the possibility of change meant being able to write the past *into* the past and *as* the past, rather than as an inescapable present.

Endings are not everything: it would be six years before he found a way to begin. Juan Rulfo's *Pedro Páramo* proposed a world where the characters were already dead, and García Márquez's performative fiction liberated his dead. For the first time, the dead come back. They come back in three ways: as psychological reality and authorial power in *One Hundred Years of Solitude* and as reality's political nightmare in *The Autumn of the Patriarch*. They do not come back in any form that a Colombian Catholic—or other Christian—should suppose or expect.

As a one-time altar boy in a nominally Catholic country, García Márquez should have believed with Catholic Christians that on death his soul is dragged to purgatory, there to be burned free of its sins, purged in purgatory for heaven. Luckier—or more deserving—souls waft directly to heaven; the unluckier—those deserving otherwise—to hell. Meanwhile all the bodies wait to be resurrected from the dead, flesh brought up from dust and reconstituted. At the Last Judgment, each body reunites with its soul to spend forever and ever in heaven or hell. Purgatory vanishes when eternity begins. That is what any Catholic should believe. Yet in spite of levitating priests, building churches, founding cemeteries, and visiting popes, that narrative is absent.

The Christian promise of eternal life has barely a walk-on in García Márquez. In "Nabo: The Black Man Who Made the Angels Wait," a man keeps urging Nabo (kicked in the head by a horse, locked in a room) to join the choir, they're waiting for him: choirs are equally African, evangelical, Catholic, and heavenly. The story ends as Nabo collapses and the mute girl cries his name; he is not seen to join any choir. The very old man with enormous wings does fly away, but where he goes remains as undefined as where he came from. Remedios rises into the heavens with the sheets, just like the Virgin, but all we see is the ascent, not the arrival. Rebeca's parents in turn have gone to God's "holy kingdom," but no one looks for them there (47, 116).

It isn't that García Márquez doesn't know his cultural options. He quotes Dante when it serves his turn. His sons were baptized, though no one knelt when the priest Camilo Torres declared the Holy Spirit's presence at Rodrigo's baptism (Martin, *García Márquez*, 253). When García Márquez won the Nobel Prize, his mother Luisa Santiaga insisted that "her father the Colonel must be celebrating somewhere; he had always predicted great things for Gabito" (Martin, *García Márquez*, 430). Where the Colonel is celebrating, Nabo's Negro saxophonist is playing a set. More folkloric than theological, such suppositions meet the need that afterlives can fill. The dead, momentarily revived, still live in those who remember them. An afterlife or realm of the dead holds little interest for García Márquez. It appears only as an indistinct watery place his characters leave whenever they can, to return to the living, to evade oblivion.

In *One Hundred Years of Solitude,* the dead walk again. Appearing first to Úrsula, rationalized by José Arcadio Buendía, the murdered Prudencio Aguilar hangs around the water jars and roams through the rooms, looking terribly sad. José Arcadio Buendía attributes Prudencio's appearance to their bad conscience until he too sees him.[17] Characteristic of death is loneliness, a "deep nostalgia as he yearned for living people," says the narrator, seconded by José Arcadio Buendía's perception that "he's so very lonely" (30).[18] Terrified of oblivion, "the other death that exists within death," Prudencio Aguilar again returns when Melquíades's second death puts Macondo on the map of the dead. This time, under the chestnut tree, José Arcadio Buendía welcomes him: "You've come from a long way off" (80).[19] But Prudencio is still dead.

In Prudencio's first return, José Arcadio Buendía knows that the living see a person who is on their minds. To that person they impute what they would feel if they were dead, here a horror of solitude, and they project onto the dead their own longing for life in death. This projecting habit in our time enables people to find solace in robot pets and to believe their cats have affection for them. People attribute mind to almost anything, and the dead are high on the list of potentially mindful inanimate things. There is equally an urgency to start over and to abandon the dead, articulated in the flight from Riohacha to a newer world. The cliché we know is "moving on, it's time to move on." So José Arcadio Buendía and Úrsula have already moved on to create Macondo when the novel opens.

Only Melquíades, magician turned author, succeeds in being alive when he returns in chapter three from his death, reported as chapter one ends. Novels are often written to bring back the dead, and their return is one effect produced by writing or reading novels. The moment of Melquíades's return is both pivotal and political. He rescues Macondo from a magical realist moment: the insomnia plague.

As Lucila Mena and Philip Swanson observe, the insomnia plague is the oblivion that has already befallen the indigenous peoples of Colombia, so rarely referred to in *One Hundred Years of Solitude* (Mena 201, Swanson 59). Their power erased, their languages forgotten, the Indians, Cataure and Visitación, once princes in the land, now servants, recognize the plague that has already destroyed their own people; they slip away as the insomnia plague descends, erasing writing's meaning, inflicting idiocy. (Sleeplessness indeed causes memory loss and prevents the formation of new memories. Insomnia is bad for the brain.) From this impending catastrophe, Melquíades rescues the town, twice over, as the magician he is, as the writer he becomes.

Returned, Melquíades finds "himself forgotten, not with the ...remediable forgetfulness of the heart, but with a different kind of forgetfulness, which was more cruel and irrevocable and which he knew very well[,] because it was the forgetfulness of death" (54).[20] The heart's forgetfulness can be restored—look! There you are again, and forgotten feeling begins to stir. In death's forgetfulness, nothing moves. The insomnia plague obliterates, and only the magician-author has the syrup of cure.

When Melquíades dies again in chapter four, he puts Macondo on the map of the dead. The dead have a map? Indeed they do—and unlike the traditional maps of the dead by Vergil or Dante, García Márquez's map leads the dead *out* of the realm of the dead *back* to the land of the living. His dead have somewhere to go, but they do not want to stay there, whether swimming in the Bay of Bengal ("The Sea of Lost Time") or with the squids off the sands of Singapore (*One Hundred Years of Solitude*). García Márquez provides a watery version of the traditional earth goddess of the dead, Greek Persephone, or Sumerian Ereshkigal, the mothering, smothering earth from which men come, to which they go. Origin meeting end, Odysseus finds his mother among the dead. "The Third Resignation" dissolves into amniotic fluids; "The Sea of Lost Time" (1961) sets the dead afloat, like Melquíades; the handsomest drowned man in the world comes from the sea and returns to it, after being tended by women. García Márquez's afterlife is uniquely watery; floating or swimming, his dead have no ground to stand on. Earth, where people die, is for the living. The map of the dead, marked with black dots, indicates places where someone has died. If no one has died, a place is unmarked, and the dead cannot find it. Traveling that map, looking for the living, the dead do not seem to interact with each other. Úrsula expects Gerineldo Márquez's corpse to greet her kin, but the narrator lends her hypothesis no support (295–96, 393).

Near Melquíades are buried the already forgotten, Rebeca's parents. Their names are known, but they are not. The letter accompanying Rebeca and their bones calls them "that unforgettable friend Nicanor Ulloa and his very worthy wife Rebeca Montiel, may God keep them in His holy kingdom, whose remains the girl was carrying that they might be given Christian burial" (47).[21] Neither Úrsula nor her husband knows the writer of the letter or remembers anyone with those names, though Rebeca is allegedly Úrsula's second cousin. Like a labeled photograph in a family album of persons now unidentifiable: though the label names them, no one any longer knows who the people in the photo were. Only names and an orphan prove they once existed, that a couple coupled.

After his burial, Melquíades shuffles through the house; Prudencio returns to the chestnut tree. Amaranta carries letters to the dead. No replies seem to be received.[22] In the final chapter, Amaranta Úrsula and Aureliano Buendía embark on their happiness and are often "awakened by the traffic of the dead." Their experience García Márquez described in "Someone Is Disarranging These Roses" and in autobiographical anecdotes. Paradoxically, that traffic gives a certainty of continuance that rolls over into certain annihilation. Like the novel's readers (and its narrator, who brings them back by naming them), Amaranta Úrsula and Aureliano Buendía hear Úrsula and José Arcadio Buendía, Fernanda, Colonel Aureliano Buendía, Aureliano Segundo—"and then they learned that dominant obsessions can prevail against death and they were happy again with the certainty that they would go on loving each other in their shape as apparitions long after other species of future animals would steal from the insects the paradise of misery that the insects were finally stealing from man" (378).[23]

In this curious sentence, Amaranta Úrsula and Aureliano Buendía promise themselves an eternity of love-making as apparitions—love constant beyond death. That spiritual spectral continuity is aborted within the sentence that supposes it. They know—or the narrator knows—that our world of humans and insects will disappear. The insects now stealing paradise from man will be displaced by "other species of future animals" of which neither we nor the insects know anything. Not even the insects are eternal. Time puts an end to every form of life the planet now knows. This ecocriticism with a vengeance looks beyond climate change to aeons of disappearance.[24]

As to those love-making apparitions, Jacques Joset notes in his superb edition of *Cien años de soledad* that "the illusion of life after (or within) death joins other illusions of the last couple that thinks to prolong the line" (486n31). Spectral love-making after death is a mirage like all the rest, a mirror that reflects only living hopes. Paradoxically, the realistic specter of annihilation is equally imaginary. The world after humanity is a reality really as unreal as the unreality of apparitions making love forever. Neither annihilation nor eternal spectral love exists. Equally produced by imagination, one is called true and realistic, the other fanciful and wish-fulfilling. Lest there be any mistake, García Márquez answered the latter fantasy in the story-title, "Death Constant beyond Love." Ironically reversed is the passionate dust of Quevedo's "Amor constante mas allá de la muerte."

Death in *One Hundred Years of Solitude* seems circumvented by Melquíades's resurrection, but Melquíades's privilege is only an author's. The pristine magical room of art is a literary fiction, juxtaposed with the overgrown, serpent-riddled room of historical, political reality. No one has a second chance outside a magician's book.

Except, it seems, the patriarch. *The Autumn of the Patriarch* (1975) is one long funeral—finding and laying out the body, which persistently comes back to life, or threatens to. Like a wilier Struldbrugg, the immortals in Jonathan Swift's *Gulliver's Travels*, the dictator seems unable to die, and then, laid out for his second funeral, parodying the beautiful drowned man, he escapes burial. All the dictators in the world, he is an Arcimboldo portrait, grotesquely assembled from disparate details of individual dictators as Arcimboldo (ca. 1526–1593) put together flowers or fruits to make his seasonal men. So a carnation thrown in the final chapter evokes Portugal's "Carnation Revolution" that overthrew Salazar's party four years after Salazar's second death. Salazar's first death was a stroke (1968); he revived to be assured for two years that he was still ruling, until he finally died again (1970). The novel ends in joyous celebration of the dictator's final passing—but that jubilant conclusion promises too much. Announced to the world is the good news "that the uncountable time of eternity had come to an end."[25]

Ending eternity is a neat trick. *One Hundred Years of Solitude* reminds us that nature will eventually play it on us as a species. When human beings vanish, human concepts, like eternity, will also vanish. Though we have no part in it, while humans persist, eternity persists. Without ephemeral us, no more eternity.

As a Marxist or secularist or modernist, García Márquez ought to believe in no afterlife at all, and that is the belief he gives to the people in *The Autumn of the Patriarch*. They ought to be Catholics or Evangelicals expecting eternal life, but they are not. They know that this life is "arduous and ephemeral but there wasn't any other" (251). Beyond this life is the patriarch's oblivion.

To his nightly address, "have a good death mother," the patriarch's mother answers from her crypt, "a very good death son" (248). In an interview, García Márquez has claimed that the patriarch's story is autobiography. Certainly the patriarch carries away with him the terror of death and oblivion from earlier stories, as he whistles "toward the homeland of shadows of the truth of oblivion, clinging to his fear of the rotting cloth of death's hooded cassock" (251).[26] These exuberant funerals are for something one wants to see ended, even as the history of *One Hundred Years of Solitude* is an unhappy one better not repeated. The joys of the master narrative about Colombia's past include the joy of that narrative's destruction. García Márquez's next fiction, *Chronicle of a Death Foretold* (1981), will focus on a death, not a funeral.

García Márquez's dead never come back again; apparitions do not appear. The dead who do not die in Miguel Littín's clandestine trip to Chile (1986) are Salvador Allende and Pablo Neruda, their immortality declared in chapter titles: "Two Dead Who Never Die: Allende and Neruda," "Two Living Dead: Allende and Neruda." If anyone ascends to heaven holding anything, it is the woman who flies Littín's clandestine film out of Chile to Italy, using the code "Grazia ascended to the heavens," as one tends to do in an airplane.[27]

Salvador Allende died in 1973, two years before *The Autumn of the Patriarch* appeared. Socialist, doctor, long-time senator and president of the senate, four-time candidate for the Chilean presidency, Allende had at last become the democratically elected socialist president of Chile in 1970.[28] Three years later he was overthrown in a CIA-supported coup that put a murderous market-oriented dictator, Augusto Pinochet, in power for seventeen years. Killed during the assault on the presidential palace in Santiago, Allende committed suicide, the new junta claimed, but no one on the left believed it. An autopsy forty years later (2011) confirmed the junta's claim, but did not mollify the disbelievers.[29]

García Márquez vowed to write no more fiction until Pinochet fell. That promise reflected two confident assumptions: that dictators would continue to fall in the late 1970s as they had in the 1950s and that a traditionally democratic nation like Chile would never tolerate a dictator for long. As it happened, Salazar's party was overthrown in Portugal's Carnation Revolution in 1974; Franco died in Spain in 1975; the eternal Somozas were routed by the Sandinistas in Nicaragua in 1979, and Latin American nations began resuming relations with Cuba in the face of US hostility, so he was not altogether in error on the first count. But on Chilean acquiescence, he was too hopeful.

Unlike many of his peers, including Pablo Neruda (they met in 1970), García Márquez had never been sanguine about Allende's chances of survival. In 1971, accidentally echoing Edmund Burke in 1789 on the French Revolution, he told an interviewer, "Chile is heading toward violent and dramatic events." The United States would not accept a socialist Chile, and others' hopes for a "peaceful and constitutional socialism [were] utopian" (Guibert 333). García Márquez's having predicted the "wall of opposition" and "violence" did not assuage his grief when his prediction came true. In an interview, he described the event simply: "The Chilean coup was a catastrophe for me" (Martin, *García Márquez*, 376).

Equally painfully, the insurrectionary hopes raised by Cuba led in the 1960s both to other insurrections and to their violent repression. Countries that had been democracies in the 1950s became military dictatorships in the 1960s and 70s: Uruguay, Bolivia, Ecuador, and Brazil. Dictatorship itself devolved into new horrors in Argentina and Guatemala. *The Autumn of the Patriarch* was nothing if not a timely book. Its readers could not fail to notice that eternity had not, in fact, come to an end.

Chronicle of a Death Foretold broke the promise not to publish. Seemingly Sophoclean, personal, and apolitical, the story goes back to an actual incident from Sucre in the 1950s. Cayetano Gentile Chimento, a friend of García Márquez, had been cut to pieces in the town's main square by the brothers of a repudiated bride. Several of García Márquez's siblings had spoken to Cayetano just before his death, and one of them saw him die.[30] In the novel, the victim's name, the place where he died, and the cuts he suffered are altered. Santiago Nasar holds his guts in his hand as he stumbles into the door of his own house to die. Salvador Allende was nicknamed "el guatón," the big belly, for his paunch. Throughout the 1950s and 60s Allende's belly and glasses identified him in Chilean political cartoons. Gerald Martin's biography reproduces the famous photograph of Allende under attack in the doorway of the president's house. He died in the president's house, his own house. Santiago, who stumbles at the threshold holding his guts, mentioned twice, is also the name of the capital of Chile, Santiago de Chile, the city where Salvador, unsaved, died. Coincidence? Accident? That seems doubtful. The novel is not an allegory; it is what it seems, but it is also a cenotaph. Allende's was a death García Márquez himself had foretold, but had not wanted to believe.

In 1982, the year after he published *Chronicle*, García Márquez received the Nobel Prize and, in his acceptance speech, re-worked the ending of *One Hundred Years of Solitude* to demand a second chance for the races of Latin America. The "utopian" expectations contemptuously dismissed in 1971 are resurrected as a forlorn hope: "a new and limitless utopia for life wherein no one can decide for others how they are to die, where love really can be true and happiness possible, where the lineal generations of one hundred years of solitude will have at last and for ever a second chance on earth."[31] That commitment to utopia and to life included the Cuban revolution, to which he had come fluttering, like one of his butterflies, and stuck to the wall. Not to have done so would have been to turn his back on a regime that had given Cubans universal literacy, health care, an unspoiled environment, and a role in the world.[32] It would also have been to acquiesce in a global turn to the right that only intensified after 1989, when the Berlin Wall fell, the Soviet Union broke up, China turned capitalist, and Marxist ideology vanished as a force for change in the world.

In the later fictions, death is not overcome with apparitions—characters cling to life, to love, to what remains, and death is irremediable and final. So *Love in the Time of Cholera* (1985) begins with a death by suicide caused neither by love nor by cholera, but by horror of old age and perhaps pain. Old age begins at a different decade for Spanish and English readers. For English readers, old age begins comfortably at 70 (15)—a person can pass through her sixties without being old. This revival of magic realism is, alas, a translator's or copy editor's error—or perhaps an infiltration from José Saramago's *History of the Siege of Lisbon*. In Spanish, old age begins at 60 (26). Jeremiah St Amour dies at the end of his fifties, killed by an author in his own mid-fifties, after his sixtieth birthday, not his seventieth.

That opening is a little gargoyle protruding from the cathedral of love. As an episode, it sets a man with a lover who refuses the indecency of old age (40, 60) against a pair of aging, aged lovers, whose alternative story occupies the rest of the novel. Not for Jeremiah, the only Old Testament prophet whose predictions come true, are the repulsive indignities of being washed and diapered, like Juvenal, or losing his teeth like Florentino. Jeremiah and his lover are forgotten by the novel—as the dead are forgotten by those to whom they do not matter. In the penultimate chapter Florentino Ariza hears the bells ringing, and someone comes to tell him that Jeremiah St Amour has died, but he knows the bells are not for the refugee, but for someone more important. They are ringing for Juvenal Urbino. So Jeremiah St Amour disappears, passed by, passed over, disregarded, dead.

Death infiltrates the title's love, though readers tend to ignore it. Even Gastón J. Fernández, addressing death's multiple aspects within the novel, ignores the title's lethal disease. Cholera kills: it causes deaths by poverty and sewage, deaths that public works could prevent. Deaths by cholera with a blow to the neck are unknown to medicine but not to politics or criminal violence—decapitation's ancient and modern terror. Dante appears. He does not, as in his own *Comedy,* meet his beloved Beatrice again, see the face of God in paradise, understand the world as a book whose leaves are bound by love, and feel 'l'amor che muove il sol e l'altre stelle," (the love that moves the sun and the other stars). García Márquez's Dante enters hell. Over the bridge to the cemetery of the poor is the inscription above hell's gate, still in Italian to make sure the reference is recognized: "*lasciate ogni speranza voi ch'entrate*" ("abandon all hope, ye who enter here") (111, 149). Whether burial or poverty means abandoning hope is not clear, but probably both.

Lacking Dante's confidence, the good Catholic Juvenal Urbino experiences the "terror of not finding God in the darkness of death" (41).[33] When Juvenal Urbino's father speaks to him of his own death, the angel of death hovers in the room for a moment and departs, with a trail of feathers in his wake—but the boy does not see him, nor does anyone else. He is merely a brief narrative flourish (114, 152). An African doll grows on Fermina Daza's pillow (125, 166). Who sent it is an unsolved mystery on the order of José Arcadio's suicide or murder in *One Hundred Years of Solitude*. The ghost of a drowned woman waves to the passing boat; Fermina sees her, certain that she did not exist yet her face seemed familiar—intersecting contradictory realities (332, 431). Florentino Ariza's love affairs are spangled with blood, from the married woman eviscerated by her husband to the molested child who kills herself. Just turned fourteen, she "was a child in every sense of the word, with braces on her teeth and the scrapes of elementary school on her knees" (272).[34] There are ecological deaths—of the river, the manatees, the alligators, despoiled.

Not even Florentino Ariza really expects to outlive the manatees. In the English translation his last word "Forever" evokes the eternities of *One Hundred Years of Solitude*, *The Autumn of the Patriarch*, the Nobel Prize speech: how long can you continue going up and down the river? "'Forever,' he said" (348). In Spanish, however, there is no echo; he speaks what the author means and wants: life, "vida." "—Toda la vida—dijo" (all life long, all my life—he said, 451). Life, not eternity, is the operative word, and "said" is the last.

So it is fitting that at the end of *The General in His Labyrinth*, its subject the death of Simón Bolívar, Bolívar does not die. The novel ends in his last moment, his last sensations of his own body, the last sounds he hears and sights he sees. They are preserved, forever, as language alone can preserve the passing moment and prevent its ending.

"Then he *crossed his arms over his chest* and began *to listen* to the radiant voices of the slaves singing the six o'clock Salve in the mills, and through the window *he saw* the diamond of Venus in the *sky that was dying forever*, the *eternal* snows, the *new* vine whose yellow bellflowers he would not see bloom on the following Saturday in the house closed in mourning, the *final brilliance of life* that would never, through all eternity, he repeated again" (268; emphases added). The unrepeatable fate of the species or race is also the unrepeatable fate of the individual, of the day, as García Márquez sketches again "the ephemeral splendor of another afternoon that would never return" (*Love in the Time of Cholera*, 41), Juvenal Urbino's experience moments before his accidental death.[35]

García Márquez's final protagonist, the Saramago-inflected, Kawabata-inspired hero of *Memories of My Melancholy Whores* puts in for a hundred after his ninety-first birthday. The novel is an apolitical catalogue of ways to think about death's approach, Shakespearean in its thoroughness. After death, unlucky souls go to New York: says the narrator, "that's where I suppose condemned souls go in order not to learn the truth of their past lives" (15). The novel ends with love and writing and life: "I was arranging my languishing papers, the inkwell, the goose quill, when the sun broke through the almond trees in the park and the river mail packet, a week late because of the drought, bellowed as it entered the canal in the port. It was, at last, real life, with my heart safe and condemned to die of happy love in the joyful agony of any day after my hundredth birthday" (115; "después de mis cien años").[36] The actual author of this story never used a goose quill. Writing at age 77, he would die at 87 in 2014. But his "cien años" will never repeat.The boat is a persistent motif. Emblem of passage, between life and death, the boat comes from elsewhere, plies the river, dwarfs the living, sounds its whistle, enters the port: it carries the living, those who will die and those who will be born.

In the 1992 "Preface" to *Strange Pilgrims/Doce cuentos peregrinos* García Márquez tells his readers that he had been dreaming his own death. He was at a great funeral party; the party ending, the celebrants dispersing, he was told he was the only one who could not leave. Then he knew that dying meant not being with your friends any more. That story he could never write, though he had tried several times. He could never make the party at his funeral "the wild revel it had been in [his] dream" (xi).[37] He had already written the wildest revel ever in "Big Mama's Funeral," but that was a revel rejoicing in something he wanted to end. Living was not something García Márquez ever wanted to see end, in spite of his clarity about, and ultimate experience of, the miserable decrepitude of age. He put in for friends and the life of writing.

At a crucial moment in his writing life, politics pulled him out from among the dead souls, beaten down by rain and bullets, man and nature. Briefly the dead walked, reviving a history and a politics, within another, later politics and history. Once a history dies, a work survives, if it survives, freed from its own causes. Its survival motivates in turn a quest for those forgotten causes. That relationship is allegorized in García Márquez's peculiar articulation of autobiography: his fictions are autobiographical, and his autobiography is a biography of his fictions, not the man. *Living to Tell the Tale* alternates pages of Colombian history and politics with anecdotes of the house, the ice, the sacred crocodile (his wife's nickname). History and politics are as much the life as the life. The memoir weaves them together in a tapestry as inextricable as the patriarch's.

An earlier version of this paper entitled "Saying Goodbye to Gabo, Gabo Says Goodbye" was delivered at "A Celebration of the Life of García Márquez," Muhlenberg College, Allentown PA, 16 April 2015, organized by Sra. Flor María Buitrago.

NOTES

1. "What man that sees the ever-whirling wheel
   Of change, the which all mortal things doth sway,
   But thereby he doth find and plainely feele
   How mutability in them doth play
   Her cruel sports, to many men's decay?" Edmund Spenser, "Mutability Cantos," 1.i, *The Faerie Queene.*

2. Focused on Colombian politics, Mena neglects regional politics. Oddly, Stephen Hart's Eréndira—who runs until she is never heard of again—runs "towards the Revolution" (*Cambridge Companion to García Márquez*, 141). The Brazilian Marcos P. Natali does not mention the Cuban revolution in "Postcolonial Writing in Latin America, 1850–2000," *The Cambridge History of Postcolonial Literature*. Mariano Siskind emphasizes the importance of that revolution for the novel's reception and readership, not authorship, "Magic Realism," *The Cambridge History of Postcolonial Literature*, II: 852–53, 860.

3. A rare exception was the Suez Crisis of 1956 when the Eisenhower administration rebuffed an attempt by France, Britain, and Israel to take back control of the Suez Canal from the nationalist, pan-Arabist president of Egypt, Gamal Abdel Nasser. A parallel recognition of national sovereignty over canals occurred in 1979, when the Carter administration made a new treaty handing back the Panama Canal to Panama. More dire in their long-term consequences were such episodes as the overthrow of democratically elected, socialist-leaning governments in Guatemala (1954) and Iran (1953). Guatemala continues to endure genocidal blood-letting; in Iran the US-installed Shah of Iran was dislodged in a revolution (1979) ultimately dominated by theocratic elements still regnant.

4. The formal alternation ended in 1974; since then Liberals have won the presidency seven times to the Conservatives' twice. See David Bushnell, *The Making of Modern Colombia: A Nation in Spite of Itself*; Marco Palacios, *Entre la legitimidad y la violencia: Colombia 1875–1994.*

5. Guillermo Cabrera Infante was at the Bay of Pigs and served as Cuba's cultural attaché in Brussels from 1962–1965; he did not leave Cuba permanently until 1965.

6. The film is difficult to secure outside Universidad del Valle de México, D.F., Mexico, but a clip is available on You Tube.

7. García Márquez's willingness to support the revolution publically when others demurred became visible in 1968, in the first Padilla affair, when his name was added to a petition to Castro against disciplining Padilla and he asked for its removal. He and Julio Cortázar remained the staunchest public supporters of the revolution among the Boom authors, continuing through 1971 and the arrest and confession of Padilla. See Martin, *Gabriel García Márquez*, 339–40, 351–53.

8. "sano y salvo a la otra acera de la muerte" (339).

9. "otra muerte irremediable y última," *Ojos*, 29. For an interesting discussion of death and burials, see Gerald Martin, "The General in His Labyrinth," in *Cambridge Companion to Gabriel García Márquez*, ed. Philip Swanson.

10. Juggling violence, resistance, and impotence in "One of These Days," the dentist removes the mayor's abscessed tooth without anesthesia, saying "Now you'll pay

for our twenty dead men" (109), "Aquí nos paga veinte muertos, teniente," *Funerales*, (22), but the town pays the dentist's bill. The forces are matched, but there is no change in view.

11. That information is singularly absent in some places where readers have a right to find it—postcolonial criticism (Natali) and Ilan Stavans' *Gabriel García Márquez: The Early Years*. Perhaps Stavans' dislike of the story prevented his seeing that a story centered on Colombia could be shaped by events occurring elsewhere shortly before it was written. He finds "Big Mama's Funeral" overrated, "somewhat stale, even unfocused" compared to unnamed other critics who regard it as a "huge step, in…. quality and maturity…at the end of the fifties." He juxtaposes the story's writing with his narrative of García Márquez and the Cuban Revolution, but makes no connection between the two (89–90). Later he invokes the pre-emptive Israeli attack in '67 on the day *One Hundred Years of Solitude* was published (159) and US popular history of the 1960s—the Beat revolution of Kerouac and Ginsburg, the Chicano movement and labor leader Cesar Chavez (169), movements of interest in the United States but of dubious relevance to *One Hundred Years of Solitude*.

12. "Big Mama's Funeral," Hart observes, "can almost be seen as a direct response to the ideology underlying the Cuban revolution," 137, citing Dasso Saldívar, *García Márquez: El Viaje a la semilla—La biografía*, 356.

13. "un taburete en la puerta para contar esta historia … y que ninguno de los incrédulos del mundo se quedara sin conocer la noticia de la Mamá Grande, que mañana miércoles vendrán los barrenderos y barrerán la basura de sus funerales, por todos los siglos de los siglos," *Los funerales de la Mama Grande*, 157.

14. García Márquez did not join other journalists visiting Sosa Blanco the night before the execution. If he did not visit Sosa Blanco the night before the execution, it seems unlikely he attended the execution. Popular sources like Wikipedia assert that he was present at the execution, but his presence was not confirmed by either Martin nor Stavans confirm.

15. Marcos Natali reports the complaints of Latin American literary figures against such postcolonial theorists as Homi Bhaba for neglecting their theoretical predecessors a century earlier in the Americas. Colonial divisions kept the Third World focused only on the metropole. "Postcolonial Writing in Latin America, 1850–2000," I: 310–12. Latins could sing whatever tune they liked; they would not be heard in India—until García Márquez.

16. The United States awarded the Cuban Pacification Medal for service in Cuba between 1906 and 1909, the Cuban Occupation Medal for service between 1899 and 1902. United States Navy Department, *General Orders of Navy Department, Series of 1913; Orders Remaining in Force Up to January 29, 1918,* Washington, D.C.: Government Printing Office, 1918.

17. At an Illinois Thanksgiving in 2015, a cousin of friends told me she had chatted with her dead grandfather, when he suddenly appeared in a hallway of her house. His widow talked to him daily. It happens here. These dead are not lonely, however, but quite cheerful, à l'américaine.

18. "la honda nostalgia con que añoraba a los vivos….'Se ve que está muy solo,'" 96.

19. "tan aterradora la proximidad de la otra muerte que existía dentro de la muerte…" "Prudencio,— exclamó—¡cómo has venido a parar tan lejos!" 154.

20. "Se sintió olvidado, no con el olvido remediable del corazón, sino con otro olvido más cruel e irrevocable que él conocía muy bien, porque era el olvido de la muerte," 125. The English calls the heart's forgetfulness "irremediable," as if the prefix "ir" made the remediation more intense, rather than nonexistent, 54. Omitting the comma after "very well" obscures the proposition that the visitor knows that forgetfulness very well because he has been through death, because of his experience of death.

21. "ese inolvidable amigo que fue Nicanor Ulloa y su muy digna esposa Rebeca Montiel, a quienes Dios tuviera en su santo reino, cuyos restos adjuntaba la presente para que les dieran cristiana sepultura," 116.

22. There are no deaths other than Melquíades's in Macondo until chapter 5. Then Remedios, the child-wife of the colonel-to-be, dies in childbirth along with the twins in her belly. This is the first massacre for which the colonel is responsible, and death descends everywhere. The chapter ends in a miniature blood bath, plotted assassinations, the plotter shot, a woman beaten to death with rifle butts, the soldiers who killed her, shot. Death once started multiplies, beginning at birth. It explodes like the belly and the babies—love and politics, birth and death.

In the penultimate chapter, when Amaranta Úrsula returns, no one dies. As if the world of the first four chapters has returned, there are references to the dead and deaths elsewhere, but in Macondo no one dies. That parenthesis soon ends, with the deaths of Amaranta Úrsula and her abandoned child in the last chapter.

23. "Muchas veces fueron despertados por el tráfago de los muertos … y entonces aprendieron que las obsesiones dominantes prevalecen contra la muerte, y volvieron a ser felices con la certidumbre de que ellos seguirían amándose con sus naturalezas de aparecidos, mucho después de que otras especies de animales futuros les arrebataran a los insectoes el paraíso de miseria que los insectos estaban acabando de arrebatarles a los hombres," 486.

24. In 1967, climate change had not yet become visible. As late as 1982 in García Márquez's Nobel Prize speech, nuclear Armageddon was the preferred anticipation of human self-destruction. The depletion of the ozone layer came to attention in the late 1970s to be addressed in the Montreal Protocol of 1987. The Kyoto Protocol was a decade later, 1997. This passage is not remarked by Raymond Williams in "An Eco-Critical Reading of *One Hundred Years of Solitude*," although the quotation he uses from Herbert Tucker, 76n3, to end his essay 75, points to the position García Márquez articulates.

25. "de que el tiempo incontable de la eternidad había por fin terminado," 271.

26. "ardua y efímera pero que no había otra," 271; "que pase buena muerte madre, le dijo, muy buena muerte, hijo, le contestó ella en la cripta," 268; "hacia la patria de tinieblas de la verdad del olvido, agarrado de miedo a los trapos de hilachas podridas del balandrán de la muerte," 271.

27. "Dos muertos que nunca mueren: Allende y Neruda," "Dos muertos vivos: Allende y Neruda," "Grazia ascendió a los cielos," 81, 84, 91–92.

28. *Clandestino en Chile* cites his comic epitaph—"Here lies Salvador Allende, future president of Chile," 82.

29. An autopsy after forty years could perhaps distinguish murder from suicide if an open-mouthed shot through the brain were the method.

30. Martin, *García Márquez*, 409. The version in *Living to Tell the Tale* identifies the woman as a schoolteacher, the murderers as her brothers, the place of death as outside the locked door of his house, but makes no reference to any marriage, 347, 382–84. "Cayetano" is coincidentally the name of the enlightened clerical lover in *Del amor y otros demonios*.

31. *Gabriel García Márquez: New Readings,* ed. Bernard McGuirk and Richard Cardwell, 211. Trans. Richard Cardwell.

32. Cuba also had in 2015 lower infant mortality and murder rates than the United States (Karl Vick, "Cuba on the Cusp," *Time,* April 6, 2015: 34). As to the Cuban revolution, Gerald Martin observes, "For the very first time since the discovery, the whole world would be touched directly by political events in Latin America," *García Márquez*, 246.

33. "el terror de no encontrar a Dios en la oscuridad de la muerte," 61.

34. "era una niña en todo sentido, con sierras en los dientes y peladuras de la escuela primaria en las rodillas," 355.

35. "Entonces cruzó los brazos contra el pecho y empezó a oír las voces radiantes de los esclavos cantando la salve de las seis en los trapiches, y vio por la ventana el diamante de Venus en el cielo que se iba para siempre, las nieves eternas, la enredadera nueva cuyas campánulas amarillas no vería florecer el sábado siguiente en la casa cerrada por el duelo, los últimas fulgores de la vida que nunca más, por los siglos de los siglos, volvería a repetirse," *General*, 269. "el esplendor efímero de otra tarde de menos que se iba para siempre," *Amor en los tiempos del cólera*, 61.

36. "es donde supongo que se van las almas en pena para no digerir la verdad de su vida pasado," 20. "Estaba ordenando mis papeles marchitos, el tintero, la pluma de ganso, cuando el sol estalló entre los almendros del parque y el buque fluvial del correo, retrasado una semana por la sequía, entró bramando en el canal del puerto. Era por fin la vida real, con mi corazón a salvo, y condenado a morir de buen amor en la agonía feliz de cualquier día después de mis cien años," 109.

37. "una parranda como la del sueño," 17.

WORKS CITED

Bucheli, Marcelo. *Bananas and Business: The United Fruit Company in Colombia, 1899–2000.* New York: New York University Press, 2005.

Bushnell, David. *The Making of Modern Colombia: A Nation in Spite of Itself.* Berkeley: University of California Press, 1993.

Chapman, Peter. *Bananas: How the United Fruit Company Shaped the World.* New York: Canongate, 2007.

Ésteban, Ángel y Stéphanie Panichelli. *Gabo y Fidel: El paisaje de una amistad.* Madrid: Espasa, 2004.

Fernández, Gastón J. "La función de la muerte en *El amor en los tiempos del cólera.*" *Discurso literario* 10.2 (1993): 97–105.

García Márquez, Gabriel. *El amor en los tiempos del cólera.* Buenos Aires: Sudamericana, 1985.
———. *La aventura de Miguel Littín clandestino en Chile.* Mexico, D.F.: Editorial Diana, 1986.
———. *The Autumn of the Patriarch.* Trans. Gregory Rabassa. New York: Harper and Row, 1976.
———. "Big Mama's Funeral." *Collected Stories.* Trans. Gregory Rabassa. New York: Harper and Row, 1984.
———. *Cien años de soledad.* (1967) Ed. Jacques Joset. 3rd ed. Madrid: Cátedra, 1987.
———. *Del amor y otros demonios.* Barcelona: Mondadori, 1994.
———. *Doce cuentos peregrinos.* Buenos Aires: Sudamericana, 1992.
———. *Los funerales de la Mama Grande.* (1962) Barcelona: Bruguera, 1980.
———. *El General en su laberinto.* Buenos Aires: Sudamericana, 1989.
———. *The General in His Labyrinth.* Trans. Edith Grossman. New York: Alfred A. Knopf, 1990.
———. *In Evil Hour.* (1968) Trans. Gregory Rabassa. New York: Harper and Row, 1979.
———. *Living to Tell the Tale.* Trans. Edith Grossman. New York: Alfred A. Knopf, 2003.
———. *Love in the Time of Cholera.* Trans. Edith Grossman. New York: Alfred A. Knopf, 1988.
———. *Memoria de mis putas tristes.* Buenos Aires: Sudamericana, 2004.
———. *Memories of My Melancholy Whores.* Trans. Edith Grossman. New York: Alfred A. Knopf, 2005.
———. *One Hundred Years of Solitude.* Trans. Gregory Rabassa. New York: Harper and Row, 1970.
———."The Other Side of Death." *Collected Stories.* Trans. Gregory Rabassa. New York: Harper and Row, 1984.
———. *Strange Pilgrims.* Trans. Edith Grossman. New York: Penguin Books, 1993.
———. "The Third Resignation." *Collected Stories.* Trans. Gregory Rabassa. New York: Harper and Row, 1984.
———. "Someone Has Been Disarranging the Roses." *Collected Stories.* Trans. Gregory Rabassa. New York: Harper and Row, 1984.
Guibert, Rita. *Seven Voices.* New York: Alfred A. Knopf, 1972. 303–37.
Hart, Stephen. "García Márquez's Short Stories." *Cambridge Companion to Gabriel García Márquez.* Ed. Philip Swanson. Cambridge: Cambridge UP, 2010. 129–43.
Joset, Jacques, ed. *Cien años de soledad.* By Gabriel García Márquez. (1967) 3rd ed. Madrid: Cátedra, 1987.
Koeppel, Dan. *Bananas: The Fate of the Fruit That Changed the World.* New York: Plume, 2008.
LeGrand, Catherine C. "Living in Macondo: Economy and Culture in a United Fruit Company Banana Enclave in Colombia." *Close Encounters of Empire: Writing the Cultural History of U.S.-Latin American Relations.* Ed. Gilbert M. Joseph, Catherine LeGrand, and Ricardo D. Salvatore. Durham: Duke UP, 1998. 333–68.

Martin, Gerald. *Gabriel García Márquez: A Life.* Toronto: Viking, 2008.

———."*The General in His Labyrinth.*" *The Cambridge Companion to Gabriel García Márquez.* Ed. Philip Swanson. Cambridge: Cambridge UP, 2010. 94–112.

McGuirk, Bernard and Richard Cardwell, ed. *Gabriel García Márquez: New Readings.* Cambridge: Cambridge UP, 1987.

Mena, Lucila. *La Función de la historia en "Cien años de soledad."* Barcelona: Plaza & Janés, 1979.

Natali, Marcos P. "Postcolonial Writing in Latin America, 1850–2000." *The Cambridge History of Postcolonial Literature.* Ed. Ato Quayson. Cambridge: Cambridge UP, 2012. I: 309–28.

Palacios, Marco. *Entre la legitimidad y la violencia: Colombia 1875–1994.* Bogotá: Norma, 1995.

Saldívar, Dasso. *García Márquez: El Viaje a la semilla—La biografía.* Madrid: Alfaguara, 1997.

Shaw, Donald. "The Critical Reception of García Márquez," *The Cambridge Companion to García Márquez.* Ed Philip Swanson. Cambridge: Cambridge UP, 2010. 25–40.

Siskind, Mariano."Magic Realism." *The Cambridge History of Postcolonial Literature.* Ed. Ato Quayson. Cambridge: Cambridge UP, 2012. II: 833–68.

Spenser, Edmund. "Two Cantos of Mutabilitie."*Poetical Works of Edmund Spenser.* Ed. J.C. Smith and E. De Selincourt. London: Oxford UP, 1912.

Stavans, Ilan. *Gabriel García Márquez: The Early Years.* New York: Palgrave Macmillan 2010.

Swanson, Philip. "*One Hundred Years of Solitude.*" *The Cambridge Companion to Gabriel García Márquez.* Ed. Philip Swanson. Cambridge: Cambridge UP, 2010. 57–63.

United States Navy Department. *General Orders of Navy Department, Series of 1913; Orders Remaining in Force Up to January 29, 1918.* Washington, D.C.: Government Printing Office, 1918.

Vick, Karl. "Cuba on the Cusp." *Time* 6 Apr. 2015: 28–39.

Williams, Raymond Leslie. *A Companion to Gabriel García Márquez.* New York: Boydell & Brewer, 2010.

———. "An Eco-Critical Reading of *One Hundred Years of Solitude.*" *The Cambridge Companion to García Márquez.* Ed. Philip Swanson. Cambridge: Cambridge UP, 2010. 64–77.

Chapter 3

Translation and Apprenticeship
Cervantes, Faulkner, and García Márquez
Edith Grossman

Around the world and over the centuries, literature in translation has been exceptionally important to countless writers who are frequently indebted to foreign authors, whose work in turn they have mined for nuggets of insight and revelation. Writers generally learn from other writers the lessons they need to know about stylistic and thematic devices, or narrative and structural techniques. Long before the advent and increasing popularity of university MFA programs in creative writing, young artists tended to learn their craft by working as literal or figurative apprentices to older, more experienced practitioners of the art. In our day, even graduates of MFA programs are likely to read other authors for that kind of instruction, but even if they can read only their own language, literary translation affords them the opportunity to find their mentors anywhere in the world.

 I propose to highlight an essential line of influence, acquired by means of translated books, that runs from Miguel de Cervantes to William Faulkner to Gabriel García Márquez, but first I'd like to clarify a crucial point. In no way do I intend the word "influence" to serve as a synonym for "imitation." On the contrary, for me it suggests a source of inspiration, an almost serendipitous encounter with a solution, even before the problem has been fully articulated and is still unformulated. An excellent example of this phenomenon is found in García Márquez's memoir, *Living to Tell the Tale*, when he recalls his initial reading of James Joyce's *Ulysses*, a book in translation he was first introduced to by a friend who, as García Márquez puts it, told him with the authority of a bishop, "This is the other Bible." At first he dismissed the book, reading it, as he says, "in bits and pieces and fits and starts until I lost all patience. It was premature brashness." Then, García Márquez tells us: "Years later, as a docile adult, I set myself the task of reading it again in a serious way, and it not only was a discovery of a genuine world that I never suspected inside me, but it also provided invaluable technical help to me in freeing language and in handling time and structures in my books" (*Living* 247).

The worldwide influence of Miguel de Cervantes Saavedra, the indisputable creator of a modern literary language and a modern literary genre, is so profound and so widespread that attempting to track it in a complete and thorough way, even if we limited ourselves to the Spanish-speaking world, would take more time than any of us have at our disposal, but I can offer a thimble-sized synopsis. Part One of *Don Quixote* was published in 1605, Part Two in 1615; translations into other European languages followed very quickly, considering that this happened in the early seventeenth century. The first of them was Thomas Shelton's 1612 English translation of Part One (his translation of Part Two appeared in 1621). Ensuing contemporary versions included the French (1614), the Italian (1622), and the German (1621, though it was incomplete and not actually published until 1648). Following Shelton's translation, which made the complete novel accessible in English only six years after it was available in Spanish, the story of *Don Quixote* in English is varied, constant, and profound. It very well may have begun before 1616, the year both Cervantes and Shakespeare died, with the tortuous saga of a play called "Cardenio," or "The History of Cardenio," long considered lost, though recent news items contained unsubstantiated reports of a manuscript of the play discovered in the effects of a deceased English lord whose very existence has been called into question. The drama, presumably written by Shakespeare and a collaborator, John Fletcher, was based on one of the interpolated tales in Part One of *Don Quixote*, a story that recounts the trials and travails of a wealthy young gentleman driven mad by love. Cardenio's love sickness proves to be a kind of contemporary—that is, mid-Renaissance—ironic mirror image of Don Quixote's literary and somehow willful faux-medieval madness.

If we skip to the eighteenth century, we encounter the widely celebrated influence of Cervantes's *Don Quixote*, often acknowledged by the authors themselves in their books, on the development of the early English novel, notably Henry Fielding's *Joseph Andrews* and Laurence Sterne's *Tristram Shandy*. Tobias Smollett, who wrote satirical picaresque novels in imitation of Spanish models, even published an English version of *Don Quixote* in 1755, which has become a classic in the history of translation. These books, and others like them, were the fertile soil that helped to nourish the great flowering of European and American prose fiction in the nineteenth century and its continuing expansion in the twentieth and twenty-first. There are well known, frequently analyzed connections between Cervantes and Gustave Flaubert in *Madame Bovary*, Cervantes and Mark Twain in *Huckleberry Finn*, Cervantes and Fyodor Dostoevsky in *The Idiot*, but I'll pass over those intriguing relationships and race headlong into the twentieth century to consider the thematic and stylistic impact of *Don Quixote* on the writing of William Faulkner, arguably the foreign novelist with the strongest connection to and greatest influence on Latin American literature in the twentieth century. He has even been called the best-known Latin American author writing in English.

Faulkner often said that *Don Quixote* was one of the novels he returned to over and over again, claiming he usually read it once a year (his home library contains three editions of the novel in translation, as well as a wooden bust of Don Quixote). Critics and commentators have found a family resemblance between the failed idealists in Faulkner's novels, those damaged, genteel people attempting to hold on to their dream of a mythic South's traditional agricultural society in the face of a contemporary rampaging urban capitalism, and Don Quixote, who feels compelled to revive and re-establish in the modern world of sixteenth-century Spain his anomalous literary vision of a chivalry that never was. Although Cervantes alludes to historical knights in the novel—the Spanish crown's renowned crusaders and conquerors—Quixote's most significant and revered models are fictional warriors like Amadís of Gaul and other exemplary heroes of the chivalric novels. To oversimplify this important point, for the deluded characters of both Faulkner and Cervantes, historical reality has become irrelevant. For them, only fictional reality matters, a reality that is the product of purposeful invention—theirs, of course, and the imaginations of writers of fiction.

Faulkner seems to have been consistently intrigued by the figure of the failed Manchegan knight. For example, on a 1962 visit to West Point, where he spent several days, he had multiple exchanges with the cadets as well as the press. During one interview, he was asked, "Could you tell us, Mr. Faulkner, exactly what qualities Don Quixote has that make him one of your favorite characters?" Faulkner's trenchant response was this:

> "It's admiration and pity and amusement—that's what I get from him, and the reason is that he is a man trying to do the best he can in this ramshackle universe he's compelled to live in. He has ideals which are by our—the pharisaical standards, nonsensical. But by my standards they are not nonsensical. His method of trying to put them into practice is tragic and comic. I can see myself in Don Quixote by reading a page or two now and then, and I would like to think that my behavior is better for having read *Don Quixote*." (Fant & Ashley 94)

But more important, I think, than the similar personality traits and dashed hopes of Cervantean and Faulknerian literary characters, is the spell cast over the American's writing by the convolutions and meanders of the Spanish baroque style. Cervantes's language, though typically filled with long, complex sentences that accumulate subordinate clauses and wind their leisurely way to the end of the paragraph, was perfectly straightforward and direct compared to that of many other seventeenth-century authors. But it seems that Faulkner could not resist the allure of circumlocution in spite of Cervantes's relative simplicity. In fact, his style was once described as "Dixie Gongorism," Góngora being the early-seventeenth-century Spanish poet responsible for *The Solitudes*, almost 2000 lines of the most difficult and complex poetry ever written in any language (I know this in my bones: I took on the glorious, quixotic task of translating that gorgeous poem a few years ago). I find it fascinating that Faulkner's New World absorption of a decidedly florid, circuitous, and ornate style is at odds with a characteristic, deep-rooted tendency toward directness in syntax and simplicity in diction that had been dominant in English for several centuries. This preference for concision and clarity probably reached its unqualified literary zenith in the writing of Ernest Hemingway, who shared with William Faulkner a mid-twentieth-century position of novelistic pre-eminence though they were at opposite ends of the stylistic spectrum. It has occurred to me that Faulkner's English-language version of a seventeenth-century style may very well be what Latin Americans found so attractive in his writing. Baroque language and style, particularly in the person of Cervantes, are there like a subliminal drumbeat at the back of every Spanish-language writer's mind, and for this reason the circumlocutions of Faulkner probably seemed familiar—almost classic—to Spanish-language readers and writers.

In an attempt to demonstrate this point, I'd like to cite a portion of Quixote's first words to Cardenio when the two men finally meet in the Sierra Morena. Cardenio in his madness is living rough in the mountains, wearing the tatters of his once fine clothes, sleeping outdoors, surviving on the charity of shepherds, goatherds, and whatever he can pilfer or scavenge. He has moments of lucidity, however, and is perfectly rational during the first part of this encounter. The fairly substantial paragraph contains only four sentences. Following that is an excerpt from Faulkner's *The Sound and the Fury*, a three-sentence paragraph that began as an entry in the index he added to the novel for *The Portable Faulkner*, and which was then used in later editions as an author's foreword—a publication history that is baroque in every way.

Don Quixote and Cardenio exchange formal and rather formulaic courtesies, with Cardenio telling the pseudo knight that his only desire is to reciprocate Quixote's kindness.

"And mine," responded Don Quixote, "is to serve you; indeed, I had resolved not to leave these mountains until I had found you and learned from you if your sorrow, which your strange way of life indicates you are suffering, might have some kind of remedy, and if it did, to seek it with the greatest possible diligence. If your misfortune were one that had all doors closed to any sort of consolation, I intended to help you weep and lament to the best of my ability, for it is still a consolation in affliction to find someone who mourns with you. And if my good intentions deserve to be thanked with some courtesy, I entreat you, Señor, for the sake of the great courtesy I see in you, and I implore you, for the sake of the thing you have loved or do love most in this life, to tell me who you are and the reason that has compelled you to live and die in this desolate place like a wild animal, for you dwell among the beasts estranged from your true self, as demonstrated by your dress and your person. And I swear," Don Quixote added, "by the order of chivalry which I have received, though unworthy and a sinner, and by the profession of knight errantry, that if, Señor, you satisfy me in this, I shall serve with the devotion to which I am obliged by being the man I am, whether to remedy your misfortune, if it has remedy, or to help you lament it, as I have promised you I would." (Cervantes 183)

And here is the first entry in the Appendix, which is actually the Foreword, of *The Sound and the Fury*:

IKKEMOTUBBE. A dispossessed American king. Called "l'Homme" (and sometimes "de l'homme") by his fosterbrother, a Chevalier of France, who had he not been born too late could have been among the brightest in that glittering galaxy of knightly blackguards who were Napoleon's marshals, who thus translated the Chickasaw title meaning "The Man"; which translation Ikkemotubbe, himself a man of wit and imagination as well as a shrewd judge of character, including his own, carried one step further and anglicised it to "Doom." Who granted out of his vast lost domain a solid square mile of virgin North Mississippi dirt as truly angled as the four corners of a cardtable top (forested then because these were the old days before 1833 when the stars fell and Jefferson Mississippi was one long rambling onestorey mudchinked log building housing the Chickasaw Agent and his tradingpost store) to the grandson of a Scottish refugee who had lost his own birthright by casting his lot with a king who himself had been dispossessed. This in partial return for the right to proceed in peace, by whatever means he and his people saw fit, afoot or ahorse provided they were Chickasaw horses, to the wild western land presently to be called Oklahoma: not knowing then about the oil. (3)

There is a notable difference between the Cervantean paragraph and the Faulknerian: Cervantes's writing is elaborate and embellished, but it follows a logical, coherent, and linear narrative sequence. Each statement follows from the previous one. Don Quixote may be mad, but his derangement never interferes with his ability to speak cogently. Faulkner, on the other hand, does not even attempt a straightforward or linear telling of a tale. He has no interest in progressive sequencing. His account creates a kind of spiral that disavows the rectilinear for the circular, the chronological for a sinuous movement through and around time and space, as each reference seems to acquire at least one explanatory, ancillary phrase. This was a lesson that

García Márquez took to heart and held close for his whole life, extending the notion of narrative circularity past the kind of material contained in a single passage, as in the paragraph just cited, and applying it to the structure of entire books. Not even his works of nonfiction, such as *News of a Kidnapping* or *Living to Tell the Tale*, are organized in a simple, chronological pattern.

García Márquez always acknowledged the immense influence that Faulkner had on his writing. In the speech he gave when accepting the Nobel Prize in Literature, he called Faulkner his *maestro*, his master and teacher. His memoir, *Living to Tell the Tale*, opens with an evocation of the boat trip he took with his mother through the great swamp to the town of Aracataca to sell his grandparents' house. During the trip, his primary occupations seemed to have been chain smoking and rereading *Light in August*, in Spanish translation. As he describes the uncomfortable, mosquito-plagued, overnight voyage, he mentions the importance Faulkner had for him, calling him "the most faithful of my tutelary demons" (*Living* 6). Faulknerian spiraling, though more evident in the narrative structure of García Márquez's novels than in particular passages, can be glimpsed in this excerpt from *The General in His Labyrinth*. It is part of a compelling evocation of the liaison between the Liberator Simón Bolívar and Manuela Sáenz, his companion for nearly ten years, and the woman who fearlessly saved his life when assassins stormed into their bedroom one rainy night in an attempt to kill him. The essential point made in these pages is that Sáenz remained faithful and loyal even though Bolívar repeatedly abandoned her, if not for another woman then for the irresistible call of the War for Independence:

> Early the following year he left her again, to complete the liberation of Perú, which was the final enterprise of his dream. Manuela waited four months, but she set sail for Lima as soon as letters began to arrive that not only were written by Juan José Santana, the General's private secretary, which was not unusual, but were thought and felt by him as well. She found him in the pleasure palace of La Magdalena, invested with dictatorial powers by the Congress and besieged by the beautiful bold women of the new republican court. The Presidential Palace was so disorderly that a colonel of the lancers had moved out one midnight because the agonies of love in the bedrooms did not let him sleep. But Manuela was now in territory that she knew all too well. She had been born in Quito, the illegitimate daughter of a wealthy American landowner and a married man, and at the age of eighteen she had jumped out the window of the convent where she was a student and run off with an officer in the king's army. Nevertheless, two years later she was married in Lima, and with a virgin's orange blossoms, to Dr. James Thorne, a complaisant physician who was twice her age. And therefore, when she returned to Perú in pursuit of the love of her life, she did not need lessons from anyone on how to hold her own in the midst of a scandal. (*General* 150–151)

The recounting is circuitous, but the language and sentence structure are fairly conventional. This may be due to the moderating effect of the eminently rational Cervantean style on prose in Spanish in spite of the Faulknerian influence. How odd to think that the work of the baroque writer in Spanish is more pellucid and more straightforward than that of the twentieth-century author in English. That kind of convolution is comparable to the somewhat winding path of influences between languages that we have been following: Cervantes to Faulkner to García Márquez and then on to contemporary English-language novelists whom we haven't mentioned but who are certainly the Colombian's legitimate heirs, and include Toni Morrison and Salman Rushdie.

I'd like to conclude by going back to the Faulkner-Latin America connection. García Márquez is not the only writer who has acknowledged Faulkner's huge impact on his artistic development. So have Carlos Fuentes, Mario Vargas Llosa, and other members of what has been called the Boom generation, who have made Faulkner's linguistic circularity and complex serpentine structures their own. One of the links among them is surely the Cervantes connection, but I believe there is something else as well, something exclusively American. Just as Faulkner and García Márquez each created a semi-mythic, prototypically American place—Yoknapatawpha County and Macondo—as the setting for many of their stories, they and their colleagues employed a circuitous style in what I believe was an attempt, perhaps unconscious, to overcome the great linguistic problem of temporality. Unlike music and its wonderful ability to express many things at the same time in chords, literature, because it is language, is obliged to speak sequentially and say only one thing at a time. We have become so accustomed to linearity in language that we are hardly even aware of the limitation. But consider this: these writers were intent on recreating in their novels a kind of New World geology of their respective societies, which certainly differed from one another but had something uniquely American in common: they were multilayered, and in all the Americas—South, Central, North, Caribbean—those layers were comparable. They consisted of an indigenous population who were forcibly repressed and sometimes eradicated, African slaves who were forcibly imported and brutalized, and European settlers who forcibly made themselves masters of everyone and everything and occupied the top stratum. But the layers were not rigidly separated even when legally segregated, and they were never impermeable. Their on-going interpenetration and commingling, however unwilling, however fraught with crisis and calamity, could perhaps have been expressed most adequately in a chord: an American music not of the spheres but of the Hemisphere. But since writers are not composers, they have to settle for wrestling into existence a language whose complexity and circularity can seem to say several things at once and evoke multiplicity. Perhaps this is the bridge that spans the apparent differences between south and farther south, between Mississippi and Mexico, Mexico and Colombia, Colombia and Peru; perhaps the bridge that allowed Cervantes to influence Faulkner and Faulkner to influence García Márquez could only have been constructed through the medium of translation; perhaps translation is literature's approximation of a chord.

This essay originally appeared in the Summer 2016 issue of In Other Words, *published by the Writers' Centre, Norwich (UK).*

WORKS CITED

Cervantes, Miguel de. *Don Quixote.* Tr. Edith Grossman. New York: Ecco Press, 2003.

Fant, Joseph L. and Robert Ashley, eds. *Faulkner at West Point.* Jackson: University Press of Mississippi, 2002.

Faulkner, William. *The Sound and the Fury/ As I Lay Dying.* New York: The Modern Library, Random House, 1946.

García Márquez, Gabriel. *Living to Tell the Tale.* Tr. Edith Grossman. New York: Alfred A. Knopf, 2003.

———. *The General in His Labyrinth.* Tr. Edith Grossman. New York: Alfred A. Knopf, 1990.

Chapter 4

García Márquez and *Mamagallismo*

On Fatigued Roosters, Resistance, Sense of Humor, and the Colombian Character

Marcela Velasco

Big Mama's funeral is notoriously attended by an irreverent pilgrimage of snake doctors, prostitutes, fried food hawkers, sorcerers, banana workers, bagpipers, the President of the Republic, and every conceivable representation of Colombia's flamboyant civil and political society (García Márquez, 1984: 198). In J.S. Bernstein's English translation of Gabriel García Márquez's short story, one delegation misses the event: the "cock breeders from la Cueva" who are actually "*mamadores de gallo*" in the original (García Márquez, 1979: 188). As I will suggest, there is a world of difference between breeding cocks and exhausting them.

Los mamadores de gallo refers to *mamagallismo* or *mamar gallo*—a widely used polysemous expression of Caribbean origin—defined as "the failure to comply with a promise to someone; to stealthily mock someone; or to be idle" (Academia Colombiana de la Lengua, 2012: 71). Close English translations include "kidding" or "goofing off." According to Samper, in 1968 García Márquez suggested the expression's broader Caribbean origins when he described Venezuelans as "enormous *mamadores de gallo*" (2014: 45). Indeed, the Venezuelan philologist Angel Rosenblatt traced the expression back to an 1887 Caracas satirical newspaper which used "*mamándole gallo*" to describe someone's mockery (Samper, 2014: 46). However, it is García Márquez who has been widely identified as the main voice of *mamagallismo* (Samper, 2014: 46).

The origin of the expression, however, is as uncertain as translating it into English is perplexing or vulgar.[1] In Colombian vernacular *mamar* means to be exhausted, drained, or enfeebled, especially in a frustrating and impatient manner (Academia Colombiana de la Lengua, 2012: 71). The expression might refer to wearing down cocks in fights or to an inferior rooster's ability at beating his superior by exhausting it with trickery. All the same, *mamagallismo* denotes procrastination, chicanery, and irresponsibility. But a positive construction of the term reflects a particularly Colombian way of living well, in bliss, playfulness, and naughtiness, and in full engagement with the joys and tragedies of the human experience. Making sense of context is thus warranted to grasp the full meaning of the term.

I build on these ideas and add that *mamagallismo* represents a major vein in the Colombian character. It occurs at both individual and collective levels, and is both public and private. I also offer that in contexts of abuse of power, *mamagallismo* turns into a "weapon of the weak" or passive, low impact, behavioral strategies such as quiet strikes, theft, or malicious gossip used by subaltern groups or individuals to undermine, evade, or resist the powerful (Scott, 1985: 304). García Márquez offers rich material to describe *mamagallismo* as the complex sociocultural phenomenon that it represents, while studies of his work, particularly those that highlight the role of satire and the influence of Amerindian culture on his art, allow me to tentatively assert that the expression found a strong foothold in Colombia's inter-ethnic relations and fluctuating regional political economies.

GARCÍA MÁRQUEZ, A *MAMAGALLISTA*

"*Los mamadores de gallo de la Cueva*" is a reference to García Márquez's circle of literary friends that frequented the restaurant "la Cueva" in Cartagena and "*el Japy*" in Barranquilla in the 1950s (García Márquez, 2003: 332, 362). In his autobiography, García Márquez refers to the "group" of writers and journalists including Manuel Zapata Olivella, whom he met at "la Cueva" in Cartagena, and Germán Vargas, Alfonso Fuenmayor and Álvaro Cepeda Samudio, among other members of Barranquilla's artistic circles who famously celebrated their love of literature and friendship at "*el Japy*" (García Márquez, 2003: 316, 632). They met during the dark years of "*La Violencia*"—the devastating bipartisan conflict that left thousands dead in the countryside and was followed by the dictatorship of Gustavo Rojas Pinilla. Cartagena and Barranquilla, however, were spared the conflict. At that time, the Barranquilla "group" gathered to rejoice, but also to criticize each other's writing, share great works of literature, and survive Colombia's troubled politics and insular literary traditions (Bell-Villada, 2010: 71).

According to Samper, for Dasso Saldívar, a García Márquez biographer, *mamagallismo's* biggest followers are the people from the Colombian Caribbean who as a general rule are anti-solemn pranksters for whom "sense of humor is the most serious thing in the world" (Samper, 2014: 46).[2] This statement perfectly characterizes the essence of "the group." Jacques Gilard claims that *mamagallista* philosophy was popularized in the rest of Colombia during the political stalemate of the National Front (cited in Samper, 2014: 47). But it was García Márquez who propagated the term in the 1970s and turned the expression into a "religion whose followers recognize García Márquez as its Supreme Pontiff" (Samper, 2014: 46). He cultivated the *mamagallista* tone in his journalistic and literary work, which contain large doses of humor and satire that stood in sharp contrast to Bogotá's stiff and peremptory academic seriousness (Gilard, 1981: 43). García Márquez disseminated Colombia's Caribbean folklore, music, and popular values, and raised them to universal status (Gilard, 1981: 44).

MAMAGALLISMO, POLITICAL ECONOMY, AND CULTURE

So why did *mamagallismo* take root during the stalemate of the National Front? The 1958 National Front was a coalitional government of Liberal and Conservative elites that ended partisan conflict and represented a bipartisan alliance of coffee growers, industrialists and landed oligarchy that steered economic policy to favor their respective sector's interests (Palacios, 2001: 14). This period coincided with the economic decay of the Atlantic coast, which lasted from 1940 until the 1990s. The region had thrived during the colonial period, declined in the nineteenth century and revived in the early twentieth century with the commercial rise of Barranquilla (Kalmanovitz, 2011). Economic historians have puzzled over the failure of the Atlantic coast to follow the economic pace of the more dynamic Andean economies.

Meisel argues that this was the result of a protectionist political economy, prohibitive transportation costs that discouraged the sale of Barranquilla's manufactured goods in Andean markets, and the reinvestment of coffee profits in the producing regions (2009: 247–248). In contrast, the Andean regional economies propped a relatively more prosperous peasant economy of small landowners capable of buying locally manufactured goods (Meisel, 2009: 40). Colombia's Caribbean coast, meanwhile, remained under the yoke of large landowners who denied peasant property rights, leading to unproductive peasant economies and, consequently, weak regional demand for modern services or manufactured products (Kalmanovitz)

Orlando Fals Borda's groundbreaking work on the regional history of the Atlantic coast describes the sociocultural dynamics of such unproductive (or pre-capitalist) peasant societies. In the Magdalena River's hinterland, interethnic groups survived in primitive riverbank and wetland societies out of the purview of large hacienda owners (1979: 21B). To adapt, people mixed hard work and diversion and produced what Fals Borda termed "*el dejadismo costeño*" or "Caribbean abandonment" to keep suffering at bay with a blissful, laid-back attitude (1979: 158B). Fals Borda proposes the concept of *dejadismo* based on field notes where his sources extensively use the expression *mamar gallo* to describe their people's sense of black humor, indiscipline, flexibility and solidarity—the required behavioral adaptation to a harsh environment (Fals Borda, 1979: 161A). One informant identified Candelario Obeso, the black poet intellectual from Mompox (1849–1884), as an early exponent of the region's flexible attitude. Interestingly, some sources correlated *mamagallismo* with lack of authority. Historically, centralized authorities—in Spain or later in Bogotá—offered little backup protection to the region's elites at the same time that local elites undermined centralized political and social powers by practicing contraband or loosening their social morals (Fals Borda, 1979: 155A). Local elites therefore knew that they could not control the hinterland, a fact that hinterland societies used to their advantage. From this Fals Borda extrapolates that *dejadismo* characterizes Caribbean elite sociocultural attitudes, differentiating the whole region from the more austere Andean cultures (1979: 160B).

Bergquist's critique of Fals Borda, however, addresses the important point of elite fear of revolt in characteristically slave societies such as Colombia's Caribbean, explaining the development of a paternalistic ethos of mutual tolerance (1990: 165). Fals Borda in Bergquist's view is remiss for taking the region's peacefulness and agreeable intercultural relations at face value and not highlighting the cultural tensions they conceal (Bergquist, 1990: 165). The journalist Antolín Díaz did not miss that point. Commissioned in the 1930s to write a chronicle on the Bolívar province by the Liberal President Alfonso López Pumarejo, who was determined on modernizing rural relations, Díaz masterfully described the despotic and violent relations in the region's backwaters, and the role of religion, carnivals, music and dance in covering it all up (Díaz, 2006).

All of the above creates an image of an idle Caribbean upper class in the decades of the fifties through the seventies that is anachronistically holding on to its diminishing material power and perhaps sending its children off to find opportunities in the more dynamic Andean economies. As some of them flocked to Andean cities, they helped spread Caribbean cultures. García Márquez, for example, describes Sunday afternoons spent dancing at the Bogotá radio station that transmitted *vallenato*—a Caribbean Colombian musical genre—and helped popularize the genre in other parts of the country (García Márquez, 2003: 272).

MAMAGALLISMO, MAGICAL REALISM, AND HUMOR

So *mamagallismo* could play the nefarious role of covering up with pleasantries the chasms that separate cultural and economic groups who nevertheless manage to live in peace. Based on an analysis of *The Kingdom of This World* by Alejo Carpentier, Fishburn argues that this sort of "oppositional duality" is the driving force behind both humor and magical realism (2005: 155). Carpentier offered the idea that Latin America's cultural plurality created "*lo real maravilloso*" and Fishburn adds that both magical realism and humor derive from the "sparks" produced by the collision of different cultures and coexisting, yet incompatible contexts (Martin, 1989: 142, cited by Fishburn, 2005: 155). The Caribbean coast's clash was both cultural and economic; its elites not only hoarded land and economic assets, they also despised popular culture. For example, *vallenato* music, which was so influential in the work of García Márquez, was proscribed from elite social circles (Samper and Tafur, 1997: 167). In sum, magical realism accords equal status to different belief systems and contrasts them starkly, often producing a humorous effect.

Building on Fishburn, humor confronts intercultural tensions by making connections between dissimilar cultures, unmasking authority, and misreading cultural mores in order to draw attention to particularly odd or intriguing values. Analyses of the work of García Márquez have examined the role of humor in his narrative (Bell-Villada, 2010: 69–81, 117). But as Samper asks, was he tenderly funny or ferociously *mamagallista*? Rodríguez-Vergara helps settle the score for the latter by asserting that his work represents a type of carnivalesque satire. Building on Mikhail Bakhtin, carnivalesque satire is a form of "dialogic" and "polyphonic" genre that is simultaneously solemn and comical, producing both laughter and indignation (Rodríguez-Vergara, 1991: 27, 29).[3] Carnival rituals allow the inversion of rules and hierarchies, tolerate blasphemy, obscenity, and parody, and erase the boundaries between spectators and participants (Rodríguez-Vergara, 1991: 31). As with magical realism, carnivalesque satire exposes different perspectives, allowing a dialogue between them in order to arrive at a collective truth (Rodríguez-Vergara, 1991: 30).

MAGICAL REALISM, *MAMAGALLISMO*, AND AMERINDIAN CULTURES

It appears that the influence of carnivalesque culture in García Márquez is well-known. In contrast, Amerindian orality in general, and Wayúu traditions in particular have been less explored in most intertextual analyses of his work that rely exclusively on archival research (Moreno, 2015: 38). Even those who place García Márquez in the Greater Magdalena region ignore the impact of Amerindian cultures (Moreno, 2015: 23). Moreno addresses this gap with a transcultural narrative study to estimate the effect of Wayúu traditions on García Márquez's brand of magical realism (2014: 141).

The author's great-grandmother, the mother of Tranquilina Iguarán, was a Wayúu, while his grandfather Colonel Nicolás Márquez owned Wayúu slaves in 1910 who served the household and followed him in his expeditions (Ayén, 2015).[4] In *One Hundred Years of Solitude,* Guajiro (Wayúu) servants raise the Buendía children teaching them their language and traditions, an autobiographical detail confirmed by the author. As a child, household servants taught him Wayuunaiki, their language, but most significantly shared their extraordinary tales and superstitious sensibilities (García Márquez, 2003: 64–65).

Moreno identifies many parallels between Wayúu stories and specific episodes in *One Hundred Years of Solitude* and in other works, such as the ascension of Remedios the Beauty, which was based on a story heard by García Márquez of a Wayúu grandmother trying to cover up her granddaughter's disgraceful escape with risible claims that the girl had ascended to heaven, and Rebeca's hauling the bones of her diseased relatives in a bag, capturing the Wayúu tradition of not abandoning family remains in strange lands (Moreno, 2015: 93, 143).

The Wayúu are part of the Arawak family and their ancestral land spans both Colombian and Venezuelan territory in the inauspicious natural environment of the Guajira desert. This environment has forced them to wander across the Caribbean. The peninsula's geography has historically served the purpose of resisting conquest in colonial times and, more recently, tax authorities. For this reason Guajiros have gained a reputation for being a fierce and proud people, but also great contrabandists. Nevertheless, ordinary Wayúu are generally victims of Colombia's dominant culture and their own strict hierarchical society, where powerful clans hoard the best resources. Conflict in these lands is an ever-present threat and the magic of words serves to keep the social peace.

Just as Wayúu myths and tradition are sources of magical realism, I tentatively suggest that Wayúu culture influences both Caribbean identity and its brand of sarcastic humor. My work on ethnic politics and social movements has brought me into contact with different indigenous communities. In this capacity I visited southern Wayúu communities in the Guajira department in 1995 and was struck by the way many people whom I talked to used sarcasm, irony, and exaggeration to describe poverty, violence, and discrimination. Clearly humor was a rhetorical "weapon" that helped people dialogue, but also dissipate conflict, resist acculturation, and mock the powerful.

Wayúu oral culture may offer some clues as to the role of humor in their society. For example, the best practitioners of Wayúu oral literature must have "a good sense of humor and a calm mood" (Ministerio de Educación Nacional, n.d.). But I think that it is the institution of "*pütchipü'ü*," "*palabrero,*" or "master of words," which is a central component of the Wayúu oral tradition, and offers clues into the practice of *mamagallismo*. In interviews, *pütchipü'üs* describe various types of word masters, ranging from those who only deal with conflicts involving drunks, lovers, or petty crime, to those who expertly solve intractable problems ("El palabrero wayúu," 2014). Rosa Matilde López, a Wayúu indigenous leader explains that, in addition to using wise words, a *pütchipü'ü* may decide to "*chistear*" or joke around to soften hearts and minds before beginning the actual negotiation ("El palabrero wayúu," 2014).

The "word master" has received widespread exposure. For example, in 1996, the *telenovela* by the name of *Guajira* delighted Colombians with Sidro "*el palabrero*" ("Luis, Lucho Tamayo," n.d.). As so often happens, secondary characters steal the show if they faithfully capture something fresh and real about Colombian culture. In this badly rated melodrama filmed in the Guajira desert, Sidro's conflict resolution antics and hilarious ways of facing trouble seemed to be giving the audiences more than the ludicrous love story between a *gringo* engineer and his Colombian love interest.

Though Sidro was a humorous sidekick, the institution of the *pütchipü'ü* is not. The *pütchipü'ü* mediates with good words to peacefully solve conflicts between families or other parties in the Guajira peninsula. As an interlocutor, a good *pütchipü'ü* may use irony and chicanery as a decentering strategy to neutralize the party with whom he is engaging. The following examples explain how. A legendary master of words was once sent to represent a Wayúu family whose child had been accidentally killed by the coal company's train as it transited through Wayúu territory. The *pütchipü'ü* exchanged words with a company representative to make reparation claims for the death of the child. An exasperated company official sardonically yielded to the idea, but demanded to know what use the family would have for this train. The *pütchipü'ü* retorted that the family had no use for it but would sell it back to the company ("El poder de la palabra," 2009). The *palabrero* masterfully and with fine humor won the point, at least rhetorically.

The testimony of Angel Amaya Uriana, a *pütchipü'ü* elder who mediated in the uncharted territory of kidnapping, an unknown practice for the Wayúu, exemplifies the use of rhetoric to create a negotiation position ("La Guajira del palabrero," 2014). In the late 1990s, Amaya Uriana traveled from the northern Guajira department to Envigado, Antioquia, to meet Francisco Caraballo, the jailed leader of the Popular Liberation Army (EPL). The guerrilla group had kidnapped a wealthy female Wayúu doctor, and Amaya Uriana calmly told the guerrilla strongman that in the Wayúu tradition, females cannot be taken in such a way ("La Guajira del palabrero," 2014). Amaya Uriana admitted to Caraballo his willingness to accept that the EPL had acted in retaliation for a wrong committed by their Wayúu victim, in which case, they had to reveal the nature of the original crime. If the kidnapped Wayúu had indeed committed a crime, they could expect compensation following Wayúu customs. But, Amaya Uriana warned, if the EPL had taken her with no clear reason, then it was the EPL who had to pay the Wayúu ("La Guajira del palabrero," 2014). The *palabrero's* linguistic strategy is seriously humorous as it involves deliberation with regard to a crime against humanity while upholding his culture's traditions to speak the truth.

After acknowledging the importance of Wayúu culture for "his essence and way of thinking," a group of Wayúu word masters offered García Márquez a *guararo* (Ayén, 2015). The *guararo* is a staff that identifies the authority of a *pütchipü'ü*. The symbolic act of accepting a *guararo* from Wayúu word masters at a ceremony in Cartagena's 2006 Hay Festival of Literature and the Arts[5] recognized García Márquez as a great *pütchipü'ü*. The ceremony was held at the headquarters of the Observatory of the Colombian Caribbean, a social science research institution ("Reconocimiento wayúu a Gabo," 2006).

SATIRE AND EXAGGERATION IN THE WORK OF GARCÍA MÁRQUEZ

Mamagallismo contains a "degrading trend" that is conspicuously displayed in *The Autumn of the Patriarch* and "Big Mama's Funeral," two works that piece together fear and filth to describe dictators and petty despots (Mose, 1992: 838). Such images of fear and filth were inspired by real life. In 1958, García Márquez went to cover the surrender of Venezuelan dictator Marcos Pérez Jiménez. In a conversation with Plinio Mendoza, published in *Fragrance of Guava,* García Márquez describes how he saw an official stepping out of the presidential palace at Miraflores. According to García Márquez, this official—purportedly Pérez Jiménez—came out walking backwards in battle uniform while brandishing a semiautomatic weapon and muddy boots; it was then, García Márquez says, when he had the intuition of "the mystery of power" (cited in Mose, 1992: 837–838). Such an image inspired his selective use of "incongruent, degrading, and extreme details" to disparage the figure of the strongman in his work (Mose, 1992: 838).

The *Autumn of the Patriarch* presents one of the "fundamental structures of long-term mamagallismo," which is to elevate someone's stature to later ridicule him (Mose, 1992: 841). This rhetorical waxing and waning is masterfully achieved in *Love in the Time of Cholera*, which in many ways parodies romantic novels (Bell-Villada, 2010: 212). Our author delights us with luxurious details on the passionate and empathetically comical, but nevertheless purely romantic, platonic, and prohibited love affair between the adolescent Fermina Daza and the young Florentino Ariza. But after dozens of pages delighting the reader with letters written in miniature version, on pieces of toilet paper, on notes smeared with bird turds, or sent with the coordinated help of dutiful telegraphers, García Márquez bluntly abandons the sappiness when a love-dazed Florentino Ariza stunningly underwhelms Fermina Daza, who is back from a two-year exile orchestrated by her father, by whispering in her ear "this is not a place for a crowned goddess," a reference to a *vallenato* lyric by the composer Leandro Díaz (García Márquez, 1988: 102). Fifty-three years, seven months and eleven days later, the lovers consummate their affair toward the end of their lives. The love story depicted in the novel transpires in the backdrop of carnivalesque conditions of life and death, rot, violence and poverty (Rodríguez-Vergara, 164, 181).

"Big Mama's Funeral" represents the chaotic death of *la Colombia tradicional*—the carnivalesque old order of despotism, superstition, incest, wealth concentration, and indentured labor created by Big Mama's clan. Before she burps and dies, Big Mama bequeaths tangible and intangible wealth of such ridiculous proportions that only underscore the madness and imbalance of the defunct order, but also its impossibly weak foundations. Her invisible patrimony for example, contains more than forty items including the wealth of the subsoil, the territorial waters, the colors of the flag, national sovereignty, the traditional parties, the rights of man, beauty queens, the purity of language, public opinion, the communist menace, the high cost of living, and the statements of political support (García Márquez, 1984: 192).

The sardonic amplification of Big Mama's bounties exposes the vaporous, but nonetheless real edifice of power. As the old order fades away it leaves no rules. Big Mama's laws offer no guidance for how the President of the Republic should participate in her funeral. Sage doctors and legal alchemists with minds constrained by big mama's rules, toil away in abstract congressional debates, while ignoring the commonsensical fact that Big Mama's corpse is decaying at 40 degrees Celsius (García Márquez, 1984: 195). Finally, at the funeral, the delirious crowd of washerwomen, salt miners, accordionists, oarsmen, and dandies "emit a cry of jubilation" as the president and his ministers, the parliament, Supreme Court, and representatives of banks, commerce, and industry make their way into the funeral procession (García Márquez, 1984: 198–199). Meanwhile, no one notices Big Mama's clan busily taking apart her house, which most likely represents the extent of her material possessions (García Márquez, 1984: 199–200). In this work García Márquez acquires full consciousness of the tragic and risible sense of Colombian history (Gilard, 1983: 73).

Exaggeration of this sort distorts reality, but also lays it bare. However, no one seems to be reacting in a reasonable fashion. Hence, is *mamagallismo* an example of social dysfunction? *Chronicle of a Death Foretold* may offer some clues. Arguably, this piece points to the confusions produced in the vacuum of social change as new values seemingly take hold but overlap with stubborn older ones. In this story, Santiago Nasar famously loses his life because no one believes the Vicario brothers' intention of murdering him. As the butcher Faustino Santos reveals to the chronicler, he thought at the time that the brothers *"estaban mamando gallo"* or were "kidding around" (García Márquez, 1981: 79; 2006: 59). The brothers are in effect engaging the entire town in an elaborate sort of "kidding around" involving the skillful yet languid avoidance of duty, in this case going through with the obstinate tradition of avenging the family's honor. They conspicuously sharpen knives and visit everyone to let them know of their intentions, so much so, that the authorities act, take away the knives and send the brothers off to sleep. While the brothers seemingly wish to be saved by the entire town from having to execute the atavistic tradition, no one cares to believe that they are serious about it, even after the brothers come back with new knives to replace the confiscated ones. No one says anything to Santiago Nasar. Society misreads the signals and fails to act, turning the event into a "communal crime" (Rodríguez-Vergara, 1991: 96). The sacrifice of Santiago Nasar not only parodies the Dionysian rites in Catholicism; it also suggests that communal values are endangered (Rodríguez-Vergara, 1991: 111).[6]

MAMAGALLISMO AS OFFICIAL NEGLIGENCE AND WASTE OF TIME

No One Writes to the Colonel offers one of the best descriptions of incompetence, dereliction of duty and malfeasance, which characterizes to this day the affairs of government in Colombia. The eponymous colonel, a veteran of the War of the Thousand Days, has waited for fifteen years to receive his war pension. Sixty years have passed since the Treaty of Neerlandia ended the War and the government promised "travel assistance and indemnities to two hundred revolutionary army officers" (García Márquez, 1979b: 24). However, the tyrannical passing of time has slowly converted the glory days that earned the colonel a pension into events barely registering in the collective memory. Scraping by with an asthmatic wife, the old colonel's life revolves around routine Friday visits to deliveries by the postman.

The government has passed a law without budgetary allocation fifteen years back and a lawyer diligently represents his claims in the administrative affairs of the government; however, his job has turned more difficult since the "city's veterans' organization, with members of both parties" has waned as the colonel's older comrades "died waiting for the mail" (García Márquez, 1979b: 24). Decision-makers seemingly work with the forces of history to not do their duty. The passing of time is the most democratic force in place, consuming expectations, and keeping claimants at bay. People and groups can be wasted away in the exile of hopeful waiting.

The verbal exchange between the desperate colonel determined to change his lawyer confronts him with the truth of government malfeasance. When the colonel demands the original "proof of claim" to his pension, signed sixty years before by the quartermaster general of the revolutionary forces on the Atlantic coast—Colonel Aureliano Buendía himself—the lawyer explains that these documents cannot be produced because they have been passing through "thousands and thousands of hands, in thousands and thousands of offices, before they reached God knows which department in the War Ministry" (García Márquez, 1979b: 26). The following dialogue between the colonel and his lawyer is an impeccable snapshot of the bureaucratic procedure of failed governance in a country in constant turmoil:

> "No official could fail to notice documents like those," the colonel said. "But the officials have changed many times in the last fifteen years," the lawyer pointed out. "Just think about it; there have been seven Presidents, and each President changed his cabinet at least ten times, and each Minister changed his staff at least a hundred times." "But nobody could take the documents home," said the colonel. "Each new official must have found them in the proper file." The lawyer lost his patience. "And moreover if those papers are removed from the Ministry now, they will have to wait for a new place on the rolls." "It doesn't matter," the colonel said. "It'll take centuries." "It doesn't matter. If you wait for the big things, you can wait for the little ones." (García Márquez, 1979b: 26–27)

The lawyer shines as a diligent messenger and manager of other people's wasted time. Ultimately the colonel comes to understand his reality with the celebrated answer to his wife's question "what will we eat today?" "Shit" (García Márquez, 1979b: 62). Waiting is the most staggering form of discrimination and reveals the meaninglessness of the has-been, the retired, the no longer useful—the one who eats *mierda*. García Márquez encapsulates an entrenched form of government, the politics of procrastination, as carried out in societies living in stalemate. Colombian politics offers plenty of evidence on the use of procrastination to subject people to the tyranny of delay and waiting. Postponement is especially evident in government strategies to disband any opposition. People commonly describe this as government *mamagallismo*, amply using the expression in press interviews, blogs, and online debates.[7]

Finally, can an author "exhaust the rooster" and violate some type of tacit "social pact" with his or her readers? Presenting a proper answer to this question matters to me less than the actual events that made me think about it. García Márquez has earned the status of great thinker in Colombian arts and culture for his role in exalting ordinary people and their history. When the original *Memories of My Melancholy Whores* was published in Spanish in 2004, it was becoming increasingly clear that Colombia's internal war was having a particularly devastating effect on the lives of women, who in addition to making up the vast majority of the country's five million internal refugees, were being subjected to special forms of sexual violence (Meertens, 2004: 197). Poor and victimized girls, comparable to Delgadina in the novel, were easily trafficked by prostitution mafias connected to the armed groups. García Márquez's novel tackling the subject of ageless sexuality and male vigor, as vicariously experienced in a borderline pedophiliac relationship with a young prostitute, is clearly placed in that particular vein of world literature that explores male fantasies of love affairs with pubescent girls. The work however, could not have appeared at a worse time in Colombian history. When news of the country's humanitarian crisis comingled with delirious literati repeating the word *puta* as with the holiest of permissions, it exposed the ferocious triumph of a particularly male-centered *joie de vivre*.

MAMAGALLISMO, ANALYSIS AND CONCLUSIONS

This chapter argues that *mamagallismo* is a particularly Colombian construction of satirical humor that developed in the backdrop of remarkable political and social transitions as well as in the intermingling of diverse cultures and frameworks of knowledge. Arguably, contact between different cultural and economic identities within the Caribbean and between the Caribbean and the Andean regions of Colombia both helped spread *mamagallismo*. And, García Márquez further disseminated the practice and attitude of *mamagallismo* through his work, which offers rich material to contextualize the polysemous expression and understand its fluctuating meaning.

The paper tentatively concludes that the author's early life, which was in full contact with Amerindian traditions, sheds light on the intercultural character of the expression. This conclusion is supported by evidence from García Márquez's biography and from intertextual analysis featuring Wayúu oral tradition. Also, the author's freethinking, joyful Caribbean peers who helped him launch his writing career were faithful practitioners of *mamagallismo*. Finally, García Márquez was writing in the backdrop of remarkable political and economic disparities.

The Atlantic coast was relatively more peaceful than other regions of Colombia, but significantly less dynamic economically. Local elites constrained the socioeconomic advance of subaltern groups, and produced sociocultural gaps that were covered up with a blissful attitude of abandonment. Such structural and behavioral conditions created the humorous sparks that characterize magical realism. True to the form, García Márquez reflects this reality through carnivalesque humor and solemn social critique; humorous images thus wonderfully and lovingly describe the real Colombia.

In conclusion, *mamagallismo* captures elements of satire, parody, and farce in order to mock established power and social conventions, and to grotesquely fuse the serious and the risible so that the same smile reflects both fear and happiness (Samper, 2014: 47). *Mamagallismo* is private and public, individual and collective. It is used to discuss traumatic events solemnly but in a shroud of irony, fine humor and exaggeration. Colombians value *mamagallismo* as a conversational art form, but also as a way of making sense of reality. Coating contemptible facts with humor accomplishes various social and psychological effects: the event is decentered from its context and brought to a safe space to be described and examined. *Mamagallismo* therefore offers a harmless framework to talk, analyze and act, and has been enriched by Colombia's intercultural orality embedded in dramatic socioeconomic and political transformations that subject ordinary people to extraordinary life events. This linguistic framework offers a language to interpret reality and a strategy to speak truth to power and perhaps, to change it. As people struggle to find their collective and individual places in the voids left by changing social backdrops, *mamagallismo* takes on new meaning and serves both negative and positive purposes.

I would like to thank María Mercedes Jaramillo and Betty Osorio for their helpful comments.

NOTES

1. The verb *mamar* is to suck, overeat, or drink too much, while the noun *gallo* means rooster or cock.
2. "Los costeños son, por regla general, gente anti-solemne, bromistas para quienes el sentido del humor es la cosa más seria del mundo."
3. "géneros serio-cómicos."
4. Mario Vargas Llosa speculated that García Márquez's early family life in Aracataca brought him into close contact with indigenous groups who became a source of inspiration for his work (cited in Ayén).
5. The Hay Festival of Literature & the Arts began in 1988 in the town of Hay-on-Wye in Wales. It later spread to other parts of the world, including Cartagena.
6. "El sacrificio comunal de Santiago Nasar como parodia al catolicismo y como rito dionisíaco [...] no significa más que los valores de la comunidad están en extinción y que ellos llevarán al exterminio de la cultura."
7. A casual google search of *"mamar gallo," "gobierno"* and *"Colombia"* will produce accusatory comments of *"mamagallismo"* in the government's handling of peace negotiations, infrastructure projects, health policy, among others.

WORKS CITED

Academia Colombiana de la Lengua. *Breve diccionario de colombianismos*. Cuarta edición revisada. Bogotá: Academia Colombiana de la Lengua, 2012. Web. 5 Nov. 2015. <http://academiacolombianadelalengua.co/sites/default/files/BREVE%20DICCIONARIO%20PDF%20FINAL%20JUNIO%207%20DE%202013(1).pdf>

Ayén, Xavi. "Wayúu, los indios de García Márquez." *Vanguardia,* 15 February 2015. Web. 17 Nov. 2015. <http://www.lavanguardia.com/cultura/20150215/54427247275/wayuu-indios-garcia-marquez.html>

Bell-Villada, Gene H. *García Márquez: The Man and His Work*. Chapel Hill: The University of North Carolina Press. 2010. Print.

Bergquist, Charles. "In the Name of History: A Disciplinary Critique of Orlando Fals Borda's *Historia doble de la costa*." *Latin American Research Review* 25.3 (1990): 156–176. Web.

Díaz, Antolín. *Sinú: Pasión y vida del trópico*. Bogotá: Editorial El Garfio, 2006.

"El palabrero Wayúu." *Que el mundo lo sepa*. Dir. Néstor Oliveros. Señal Colombia, 2014. Television.

"El poder de la palabra." *Wayúu, gente de arena*. Dir. Andrés Arias García. Señal Colombia, 2009. Television.

Fals Borda, Orlando. *Historia doble de la costa. Mompox y Loba*. Tomo 1. Bogotá: Carlos Valencia Editores, 1979. Print.

Fishburn, Evelyn. "Humour and Magical Realism in *El reino de este mundo*," in Stephen Hart and Wen-chin Ouyang, eds. *A Companion to Magical Realism*. Rochester, NY: Tamesis, 2005, 155–167. Print.

García Márquez, Gabriel. "Big Mama's Funeral." *Collected Stories*. Trans. Gregory Rabassa and J.S. Bernstein. New York: Harper & Row, Publishers, 1984, 184–200. Print.

———. *Chronicle of a Death Foretold*. Trans. Gregory Rabassa. New York: Alfred A. Knopf, 2006. Print.

———. *Crónica de una muerte anunciada*. Bogotá: Editorial la Oveja Negra, 1981. Print.

———. *Living to Tell the Tale*. Trans. Edith Grossman. New York: Alfred A. Knopf, 2003. Print.

———. *Love in the Time of Cholera*. Trans. Edith Grossman. New York: Alfred A. Knopf, 1988. Print.

———. *No One Writes to the Colonel and Other Stories*. Trans. J.S. Bernstein. New York: Harper & Row, Publishers, 1979b. Print.

———. *Los funerales de la mamá grande*. Madrid: Ediciones Alfaguara, 1979. Print.

Gilard, Jacques. "Prólogo." In *Gabriel García Márquez, Obra periodística Vol. 1. Textos costeños*. Edited with an introduction by Jacques Gilard. Barcelona: Bruguera, 1981, 7–72. Print.

———. "Prólogo." In *Gabriel García Márquez, Obra periodística Vol. 3. (1955–1960). De Europa y América*. Edited with an introduction by Jacques Gilard. México: Editorial Diana, 1983, 13–75. Print.

Kalmanovitz, Salomón. "Por qué perdió la costa Caribe el siglo XX?" *El Espectador.* 26 June 2011. Web. 7 Dec. 2015. <http://www.elespectador.com/opinion/perdio-costa-caribe-el-siglo-xx>
"La Guajira del palabrero." *Con los caminos abiertos.* Doménicotv S.A.S, 2014. Web. 23 Nov. 2015. <https://www.youtube.com/watch?v=uju3EYRvc4c>
"Luis, Lucho Tamayo." *COLARTE, Patrimonio cultural colombiano.* N.D. Web. 23 Nov. 2015. <http://www.colarte.com/colarte/ConsPintores.asp?idartista=13864&pest=busqueda>
Martin, Gerald. *Journeys Through the Labyrinth: Latin American Fiction in the Twentieth Century.* London: Verso, 1989. Print.
Meertens, Donny. "Género, desplazamiento, derechos," in Martha Nubia Bello, ed. *Desplazamiento forzado. Dinámicas de guerra, exclusión y desarraigo.* Bogotá: Universidad Nacional de Colombia/ACNUR, 2004, 197–204. Print.
Meisel Roca, Adolfo. *¿Por qué perdió la costa Caribe el siglo XX?* Bogotá: Banco de la República, 2009. Web. 7 Jan. 2016. <http://www.banrep.gov.co/es/por-que-perdio-costa-caribe-siglo-xx>
Mendoza, Plinio and Gabriel García Márquez. *The Fragrance of Guava: Conversations with Gabriel García Márquez.* Trans. Ann Wright. London: Verso, 1983. Print.
Ministerio de Educación Nacional. República de Colombia. Poéticas de la literatura Wayúu. Bogotá, N.D. Web. 7 Dec. 2015. <http://www.colombiaaprende.edu.co/html/home/1592/article-226630.html>
Moreno Blanco, Juan. "Gabriel García Márquez en clave wayúu," in Biblioteca Mexicana del Conocimiento, ed. *Gabriel García Márquez. De la letra a la memoria.* México: Programa Editorial del Gobierno de la República, 2014. Print.
———. *Transculturación narrativa: la clave wayúu en Gabriel García Márquez.* Cali, Colombia: Programa Editorial Universidad del Valle, 2015. Print.
Mose, Kenrick. "Formas de crítica social en Gabriel García Márquez." Actas del X Congreso de la Asociación Internacional de Hispanistas, Barcelona 21–26 agosto de 1989, ed. Antonio Vilanova, Vol. 4. Barcelona: Promociones y Publicaciones Universitarias, 1992. Web. 22 Nov. 2015. <http://cvc.cervantes.es/literatura/aih/pdf/10/aih_10_4_004.pdf>
Palacios, Marco. *De populistas, mandarines y violencias. Luchas por el poder.* Bogotá: Editorial Planeta, 2001. Print.
"Reconocimiento wayúu a Gabo." *El Tiempo.* 16 February 2006. Web. 7 Jan. 2016 <http://www.eltiempo.com/archivo/documento/MAM-1917778>
Rodríguez-Vergara, Isabel. *El mundo satírico de Gabriel García Márquez.* Madrid: Editorial Pliegos, 1991. Print.
Samper, Daniel. "García Márquez el humorista." *Boletín de la Academia Colombiana, número extraordinario* (2014): 43–55. 23. Web. 7 Jan. 2016 <http://academiacolombianadelalengua.co/academia/sites/default/files/BOLETIN_EXTRAORDINARIO.pdf>
Samper, Daniel and Pilar Tafur. *100 años de vallenato.* Bogotá: Música, Talento y Mercadeo, 1997. Print.
Scott, James. *Weapons of the Weak: Everyday Forms of Resistance,* New Haven: Yale University Press, 1985. Print.
Vargas Llosa, Mario. *García Márquez: Historia de un deicidio.* Barcelona: Barral Editores, 1971.

Part II

RE-READING THE HISTORY OF MACONDO

Chapter 5

Names and Narrative Pattern in *One Hundred Years of Solitude*

Gene H. Bell-Villada

The casual, first-time reader of *One Hundred Years of Solitude* is inevitably struck by the vast array of recurring names with which García Márquez constructs his narrative. There are five characters named "José Arcadio" (including the morose and short-lived Arcadio). There are three important personages named "Aureliano"—a group further complemented by the marginal Aureliano José, the seventeen illegitimate children of the Colonel, and the newborn baby Aureliano who is devoured by ants. There are three young women characters christened "Remedios" (Remedios Moscote, daughter of the magistrate Apolinar; Remedios, the Beauty; and Renata Remedios, known as "Meme"). The very last female Buendía—the ultra-modern, Europeanized swinger Amaranta Úrsula—bears the names of her two weightiest women ancestors.

In 2004, when Oprah's Book Club featured Gabo's monumental work as her Spring selection, I served as an invited consultant to the TV program for six weeks. Among my duties over that period was to respond to selected readers' questions and criticisms on the show's website. The most common of gripes had to do with the constant repetition of names in the book. This of course should come as no surprise. Any instructor who has used García Márquez's novel in the classroom (especially one having non-Hispanic students) well knows the difficulty of keeping so many sound-alike characters clear in one's mind, of distinguishing this Aureliano from that one, of remembering which José Arcadio it is that sleeps with which woman. Even so authoritative a critic as Emir Rodríguez Monegal, when first reviewing the book, made a minor slip in this area: "Tantos Aurelianos acaban por confundirse en un solo Aureliano; tantas Rebecas (*sic*) terminan por solaparse en una sola" (34–35; "So many Aurelianos end up blurring into one Aureliano; so many Rebecas (*sic*) finally blur into one"). Unless this is an error from the printing shop, Rodríguez Monegal shows a slight lapse here, in as much as there is only one character named Rebeca in *One Hundred Years*. In a similar instance, Carlos Blanco Aguinaga refers to an "Arcadio José" (a combination that never comes up in García Márquez's narrative) and speaks of there being two women named Remedios (when actually, as we noted above, there are three) (38).

Despite the confusing aspect that such an abundance of José Arcadios and Aurelianos can present on first (even on second or third) reading, a careful examination reveals that these names present a lucid, rigorously consistent and fairly simply pattern of character traits and biological trajectories. Úrsula herself hints partly at this system when, midway through the novel, she concludes that, "while the Aurelianos were withdrawn, but with lucid minds, the José Arcadios were impulsive and enterprising, but they were marked with a tragic sign" (174).

Because the division between the Aurelianos and the José Arcadios is so basic to the structure of *One Hundred Years of Solitude*, it would be most fruitful at this point to enter directly into the matter of the male Buendías and classify the types of actions associated with their names. For, as we shall soon note, the Aurelianos pursue one line of activities, the José Arcadios another— and never do the twain meet. Throughout the following discussion it must be borne in mind that, as a result of a childhood prank, the respective identities of the Segundo twins are reversed; José Arcadio Segundo is really Aureliano Segundo and vice-versa. This long-standing error is accidentally righted after their simultaneous deaths, when the drunken pallbearers mix up the coffins and inter their respective bodies in the "wrong" graves.

From the very first presentation and description of the two brothers there is an indication of the basic contrast that will distinguish the José Arcadios from the Aurelianos:

> José Arcadio, the older of the children, was fourteen. He had a square head, thick hair, and his father's character. Although he had the same impulse for growth and physical strength, it was early evident that he lacked imagination... Aureliano, the first human being to be born in Macondo, would be six years old in March. He was silent and withdrawn. He had wept in his mother's womb and had been born with this eyes open. As they were cutting the umbilical cord, he moved his head from side to side, taking in the things in the room and examining the faces of the people with a fearless curiosity... Úrsula did not remember the intensity of that look again until one day when little Aureliano, at the age of three, went into the kitchen at the moment she was taking a pot of boiling soup from the stove and putting it on the table. The child ... said, ... "It's going to spill." The pot ... began an unmistakable movement ... and it fell and broke on the floor. (23)

The passage sets up a dual opposition between physicality and intelligence, body and mind, brawn and brain. At the outset the narrator establishes that

José Arcadio—with his caricaturesque square head and hairy aspect, his impulsiveness and lack of imagination—is the irrational type, an animal-like creature of instinct who either tends not to use his brain or isn't terribly bright. Aureliano on the other hand immediately comes across as clear-headed, rational and insightful, native traits symbolized by his wide-open eyes at birth, his dispassionate examination of those in attendance at the delivery room, and his uncanny ability to foresee future events. Of a piece with these fancifully exaggerated mental qualities is Aureliano's youthful taciturnity, the aloofness of a personality type that holds back impulses and passions. It is worth noting that the above description of Aureliano employs the same adjective—"retraído" ("withdrawn")—later to be used by Úrsula when she formulates her own distinction between the two groups.

These sets of traits, and the logical oppositions between them, are consistently maintained throughout the narrative. All of the José Arcadios (to take at this point just one grouping) exhibit forceful drives, a raw, animal energy that impels them to awesome activities of the moment: José Arcadio flees with the gypsies and, as a sailor, circumnavigates the globe; Aureliano (i.e. José Arcadio) Segundo rescues Fernanda from a riot, traverses mountains in wooing her, angrily destroys all the family crystal ware in response to her harangue, and then storms out to return with food in abundance; even the effete José Arcadio the Seminarian furiously expels, whip in hand, the unruly adolescents who have made a shambles of his bedroom. None of the Aurelianos are given to such irrational impulsiveness. On the other hand, owing to a lack either of intelligence or intellectuality, the José Arcadios seem incapable of undertaking or even understanding long-range projects that may require abstract planning, calculation, or imagination: José Arcadio is indifferent to the civil wars; the adult Aureliano Segundo has little interest in Melquíades's manuscripts and stands apart from the banana-workers' struggles; José Arcadio the Seminarian drops out of his Divinity studies soon after arrival in Rome, and will later find Aureliano Babilonia's scholarly pursuits quite baffling.

Precisely because of their intellectual limitations, the José Arcadios yield readily to physical comforts, sensual temptations, and sex. They are essential hedonists for whom personal attachments and simple pleasures are the natural domain; one important consequence of this latter predisposition is that they tend to be more or less dominated by women. Hence, José Arcadio falls under the thrall of Rebeca's "voracious" womb; Aureliano Segundo is a fulltime drinker, gourmandizer, and fornicator—indeed, he is one of literature's most memorable portraits of personal dissipation (a Colombian Falstaff, as it were)—who depends in an almost child-like way on his mistress Petra Cotes; José Arcadio rises at eleven every morning, never does a day's work, spends much of his time entertaining young boys, and is inordinately attached to the memory of his mother Fernanda. Significantly, though all these José Arcadios live in times of momentous historical change—civil conflict; economic boom; foreign takeover; class struggle; social decay—they demonstrate not the slightest involvement with or concern about these larger situations. So tied are they to the immediate realities of food and sex that they are profoundly apolitical (Aureliano Segundo befriends the banana company children) and even amoral in their actions (José Arcadio the first-born seizes neighboring peasants' properties).

On the other hand, the Aurelianos are all sober, quiet, rational men whose most telling trait is their clear and calculating minds. By opposition to the compulsive fitfulness of the José Arcadios, the Aurelianos are born thinkers with a natural capacity for extended projects. It is this fundamental intellectual quality which provides them their long-range stamina, their skill and resourcefulness in organizing plans of action and performing major duties. Hence, Colonel Aureliano Buendía is the great Liberal *caudillo* and later a conscientious artisan, a painstaking maker of gold fishes; Aureliano Centeno and Aureliano Triste are both highly effective inventors and entrepreneurs (one learns how to manufacture sherbet, the other brings the yellow train); José Arcadio Segundo starts out as an organizer of cockfights, later becomes a labor leader, and finally lays some of the groundwork for the study of Melquíades's manuscripts; Aureliano Babilonia makes a lifetime of deciphering the mysterious parchments and ultimately succeeds in his chosen enterprise.

In marked contrast to the sexual needs and hedonistic excesses of the José Arcadios, the Aurelianos have no overriding interest in sex. If there is a woman at hand, an Aureliano will so indulge and even become infatuated (as does young Aureliano Buendía with Remedios Moscote), but this sentiment never manages to become a full-time, lifelong, passionate obsession. The Colonel may have engendered seventeen sons from seventeen mistresses, yet this marginal activity never intrudes on his life as military leader; José Arcadio Segundo hangs around Pilar Ternera's brothel, though this he appears to do more for social life than physical pleasures, and he lives out his later years in the utter isolation of Melquíades's room. Admittedly, Aureliano Babilonia spends entire months making love with Amaranta Úrsula, but this erotic fact stands out precisely because it is so contrary both to his scholarly nature and his personal history; it is after his lover dies that Aureliano Babilonia re-discovers his intellectual vocation, experiencing his brief yet magical moment of personal triumph when he deciphers Melquíades's manuscripts.

In a neat parallel to Aureliano Buendía's having been born with his eyes open, he and his other namesakes all will die with their eyes open. And just as the newborn Aureliano's open eyes vividly symbolize his native intelligence, all the other Aurelianos breathe their last with their mental faculties and physical senses intact. Colonel Aureliano Buendía ends his days while actively urinating on a chestnut tree, remembering a circus he had seen earlier that day. José Arcadio Segundo's last words are an exhortation to young Aureliano Babilonia never to forget the three thousand massacred workers—at which point the former labor leader drops dead, eyes open. Our very last image of Aureliano Babilonia is of him reading slowly about his imminent doom; although he will perish immediately after the final line in *One Hundred Years of Solitude*—outside the text as it were—in his last moments he achieves an absolute understanding of himself, of his secret family history and of his town, he thereby bringing to a grand culmination the intellectual aptitudes of all the Aurelianos.

The José Arcadios, by contrast, all die sordid and painful deaths—an instance of the "tragic sign" noted by Úrsula: José Arcadio either shoots himself or is murdered by his wife Rebeca; Aureliano Segundo dies after a protracted illness, apparently a throat tumor; and José Arcadio the Seminarian is drowned by juvenile delinquents.

This pattern of name-based traits, and the resultant system of oppositions, are, within the Buendía household, remarkably clear and consistent. Of course, as with every system, there are the exceptions—though these divergences, it will be seen, have a logic of their own. The most notable instance here is José Arcadio Buendía, the Founder of the clan. And being the original patriarch, this *Ur*-Buendía carries in his person the characteristics of José Arcadios and Aurelianos both. With his wife Úrsula he exhibits (at the beginning of their marriage) sexual desires later to become pronounced in his like-named descendants; his skewering of Prudencio Aguilar and his confrontation with don Apolinar Moscote well illustrate the impulsiveness that typifies all José Arcadios. At the same time, however, José Arcadio Buendía is a natural intellectual—the turf of the Aurelianos. Neatly exemplifying Gramsci's idea of the "organic intellectual" (118–25), José Arcadio Buendía is a masterful leader when the tasks of founding, organizing, and defending Macondo society are the historical imperatives of the moment. Beyond this, José Arcadio Buendía is an intensely dedicated experimental scientist who comes up with legitimate discoveries—for example, his realization that "the Earth is round like an orange." With his capacity of endless study, the Founder of the Buendía line anticipates Aureliano Babilonia, whose researches and findings will illuminate as well as put an end to the Buendía clan.

Both these radically different human personalities are fully present—coexisting if not exactly harmonized—in José Arcadio Buendía. It is with the Founder's offspring that these two opposing strands—instinct/reason, impulsiveness/calculation, Eros/Civilization—will split into separate entities, never to reappear within one man.

The other exceptions to the José Arcadio/Aureliano doublet can be found among those characters who, while bearing one or another of these names, are christened slightly differently. These special cases include the seventeen illegitimate children of the Colonel (Aureliano Amador, Aureliano Centeno, etc.), as well as Arcadio and Aureliano José (respectively the natural sons, through Pilar Ternera, of young José Arcadio and Aureliano). Bastard offspring all, they nonetheless share with their paternal namesakes certain familiar traits and destinies: Aureliano Triste and Aureliano Centeno prove to be highly skilled craftsmen and businessmen; Arcadio, harsh and impulsive as military dictator, is easily thrashed into submission by his grandmother Úrsula, and later dies violently before a firing squad. At the same time, however, these minor figures deviate from the fixed ways of their respective name-series. For example, all seventeen of the Colonel's out-of-wedlock Aurelianos are shot by the police. They thus replicate the José Arcadios' violent deaths, while also differing from them in being victims not of gratuitous murder but targets of political, ideologically motivated assassination. Arcadio in turn transcends his name-set in acquiring some standing as a military officer, though this particular development can be accounted for by the fact of his illegitimacy, which bars Arcadio from many of Macondo's more normal and mundane pleasures. Arcadio's truncated name, it might be mentioned, suggests his marginal quality, the social incompleteness and personal freakishness characterizing his short, skewed life.

A similar if less-developed system of differences built on given names also divides the Buendía females into two sets. On one hand there are those women notable for their dynamism and common sense: the materfamilias Úrsula, her daughter Amaranta, and (the last of the female Buendías) Amaranta Úrsula. On the other hand there is a group of women called Remedios, all of them varyingly childish, innocent, and immature: Aureliano's ill-fated young bride Remedios Moscote; the apparently retarded Remedios, the Beauty; and the scatterbrained daughter of Fernanda del Carpio and Aureliano Segundo, known as "Meme" but originally christened Renata Remedios. The first of these two groups might be said roughly to correspond, among the males, to the Aureliano series, whereas the Remedios grouping approximates the spirit and function of the José Arcadios.

If *One Hundred Years* has any positively heroic figure, any major character depicted without humor or irony, with reverence and awe, it is Úrsula Iguarán de Buendía, whose unflagging energy and "invincible heart" help keep the family a going concern. It is she who runs the day-to-day affairs of the household and restrains the wilder impulses of the men. Her narrow traditionalism notwithstanding, this sober, solemnly practical woman of action finds the path to the town with the inventions, starts the animal-candies business, tames Arcadio, manages the family budget, feeds her demented husband, cleans and grooms José Arcadio Segundo hidden in Melquíades's room, and takes in and raises several bastard children. These qualities of fortitude and good sense are transmitted to Úrsula's daughter Amaranta, who never yields to immediate emotion, maintaining her equanimity throughout, shedding not even a tear when Remedios, the Beauty, rises to heaven.

As is only to be expected, Amaranta Úrsula recapitulates her ancestral namesakes' positive traits. These resemblances are singled out early in her childhood, when there emerges a special bond of affection between Úrsula and the young girl, who is described as being "just like" (263) her great-great-grandmother. Later, when Amaranta Úrsula sets sail for Brussels, it is remarked of her that she has the same "lively eyes that Úrsula had had at her age," and moreover that her tearless, taciturn farewell "revealed the same strength of character" (326), a self-control we noted previously in Amaranta as well. Later, upon Amaranta Úrsula's return to her native Macondo, the narrator employs the very same language used when earlier characterizing Úrsula, who in her youth is "*active, small*, severe" (18), while Amaranta Úrsula is "*active, small* and indomitable like Úrsula" (348; all emphases added). And, like Úrsula, it is she who makes the house livable, ridding it of the ants, planting flowers, weeding the garden, and recruiting an army of artisans to restore the furniture and the floors. It is only when Amaranta Úrsula casts aside the best traditions embodied in her names that the family mansion finally succumbs to the ravages of nature—and she herself dies in childbirth.

The seriousness and strength of the women in *One Hundred Years* and the capriciousness and frivolity of the men is a contrast frequently singled out in García Márquez criticism. Luis Harss and Barbara Dohman long ago noted that Gabo's male characters are "flighty creatures, governed by whim, fanciful dreamers given to impossible delusions, … basically weak and unstable." The women, on the other hand, are "solid, sensible, unvarying and down to earth, paragons of order and stability." The Colombian novelist himself admitted to Harss and Dohman, "My women are masculine" (327). And yet, this distinction, though obviously applicable to the Úrsula/Amaranta group (as well as to such non-Buendía women as Pilar Ternera and Petra Cotes) tells only about half of a more complex story. For throughout *One Hundred Years of Solitude* there also runs the Remedios line, whose essential traits are stunted emotional growth and a resulting lack of contact with the realities of the adult world. In this group one might also include Rebeca, whose name shows the same initial syllable "Re-" and who, true to the pattern, sucks her thumb until late in life and exists mostly in a personal world of her own.

This trait of immaturity stands out among all the Remedios characters. The nine-year-old Remedios Moscote still wets her bed, soils her underwear, and on the very evening of her wedding is clueless about the birds and the bees. She dies in puberty at age thirteen. Remedios, the Beauty is an extreme version of the little-girl Moscote: she reaches age twenty without having learned how to read, write, or dress herself; she further pushes Remedios Moscote's backwardness in toilet matters by daubing the house wells with her excrement; and, with her inability to comprehend why men die of love of her, Remedios, the Beauty stretches to absurd heights the sexual innocence of her former namesake. Although Renata Remedios—Meme—leads more of a normal life, she too remains little-girlish, a fact suggested by her nickname (she is the only character in the entire book to possess one) and by her initial name "Renata," which signifies "reborn" (she is Remedios born-again). Meme's infantilism is evinced in her lighthearted love of partying and her lack of discrimination in friendships. She becomes a clavichord virtuosa only as a result of Fernanda's tyrannical discipline rather than from any will of her own—Meme's musical skills thus being a measure of her obedience and passivity. Though she lives to a ripe old age in a convent in Krakow (a thoroughly preserved medieval town, in the Catholic country at a farthest remove from Macondo), Meme's life as a Buendía is effectively terminated during her teens or early twenties.

In addition to these Buendía name-sets, with their fixed personalities and repeated destinies, two female outsiders play fundamental and parallel roles in the clan's sexual history. I am referring of course to Pilar Ternera and Petra Cotes, who exert a primordial influence on all those Buendía blood-kin who enjoy erotic relationships with the opposite sex. Pilar Ternera in particular has the crucial function of sexual teacher, initiator, provider, and mediator: She first "deflowers" José Arcadio and Aureliano; she later gives birth to Arcadio, who incestuously desires her but to whom she sends as substitute the silent Santa Sofía de la Piedad; from this chance union Aureliano Segundo, future father of Meme, is born, whom Pilar Ternera will then advise to sleep with auto mechanic Mauricio Babilonia; from this torrid and clandestine amour there issues scholar Aureliano Babilonia, whom Pilar will eventually urge to go and seduce his aunt Amaranta Úrsula... In fact, the only blood-Buendías whom Pilar Ternera does not directly aid in bedding down with the opposite sex are the Segundo twins. Here the narrative gap is filled by Petra Cotes, who for a period of several weeks sleeps alternately with José Arcadio Segundo and Aureliano Segundo, not realizing at first that her bed partner is not one man, but two. This narrative divergence, however, also contains a repetition; for, just as Pilar Ternera did initiate José Arcadio and Aureliano sexually, now, many years later, Petra Cotes sexually initiates their grandnephews, who happen to bear their very same given names.

These two local Venuses stand as polar opposites to the conservatism of Úrsula and (it goes without saying) to the icy prudishness of Fernanda del Carpio. In contradistinction to the traditionalism, the mainstream respectability and instinctual restraint symbolized in the great mother of all Buendías,

Pilar Ternera the fortune-teller, prostitute, and brothel keeper vividly embodies free-floating marginality, a gay and joyous sinfulness, an irresponsible and insouciant physicality. Though not as disreputable, Petra Cotes too lives from marginal activities (raffles, a form of gambling) and moreover recapitulates Pilar's radiant sexual presence and skill. Finally, the fact that the names "Petra" and "Pilar" begin with the same phoneme and also carry comparable connotations of stone and strength, demonstrates their parallel roles as female figures and as material means of support for the men in García Márquez's narrative.

This treatment of character, whereby a set of traits is invested upon someone by means of a signal so handy and recognizable as a proper name, has a number of functions. First, it demonstrates tendencies and idiosyncrasies persisting within a clan—which long-range dynamic is a commonplace of family histories, in literature and in real life both. At the same time the repetition of names inevitably disperses the individuality of all relevant characters, stressing a generic, collective temperament that presides over and broadly shapes a particular José Arcadio or Aureliano. Those qualities peculiar to any Buendía, arising largely from circumstances of the moment, are ultimately subordinate to what Rodríguez Monegal calls "la repetición de la estirpe que doblega brutalmente el curso de cada destino individual" (34–35; "the forces of familial repetition, which holds brutal sway over the course of each individual destiny"). Like those characters in Borges and Cortázar stories, who unknowingly carry out actions dictated by past forces whose existence they scarcely suspect, the Buendías are systematically channeled into patterns established generations ago by their namesakes.

García Márquez's formidable system of names and narrative patterns is a rigorous and consistent construct. (In an earlier, classic instance of the family-chronicle genre, Thomas Mann's *Buddenbrooks* features a "Johann" among each of its four generations.) The many repeated Buendía names may at first confuse a reader, but together they constitute a necessary formal recourse. For, at the same time that the repetitions signal the successive transmission of family temperaments, the paradox is that this latter phenomenon—so banal, so much taken for granted—has become, in Viktor Shklovsky's term, "defamiliarized" (13–14). It can safely be said that any author of a family saga is under virtual obligation to depict the re-production of personality, to show that in a family there are, as is were, "family resemblances" (or family differences, which is the obverse side of the same idea). Had García Márquez employed a more ample variety of names, and not applied them as self-contained rubrics, the effect may have been more "lifelike," but the text would not have been empowered so to signify so basic and commonplace a topic of family existence. With his striking but artfully developed device, García Márquez imparts new life to a well-known social, vital, and narrative experience.

This chapter originally appeared as an article in Latin American Literary Review 9, no 18 (1981), pp. 37–46.

WORKS CITED

Blanco Aguinaga, Carlos. *De mitólogos y novelistas.* Madrid: Ediciones Turner, 1975.

García Márquez, Gabriel. *Cien años de soledad.* Buenos Aires: Editorial Sudamericana, 1969.

———. *One Hundred Years of Solitude.* Trans. Gregory Rabassa. New York: Avon, 1971.

Gramsci, Antonio. "The Formation of Intellectuals." In *The Modern Prince and Other Writings.* Trans. Louis Marks. New York: International Publishers, 1957, pp. 118–25.

Harss, Luis and Barbara Dohman. *Into the Mainstream: Conversations with Latin American Writers.* New York: Harper & Row, 1967.

Rodríguez Monegal, Emir. "Novedad y anacronismo de *Cien años de soledad.*" *Revista Nacional de Cultura* (Caracas), no. 185, julio-agosto-septiembre 1968. Reproduced in Helmy F. Giacoman, ed., *Homenaje a Gabriel García Márquez.* Long Island City, NY: Las Américas, 1972, pp. 15–42.

Shklovsky, Viktor. "Art as Technique." In Lee T. Lemon and Marion J. Reis, eds. and translators, *Russian Formalist Criticism: Four Essays.* Lincoln: University of Nebraska Press, 1965, pp. 3–24.

Chapter 6

The Enlightened Blindness of Úrsula Iguarán

María del Mar López-Cabrales

> When most I wink, then do mine eyes best see,
> For all the day they view things unrespected;
> But when I sleep, in dreams they look on thee,
> And, darkly bright, are bright in dark directed.
> Then thou, whose shadow shadows doth make bright,
> How would thy shadow's form form happy show
> To the clear day with thy much clearer light,
> When to unseeing eyes thy shade shines so!
> How would, I say, mine eyes be blessed made
> By looking on thee in the living day,
> When in dead night thy fair imperfect shade
> Through heavy sleep on sightless eyes doth stay!
> All days are nights to see till I see thee,
> And nights bright days when dreams do show thee me
> William Shakespeare, *Sonnet 43*

> What I see not, I better see—
> Through Faith—my Hazel Eye
> Has periods of shutting—
> But, No lid has Memory—
> For frequent, all my sense obscured
> I equally behold
> As someone held a light unto
> The Features so beloved—
> And I arise—and in my Dream—
> Do Thee distinguished Grace—
> Till jealous Daylight interrupt—
> And mar thy perfectness—
> Emily Dickinson, *What I see not, I better see*. 939

The last time I read *One Hundred Years of Solitude*, a couple of years ago, I repeatedly burst out laughing, and the book moved me once again with its sheer genius. In one of the most emotive episodes of the novel, Úrsula Iguarán goes to visit her son Aureliano Buendía in jail, minutes before his scheduled appearance before the firing squad. Úrsula finds him "paler [...] than when he had left, a little taller, and more solitary than ever. [...] [And] Úrsula felt inhibited by the maturity of her son, by his aura of command, by the glow of authority that radiated from his skin" (123–24). But in the end, after all the emotion prompted by the imminence of death, the encounter turns into an everyday conversation between mother and son. As she takes her leave, Aureliano hands over to his mother some verses, dedicated to his wife Remedios, which he had composed before and during the war, so that she, Úrsula, will have them burned.

> ...Úrsula promised and stood up to kiss him good-bye.
> "I brought you a revolver," she murmured.
>
> Colonel Aureliano Buendía saw that the sentry could not see. "It won't do me any good," he said in a low voice, "but give it to me in case they search you on the way out." Úrsula took the revolver out of her bodice and put it under the mattress of the cot. "And don't say good-bye," he concluded with emphatic calmness. "Don't beg or bow down to anyone. Pretend that they shot me a long time ago." Úrsula bit her lip so as not to cry. "Put some hot stones on those sores," she said. (124–25)

With the precision of a philatelist, García Márquez is able to present to us, in the figure of Úrsula, an ordinary mother who visits her son in jail and is worried about basic matters: his feeding, his health, his personal hygiene. She is a mother whose sole interest is in her son's getting his sores cured, in her giving him *dulce de leche* so that he will have energy, and in making sure he puts on clean underwear and new shoes when his time comes (123).

From every nook and cranny of *One Hundred Years of Solitude* something surprising comes our way. Its universe is filled with mirages, labyrinths, and dualities. No wonder, then, that it continues to be the most widely read book in the history of Latin American literature.

In the approach to be taken in this essay, I shall endeavor to demonstrate that, though critics have tended to analyze the characters in *One Hundred Years* as archetypes, its female characters show dualities and contradictions that render such reductionism untenable. In so demonstrating, I shall concentrate on analyzing Úrsula Iguarán and, in particular, on the blindness and elderliness experienced by her at the end of her days as a condition that, ultimately, helps her stay alert and develop her other senses to the maximum. Indeed, Úrsula will die in old age without anyone realizing she is blind.

In those last years of her life, Úrsula will be granted light in darkness and be capable of understanding and "seeing" what others cannot. Blindness as a form of enlightenment, let us not forget, has also been depicted by García Márquez in two of his short stories: "Artificial Roses" (in *Big Mama's Funeral*) and "Someone Has Been Disarranging These Roses" (in *Eyes of a Blue Dog*).

AN IMPOSSIBLE TAXONOMY

Countless studies have been devoted to analyzing the symbolism of the feminine characters in the work of García Márquez and, more precisely, in *One Hundred Years*. Lorraine Elena Roses states in "The Sacred Harlots of *One Hundred Years of Solitude*" that vast amounts have been written about the dichotomy in the representation of women in this novel as either virgin or whore. "Many [...] critics have established a [...] Manichaean typology of García Márquez's female characters, ultimately coming to the conclusion that women cannot transcend the limited space assigned to them in the novel" (Roses 68). Following her analysis of some reductive studies by critics such as Ernesto Volkening, who asserts that the women in this narrative are "deprived of the gift to slip away to fantastic regions" (Roses 68), or the well-known article by Margaret Sayers Peden that divides up the female characters between positive and "bad" ones, Roses proposes the following:

> [...] the dichotomy between the "good" and the "bad" women should be dismantled and reconfigured as a dialectic and progression in which the socially elite women struggle to wield social power over the transgressive or abject members of their sex, while simultaneously being challenged and influenced by them. [...] the socially marginal, abject women occupy, alongside the elites, a privileged space in the novel. [...] they follow a path to knowledge in a transcendent sense, one of mythic and quasi-biblical dimensions. With a sustaining immanent wisdom complementary to that stored in the manuscripts of Melquíades, these female characters, down the generations, illuminate a path toward possible redemption through love. (69–70)

Roses ends by arguing that those women considered "bad" in the novel rather can be seen as an "avatar of the female deities and sacred harlots of pre-Judeo-Christian antiquity that populate the visionary utopias of feminist thought" (Roses 76). *One Hundred Years of Solitude* shows us a small utopian community where, at the start, everyone has the same rights and is placed at the same level, with neither laws nor security forces being necessary—yet it is also a space where everything gets complicated. Even the mother—son tie is an intricate one, owing to Colonel Aureliano Buendía's incapacity to love or to reciprocate his mother's love (249):

> Then Colonel Aureliano Buendía realized, without surprise, that Úrsula was the only human being who had succeeded in penetrating his misery, and for the first time in many years he looked her in the face. Her skin was leathery, her teeth decayed, her hair faded and colorless, and her look frightened, He compared her with the oldest memory that he had of her, the afternoon when he had the premonition that a pot of boiling soup was going to fall off the table, and he found her broken to pieces. In an instant he discovered the scratches, the welts, the sores, the ulcers, and the scars that had been left on her by more than half a century of daily life, and he saw that those damages did not even arouse a feeling of pity in him. Then he made one last effort to search in his heart for the place where his affection had rotted away and he could not find it. [...] The only affection that prevailed against time and the war was that which he had felt for his brother José Arcadio when they both were children, and it was not based on love but on complicity. (173)

This situation complicates human relations in the whole novel, although it is not capable of entirely defeating Úrsula, who begins to fade only following the death of her daughter Amaranta during the five-year rains.

Bell-Villada proposes the following classification to identify the different characters in the novel: "[...] there are the assorted erotic (or anti-erotic) types: José Arcadio the impetuous stud; Rebeca the insatiable wife; Remedios the Beauty, a femme most fatale; Fernanda the haughty and beautiful prude; Petra the eternal mistress; and Amaranta the anguished virgin and the tease, destructive and sad, whose name, ironically, contains the Spanish verb *amar*, but who is herself incapable of love, wanting only those men whom she cannot have while summarily rejecting those whom she can" (2010: 101). Montaner Ferrer remarks with regard to Úrsula that, even as she assumes the leading voice of the narrative, she also must suffer different indignities (91), such as having to raise not only her biological offspring but also to adopt Rebeca, and to accept the seventeen children who were engendered by Colonel Aureliano Buendía and are marked by an ashen cross. Úrsula also opens the family home to Pietro Crespi and Santa Sofía de la Piedad, and is even able to save Colonel Gerineldo Márquez from an unjust death by threatening her own son. Montaner Ferrer classifies the female characters thus:

> Between an Úrsula who is prone to fantasizing, to a scatterbrained Amaranta Úrsula, there is a colorful slate of matriarchs. One of them holds back willingly from the honor of this role—Santa Sofía de la Piedad; another is definitively rejected—Rebeca; another one acts without restraint or measure—Fernanda. But these are neither all of the women nor all the matriarchs: Remedios, the

Beauty, disappears, more suspiciously than fantastically. The listing is completed with two more matriarchs, though carefully camouflaged by Gabriel García Márquez: Pilar Ternera—long-lived, vital, patient—and Mercedes, the stealthy pharmacist, a matriarch who stands outside the novel. (90)

[Entre Úrsula la fantasiosa y Amaranta Úrsula la despistada hay una jugosa nómina de matriarcas. Una se inhibe voluntariamente del honor de ese puesto—Santa Sofía de la Piedad; otra es rechazada definitivamente—Rebeca; otra actúa sin tasa ni medida—Fernanda. Pero éstas no son todas las mujeres ni todas las matriarcas: Remedios, la bella, desaparece más sospechosa que fantásticamente. La cuenta se completa con dos matriarcas más, aunque cuidadosamente camufladas por Gabriel García Márquez: Pilar Ternera—longeva, vital, paciente—y Mercedes, la farmacéutica sigilosa—matriarca fuera de la novela. (90)

In "Una lectura arquetípica de los personajes femeninos de *Cien años de soledad*," Laura Verónica Rodríguez Imbriaco posits a relationship between the most outstanding female characters in the novel—Úrsula Iguarán; Pilar Ternera; Amaranta Buendía; Remedios, the Beauty; and Amaranta Úrsula—and several goddesses from Greek mythology. Úrsula, the character that concerns us here, is associated with Gea—mother goddess, earth goddess—and at the same time with Demeter—the goddess of grain and harvest who lived through various phases: a happy mother prior to the abduction of her daughter Persephone; disillusioned and sad after the kidnapping; and finally, happy once again at Persephone's return.

According to Valverde Barrenechea, Úrsula is the founding "she-bear" of the tribe and has a lunar quality (47): "Úrsula is fundamentally the Earth, human settlement; Pilar Ternera constitutes above all the EROTIC 'PILLAR' of Macondo; and Petra Cotes is FERTILITY. Earth, Eros, and fertility are elements that, in mythological thinking, are associated with the moon or evolve from it" (46). This scholar also claims that all of the characters in the novel die either in the house or thinking of founder Úrsula, and that the only woman who disappears by rising to heaven is Remedios, the Beauty, who receives a treatment resembling that of the Blessed Virgin in her Assumption. By contrast, Petra Cotes, who represents fertility in Macondo, does not die but rather disappears without explanation; the narrator simply ceases to make mention of her.

Rodríguez-Vergara asserts that, in *One Hundred Years of Solitude*, the male-patriarchal myth of founding of the community is imposed, along with the "establishing of order within chaos, in which men have the patriarchal duty of writing and enforcing the laws and thus protecting the women and children ... In this novel, the men set out to organize the community and soon tire of the effort, leaving the task to the women" (20). And without doubt Úrsula Iguarán is the woman who organizes and structures the life of

Macondo and of all those who live in and go through the town. Although she has been branded a conservative, a woman who represents the traditional, bourgeois values of Creole society in Latin America, and although she imposes her will in at times tyrannical ways and is always aiming to control and question the lives of the inhabitants of Macondo, Úrsula is an intimately drawn character who represents her own ambivalences and dualities, her contradictions and rough edges, like many or most of the characters in this novel.

To end this review summary of some of the articles that set forth an impossible taxonomy of the female characters in *One Hundred Years of Solitude*, I wish to cite Bell-Villada's (2010) quotation from the magnificent article by Reinaldo Arenas, "En la ciudad de los espejismos," in which Úrsula is described as one of the great women in the history of Latin American literature. In Arenas's (translated) words, she is

> [...] the bride filled with prejudices on her wedding night; she is the loving mother, concerned at times intolerable, at times heroic; she is the inconsolable widow who weeps under the almond trees in the afternoons...; she is the centenarian who conceals her blindness so as to avoid pity; she is the almost delirious and withered great-grandmother who knows that preparing a dessert in the kitchen is one of the indispensable rituals for maintaining the equilibrium at home. (103)

Úrsula, as small and diligent as a worker-bee, and, at the same time, as grand and protective as a mother-bear, "stands out as an instance of the potential for simple human greatness," Bell-Villada notes (2010: 103).

ENLIGHTENED BLINDNESS

The first time we read about Úrsula's blindness and old age is when she decides to assume the task of raising the son of Aureliano Segundo: "Although she was already a hundred years old and on the point of going blind from cataracts, she still had her physical dynamism, her integrity of character, and her mental balance intact. No one would be better able than she to shape the virtuous man who would restore the prestige of the family, a man who would never have heard talk of war, fighting cocks, bad women, or wild undertakings, four calamities that, according to what Úrsula thought, had determined the downfall of their line" (188–89). That is how Úrsula decides that the boy will be a priest and, God granting, will become Pope.

When Remedios, the Beauty, rises to heaven, Úrsula's blindness also appears mentioned:

Úrsula, almost blind at the time, was the only person who was sufficiently calm to identify the nature of that determined wind and she left the sheets to the mercy of the light as she watched Remedios the Beauty waving good-bye in the midst of the flapping sheets that rose up with her. (236)

Not everything about Úrsula is fortitude, however. Like any human being she also suffers doubts:

Úrsula felt tormented by grave doubts concerning the effectiveness of the methods with which she had molded the spirit of the languid apprentice Supreme Pontiff, but she did not put the blame on her staggering old age or the dark clouds that barely permitted her to make out the shape of things, but on something that she herself could not really define and that she conceived confusedly as a progressive breakdown of time "The years nowadays don't pass the way the old ones used to," she would say, feeling that everyday reality was slipping through her hands. In the past, she thought, children took a long time to grow up. (245)

As is noted in this quotation, Úrsula perceives as obstacles to achieving goals not her blindness and old age, but rather the lack of time. At precisely this instant, the narrative stops midway in order to recount the history of the Buendías up to the present moment. And immediately, the gaze turns to the elderly woman, describing her blindness in greater detail:

The truth was that Úrsula resisted growing old even when she had already lost count of her age and she was a bother on all sides as she tried to meddle in everything and as she annoyed strangers with her questions as to whether they had left a plaster Saint Joseph to be kept until the rains were over during the days of the war. No one knew exactly when she had begun to lose her sight. Even in her later years, when she could no longer get out of bed, it seemed that she was simply defeated by decrepitude, but no one discovered that she was blind. She had noticed it before the birth of José Arcadio. At first she thought it was a matter of a passing debility and she secretly took marrow syrup and put honey on her eyes, but quite soon she began to realize that she was irrevocably sinking into the darkness, to a point where she never had a clear notion of the invention of the electric light, for when they put in the first bulbs she was only able to perceive the glow. She did not tell anyone about it because it would have been a public recognition of her uselessness. She concentrated on a silent schooling in the distances of things and people's voices, so that she would still be able to see with her memory what the shadows of her cataracts no longer allowed her to. Later on she was to discover the unforeseen help of odors, which were defined in the shadows with a strength that was much more convincing than that of bulk and color, and which saved her finally from the shame of admitting defeat. In the darkness of the room she was able to thread a needle and sew a buttonhole and she knew when the milk was about to boil. She knew with so much certainty the location of everything that she herself forgot that she was blind at times. On one occasion Fernanda had the whole house upset because she had lost her wedding ring, and Úrsula found it on a shelf in the children's bedroom. Quite simply, while the others were going carelessly all about, she watched them with her four senses so that they never took her by surprise, and after some time she discovered that every member of the family, without realizing it, repeated the same path every day, the same actions, and almost repeated the same words at the same hour. [...] the search for lost things is hindered by routine habits and that is why it is so difficult to find them. (246–47)

This concept of blindness illumined by memory and the retelling of things is expressed by one of the characters who suddenly go blind in the novel *Blindness*, by another great fabulist, in this case José Saramago, the Portuguese Nobel laureate:

[...] he had reached the conclusion that blindness, undoubtedly a terrible affliction, might still be relatively bearable if the unfortunate victim had retained sufficient memory, not just of the colors, but also of forms and planes, surfaces and shapes, assuming of course, that this one was not born blind. He had even reached the point of thinking that the darkness in which the blind live was nothing other than the simple absence of light, that what we call blindness was some that simply covered the appearance of beings and things, leaving them intact behind their black veil. (6)

Indeed, Úrsula's years, and her "honorable pact with solitude" that Colonel Aureliano speaks about when he shuts himself off to craft his little golden fishes (199), are what allows her to perceive more clearly what is going on in the house: "[...] in the impenetrable solitude of decrepitude she had such clairvoyance as she examined the most insignificant happenings in the family that for the first time she saw clearly the truths that her busy life in former times had prevented her from seeing" (248). Through the clairvoyance granted her by blindness, precisely at that moment Úrsula realizes that Aurealiano is a man incapable of love because she heard him cry when she had him in her womb; that Amaranta is not bitter and cruel but a woman suffering an atrocious fear from the torments of her own heard; and that the only strong, courageous being whom Úrsula had also loved for the purposes of continuing the family line is her adoptive daughter Rebeca. That is why she states, as she touches the walls, "Rebeca... how unfair we've been to you!" (250). ... there was a sun of clairvoyance in the shadows of that wandering ... [because] an alert old age can be more keen than the cards" (250).

Another moment in which Úrsula demonstrates her enlightened blindness is when, after the death of Amaranta, she finds out about Meme's murky ties with someone:

"It was too obvious that Meme was involved in secret matters, in pressing matters, in repressed anxieties long before the night that Fernanda upset the house because she caught her kissing a man in the movies" (283). Úrsula will question Meme and thus discover the young girl's relationship with Mauricio Babilonia, which allows the narrative voice to state that: "Her lucidity, the ability to be sufficient unto herself made one think that she was naturally conquered by the weight of her hundred years, but even though it was obvious that she was having trouble seeing, no one suspected that she was totally blind. She had so much time at her disposal then and so much interior silence to watch over the life of the house that she was the first to notice Meme's silent tribulation." (283)

Following this episode, the elderly matriarch's end rushes on. Úrsula stands at the door to "watch" the funeral of Gerineldo Márquez go by and, presaging her own last breath, asks him to give regards to his people because they will all see each other when the weather clears. Absent-minded, and conversing with her ancestors, as the children play with her she continues to ask them about the whereabouts of the person who had brought a plaster, life-size statue of Saint Joseph, in order that she may retrieve it once the rains are over. Aureliano Segundo, fearing that the old lady will go to her grave with the knowledge of the whereabouts of the fortune stored away in that statue, questions Úrsula uselessly "because in the labyrinth of her madness she seemed to preserve enough of a margin of lucidity to keep the secret which she would reveal only to the one who could prove that he was the real owner of the buried gold" (328).

When it stops raining after almost five years, Úrsula totally regains her lucidity. She weeps on seeing that during all those years she had become a mere toy for the children; with no one's help, she washes her face and gets out of bed to join the family fold.

> The spirit of her invincible heart guided her through the shadows. Those who noticed her stumbling and who bumped into the archangelic arm she kept raised at head level thought that she was having trouble with her body, but they still did not think she was blind. She did not need to see to realize that the flower beds, cultivated with such care since the first rebuilding, had been destroyed by the rain and ruined by Aureliano Segundo's excavations, and that the walls and the cement of the floors were cracked, the furniture mushy and discolored, the doors off their hinges, and the family menaced by a spirit of resignation and despair that was inconceivable in her time. (333–34)

Despite her blindness and old age, Úrsula witnesses the destruction of her home by termites and cockroaches; yet she doesn't give in and exclaims, "A person can't live in neglect like this [...]. If we go on like this, we'll be devoured by animals" (334). And from that moment on, until her time comes she will not stop working. The moment when Úrsula loses completely the use of her reason occurs when she discovers Meme's child and thinks it her son, Colonel Aureliano Buendía. Nevertheless, Úrsula will resist even her own death. When she is finally found lifeless inside the house, her great-great-granddaughter Amaranta Úrsula says, "Poor great-great-grandmother, [...] she died of old age" (341), and a startled Úrsula shouts, "I am alive" (342), but no one can hear her.

Aureliano (Babilonia) says that she can't even speak and that she died like a little cricket precisely when she asks to be listened to, because she is speaking. After this, though, she resigns herself to her own death:

> "My God," she exclaimed in a low voice. "So this is what it's like to be dead." She started an endless, stumbling, deep prayer that lasted more than two days [...]. They found her dead on the morning of Good Friday. The last time that they had helped her calculate her age, during the time of the banana company, she had estimated it as between one hundred fifteen and one hundred twenty-two. (342)

After this, we witness the precipitous end of Macondo and of the Buendía family.

CONCLUSION

For personal reasons that are not relevant here, the subject of old age and blindness are topics that have obsessed me lately. Perhaps because of that, in my re-reading of *One Hundred Years of Solitude* the character of Úrsula grew into a recurrence, not only for her central role as origin and foundation of the plot, but also as a way of finding a bit of light in darkness and a ray of hope within the somber prospect of an old age in the shadows.

A few months ago, during a visit to Rome, I entered the church of Santa Maria del Popolo on a rainy afternoon. I was reminded of the great deluge of Macondo; and I had the presentiment of something magical about to take place. In the Cerasi Chapel of that church, I found a series of extraordinary works of art. On the altar there was a magnificent Assumption of the Virgin Mary, by Annibale Caracci. On each side were two masterpieces by his chief rival Caravaggio: To the left of the altar was the Crucifixion of Saint Peter. Thinking himself not worthy of dying as Christ had perished, Saint Peter had asked to be crucified upside down, and this sacrifice in a darkness inhabited by diagonals evoked for me Julio Cortázar's short story "The Night Face up."

It was my looking left, however, that elicited the true miracle: there stood a painting of the Conversion of Saint Paul. The intense, inward worlds of Caravaggio are condensed in so singular a work that was touching my soul. The persecutor of Christians, Saul of Tarsis, has just plummeted to the ground from the force of a divine stroke of lightning. The voice of the Maker can be heard: "Saul, Saul, why dost thou persecute me?" The painting seems made of silence and shade, and, truth to tell, it is a work contemplated by an abundant assembly usually gathered in church without uttering a word. (Or so it seemed to me.) The back of an impeccably drawn horse, held by a servant, demarcates the scene at the top; and at the bottom Saul, Saint Paul, with his arms spread, delineates a perfect concavity on the verge of being filled, and gives off an expression of severe concentration and an Apollonian profile allowing us to contemplate an eye, shut on account of the profuse light. I too felt briefly enraptured by the intense light of truth, the light that dazzles any onlooker who comes too close to the canvas. The paradox: What is up is down; on seeing the light, Saul is blinded.

The play of light and shade of such *tenebrismo* (the technical term in painting for extreme chiaroscuro) struck me as the most appropriate artistic language for representing a scene related to a blindness that had me obsessed. The blindness of Úrsula. The blindness as metaphor for a terrible illness in Saramago's novel: Woe to us and to our world if we could all succeed in seeing, perhaps precisely from having lost our vision, the incidental, the banal, the circumstantial. The epidemic of blindness thus must be eradicated, encapsulated, annihilated. Many elderly people go blind. They live it as a terrible, depressing reality, without recognizing that perhaps they may be better off on the threshold of a type of vision in which eyes are no longer needed. Many blind people are musicians—Joaquín Rodrigo, Andrea Boccelli, Stevie Wonder, or the Japanese pianist and composer Nobuyuki Tsujii (b. 1988). Music opens the doors to other truths for which sight is not indispensable. And there are blind bards who are masters at spinning tales, as were the first narrator Homer, and one of the greatest short-story writers of the twentieth century, Jorge Luis Borges—blind men whose transcendent gaze helps us enter a reality different from the one delineated by the light of what we see every day, leaving us with the sense of being capable of intuiting another world that is more real than ours, filling us with a nostalgia that engulfs us when we close the final page of a novel so unrepeatable as is *One Hundred Years of Solitude*.

In this chapter, I have aimed to demonstrate that, beyond constituting a character that can be reduced to a simple archetype, the enlightened blindness and the later years of Úrsula provide her a motive for discovering the secret of a satisfying old age and for signing an honorable pact with solitude. In constructing this character and the magical world of Macondo, García Márquez displays an exercise of creative mastery that, with its unlimited powers of suggestion, eludes any attempt at reductionism.

Translated by Gene H. Bell-Villada

WORKS CITED

Arenas, Reinaldo. "En la ciudad de los espejismos." *Casa de las Américas* (Havana) 7, no. 43 (May–June 1968): 134–38. Reprinted in *Sobre García Márquez*, edited by Pedro Simón Martínez (q.v.), pp. 139–46.

Bell-Villada, Gene (ed.). *Gabriel García Márquez's One Hundred Years of Solitude: A Casebook.* Oxford: Oxford University Press, 2002.

———. *García Márquez: The Man and His Work.* Chapel Hill: The University of North Carolina Press, 2010. 2nd. ed., rev. and expanded.

García Márquez, Gabriel. *Big Mama's Funeral* in *Collected Stories.* Trans. J. S. Bernstein. New York: Harper Perennial Modern Classics, 1999.

———. "Eyes of a Blue Dog." In *Collected Stories.* Trans. Gregory Rabassa. New York: Harper Perennial Modern Classics, 1999.

———. *One Hundred Years of Solitude.* Trans. Gregory Rabassa. New York: Harper Perennial Modern Classics, 2006.

Monet-Viera, Molly. "Brujas, putas y madres: el poder de los márgenes en *La Celestina y Cien años de soledad.*" *Bulletin of Hispanic Studies*, LXXVII (2000): 127–46.

Montaner Ferrer, María Eulalia. "Falaz Gabriel García Márquez: Úrsula Iguarán, Narradora de *Cien años de soledad.*" *Hispanic Review* 55 (1987): 76–93.

Peden, Margaret Sayers. "Las buenas y las malas mujeres de Macondo." In *Explicación de Cien años de soledad* 4, mo. Supp. 1 ed. Francisco De Porrata. San Jose, CA: Porrata Avendaño, 1976, pp. 313–27.

Rodríguez Imbriaco, Laura Verônica. "Una lectura arquetípica de los personajes femeninos de *Cien años de soledad*" *Espéculo.* https://pendientedemigracion.ucm.es/info/especulo/numero39/ciensole.html

Rodríguez-Vergara, Isabel. "Mujeres. Desmantelando el sistema patriarcal en las novelas de García Márquez." In Rodríguez-Vergara, Isabel (ed.). *Colombia: Literatura y cultura siglo XX.* Washington: OAS,1995.

Roses, Lorraine Elena. "The Sacred Harlots of *One Hundred Years of Solitude.*" In Bell-Villada, Gene, ed. *Gabriel García Márquez's One Hundred Years of Solitude: A Casebook,* pp. 67–78.

Saramago, José. *Blindness.* Trans. Margaret Jull Costa. Orlando: Harvest Books, 1998.

Valverde Barrenechea, Leticia. "Úrsula, Petra Cotes y Pilar Ternera. Una triada mítica de lo inconsciente colectivo." *Káñina*, Rev. Artes y Letras. Univ. Costa Rica. Vol VII, (2) 1983, pp. 43–57.

Volkening, Ernesto. "Gabriel García Márquez, o el trópico desembrujado." In *9 asedios a García Márquez.* Ed. Mario Benedetti. Santiago de Chile: Editorial Universitaria, 1979, pp. 147–63.

Chapter 7

Satire, Ecocentrism, and Luddite Discourse in *One Hundred Years of Solitude*

Regional Approaches for a Global Environmental Crisis

William Flores

This chapter examines *One Hundred Years of Solitude* to identify the kind of ecological consciousness present in the novel and to suggest how the work conveys environmental apocalyptic imaginations that depict a nonfictional environmental crisis. Raymond L. Williams explains that *One Hundred Years of Solitude* is "the total story (and history) of Macondo from an oral, prewriting society to its development as a sophisticated writing culture in the final chapters" (1991: 116). In the novel, García Márquez at first describes Macondo, the place where the events occur, as a natural paradise where its inhabitants live together with nature, respecting it. Concerning this utopian world, Rosario Curiel notes that, during Macondo's earlier years, people and nature live in harmony. From her article, it can be inferred that this harmony is based on the "arcadia-utopia of José Arcadio Buendía's dreams, a happy, well-administered village" (447; my translation). Curiel suggests an anthropocentric rule of government over the natural environment as a reason for the utopia of early Macondo. The question then is whether or not García Márquez's text evidences an anthropocentrism that emphasizes good stewardship over nature as the ideal or a biocentrism that promotes coexistence between humans and nature.

One Hundred Years of Solitude describes the recently founded Macondo as "a village that was more orderly and hard-working than any known… a truly happy village" (10–11). The early settlement is further described as "a village of twenty adobe houses, built on the bank of a river of clear water that ran along a bed of polished stones, which were white and enormous, like prehistoric eggs" (1). The narrator not only states that its population lives happily but also describes the environment in which this population lives: rudimentary houses, made of biodegradable materials in the midst of a natural paradise, where society respects and appreciates the natural environment. This description follows fundamental precepts of the philosophy of deep ecology, as proposed by Bill Devall and George Sessions. The two authors recognize the existence of a dominant worldview—the appreciation of the Earth as if it were a mere set of natural resources (Devall & Sessions 43). According to Devall & Sessions (65), deep ecology fully contrasts the dominant worldview. A significant part of the dominant worldview is the presence of a constant faith in human civilization surviving any catastrophe, saved through the use of advanced technology. This chapter then uses such contrast as a means to identify the environmental consciousness in *One Hundred Years of Solitude*. Deep ecology, for example, advocates or argues for the sustainable use of other living beings only to satisfy vital needs (Devall & Sessions 70). *One Hundred Years* thus portrays the early days of Macondo as a place in which the inhabitants coexist with nature without damaging it—a depiction that is consistent with deep ecology.

As events unfold in the narrative, the text reveals that it is not the lack of order that destroys the harmonious coexistence and happiness in Macondo, but rather the utilization of the natural environment as a set of natural resources that exist for the sole purpose of satisfying consumer interests. As the novel progresses, the harmonious coexistence between people and nature begins to deteriorate quickly. One of the events that complicate this harmony is the arrival of the banana company in Macondo. The greedy abusive practices of the company produce a transformation in the natural world characterized as follows:

> Endowed with means that had been reserved for Divine Providence in former times, they changed the pattern of the rains, accelerated the cycle of harvests, and moved the river from where it had always been and put it with its white stones and icy currents on the other side of the town, behind the cemetery. (245)

The banana company utilizes the natural environment of Macondo to meet the company's economic ambitions. In the narrative, the banana company is able to alter the normal rain cycle, advancing it or delaying it according to the company's interests. Concerning this type of weather modification, Olga Carreras González asserts the following:

> The flood is "summoned" by Mr. Brown, who in the midst of a dry season… looks at the sky and promises to announce the signing of the agreement with the workers from the banana company when the rain stops. And the rain begins obediently as if under a spell…. And it rains for "four years, eleven months and two days." (82; my translation)

As Gary S. Elbow indicates, when García Márquez's descriptions depart from reality, they do so for a specific purpose (80). One of these occasions is this description of the calling for a flood-like rain to fall over Macondo. In this passage, García Márquez uses his extraordinary management of hyperbole to depict the magnitude of the interference that the agribusiness firm will have over the local natural environment. In the wake of the transformation that follows the arrival of the banana company, the "river of clear water" (García Márquez 1) no longer exists in a pristine condition. The text emphasizes that the company "moved the river from where it had always been" (245). Although the narrator does not specify why the banana company relocates the river, one can infer that the move takes place in order to irrigate their plantations. The work evidences an environmentalist consciousness accentuating the effects that changes in Macondo have on the natural environment. In the novel, the utilization of nature for the purpose of satisfying economic ambitions triggers a series of events that leads to the destruction of the town. Consequently, the detailed descriptions of the sustainable use of natural resources as the basis for the harmonious coexistence between the Macondo of the first chapters and its natural environment; the environmental consciousness evident in the episodes analyzed in this essay; and the portrayal of a series of cataclysms that occur in Macondo when the banana company begins to exploit the environment—these all suggest that the text aligns with a biocentric perspective concerning the natural world.

Another episode often examined by scholars of *One Hundred Years of Solitude* is the massacre of three thousand banana-company workers. Numerous studies analyze the sociopolitical implications of this episode. *García Márquez: The Man and His Work* by Gene Bell-Villada, *Gabriel García Márquez* by Raymond L. Williams, and *García Márquez: el viaje a la semilla* by Dasso Saldívar are instances of relevant scholarship that delve into this topic; nonetheless, there is still room for further examination of the environmental manifestations surrounding this bloodbath. Following the mass murder, Mr. Brown, one of the managers of the banana company and therefore one of its perpetrators, reportedly summons a storm over Macondo that will last nearly five years. This deluge serves as an alibi for Mr. Brown to hide his crimes and concurs with the depiction of the banana company executives as being able to change "the pattern of the rains" (García Márquez 337). The same imagination that creates Mr. Brown, who is able to alter the climatological cycle of a geographical Macondo, is also the imagination that creates Macondo's environmental apocalypse. García Márquez thus provides a portrayal of an ecocatastrophe that can occur if humans continue to manipulate the environment for personal economic ambitions. The author conveys a message of careful sustainable treatment toward the environment inasmuch as altering its ecological balance can cause an environmental apocalypse.

As Gema Areta Marigó points out, in *One Hundred Years of Solitude* "nature becomes the primary culprit of the end of the Buendía dynasty" (363; my translation); but what moves nature to destroy the world of the Buendía family, and how that apocalyptic narrative evidences ecological wisdom, are questions that still need to be explored. Thus far we have established that Mr. Brown personifies the exploitation of natural resources to meet economic ambitions and is the character who summons the deluge that befalls Macondo. The destruction caused by that deluge falls mainly on the buildings of the banana company as well as on the town itself, as the narrator indicates:

> On Friday at two in the afternoon the world lighted up with a crazy crimson sun as harsh as brick dust and almost as cool as water, and it did not rain again for ten years. Macondo was in ruins. In the swampy streets there were the remains of furniture, animal skeletons covered with red lilies, the last memories of the hordes of newcomers who had fled Macondo as wildly as they had arrived. The houses that had been built with such haste during the banana fever had been abandoned. The banana company tore down its installations. All that remained of the former wired-in city were the ruins. The wooden houses, the cool terraces for breeze card-playing afternoons, seemed to have been blown away in an anticipation of the prophetic wind that years later would wipe Macondo off the face of the earth. (García Márquez 355–356)

Hence, like Frankenstein's monster or Lucifer, who turn against their masters, nature turns against the entity that dared to dominate her. Even so, the banana company is not the only entity at fault for the destruction of Macondo, but also the people of Macondo and elsewhere who welcome and allow the company to take advantage of the town even though they know about the firm's abusive practices toward nature. Based on the text, this type of treatment toward the natural world is the reason why nature turns against Macondo.

The environmental imagination in *One Hundred Years of Solitude* presents an apocalypse brought about by a reaction committed by nature; in the novel, nature acts as a living being that is angry for the abuses committed against her and, at the end, exerts her force to destroy the town. The ecosophy in *One Hundred Years* depicts a natural environment that has flourished while coexisting in harmony with humanity, an environment that adapts to the changes that take place in the living habits of the population of Macondo, yet that also has the potential to destroy Macondo when its population interferes with the cycles and balance of nature. According to the narrator, soon after human beings achieve the ability to modify the rainfall, speed up the crop cycles, and relocate the local river, the signs of the "prophetic wind that years later would wipe Macondo off the face of the earth" (García Márquez 356) begin to be displayed. The tension between nature and mankind at the end of the novel is described as follows:

Surrounded by the voracity of nature, Aureliano and Amaranta Úrsula continued cultivating the oregano and the begonias and defended their world with demarcations of quicklime, building the last trenches in the age-old war between man and ant.... At night, holding each other in bed, they were not frightened by the sublunary explosions of the ants or the noise of the moths or the constant and clean whistle of the growth of the weeds in the neighboring rooms. (García Márquez 441–442)

This quotation presents nature as a voracious phenomenon. Far from the idyllic natural environment of the beginnings of Macondo, the last chapters portray a distorted, personified natural environment that is able to threaten and destroy humanity. In the apocalyptic imagination of *One Hundred Years of Solitude*, some of the remaining inhabitants of Macondo, such as Aureliano and Amaranta Úrsula, try to defend "their world with demarcations of quicklime." The passage presents humans, not as the powerful entities often conceived of in modern culture, but as weak and minute in comparison with the magnificence of the natural world and its strength.

Just prior to the destruction of the world of the Buendía family, mankind is portrayed as attempting to appease nature; nature, however, has been damaged beyond repair and has transposed from victim to unstoppable executioner. The imagination that creates the apocalypse of the world of the Buendía family demonstrates parallels with the philosophy of deep ecology, inasmuch as this apocalypse is produced by excessive human interference in nature. García Márquez's novel is thus consistent with the fifth basic principle of deep ecology: "Present human interference with the non-human world is excessive, and the situation is rapidly worsening" (Devall & Sessions 70).

In addition to providing an original version of a possible environmental apocalypse, *One Hundred Years of Solitude* portrays humanity's tendency to exploit natural resources. In the apocalypse of the world of the Buendía family, living creatures that are often regarded as insignificant, such as an ant or moth, become a threat of destruction. The author chooses these seemingly insignificant beings as a means of suggesting the importance of respecting each member of the ecosystem in which we live.

In the novel's last pages, García Márquez presents an apocalypse in which there is no second chance to mend past mistakes. To finish with the destruction of the Buendías' world, nature displays its force by a powerful wind that completely extinguishes local humanity. The concluding sentence, "races condemned to one hundred years of solitude did not have a second opportunity on earth" (García Márquez 448), stresses how improbable it is for humanity to gain a second chance at re-establishing a harmonious relationship with the natural world once nature is damaged beyond repair. The exploitation of natural resources for the purpose of satisfying economic ambitions triggers the events leading to the utter effacement of Macondo. The creative imagination underlying *One Hundred Years of Solitude* displays a magical-realist world where humanity has reached the ability to alter the natural climatological cycles, hasten crop rhythms, and relocate rivers. This same environmental imagination also creates the ecological apocalypse of the Buendías' world, thus paralleling additional tendencies from the philosophy of deep ecology: the presentation of ecocatastrophes produced by excessive human interference in the natural world. Furthermore, the ecosophy evident in the text rejects the dominance of man over nature and, at the same time, suggests that a harmonious coexistence of mankind and nature is the optimal relationship required for the survival of all. This ecosophy is consistent with the basic principles of deep ecology, such as the recognition of the right of every life form to flourish and reach a positive development (Devall & Sessions 70; Foucault 369), the appreciation of nature for its intrinsic value, and the recognition of excessive human interference in balanced ecosystems (Devall & Sessions 70–71). Thus, the environmental imagination in the novel, far from manifesting anthropocentric notions concerning the natural world, rejects such notions and demonstrates tendencies consistent with the philosophy of deep ecology.

In addition to the coexistence between mankind and nature and the apocalyptic imagination depicted in *One Hundred Years of Solitude*, another theme worthy of analysis is the treatment of animals. Indiscriminate hunting, for example, has strong negative implications for the balance of ecosystems. Within the scope of this topic, the most notorious nonfictional character is Francis Drake. José Camacho Delgado (425) describes the English pirate as a scourge for the people of the Colombian coast. Concurrently, Gene Bell-Villada notes that the pirate's raids function "as prime mover in the chain of events starting with the southward flight of Úrsula's great-great-grandmother" (104). Moreover, the novel describes the fact of indiscriminate hunting as follows: "[José Arcadio Buendía] knew that... Sir Francis Drake had gone crocodile hunting with cannons and that he repaired them and stuffed them with straw to bring to Queen Elizabeth" (10–11). The text highlights Drake's hunting of alligators for their skin, a practice that, while damaging biodiversity, is still often performed in South America and the Caribbean. In the context of the novel, Francis Drake is portrayed as an evil person not only because of his assault on the city of Riohacha, but also because, as a result of the assault, Úrsula's great-great-grandmother gets burned and is left handicapped for life. Úrsula hence blames the pirate for every problem that she has with her husband. Thus, in the novel, Francis Drake not only is an evil person but also represents all who engage in the lucrative hunting of animals.

While in *One Hundred Years of Solitude* those who contribute to the destruction of biodiversity are initially personified in Francis Drake (including hunters of endangered species and those who hunt for pleasure), those who hunt for food, by contrast, are represented by José Arcadio Buendía and the happy inhabitants of early Macondo. As the narrative unfolds, José Arcadio Buendía and the men who help him establish Macondo enter into the forest to hunt deer and macaws for food. The ecosophy evident in *One Hundred Years* does not prohibit all hunting, only the kind that is not used for the purpose of human consumption, the kind that harms ecosystems. This ecosophy is consistent with the third basic principle of deep ecology, which states that human beings have no right to reduce biodiversity unless it be to satisfy vital needs (Devall & Sessions 70–71).

The theme of cruelty to animals in *One Hundred Years of Solitude* is not only present in the portrayal of Drake's lucrative hunting but also in the sport of cockfighting. Two of the novel's main characters start out practicing this cruel sport: Founder José Arcadio Buendía and his great-grandson José Arcadio Segundo. Concurrently, the episodes depicting the sport present a causal relationship between cruelty to animals and the statements and acts of violence performed between the two main characters involved in raising the gamecocks. The phrase "aroused by the blood of his bird" (García Márquez 23) indicates that it was precisely the cruelty committed against his gamecock that led Prudencio Aguilar to attack José Arcadio Buendía verbally and, in turn, led José Arcadio Buendía to murder him.

Later in the narrative, Prudencio Aguilar's ghost continually haunts Úrsula and José Arcadio Buendía. Due to these constant re-appearances, Úrsula and her husband decide to leave the town where they have been living. They cross over the mountain range that has delimited the Buendía world and, with the help of a few dozen followers, eventually establish Macondo. Just prior to the journey, José Arcadio Buendía slaughters all his gamecocks and forbids himself and all those traveling with him to rear these creatures in their new settlement. The depictions of the practice of raising gamecocks show us a dangerous practice in the sense that it has the potential to destroy not only the lives of the animals used in the sport, but also the lives of the people so involved. The text suggests that there is a relationship between the violence produced in the cockfights and the constant verbal and physical violence present in the lives of the owners of the birds. The fact that violence and murder are described in association with the practice of raising gamecocks is not coincidental; that episode is not the only occasion in which the narrative suggests that cockfighting produces violence, cruelty, or some kind of curse to characters in the novel.

Later in the work, José Arcadio Segundo starts raising gamecocks even though cockfights are prohibited in Macondo. José Arcadio Segundo ignores the ban despite the fact that Colonel Gerinaldo Márquez and Úrsula both berate him for reviving that practice. Even Úrsula tells him: "'Take those creatures somewhere else,' Úrsula offered him the first time she saw him come in with his fine fighting birds. 'Roosters have already brought too much bitterness to this house for you to bring us any more'" (203). The fact that it is precisely Úrsula who states that the gamecocks are what brings bitterness to the Buendía family, and subsequently to Macondo, is noteworthy because Úrsula's is the prime point of view in *One Hundred Years of Solitude*. Indeed, María Eulalia Montaner Ferrer goes so far as to argue that Úrsula holds the title of narrator in the novel (89). Consequently, when Úrsula rebukes José Arcadio Segundo, the text itself, and not only a protagonist, is all but presenting the reproof.

As Úrsula suggests, then, in *One Hundred Years of Solitude*, the practice of raising gamecocks brings with it a curse. Ignoring Úrsula's warning, José Arcadio Segundo continues covertly raising gamecocks, and then, like his great-grandfather, his life becomes filled with bitterness. José Arcadio Segundo in time becomes one of the organizers of the strike against the banana company that ends with the notorious massacre of the three thousand workers. His efforts are not blessed in the narrative; as a survivor, his life is haunted by the terrible memory of the massacre of his followers. Ironically, the character who used to delight himself in bloody cockfights is portrayed hiding inside a train car, immersed in a pool of blood and bullet-riddled bodies on their way to being dumped into the sea. Analyzing textual parallels, one should note that José Arcadio Segundo and his great-grandfather both lose their sanity during the last days of their lives. José Arcadio Segundo hides from the military by secluding himself in the same old room where Melquíades had hid while José Arcadio Buendía was spending his last days tied to a tree. Both are violent men who had enjoyed cockfighting. One lives his life with guilt over having killed Prudencio Aguilar; the other, with the memory of witnessing the massacre of three thousand of his own followers.

The practice of raising gamecocks converts these birds into simple resources utilized to satisfy sadistic desires and economic ambitions. This activity is consistent with the dominant anthropocentric worldview; however, the custom and thus the dominant worldview are rejected in the text. *One Hundred Years of Solitude* suggests that the practice of raising gamecocks creates dysfunctions and constant conflict in the lives of those who abuse animals. Hence, the ecosophy evidenced in *One Hundred Years* rejects cruelty committed in cockfighting, and by extension, abuse committed against all animals. Such a rejection is consistent with the concept of biocentric equality, which consists in the assumption that "all things in the biosphere have an equal right to live and blossom and to reach their own individual forms of unfolding and self-realization" (Devall & Sessions 67). A sense of biocentric equality is illustrated throughout the text in various instances when animal life is protected. Furthermore, the novel's ecological imagination serves to illustrate a proposal found in the philosophy of deep ecology: the need not only to change the laws but to transform ideological and economic structures that consent to animal cruelty (Devall & Sessions 70). While *One Hundred Years* suggests the need for change, the text also clearly implies that customs deeply rooted in a culture, such as cockfighting, require a gradual change that can be accomplished through the transformation of ideological and economic structures, rather than by creating new laws that attempt to protect the environment. This transformation and its subsequent move away from practices that harm the ecosystem are some of the most important challenges in the modern environmental movement.

An essential part of the philosophy of deep ecology is the belief that all living beings possess an intrinsic value in themselves independent from their usefulness to humanity (Devall & Sessions 70). US author Nicols Fox examines the relationship between deep ecology and the Luddite tradition and finds that this relationship is based on the notion that "deep ecology questions the assumptions and domination of the technological culture; defends low-tech cultures against the imposition of these technologies; and encourages soft and appropriate technologies that require fewer resources and less energy and that produce less environmental, social, and cultural damage" (218). The following pages explore how technology is presented in *One Hundred Years of Solitude* in order to determine whether or not the work evidences Luddite tendencies.

In *One Hundred Years of Solitude*, technological advances unfold in stages: first, the construction of wooden houses with zinc roofs in Macondo, forsaking mud and reeds as building materials; next, the presence of technological devices such as the machines brought by the periodically visiting gypsies; and finally, the arrival of the train and cinema to Macondo. In each of these stages, the people of Macondo begin changing their ways; the characteristic industriousness of early Macondo is replaced by mechanization, which becomes a colonizing tool used against the inhabitants of Macondo and its natural environment. From a Luddite perspective, it seems as if "the presence of the machine would begin to change the way individuals thought and acted" (Fox 124). But is it truly the presence of the technological machines that destroys the town of Macondo? Does *One Hundred Years* present an antagonistic feeling toward technological progress?

Some of the technological devices that gypsies bring to Macondo are the magnet and the magnifying glass; however, these devices do not carry an intrinsically evil value. On the contrary, the beneficial purposes of these instruments are implicit in the arrival of doctors and other professionals to Macondo following the construction of the train. In the hands of an ophthalmologist, a lens can be used to correct vision. In real life, the magnifying glass has been used to look into space and study the stars, to create microscopes, detect diseases, and increase the quantity and quality of life for humans and animals. While the text does not present a magnifying glass as an evil instrument, García Márquez's novel does show the dominant characteristic of human beings to use technology as an instrument of oppression.

In several episodes of the novel, the use of technology as a means of oppression manifests itself in a satirical way: First, José Arcadio Buendía tries to use the magnifying glass to train hypothetical soldiers in "the complicated art of solar war" (García Márquez 4). Next, in the hyperbolic description of the massacre of three thousand workers, the machine gun is presented as a tool of domination and mass destruction in the context of a surreal world that covers up such an atrocity; as Leonard Feinberg has argued, a world turned upside down and hyperbole are among the major characteristics of satire.[1] Additionally, the narrative presents the banana company using technology to alter rain cycles and change the course of rivers with the purpose of gaining control over nature.

One of the main tools of domination and a symbol of progress that is satirized in *One Hundred Years of Solitude* is the "innocent yellow train" described as a development that was to bring "changes, calamities, and feelings of nostalgia" to Macondo (García Márquez 239). Using the adjective "innocent," the narrative explicitly states that the responsibility for the calamities that are to occur in Macondo would not fall on the machine itself; for this reason, the responsibility should devolve onto those who utilize the machine in an evil way. This wrongful utilization of technology is the object of satire in at least part of the novel. The work indicates that it is not the technological tool that brings negative consequences to Macondo, but rather the ways in which people with ambitions for power and control make use of this kind of instrument.

The references to the "innocent train" and the ironic allusions to the magnifying glass as a weapon of war rule out the possibility that the text expresses antagonism toward technological advances. Concurrently, the representation of the dominant nature of human beings, and of the utilization of technology as an oppressive tool, fundamentally questions the belief that any optimal progress can only be achieved through the use of advanced technology— a type of inquiry that is consistent with the philosophy of deep ecology. Concerning the harmonious relationship between the inhabitants of early Macondo and the natural environment, the text presents early Macondo as an ideal world, a utopia based not on luxury or on an idealized technocentric society, but one that is based on order and on the disciplined labor of its first inhabitants. The fact that the text describes that community with the phrase "It was a truly happy village" (García Márquez 11) points toward a Luddite perspective by implicitly defending cultures that use only basic technology and wish not to be imposed upon by the use of advanced technology.

Recent ecocritical analyses find that environmentally inclined modern literature often focuses on "exposing crimes of eco-injustice against society's marginal groups" (Buell, 2005: 24). *One Hundred Years of Solitude* follows this pattern of exposure by describing various abuses and even a massacre committed in an imaginary Macondo—crimes that are based on real events such as the inadequate working conditions and the 1928 massacre of the United Fruit Company's workers in the Colombian town of Ciénaga—and by denouncing the excessive human interference in the natural world with the sole aim of satisfying economic ambitions. The novel's apocalyptic imagination depicts an ecocatastrophe in which the following key is given: "Races condemned to one hundred years of solitude did not have a second opportunity on earth" (448). More broadly, the author's final sentence expresses the impossibility of obtaining a second chance at reestablishing a harmonious relationship with the natural world once the latter is damaged beyond repair. Thus, the apocalyptic imagination in *One Hundred Years* illustrates the responsibility that humanity has of learning to coexist with the natural world, a challenge given to modern man in any environment, be it rural, urban, or a merger of both.

According to ecocritical scholar Lawrence Buell, there are two trend-lines marking an evolution in ecocriticism: "'first wave' of ecocriticism" and "'second' or newer revisionist wave" (2005: 17). Of the two trend-lines, an interpretation of first-wave ecocriticism might conclude that *One Hundred Years of Solitude* suggests a return to a pre-modern past as the solution to the current ecological problems. In the view of this essay, however, such a reading would ignore key passages requiring a different interpretation, passages referring to technology, among them the ironic textual references to the "innocent train" or the satirical allusions to the magnifying glass when utilized as an instrument of war. These key passages rule out the possibility that García Márquez's novel could express antagonism toward technological instruments; conversely, they reflect on the ways in which people with selfish ambitions transform these instruments into destructive tools, indicating that modernity is not the problem in itself, but rather that the utilization of modern tools by unqualified people is the factor that can bring about the self-destruction of the human race. Thus, *One Hundred Years* suggests the appropriate use of modern technology and the process of learning to coexist with nature as a solution to the current environmental dilemma. For all these reasons, *One Hundred Years*, besides being a fictional narrative that contains themes related to the environment, can also be seen as a work that is consistent with the principles of deep ecology discussed in these pages. It can also be inferred that García Márquez has had these insights that predate and coincide with the fundamental tenets of deep ecology.

One Hundred Years of Solitude illustrates the need to adapt environmental laws and regulations to diverse local socio-cultural realities and that, more important than creating new laws for the preservation of the environment, in our time it is critical to transform ideological and economic local structures so that societies and their natural environments may be able to coexist in a sustainable manner. Lawrence Buell (1995: 285) points out that the greatest danger to the environment is not the magnitude of environmental damage but rather the perception that most of the world's population has of the damage—a majority still unaccepting of the fact that the ecological crisis is extremely serious. Through the exposure of crimes of eco-injustice, the presentation of some possible effects of local practices that are consistent with anthropocentrism, and the portrayal of an environmental apocalypse, *One Hundred Years* offers the reader an opportunity to respond and create an alternate future to the grim fate that awaits us all if societies do not learn to coexist with nature.

NOTE

1. For general observations concerning the space of satire, see the chapter titled "Image of the World" in *Introduction to Satire* by Leonard Feinberg. Additionally, this essay uses Matthew Hodgart's theoretic model found in his book titled *Satire* and Gilbert Highet's tests, such as the "choice of some traditionally satiric subject and treatment" in a given work (Highet 15–18).

WORKS CITED

Areta Marigó, Gema. "García Márquez y el discurso de la naturaleza." *Quinientos años de soledad: actas del Congreso "Gabriel García Márquez" celebrado en la Universidad de Zaragoza del 9 al 12 de diciembre de 1992*. Eds. Rosa Pellicer & Alfredo Saldaña Sagredo. Zaragoza: Navarro & Navarro (1997): 361–368. Print.

Bell-Villada, Gene H. *García Márquez: The Man and His Work* (2nd ed.). Chapel Hill: The University of North Carolina Press, 2010. Print.

Buell, Lawrence. *The Environmental Imagination: Thoreau, Nature Writing, and the Formation of American Culture*. Cambridge, MA: Harvard University Press, 1995. Print.

———. *The Future of Environmental Criticism: Environmental Crisis and Literary Imagination*. Malden, MA: Blackwell, 2005. Print.

Camacho Delgado, José Manuel. "José Arcadio y el mundo de los piratas." *Quinientos años de soledad: actas del Congreso "Gabriel García Márquez" celebrado en la Universidad de Zaragoza del 9 al 12 de diciembre de 1992*. Eds. Rosa Pellicer & Alfredo Saldaña Sagredo. Zaragoza: Navarro & Navarro (1997): 425–432. Print.

Carreras González, Olga. *Macondo en la obra de Gabriel García Márquez: Caracteres y significación*. Diss. University of California, Riverside, 1970. Print.

Curiel, Rosario. "Carpentier y Gabriel García Márquez: maravilla y magia de la utopía." *Quinientos años de soledad: actas del Congreso "Gabriel García Márquez" celebrado en la Universidad de Zaragoza del 9 al 12 de diciembre de 1992*. Eds. Rosa Pellicer & Alfredo Saldaña Sagredo. Zaragoza: Navarro & Navarro (1997): 443–452. Print.

Devall, Bill & George Sessions. *Deep Ecology: Living as if Nature Mattered*. Salt Lake City, UT: Gibbs M. Smith, 1985. Print.

Elbow, Gary S. "Creating an Atmosphere: Depiction of Climate in the Works of Gabriel García Márquez." *Climate and Literature: Reflections of Environment*. Ed. Janet Pérez & Wendell Aycock. Lubbock: Texas Tech University Press, (1995): 73–81. Print.

Feinberg, Leonard. *Introduction to Satire*. Ames: Iowa State University Press, 1967. Print.

Foucault, Michel. *The Order of Things*. New York: Vintage Books, 1970. Print.

Fox, Nicols. *Against the Machine: The Hidden Luddite Tradition in Literature, Art, and Individual Lives*. Washington, DC: Island Press, 2002. Print.

García Márquez, Gabriel. *One Hundred Years of Solitude*. Trans. Gregory Rabassa. New York: Perennial Classics, 1998. Print.

Highet, Gilbert. *The Anatomy of Satire*. Princeton: Princeton University Press, 1962. Print.

Hodgart, Matthew. *Satire*. New York: McGraw-Hill, 1969. Print.

Montaner Ferrer, María Eulalia. "Falaz Gabriel García Márquez: Úrsula Iguarán, narradora de *Cien años de soledad*." *Hispanic Review* 55.1 (Winter 1987): 77–93. Print.

Saldívar, Dasso. *García Márquez: El viaje a la semilla. [LA BIOGRAFIA.]* Madrid: Alfaguara, 1997. Print.

Williams, Raymond L. *The Colombian Novel, 1844–1987*. Austin: University of Texas Press, 1991. Print.

———. *Gabriel García Márquez*. Boston: Twayne, 1984.

Chapter 8

Rediscovering Ice

García Márquez, Aira, and Vallejo on Chilling Memories

Héctor Hoyos

In this brief essay, I would like to make a proposal about a fruitful way to read García Márquez today. Homage can be trite, and institutionalization stultifying. Modifying a felicitous phrase Bruno Latour borrows from Whitehead, the goal is rather to "extend the eventfulness of literature" (2008: 94). In that spirit, I'll make the case to approach the author, his legacy, and the manuscripts recently acquired by the Harry Ransom Center (University of Texas, Austin) in a manner akin to how the opening chapter of *One Hundred Years of Solitude* (1967) approaches ice. This is no simple task—not just *despite* our familiarity with this famous trope, but *because* of it. There is much to unlearn, as I will show, by relying on César Aira's rewriting of the discovery-of-ice scene in *Cómo me hice monja* (1993, trans. *How I Became a Nun*, 2007); on that same writer's idiosyncratic take on García Márquez in *Diccionario de autores latinoamericanos* (2001, Dictionary of Latin American Authors); and on Fernando Vallejo's mordant "Cursillo de orientación ideológica para García Márquez" (1998, A Short Course in Ideological Orientation…). Throughout, I will also draw inspiration from different strands of new materialism.[1] This multifarious critical current allows us to reassess the continuing agency of García Márquez past the 2014 demise of the man who bore that name.

The discovery of ice provides unity of action to the first chapter of García Márquez's book. In a novel that is a world of wonders—a *Wunderkammer* that counteracts the logic of imperial collecting, as Jerónimo Arellano puts it (374)—the chapter is already a world in miniature. It is also an advance and a promise, which made physical copies of the book fly off bookstore shelves for the first time in Buenos Aires in 1967. Pedagogically, it sensitizes readers to peripheral modernism and undertakes the seemingly miraculous task of bridging the gap between high and popular culture. Meanwhile, the storage and display of the draft itself puts the city of Austin, Texas on the map of world literature, consolidating cultural capital and capital *tout court*, alongside that of Woolf, Proust, and others. Back at the start of the story, Colonel Aureliano Buendía's inaugural flashback takes him from the firing squad to childhood recollections of his father and his many objects, building up to the ice by way of magnets, magnifying lenses, and molten gold coins, among several others. The heterogeneous collection of collections, including objects from the realms of alchemy, navigation, everyday life, and the absurd, can easily be construed as an allegory of uneven development—think of José Arcadio Buendía arriving late to astronomical discovery. It also carries out a Lefebvrian autonomization of narrative space, bringing together objects that, beyond the household, define the confines of Macondo and what is possible there. Yet it also plays out an accrual of value. At one point, ice is taken for the greatest diamond in the world; the author's manuscript itself is worth hundreds of thousands of dollars.[2] In short, the quest for ice is, borrowing Donna Haraway's term, a material-semiotic affair.

Appreciating the agentic properties of ice, the crown jewel of the chapter, is a valuable starting point when it comes to defamiliarizing García Márquez once again. Liberated from a reductionist view that sees allegorization and symbolization as the only possible effects of fiction, our regarding ice as actor allows us to potentiate the aspirations of *Neue Sachlichkeit*, the "new way of objects" behind Carpentier's *real maravilloso*. It allows us to understand the force of García Márquez beyond patrimonialization and kitsch. A central, if overlooked, achievement of the author's oeuvre is estranging readers' relationship to objects, or in other words their sense of belonging within the continuities of what new materialism likes to refer to as "nature-culture" and the human/nonhuman (Latour 1993: 7). This project, fully realized in the later, highly economical short story "Light Is Like Water," belongs to a parallel tradition of materialist thinking in Latin America. As I discuss elsewhere, that intellectual lineage takes from Fernando Ortiz and José Eustasio Rivera, among others, the use of narrative and metaphor to destabilize our rapport with nonhumans.[3] Turning the author's manuscripts into the gold reserves of a modern American university's financial portfolio is, at best, the kind of tension that fuels debate and interest; at worst, a cancellation, a domestication of things.

The strategic antagonizing of García Márquez and of his contemporaries has left us famous coinages such as Alberto Fuguet's "McOndo" or Jorge Volpi et al.'s "Crack Movement." However, of all writers, it is the Argentine César Aira (b. 1949) who best understands the power of the Colombian author's things, let alone his words. In the two opening chapters of *Cómo me hice monja*, Aira gives us a first-person account of a six-year old boy whose father takes him to have strawberry ice cream for the first time. The father becomes furious when the kid tastes the ten-cent cup and finds it revolting; he, the parent, has finished his own fifty-cent pistachio, sweet cream, and whiskey-kumquat ice cream and found it delicious. In *Cien años de soledad*, a change of focalization reveals that the quixotic, absent-minded patriarch actually has children to care for: "he looked out the window and saw the barefoot children in the sunny garden and he had the impression that only at that instant had they begun to exist" (14). In *Cómo me hice monja*, the boy-girl narrator utters the curt phrase "he looked at me almost as if I had become an object [como si yo me hubiera objetivado]" when the father notices the child's retching (13, 16). A silly but not entirely unrealistic contest follows, in which the father tells the child to at least try some, and the child refuses. Readers will recall that young Aureliano Buendía courageously takes a step forward to touch the ice and finds it boiling hot. In Aira, by contrast, the father, who hasn't tried the kid's ice cream, simply knows it to be delicious and sweet; the child, who has barely had any, finds it disgusting and bitter. At one point the ice cream starts to drip onto the child's legs—*her* legs, in this instance. The pronoun changes as if to signal a major event in psychic life, the kind of childhood memory that pops up at a firing squad (*mnemosyne*). The girl feels "dry retches"—take note of the avant-garde simile that follows—like "a car slamming on the brakes" (12, "las frenadas de un auto loco," 16). At last the father tries some of the strawberry ice cream and realizes it has indeed gone horribly bad. The story unfolds at breakneck pace: he wants to confront the vendor but two other boys, who order a gargantuan ice cream of one peso each, stand in his way. The vendor tries to pass off a fresh batch of strawberry ice cream on to him for the one he sold before; the father, in a fit of rage and desperation, shoves the vendor's face into the drum of strawberry ice cream until the latter's limbs stop moving.

Aira offers a lesson in the smart art of literary parricide. In psychoanalytic terms, he *condenses* again death and childhood; he *displaces* the wonders of ice in the tropics to comfort food in the Southern Cone, pun intended. Rather than replace the abrupt mnemosyne of ice for elaborate anamnesis, as in the measured recollection of the past that the title *Cómo me hice monja* suggests, he unleashes word-deeds, trading sound for meaning: via homophony, the alluded phrase is *cómo me hice jamón* ("how I became ham"), Buenos Aires slang for "how I died." At one point, nonsensically, the by-then imprisoned dad is referred to as "Su Jamestad," a made-up word that inverts the vowel sounds and syllable order in "Su Majestad"—approximately, from "His Majesty" to "His Jamesty" (60). *Cien años*'s flashback becomes two disjointed moments that draw attention to their own artifice: a childhood memory as told both in real time and from beyond the grave. Fittingly, Francine Masiello describes Aira's reference to García Márquez as a form of "teasing." She rightly notes that one novel is an epic of conquest and discovery "in which the father of the Buendía tribe unleashes his heterosexual passion as a model for generations to come," whereas "the father in Aira's novel suggests father-son incest, beginning with a description of his enforced 'pleasures'" (10). At one point, the words of the father "cannot reach" César, now the girl (10, 14). García Márquez's words do catch up with César, the author, whose rewriting amounts to a materialist cultural critique of *macondismo*, male privilege included. "Critique" in the two senses of the word: a study of things García Márquez and also of their limits. Masiello focuses on the latter, but the former is just as crucial: for a hyperbole of homosexual penetration, recall José Arcadio Buendía's foundational skewering of his good friend Prudencio Aguilar, the ghost that would haunt the young patriarch.

Culling together various strands of research, musicologist Ana María Ochoa defines *macondismo* as "an ideology that is celebratory of magical realism's trait of seeing Latin America as undecipherable, beyond the code, and as a place whose very disjunctures are, in and of themselves, identifying characteristics" (207). I contend that García Márquez, much as he benefitted in life from that misguided ethos, is ultimately its first casualty. It is a small step, for an author who has been a metonym of the region as a whole, to become a bastion of whimsical, baffling contradiction. It is an even smaller step for that widely read author to become, in a sense, unread: impossible to regard but through the lens of the ideology that he is supposed to affirm. Aira provides a way out of such circular logic. García Márquez may at times represent Latin America as beyond rationality, but this is something he celebrates as much as decries—think, for instance, of how *Noticia de un secuestro* (1996; trans. *News of a Kidnapping*) dissects the times of Pablo Escobar. The Carpentier dyad *real maravilloso* was more about tension, than about the resolution of contradiction. Both exceptionalizing García Márquez and making him the figurehead of *macondismo* render the author's oeuvre into an ineffective, uneventful monument.

Aira's other major intervention into the legacy of García Márquez is just as illuminating. His *Dictionary of Latin American Authors*, as yet untranslated, initially was issued and circulated, in playful and misleading fashion, as a work of reference (as was once the case with Bolaño's *Nazi Literature in the Americas*); to this day, libraries often feature it alongside scholarly works of a similar title in their reading rooms. There is plenty to learn about the region's literature by consulting it, but conventional scholarship is not something it delivers. By way of a prologue, an "Advertencia"—in this case, both a Warning and a Note—introduces the book as an "entirely domestic and personal, accumulation of commentaries, (...) this 'Dictionary' is one such work solely for being in alphabetical order" (my translation, 7). Aira leverages the force of the book-object, which smacks of an important-looking, learned work, with avant-garde, idiosyncratic interventions into literary historiography.

Significantly, the prologue, first dated in 1985 with a later postscript from 1998, addresses readers who look for "hidden treasures" (7). At the original time of writing, in the heavy-handed years of promotion that followed the Nobel Prize, García Márquez was rather a treasure one could not avoid.

In some ways, the treatment the Colombian author receives brings to mind the narrator of "Big Mama's Funeral," who chimes in "now that it is impossible to walk around in Macondo because of the empty bottles, the cigarette butts, the gnawed bones (...) [to] relate from the beginning the details of this national commotion, *before the historians have a chance to get at it*" (198; my emphasis). If literary historians—think of Enrique Anderson-Imbert—are ostensibly detached and impartial, Aira is anything but. On the other hand, the Dictionary systematically undoes the commotion, as if it had never happened. Aira is not all that impressed with García Márquez, who pretty much gets an entry *like everyone else*. Again like the narrator in Big Mama, Aira's offers jaw-dropping assertions with a straight face. It is purposefully difficult to discern dispassionate good sense from white-glove attacks and brushings off: we read that *La hojarasca* is a somewhat feeble Faulknerian exercise ("ejercicio faulkneriano algo endeble," 232); *La mala hora* a pleasant read *despite* excessive characters, programmatic Latin Americanism, and allegoric intention. In their heart of hearts, readers of García Márquez might not disagree: these are works of apprenticeship, after all. However, reatroactive greatness is so powerful that it becomes something of a taboo to criticize the master or even affect anything but reverence. This may be part and parcel of literary success, but its detriments in the case of García Márquez have nonetheless been costly: isolated from the vibrant pangs of the rest of literature, high atop a pedestal, the writer is easily misapprehended. With brevity and cleverness, Aira's "pre-historical" entry re-connects with García Márquez in thought-provoking ways.

There is a recurrent mytheme of ascent to literary glory that García Márquez himself cultivated and biographers from Dasso Saldívar and Gerald Martin onwards have echoed. It features *One Hundred Years of Solitude* as pre-climax and the Nobel Prize as climax. It can be found in the Real Academia's commemorative edition of the novel, where the merit of this ascent is extended onto none other than the Spanish language as a whole, with a remarkably unself-conscious glotopolitical language (ix). It even informs a visually pleasing graphic novel by Oscar Pantoja in which the author stands in ceremonial *liqui liqui* frame-to-frame with Remedios la Bella ascending to the heavens, boy Colonel Buendía discovering ice, and a train of murdered banana workers en route to the sea (Figure 8.1). Compare this agonistic, hagiographic structure with Aira's dry, one-line description of that famous novel: "*Cien años de soledad* (1967), colosal éxito de crítica y ventas [colossal critical and commercial success]." This is, to be sure, a brief mention

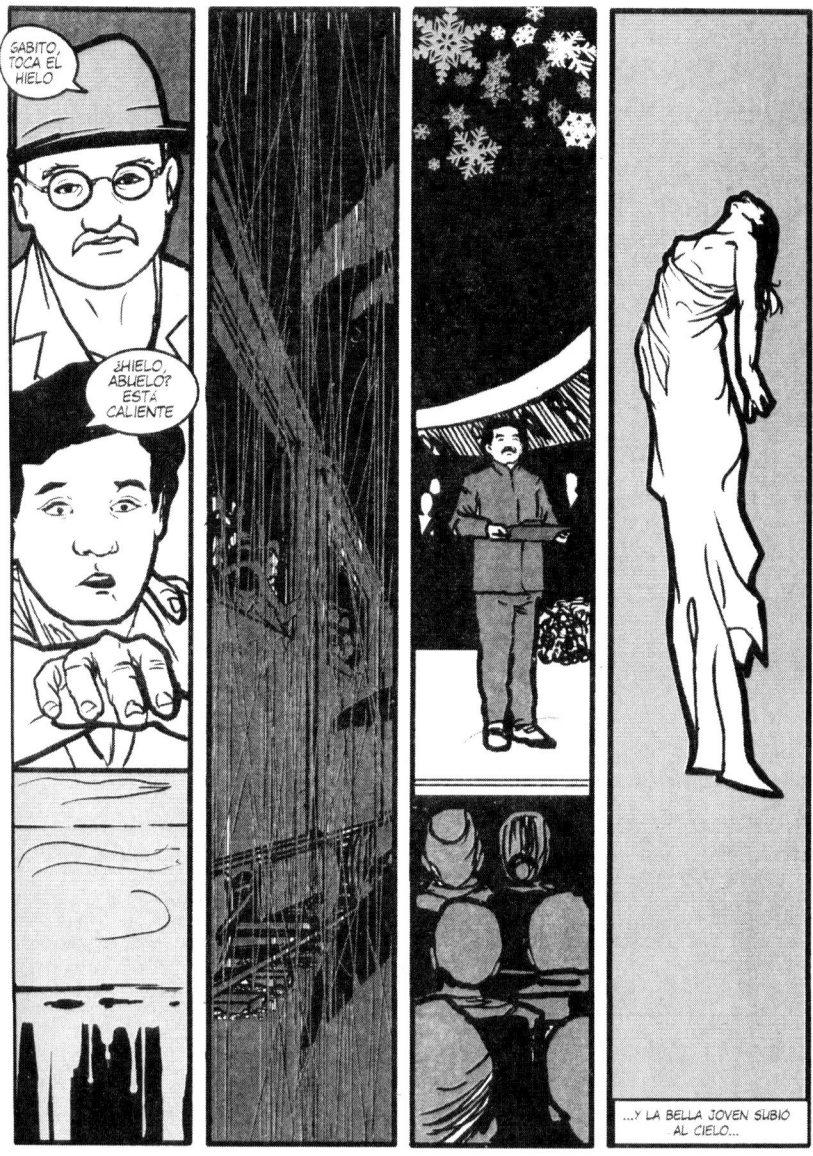

Figure 8.1 From Pantoja, Óscar et al. Gabo: Memorias de una vida mágica. Bogotá: R+N, 2014. Solamente con "®Rey Naranjo Editores, Colombia."

in a brief entry, a parody of back cover platitudes. The entry does not quite change literary history or offer an alternative, for it acknowledges the book's stature, but intervenes in its telling by conferring a differentiated attention to the work. Sometimes, extending the eventfulness of literature means questioning the event in the first place.

Bitingly, Aira emphasizes the flurry of sometimes redundant publications that followed *One Hundred Years of Solitude*. Much like The Beatles in the wake of Beatlemania, who issued various LPs with partially overlapping tracks to satisfy their fans' demand, there is a less heroic side to García Márquez's publication strategy that Aira's entry sheds light on. This happens right after the summary characterization of the masterpiece. My translation tries to approximate some of its crafty, read-between-the-lines wit:

> Immediately thereafter, there came out several short books by the author (the occasional title unauthorized): *Isabel Watching it Rain in Macondo* (1967), *The Story of a Shipwrecked Sailor* (1970) (…), *The Black Man who Made the Angels Wait* (1972), *Eyes of a Blue Dog* (1972). And in 1975 there came another long novel, *The Autumn of the Patriarch* (…)
>
> Se publicaron inmediatamente varios libros breves del autor (alguno de ellos desautorizado): *Isabel viendo llover en Macondo* (1967), *Relato de un náufrago* (1970) (…), *El negro que hizo esperar a los ángeles* (1972), *Ojos de perro azul* (1972). Y en 1975 otra novela extensa, *El otoño del patriarca* (…). (Aira 2001: 232)

It is customary to gloss over the interim, purportedly irrelevant period between the two masterpieces. Canonization shares the values emblazoned in the Real Academia's coat of arms: "limpia, fija, y da esplendor [cleans, fixes, and gives splendor]." Aira, on the contrary, muddies the waters. The result is a precarious García Márquez, who struggles to leave his mark on the dictionaries of literature, like everyone else. As it happens, Aira favors brevity over extension, so in a sense this entry judges the world-renowned Colombian author by the Argentine novelist's less universal standards. Presumably, the opposite has been the case, and Aira's accomplishments, like those of many other writers of his generation, were under-appreciated due to the overwhelmingly successful aesthetic paradigm represented by the Colombian author. This turning of the tables is not just about challenging the fetish with long novels, often taken as a sine qua non of mastery, but about making way for alternative axiologies of Latin American literature.

Similarly, the *Dictionary* features country indexes toward the end; the Colombian index closes with authors who have appeared under the shadow of the "success and charm" of García Márquez (599). All of these are humorous ways of de-eclipsing Latin American and Colombian literatures, while still engaging with the colossus. It is refreshingly irreverent to read that *Crónica de una muerte anunciada* (1981) is a short novel "of highly achieved mechanics"; *El amor en los tiempos del cólera* (1985) "a dismayed, conventional attempt at a New World *Sentimental Education*" (232); or *El general en su laberinto* the result of a quest for themes. This is not the trivialization and misrepresentation that Fuguet banked his own success on, best encapsulated in his offhand, derogatory phrase "flying *abuelitas*" (*Salon*). The goal is not to build greatness from antagonism but to question the underlying structures of accumulation of cultural prestige, and moreover, to explore how Latin American literature would look like had *macondismo* not prevailed. This results in a different valorization of individual works and their place within the familiar narrative of authorial rise. With this account of the fragility and precariousness of even the most solid of literary careers, Aira gives us back an important feature of García Márquez's ice, namely: that it can melt, too.

Fernando Vallejo (b. 1942), whose importance to the last thirty years of Mexican and Colombian literatures is arguably second only to, well, García Márquez's, also brings this point home. The author, known for such inflammatory novels as *La virgen de los sicarios* (1994, trans. *Our Lady of the Assassins*, 2001) and *El desbarrancadero* (2001, The Precipice), is not shy when it comes to calling out the powerful, be they Popes, presidents, drug lords, or fellow authors. He defames in grand style; in one of Jean Franco's later articles, she refers to Vallejo as a master of the craft of insult. The literary magazine *El malpensante*, true to its name—The Suspicious One— published an iconoclastic short piece in 1998 titled "Cursillo de orientación ideológica para García Márquez [A Short Course in Ideological Orientation for García Márquez]." There the author, in an open letter to García Márquez written in a tone of familiarity—calling him "Gabo" or "Gabito," addressing him by *tú* rather than *usted*—lectures him on his support of the homophobic, repressive Cuban regime. He does not do so directly, but through an exemplifying, purportedly autobiographical story of Vallejo's dangerous love affair with Jesús, a Cuban teenager.

Vallejo's narrator meanders before setting the passionate scene in a tightly policed Havana. As is well known, the two Colombian authors relocated to Mexico—one in close, public contact with political figures, the other in relative anonymity. So first Vallejo mentions how García Márquez sought to impress the soon-to-be-assassinated presidential candidate Luis Donaldo Colosio (1950–1994), but did not attend his funeral; then he reports the author's remark, upon chatting with Bill Clinton at the Los Pinos presidential residence in Mexico, that he was "breaking the ice." Vallejo describes the witticism as a stroke of genius—one assumes: with its overtones of communion, the novel, and the Cold War—but is otherwise not amused. He leads the reader to believe that this is yet another example of García Márquez's left and right power-grabbing antics. It is never said outright, but the implication is that Gabito has a stone-cold heart. To which Vallejo sets forth in opposition a recurrent image in his own writing: a warm, pulsating heart, rendered here as pure fire. The narrator introduces his lover to the invisible addressee, Gabo:

> I introduce him to you first on the street, dressed, so we may take off his clothes later on, one item after another, in the intimacy of the bedroom: sweet-sixteen, green-eyed, lightly dark-skinned, with a sexuality that would not fit into his pants, something one would call a hallucination. His dazzling green eyes took note of my poor dim eyes, and the spark in his eyes, looking at me, lit the air on fire. Oh, Gabo, what a blaze, what burning blaze in Cuba, the blaze of love! Fortunately we sort of put it out in the bedroom, because otherwise we would have set the canefields on fire, and done, no more sugar harvest.

> [T]e lo presento primero en la calle vestido para que le quitemos después la ropa prenda a prenda en la intimidad del cuarto: de dieciséis tiernos añitos, de ojos verdes, morenito, con una sexualidad que no le cabía en los pantalones, lo que se dice una alucinación. Sus ojos verdes deslumbrantes se fijaron en los pobres ojos míos apagados, y la chispa de sus ojos viéndome incendió el aire. ¡Uy Gabo, qué incendio, qué inmenso incendio en Cuba, el incendio del amor! Menos mal que medio lo apagamos después en el cuarto, porque si no, les quemamos los cañaverales y listo, se acabó la zafra. (*El malpensante*)

This is a far cry from the spark of Revolution. In this permutation of the discovery-of-ice scene, we are privy to the discovery of fire. Thought-provoking power imbalances are staged unabashedly, foreclosing facile identity politics: Vallejo is traveling with diplomatic immunity, while his young lover, who is barely at the legal age of consent in Cuba, is significantly more at risk. When a soldier comes out of the bushes, pointing his rifle at the couple, Vallejo saves the day by calling the soldier off by using his own, regional *antioqueño* slang: state agents do not oppress foreign travelers, let alone dignitaries. Naturally, the mood is gone, but Vallejo insists he will die if he does not sleep with Jesús. The boy responds, laconically, that he can die, too. They risk those two deaths, one metaphorical and one literal. With a clothes-switching ruse à la Don Juan, the writer smuggles the boy into his hotel room, which they finally, metaphorically, set ablaze. The text only refers elliptically to the literal consequences of the affair, as the narrator says he will spare Gabito his telling him what he found when he returned to Cuba. That ominous ellipsis of the later trip brings the picaresque to a halt. For all the jovialness in his report of the soldier writing down Jesús's last name and misspelling it, in his briefly fantasizing about a ménage à trois with soldier, or in the erotic charge of addressing an imaginary Gabo as witness to the scene, the boy remains, as his first name suggests, a sacrificial victim. And García Márquez, by siding with the Revolution, remains complicit with its homophobia.

Given the complex power dynamics in the fable, Vallejo does not come across as proxy advocate of anti-establishment Cubans—nor as a champion of gay rights in general (he is indeed a defender of animal rights), nor as a supporter of suppressed homosexual Cuban writers like Virgilio Piñera in particular. What he does offer is pathetic appeal, presenting a negative of sorts of the father-son ice scene, to shake the heteronormative foundations of García Márquez's myth. Most importantly, he shows how his countryman's ice is the stuff of compromise. It's a political stance with a nasty underside. At one point Vallejo's character asks Jesús precisely whom is the Comité de Defensa de la Revolución defending the Revolution from. He answers his own rhetorical question: "They must be defending it, Gabo, from the *pájaros*. You get this because you are an eagle." Though *pájaro* literally means bird, its sense in Cuban slang becomes clear as Vallejo continues, "The two *pájaros* or gays [maricas] kept on walking, and walking, walking we reached the meadows of the Hotel Nacional." Vallejo employs the same informal, antioqueño pronoun *vos* that he used to call off the soldier and his "toy" gun. Consider the passage in the original: "La estarán defendiendo, Gabo, de los pájaros. Vos me entendés porque vos sos un águila (…) Los dos pájaros o maricas seguimos caminando, y caminando, caminando llegamos a los prados del Hotel Nacional" (46). Metonymic displacement leads to heightened contradiction, for the Nobel laureate appears here as a *gran marica*, in the derogatory sense (big sissy, approximately) rather than the sexual sense (queen), yet also as a different, more deadly kind of predator—a chilling thought, no doubt.[4]

I find in Vallejo's and Aira's hot and cold reconsiderations of things García Márquez a vivid reminder of the stakes and risks of writing. Buying into the idea of an author's greatness as some pre-ordained state of affairs is naïve, no matter how seductive or charming the narrative may be. Think of the domestic public anecdote of Mercedes and Gabo sending the second half of *One Hundred Years of Solitude* to the publisher in Buenos Aires: the thrust in that mytheme is that the work, and the author, are the alpha and omega of Latin American literature. It is wise to remember that this is not the case. Ice demands as much of us, for it insists on immanence in a narrative that is all about transcendence, as in earning the Nobel Prize, attaining greatness, or overcoming national and regional limits to become truly global. Ice upholds dialectics where monologic discourse is most at home. For Aira, García Márquez comes too close to formula. For Vallejo, to Stalinism. Whatever the case may be, it is valuable to question the author's uncanny convening power, his seemingly flawless harmonization of form and content.

Engaging García Márquez, instead of rehearsing his commonplaces, calls for something of a double take: both to unlearn what we think we know and to read him more thoroughly. I believe the authors under consideration here facilitate these tasks. Aira's and Vallejo's public working through of the anxiety of influence and of the trauma of magical realism builds on the cathectic force of objects and words rather than merely borrow them. Such an approach prefers to resituate, rather than to exceptionalize, thus revealing the material-semiotic treasure trove that García Márquez continues to be.

NOTES

1. For an overview of different strands of new materialism, see Coole and Frost.
2. Professor Gabriela Polit, from the University of Texas at Austin, mentioned the figure of two million dollars as the likely amount the library paid for the author's papers. This at the panel "The Legacy of Gabriel García Márquez," Modern Language Association conference, January 7, 2016, Austin.
3. In this short story, two wealthy immigrant *cartagenero* children and their classmates drown in electric light, in Madrid, in a reverse and tragic trajectory of colonialism that subverts the very term "Enlightenment." See Hoyos 2011. My current manuscript is entitled *Things with a History: Transcultural Materialism in Latin America*.
4. For a comprehensive view of the *ninguneo* (literally, treating some one as "no one") that Vallejo deploys against García Márquez across multiple sources, and the even more radical silent treatment the Nobel laureate deploys against the Rómulo Gallegos Prize, see Joset.

WORKS CITED

Aira, César. *Cómo me hice monja*. Rosario: Beatriz Viterbo, 1993.
———. *How I Became a Nun*. Trans. Chris Andrews. New York: New Directions, 2007.
———. *Diccionario de autores latinoamericanos*. Buenos Aires: Emecé, 2001.
Arellano, Jerónimo. "From the Space of the *Wunderkammer* to Macondo's Wonder Rooms: The Collection of Marvels in *Cien años de soledad*." *Hispanic Review* 78.3 (2010): 369–86.
Coole, Diana H. and Samantha Frost, eds. *New Materialisms: Ontology, Agency, and Politics*. Durham, London: Duke University Press, 2010.
Franco, Jean. "El arte de vituperar." *Cuadernos de literatura* 19.37 (2015): 177–84.
Fuguet, Alberto. "I am not a Magic Realist!" *Salon*. June 11, 1997.
García Márquez, Gabriel. *Cien años de soledad*. Madrid: Cátedra, 1984.
———. *Cien años de soledad*. Edición conmemorativa. Madrid: Real Academia Española y Asociación de Academias de la Lengua Española, 2007.
———. *One Hundred Years of Solitude*. Trans. Gregory Rabassa. New York: Harper Collins, 2003.
———. "Big Mama's Funeral." *Collected Stories*. New York: Harper Perennial Modern Classics, 2008: 197–99.
Haraway, Donna. *The Haraway Reader*. New York: Routledge, 2004.

Hoyos, Héctor. "La poesía de los objetos y la trayectoria: una lectura comparada y política de *Doce cuentos peregrinos.*" *Ensayos críticos sobre cuento colombiano, siglo XX*. Adolfo Caicedo, María Luisa Ortega, and Betty Osorio (Eds.). Bogotá: Ediciones Uniandes, 2011: 231–48.
Joset, Jacques. "Fernando vs. Gabo." *Bulletin hispanique* 112–12 (2010): 821–31.
Latour, Bruno. *We Have Never Been Modern*. Trans. Catherine Porter. Cambridge: Harvard University Press, 1993.
———. "Powers of the Facsimile. A Turing Test on Science and Literature." *Intersections: Essays on Richard Powers*. Stephen J. Burn and Peter Demsey, eds. University of Illinois: Urbana-Champaign, 2008: 263–92.
Masiello, Francine. *The Art of Transition: Latin American Culture and Neoliberal Crisis*. Durham: Duke University Press, 2001.
Ochoa, Ana María. "García Márquez, Macondismo, and the Soundscapes of Vallenato." *Popular Music* 24.2 (May 2005): 207–22.
Pantoja, Óscar et al. *Gabo: Memorias de una vida mágica*. Bogotá: R+N, 2014.
Vallejo, Fernando. "Cursillo de orientación ideológica para García Márquez." *El malpensante* 13, noviembre-diciembre de 1998: 44–48.

Part III

LATER WORKS

Chapter 9

After the End
Bolívar in the Labyrinth of History
Michael Wood

"It was the end," we read some forty pages into Gabriel García Márquez's novel *El general en su laberinto*. The passage is one of only three times in the book when we see the hero's name—the other occasions involve naming a dog, and an urgent whisper in the general's ear—and we get the spreading splendor of the full version: "General Simón José Antonio de la Santísima Trinidad Bolívar y Palacios was leaving forever."[1] This is true in the sense that he will die before this last year of his life is out; but as Gerald Martin reminds us, he will not die in these pages, and he will leave several other places before he arrives at Santa Marta, his last destination.[2] At the moment he is barely managing to get out of Bogotá.

"He won't leave and he won't die" (18).[3] The cruel slogan painted on the walls of the Archbishop's palace is not terminally true. But he takes his time, physically and mentally, and his enemies could be forgiven for believing the slogan was correct. The first words we hear the general pronounce in the novel are "Let's go." His servant José Palacios has heard him say this "so many times and on so many different occasions" that he doesn't think the general means it, in spite of the ostensible preparations for departure (9). "The truth was that even his most intimate friends did not believe he was abandoning either power or the country" (18). "His repeated renunciations of power," we are told, "had been incorporated into popular song …. His renunciations were reiterated so many times, and in such dissimilar circumstances, that no one ever knew again which to believe" (19).[4]

The narrator loves these ambiguities about the general's intentions and declarations. "Tomorrow I leave the country," the general says. The narrator adds, "It was not tomorrow, but four days later" (32).[5] This is true only if "the country" means this part of the country, namely Bogotá; and of course the slippage of time itself is part of the comic point. The decisive hero is not indecisive but he is four days behind his proposed schedule. At another point the general says he will leave and never return, but he doesn't say when or where he's going. At times he pretends he is just waiting for his passport in order to leave the country, indeed the continent. When he receives his passport, he says, "We are free." Two days later he says, "We are sad" (149).[6] And at one point when the fighting intensifies in the maritime region where he is staying, he takes a trip to see how things are going. The narrator comments, "Viewed in the proper light, he was no longer a defeated pensioner fleeing into exile but a general on campaign" (183).[7] This isn't necessarily the proper light, of course; the perspective is the narrator's sympathetic contribution.

The only person who does believe, correctly, that the general is leaving is his mistress Manuela Saenz. "But she was also the only person who had at least one telling reason for expecting him to return" (11).[8] Is the suggestion that his friends and fellow officers no longer have any expectations of him? That they have lost their faith not in him but in the sustainability of his cause: independence with unification? Manuela knows how much he loves her, and the narrator is convinced that love is the most real as well as the most enduring of reasons. The other thing that Manuela knows, we learn at a later stage, is that "her eternal fugitive no longer had a place to escape to" [139].[9] He could leave Bogotá, the implication is, he could even leave Colombia; but where could he have gone that would not be entirely defined by where and what he had been?

The time of the human body and of material events is meticulously counted in the novel. Dates are given ("Saturday, May 8, 1830," "September 25, 1828" [10, 51]), days are numbered (the general "spent twenty-nine days in Turbaco" [131]), a month is evoked ("October was reduced to the sound of rain" [197]). We hear of "the rush of history" (218), and read finalizing phrases like "just one time and forever" (214). As Bolívar is dying he looks at the sky for the last time, and we are told what he will *not* see the following Saturday: the yellow flowers on a new vine, "the final brilliance of life that would never, through all eternity, be repeated again" (232).[10]

The mental time of the narrator and his hero, however, is quite different; constantly invaded by the past and the future. Marcel Proust suggests that "from a simple realistic point of view" the places we wish for take up more room in our true life than the place where we actually are at any moment, and this proportion almost certainly applies to time as well.[11] Even by this generous standard *El General en su laberinto* seems exceptional, and wishing is perhaps not its chief mode of consciousness. The general thinks of his return from Lima three years before, of his time in the jungle scarcely three years earlier, of the longest night of his life, of the number of times he has traveled on the Magdalena River. "Memories were more of a burden than the years" (107).[12] And if the general is deeply caught up in his past, the narrator complements such views with interesting incursions into what was then the future. Doctors are still pondering the cause of the general's death a century and a half later. There are forty-nine civil wars still to come in Colombia. Even the source of this novel itself gets a mention: Álvaro Mutis's story, published "one hundred eighty years later" (169).

We may also note an intriguing stylistic trick in the prose of the novel: flashbacks are often double or even triple. A revolt of hussars and grenadiers reminds the narrator (or perhaps the general) that the viceroy Juan Samano fled through the same streets eleven years before—"after three long centuries of Spanish domination" (16). "Months before," we read at the beginning of a sentence that takes us straight to "his Babylonian nights in Lima" four years earlier (9). A sentence starts "Days later;" the following sentence opens "Three years before" (24). A memory of the general's meeting Manuela eight years previously evokes the death of his wife twenty-seven years earlier. A male servant announcing a date names it also as "the Day of the Blessed Virgin, Mediatrix of all Grace." He adds, "It has been raining since three o'clock in the morning." The general replies, "Since three o'clock in the morning of the seventeenth century" (10).[13]

These temporal shifts are quietly, gracefully signaled, but become dizzying when we pause over them. Yet they are not only dizzying. They are part of a larger, implicit view of human actions and thoughts in history. And of course, if we are interested in time and narrative, we can't afford to let García Márquez's signature phrase—"había de," (was to)—slip away as if we understood it too well. I count thirty-four uses in the novel. Not all of them are important for our purposes, but each of them helps us to understand the idiom better. The meanings range from the notion of a plan or a proposal to something like a fate, although the touches are quite light at the latter end of the scale. A similar gliding effect occurs with the Spanish word "destino," which means destination as well as destiny. There is some dazzling play with this possibility in *Cien años de soledad*, notably in the case where a young man is said to be "destined" to be happily married and live to a ripe old age, but unfortunately gets shot and killed before any of this can happen. Just in case we are not confused enough, we are told that the mishap was caused by "a wrong interpretation of the cards" offered by a fortune-teller, in this case the young man's mother.[14] She foresaw his death, that is, but shouldn't have. She turned out to be right because she was wrong. On the other hand, destiny was not cheated, since the man who was supposed to die that night did also die. The mother missed that one.

It is striking that "destino" in *El General en su laberinto* means destiny more often than it means destination, but sometimes destiny means only the way a career or a life ultimately developed, and doesn't have to imply any sort of fate. The uses of "había de" show a similar sort of balance. They do however entangle us deeply in the idea of history, and in their discreet way they structure the whole narrative. Where the usage in *Cien años de soledad* always represents a semi-secret incursion of the narrative present into the narrated past, a retrospective act of prophecy, the effects are more varied in *El general en su laberinto*, and run from simple suggestions of planning or sequence to complex intimations of necessity, psychological or political.[15] They may also imply not that the present has stolen into the past but that the past is fully alive in the present.

Edith Grossman translates all but one of the instances of "había de" as "would," a conditional mood of a verb rather than a separate idiom. This makes sense, since the idiom is perhaps more emphatic in English than in Spanish (and perhaps used less by other Spanish writers than by García Márquez). The effect remains, but becomes stealthier. The phrase may mean simply that something was going to happen, that someone was planning to do something: "In a few days the Constituent Congress would meet;" "the rumor would fly;" "he would be in Quito" ([21, 56, 22]).[16] Another set of meanings reminds how things have turned out, that this is what hindsight tells us: "a legendary legal imbroglio that would go on for two years after his death;" "Alto Peru, which would later become the Republic of Bolivia;" "Barranca de San Nicolás, which in a few years would become the most prosperous and hospitable city in the country" (58, 137, 185).[17] And finally there may be an implication that the future really was alive in the past, that some sort of special intensity or necessity was at work: "she was to remember the flash of his teeth in the moonlight;" "provocations that would end in her exile and oblivion;" "she would always remember him as a... man who seemed much older than his thirty-two years;" "slamming the door with a noise that would echo round the world;" "that would be his fixed idea;" "the path that would bring him, in time, to the designated presidency of Venezuela" (48, 68, 71, 147, 177, 218).[18]

Here are some more complicated occasions. Of the general's nephew we learn that he was planning to write a memoir, but this didn't happen. He was twenty-six when the general died, and "would live to the age of eighty-eight without writing anything more than a few disordered pages, for fate granted him the immense good fortune of losing his memory" (230).[19] The implied rational account of these events offers no mysteries, no games with time and destiny. The nephew lived until a good old age and lost his memory somewhere along the way. That is why he wrote only a few unconnected pages. But the phrase "would live," along with the words "fate" and "fortune," lends an entirely different color to the casually offered information. The language is mildly playful and ironic—especially about the good luck of losing memory—and we don't need to suspect our narrator of heavy philosophizing. The unmistakable suggestion, though, is that chance in this case gave a fine impersonation of design, and we can hardly fail to notice the success of the performance. If the novelist didn't arrange these matters, then history is a pretty good novelist.

Another instance:

> Only Manuela knew that his disinterest was not lack of awareness or fatalism, but rather the melancholy certainty that he would die in his bed, poor and naked and without the consolation of public gratitude. (13)[20]

"Disinterest" is not quite the right word for the general's lack of interest in his own safety, but the rest of the sentence works equally well in both languages. We are not asked to believe that the general was fated to die in this way, only that he was certain he would. Or rather that Manuela knew he was certain. But of course the distinction between his certainty and what we would call fatalism is all but invisible, and this is just the effect García Márquez wants— particularly since the general turns out to be right. Again, there is nothing predetermined here in any theological sense, but a sense of miserably precise foreknowledge is almost irresistible. A similar effect, but without the misery, is evoked in relation to the general's wild announcements for the future, made in 1817, including the liberation of New Granada and Venezuela, the foundation of Colombia and the conquest of the "immense southern territories all the way to Perú." "Those who heard him... thought he had lost his mind, and nevertheless it was a prophecy fulfilled in every detail in less than five years" (222–223).[21] There is no fate here, only an outsized confidence. But then what words do we use when such predictions come true?

We can ask the same question about moments in the past we take as a kind of destiny. In 1817, Bolívar ordered the execution of a rebellious general, Manuel Piar, and never forgot the occasion.

> For the rest of his life he would repeat that it was a political necessity that saved the country, persuaded the rebels, and avoided civil war. In any case, it was the most savage use of power in his life, but the most opportune as well, for with it he consolidated his authority, unified his command, and cleared the road to his glory. (201–202)[22]

Here "había de" almost means "had to" rather than "was to," and the first sentence reports only on what Bolívar said, how he justified his act to himself and others. We may think he was right or wrong in his act, but his own conscience seems to be working a little too hard to defend the decision. The next sentence has a different stance, introduced by the careful "in any case." The narrator doesn't tell us whether the result was worth the moral cost, but firmly insists on the result. Gerald Martin links the execution in the novel to the death sentence imposed on General Arnaldo Ochoa by Fidel Castro in 1989, and thinks García Márquez wanted to make this connection, implicitly criticizing both leaders. This seems very plausible, although I think the criticism might have been twinned with a sense of *Realpolitik* and an awareness that writers have a moral latitude not always available to heads of state. Even without a specific authorial intention the linkage helps us to understand what Martin calls the writer's "obsession with, indeed his sympathy with, men in power."[23] The obsession is not an infatuation. The writer doesn't have to say whether or not he approves the ferocious act, he has only—if he cares about such things—to make sure we understand the stakes, and are free to make up our own minds. Haunted as the general is by the event, he tells his servant now, in his last days, that he would do the same again. Is this stubbornness, denial, or a cool, harsh view of what was needed? It's very hard to separate the psychological question from the moral one. Does the general know his own mind, and how far is his thinking likely to be from ours? All we know is what he "would repeat."

The curious nonreporting of the general's death raises similar questions, and in this context it is worth rephrasing Martin's reminder slightly. It's not quite that the general "does not actually die in the novel." There is no doubt about the death, it's just that we hear about it only circumstantially, the narrator disappears at the actual moment. We learn of the wake, which takes place sixteen days later; of the medical specialists who have been summoned and arrive very quickly but not quickly enough. The corpse makes the return journey from a plantation to Santa Marta ten days after the living man went the other way; and in the saddest of these notations we are told that Manuela was on her way to Santa Marta when she learned that "she was a whole lifetime too late" (226).[24]

The narrator's absence at the moment of death is an important feature of the novel's systematic contrast between the inexorable linear time I have evoked and the multiple mental times of the general's memory and the narrator's knowledge. It helps us to see that for García Márquez the mortal, dying Bolívar of the last months of his life, indeed the Bolívar who made himself into a hero from his early days, and the mythical Bolívar of the countless statues and the long history of celebration are not different persons. They are a single, complicated figure, there is no transition that will take us from the literal life to the legend.

Even someone as subtle as José Enrique Rodó can miss this interwoven aspect of Bolívar's life, which may well belong to a perspective on fiction and history that was not available in the Uruguayan essayist's time. Bolívar's attitude, Rodó says, meaning his attitude in actual life, "may seem histrionic to those who have not arrived a precise understanding of his personality."[25] It may indeed; and even to those have arrived as such an understanding, which is likely to include this aspect of his life rather than correct it or deny.

García Márquez's Bolívar is a man who says "This isn't my theater," meaning not that he isn't theatrical, but that the scene is inadequate for him (35).[26] His theatrical uniforms are remarked on; and elsewhere he says "I am condemned to a theatrical destiny (75).[27] The many carefully crafted remarks Bolívar makes in the book, the "one-liners" Gene Bell-Villada has noted, certainly are a mark of the writer's style as much as of the general's; but then the double source itself tells us something.[28] We don't have to believe that history is all fiction, or that real life has been betrayed by theater; only that theaters are real, and that some lives fictionalize themselves even as they are lived.

Remarks that seem to and may indeed belong to the repertory of the narrator's critique of Bolívar—a matter not of finding fault with a great man, but of understanding the intricate composition of his greatness—take on a different tone in this context. When Bolívar finds his once voracious appetite for reading is declining, we are told, "and as always he attributed this to a cause beyond his control" (86).[29] "As always" is a piece of mischief on the part of narrator, an insertion of an invisible act of will where Bolívar pretends there isn't one. When did Bolívar ever acknowledge that anything significant was beyond his control? But then he also knows when not to play the part of the man of will. We are also told, in a rather sterner aside, that "when problems had no solution he resolved them by deceiving himself" (145).[30] This practice is undeniably a fault according to many systems of self-knowledge, from that of Socrates to that of Polonius; but then the criticism seems to backfire. What else are we to do with the irremediable, isn't there a kind of courage here? In both cases a gap between event and representation opens and closes, and this is precisely what keeps happening in the novel.

A perfect instance of this double vision, of the deep entanglement of lived time in posthumous life, is the novel's presentation of Bolívar's "dream" and what happens to it. This is "the golden dream of continental unity;" "the largest alliance of nations in the world" (21, 180).[31] The concept of unity doesn't prescribe any particular political arrangement, and the second definition leaves the idea of separate American nations intact. This isn't the usual formula for Bolívar's dream, which the narrator of the novel, perhaps articulating Bolívar's vision, perhaps slightly travestying it, also describes as "the fantastic dream of creating the largest country in the world: one nation, free and unified, from Mexico to Cape Horn" (46).[32] This is the idea that Bolívar said was too grand for his enemy Santander: "The unity of America was too much for him" (107).[33] But at one point the dream is just a dream even for Bolívar: "I've become lost in a dream, searching for something that doesn't exist" [194].[34]

As this last phrase suggests, Bolívar in his last days felt himself to be a failure. The novel and history agree perfectly on this. The novel proposes, however, in its careful, perhaps skeptical phrasing of the dream, that the failure was a more immediate and practical matter, and does not offer an opinion on the desirability of a united South America. Bolívar had led the colonies to independence, but his legacy, it seemed, was likely to be not only the abeyance of continental unity, and not only the perseverance of old colonial divisions in the liberated world, but drastic divisions even within those divisions. "Every Colombian is an enemy country," he says (209).[35] "The only ideas that occur to Colombians are for ways to divide the nation" (219).[36] It is in this mood that Bolívar speaks of the price paid "for an independence that's not worth shit;" and famously says that the United States is "omnipotent and terrible, and its tale of liberty will end on a plague of miseries for us all" (152, 196).[37] Independence, the genuine, amazing achievement, is a disappointment to the dying hero, and liberty comes to mean a kind of anarchy. Elsewhere, thinking of his own correspondence, Bolívar associates liberty with disorder. The dream had become a ruin, as Jorge Volpi says.[38]

The tone of this ending, as many critics have noted, resembles that of *Cien años de soledad*, and an important question we can address to both novels is why such desolate conclusions do not entirely have the depressing effect they may seem to require. We could transpose the question into a biographical one. Why would a progressively minded author, a believer in change and an ardent supporter of the Cuban Revolution, choose to present us with such bleak and apocalyptic plots, to offer no hope to his protagonists within their own world? The games with time I have traced in this essay may afford the beginning of an answer.

It has two parts. First, there is a lot of political realism in this magical realism; none of the magic is designed to take away or diminish the facts of historical defeat and disappointment. And second, events in history cannot be separated in any nontrivial sense from their representation or narration. This means that although we cannot alter the past we can always rethink it—and rethink its thinking. We may learn the lessons of history, not, as is often suggested, from copying its achievements or avoiding its errors, but by understanding where choices were available and what they were. For this purpose a narrative that is both fictional and historical, that knows an end is not always or immediately an end, that time can be both single and multiple, and that destiny may be an all too plausible name for what just turned out to happen, is a near-perfect instrument of understanding, as long as we recognize that irony is part of its practical use, and not a mode of denial or obfuscation.

At one point in *El general en su laberinto* we read that our hero said that his return from Caracas to Bogotá to assume the presidency in 1827 was his decisive moment. The narrator then comments, "A little more reflection would have permitted him to realize that for almost twenty years no moment of his life had not been decisive" (103).[39] This discreetly comic sentence clearly suggests that if all the general's moments were decisive, we could just as easily say that none of them was; that what counted was the whole set of his life's actions, whatever their result. It also hints, however, at a more interesting truth. What we call decisive moments are always inventions, mental versions of the idiom "was to," and there are many occasions when we simply cannot do without them. The paragraph ends with the words "It was his destiny."

NOTES

1. García Márquez 2004, p. 38, and cf. pp. 91, 123. "Era el fin;" "El general Simón José Antonio de la Santísima Trinidad Bolívar y Palacios se iba para siempre." García Márquez 1989, p. 44, and cf. pp. 107, 142. Further references to the translation are taken up into the text.
2. Martin 2012, p. 157.
3. "Ni se va ni se muere." García Márquez 1989, p. 21.
4. "tantas veces y en ocasiones tan diversas;" "La verdad era que aún sus amigos más íntimos no creían que se iba, ni del poder ni del país;" "Sus renuncias recurrentes estaban incorporadas al cancionero popular... Volvió a renunciar tantas veces, y en circunstancias tan disímiles, que nunca más se supo cuándo era cierto." García Márquez 1989, pp. 11, 21–22, 22.
5. "Mañana mismo me voy del país;" "No fué mañana mismo, pero fue cuatro días después." García Márquez 1989, p. 37.
6. "Somos libres"; "Somos tristes." García Márquez 1989, p. 173.
7. "Vista al derecho, ya no era un jubilado en derrota huyendo hacia el destierro, sino un general en campaña." García Márquez 1989, p. 212.
8. Pero también era la única que tenía al menos un motivo cierto para esperar que volviera." García Márquez 1989, p. 14.
9. "su eterno fugitivo ya no tenía ni siquiera para dónde escapar." García Márquez 1989, p. 161.
10. "Sabado ocho de mayo del ano treinta," "El miercoles 25 de septiembre de 1828;" "se quedó veintinuieve días en Turbaco;" "Octubre se redujo al rumor de la lluvia;" "la prisa de la historia;" "por una sola vez y hasta más nunca;" "los últimos fulgores de la vida que nunca más, por los siglos de los siglos, volvería a repetirse." García Márquez 1989, pp. 12, 60, 152, 229, 252, 248, 269.
11. Proust 1987, p. 383.
12. "Los recuerdos le pesaban más que los años." García Márquez 1989, p. 126.
13. "al cabo de tres siglos de dominio español;" "Meses antes... las noches babilónicas de Lima;" "días más tarde... tres años antes;" "Está lloviendo desde las tres de la madrugada... Desde las tres de la madrugada del siglo diecisiete." García Márquez 1989, pp. 19, 12, 29, 12.
14. García Márquez 2006, p. 151.
15. cf. Bell 1993, p. 32: "the ghosts of these earlier meanings constantly haunt the text."

16. "En breves días había de reunirse el congreso constituyente;" "había de correr el rumor;" "había de estar en Quito." García Márquez 1989, pp. 25, 67, 28.

17. "un embrollo judicial legendario, que había de prolongarse hasta dos años después de su muerte;" "alto Perú, que había de convertirse más tarde en la república de Bolivia;" "Barranca de San Nicolás, que en pocos años había de convertirse en la ciudad más próspera y hospitalaria del país." García Márquez 1989, pp. 69, 160, 215.

18. "había de recordar el fulgor de sus dientes a la luz de la luna;" "provocaciones…. que había de terminar para ella con el destierro y el olvido;" "había de recordarlo siempre como un hombre que parecía mayor de sus treinta y dos años;" "un portazo que había de resonar en el mundo entero;" "aquella había de ser su idea fija;" "el camino que había de llevarlo con los años a ser presidente encargado de Venezuela. García Márquez 1989, pp. 57, 81, 84, 171, 206, 252.

19. "había de vivir hasta los ochenta y ocho sin escribir nada más que unas cuantas páginas descosidas, porque el destino le deparó la inmensa fortuna de perder la memoria." García Márquez 1989, p. 267.

20. "Sólo Manuela sabía que su desinterés no era inconciencia ni fatalismo, sino la certidumbre melancólica que había de morir en su cama, pobre y desnudo y sin el consuelo de la gratitud pública." *El General,* p. 16.

21. "inmensos territorios del sur hasta el Perú"; "Quienes lo escucharon entonces pensaron que había perdido el juicio, y sin embargo fue une profecía cumplida al pie de la letra, paso por paso, en menos de cinco años." García Márquez 1989, p. 258.

22. "Por el resto de su vida había de repetir que fue una experiencia política que salvó al país, persuadió a los rebeldes y evitó la guerra civil. En todo caso fue el acto de poder más feroz de su vida, pero también el mas oportuno, con el cuál consolidó de inmediato su autoridad, unificó el mando y despejó el camino de su gloria." García Márquez 1989, p. 234.

23. Martin 2009, p. 460.

24. "que llevaba toda una vida de retraso." García Márquez 1989, p. 262.

25. "puede parecer histriónica a los que no hayan llegado a una cabal comprensión de su personalidad." Rodó 2015, p. 215.

26. "Este no es mi teatro." García Márquez 1989, p. 41.

27. "Estoy condenado a un destino de teatro." García Márquez 1989, p. 89.

28. Bell-Villada 2012, p. 230.

29. "lo atribuyó, como siempre, a una causa ajena a su dominio." García Márquez 1989, p. 101.

30. "cuando los problemas eran irremediables los resolvía engañándose a sí mismo." García Márquez 1989, p. 168.

31. "el sueño dorado de la integridad continental;" "la alianza de naciones más grande del mundo." García Márquez 1989, pp. 25, 209.

32. "el sueño fantástico de crear la nación más grande del mundo: un solo país libre y único desde México hasta el Cabo de Hornos." García Márquez 1989, p. 56.

33. "La unidad de America le quedaba grande." García Márquez 1989, p. 125.

34. "me he perdido en un sueño buscando algo que no existe." García Márquez 1989, p. 225.

35. "Cada colombiano es país enemigo." García Márquez 1989, p. 242.

36. "Todas las ideas que se les occurren a los colombianos son para dividir." García Márquez 1989, p. 253.

37. "esta mierda de independencia;" "son omnipotentes y terribles, y con el cuento de la libertad terminarán por plagarnos a todos de miserias." García Márquez 1989, pp. 176, 227.

38. Volpi 2009, p. 30.

39. "Un poco más de reflexión le habría permitido comprender que desde casi veinte años atrás no hubo un instante de su vida que no fuera decisivo." García Márquez 1989, p. 120.

WORKS CITED

Bell, Michael. *Gabriel García Márquez: Solitude and Solidarity.* Basingstoke: Macmillan, 1993.

Bell-Villada, Gene H. *García Márquez: The Man and his Work.* Chapel Hill: University of North Carolina Press, 2010.

García Márquez, Gabriel. *El general en su laberinto.* Buenos Aires: Editorial Sudamericana, 1989.

———. *The General in His Labyrinth.* Translated by Edith Grossman. New York: Knopf, 2004.

———. *One Hundred Years of Solitude.* Translated by Gregory Rabassa. New York: Harper, 2006.

Martin, Gerald. *Gabriel García Márquez: A Life.* New York: Knopf, 2009.

———. *The Cambridge Introduction to Gabriel Garcia Marquez.* Cambridge: Cambridge University Press, 2012.

Proust, Marcel. *À la recherche du temps perdu*, vol 1. Paris: Gallimard, 1987.

Rodó, José Enrique. *Cinco Ensayos.* Madrid: Sociedad Española de Librería, 2015.

Volpi, Jorge. *El insomnio de Bolívar: Cuatro consideraciones intempestivas sobre América Latina en el siglo XXI.* Barcelona: Random House Mondadori, 2009.

Chapter 10

The Magic of Love, the Horrors of Death, and Other Themes in the Short Stories of Gabriel García Márquez

Rubén Pelayo

The amalgamation of love and death—the indivisible idea of Thanatos shadowing Eros as if in a dual-natured deity—is preeminent in the works of Gabriel García Márquez. The pleasure that overrides the imaginings found in his *Strange Pilgrims*, and in all three previous short story collections, defies death and vice versa.

Gabriel García Márquez published a total of forty-one short stories. In 1947, at the tender age of twenty, he published his *opera prima* "The Third Resignation." His last tale was the 1982 sketch "Sleeping Beauty and the Airplane," inspired by Yasunari Kawabata's novel *House of the Sleeping Beauties*.[1] The four books in this genre appeared in Spanish as *Los funerales de la Mamá Grande* (1962; *Big Mama's Funeral*); *La increíble y triste historia de la cándida Eréndira y de su abuela desalmada* (1972; *The Incredible and Sad Tale of Innocent Eréndira and Her Heartless Grandmother*); *Ojos de perro azul* (1974; *Eyes of a Blue Dog*); and *Doce cuentos peregrinos* (1992; *Strange Pilgrims*).[2]

In this our second decade of the twenty-first century, the English-speaking world continues to pay attention to Hispanic culture, Hispanic issues, and the literature published by Hispanic writers. The trend started taking on international shape in the 1940s and 50s, but the veritable explosion occurred in the 1960s. The increased attention to Latin American letters was given to the novel, even if it started with the short stories of Jorge Luis Borges.

By the 1970s, based on the translations into French, Italian, English and other leading languages, the Latin American Boom was well on its way. The Spanish American names of the literary "Boom," notably Julio Cortázar, Carlos Fuentes, Mario Vargas Llosa, and Gabriel García Márquez are nowadays, in certain literary circles, virtually household names. College students majoring or minoring in Spanish are equally familiar with Jorge Luis Borges,

María Luisa Bombal, Alejo Carpentier, Juan Rulfo, Elena Poniatowska, Rosario Ferré, and many others. But no matter how ground-breaking the work of Jorge Luis Borges was and continues to be, and how experimental and well-received were the stories by Cortázar, Fuentes, Bombal, Ferré et al., the one name that resonates the most amongs English-speaking readers is that of Gabriel García Márquez. Even though it is not necessarily as a short story writer that he is best known, his *oeuvre* encompasses several genres, including a one-act theater monologue, *Diatriba de amor contra un hombre sentado* (Diatribe of Love against a Seated Man.) The 1994 premier of this play, however, did not enjoy the glowing reception in Argentina[3] that years earlier, in 1967, García Márquez had received in Buenos Aires with the publication of *One Hundred Years of Solitude*.

The wealth of the short story tradition in Latin America, González Echevarría states, shares in the fabulous richness of its literature and art in general. Furthermore, he notes, "it belies those who would naively equate economic underdevelopment and political instability with artistic poverty."[4] The inventive wealth found first in Borges' *Ficciones* (1944; *Ficciones*) and *El Aleph* (1949; *The Aleph*), and later in the above-mentioned "Boom" writers, has placed them among the best writers of the modern short story. García Márquez as an author has influenced the work of Toni Morrison, Salman Rushdie, and Mo Yan—two of them Nobel Laureates—not to mention the more visible influence in Isabel Allende's *La casa de los espíritus* (1982; *The House of the Spirits*), Laura Esquivel's *Como agua para chocolate* (1989; *Like Water for Chocolate*), and Rosario Ferré's *The House on the Lagoon* (1995). At Peru's International Book Fair 2015, an expert on Asian literature remarked, "The magical realism of Colombian writer Gabriel García Márquez has greatly influenced China's Mo Yan, winner of the 2012 Nobel Prize in literature. Outrageous and mind-bending passages in some of his stories are what draw parallels with the magical realism of García Márquez."[5]

We shall examine Gabriel García Márquez's short story writing, from all four books, with emphasis on the stories of *Strange Pilgrims*, his last publication in the genre.[6] Short story collections by Gabriel García Márquez span more than three decades, from 1947 to 1982. The first three short story collections were later compiled in English as a single text in *Collected Short Stories* (1984). Only *Doce cuentos peregrinos* (1992) was published as a single book, the next year, as *Strange Pilgrims* in the United States. The stories we consider seminal, woven into the *corpus* of this essay, are "Eyes of a Blue Dog," "Monologue of Isabel Watching it Rain in Macondo," "Death Constant Beyond Love," "The Last Voyage of the Ghost Ship," and "The Incredible and Sad Tale of Innocent Eréndira and Her Heartless Grandmother." The four stories from *Strange Pilgrims* to be closely examined are "Bon Voyage, Mr. President," "Maria dos Prazeres," "Miss Forbes's Summer of Happiness," and to end this analysis, the seemingly autobiographical "The Trail of Your Blood in the Snow."

Death, love and the lack thereof, exploitation, violence, the stranger in town, solitude—all permeate the unforgettable plots García Márquez has crafted along with the theme of the double. This latter recurring theme appears, for the first time in 1948 in "The Other Side of Death." Twenty-three years later it was masterfully developed in *One Hundred Years of Solitude* (1967), through Aureliano Segundo and José Arcadio Segundo, the great-grandchildren of the founding couple of Macondo. These two brothers are the greatest characterization of the theme of the double ever to be found in Latin American letters. Jorge Luis Borges experimented with the theme in numerous pieces, and also in a different fashion, in "The Other." What we find in Borges's story is a split of the same character, one young, one old.[7]

The last two stories García Márquez wrote were "Tramontana" and "Sleeping Beauty and the Airplane," both in 1982. The volume *Strange Pilgrims*, nevertheless, was not published in English until 1993.[8] Two of the stories in the book were written as early as 1976: "Miss Forbes's Summer of Happiness," made into a film in 1988, and "The Trail of Your Blood in the Snow." Until recently, most of the short stories by García Márquez that are read and discussed in American college classrooms were not taken from *Strange Pilgrims*. The canonical stories "Monologue of Isabel Watching it Rain in Macondo," "Balthazar's Marvelous Afternoon," "Tuesday Siesta," and "Big Mama's Funeral," among others, seemed not to allow for any alternative work. Whether for commercial reasons, or because the aforementioned stories are indeed well crafted and recognizable, there has not been much interest in including the stories from *Strange Pilgrims*. Nevertheless, that approach is beginning to change in some of the most recent anthologies of Latin American literature.

If Gabriel García Márquez had never put any of his novels to paper, writes Gene H. Bell-Villada, his shorter fiction would have still gained him a niche in literary history. Bell-Villada puts García Márquez in the company of such acknowledged masters of short fiction as Chekhov, Mann, Joyce, Cheever, and Grace Paley.[9] García Márquez was immensely popular in the Spanish-speaking world just before the end of the 1960s. In the 1970s his popularity increased, but by the 1980s the Colombian-born writer was one of the biggest names in the world of literature, and his works found circulation in all leading languages. It was as if he had been propelled into a literary orbit from a Hispanic-sphere all his own; almost as if Latin America depended on his monolithic representation. However, there were English-language critics who thought his short stories were not on a par with his novels. Michiko Kakutani, writing for the *New York Times*, judged that "the entries in the *Strange*

Pilgrims collection demonstrate that the shorter form of the story does not lend itself to Mr. García Márquez's talents."[10]

Prudencia Linero's travel to Italy—in "Seventeen Poisoned Englishmen"—from *Strange Pilgrims* is indeed a *pilgrimage*, as the book title suggests. Hers is a spiritual journey to see the Pope following the death of her beloved husband. The same ideal of a religious pilgrimage is true in the story "The Saint." However, the other ten stories from this collection refer simply to traveling, detached from the spiritual practice. In Spanish, *peregrinar* (pilgrimage) is used loosely to simply refer to the action of traveling from point A to point B (*viajar o andar de un lugar a otro.*) In "The Trail of Your Blood in the Snow," for example, Nena Daconte and Billy Sánchez de Ávila fly to Madrid and then drive to Paris on their honeymoon. That is their *peregrinar*—their pilgrimage. In addition, the septuagenarian president of "Bon Boyage, Mr. President" goes to Geneva to seek medical treatment. "Sleeping Beauty and the Airplane" is unique in its structure in that the eponymous character is actually traveling back from, and not to, Europe. "I Sell my Dreams" somewhat follows the same pattern, but the story begins with the main character deceased in Havana; the narrator then traces her back to Vienna where all she did was "dream" for a living. In this story, the beginning of it is indeed the end of it. The female protagonist of "I Only Came to Use the Phone" is a Mexican variety artist, a music-hall performer; the story does not state whether she sings or dances. She lives in Barcelona as an immigrant, as does the one in "Maria dos Prazeres," whose name and city of residence they both share. The name repetition is typical of García Márquez, but their personalities, as well as their ages, are strikingly different. One is a twenty-seven-year-old; the other is seventy-six; the older woman is a prostitute, the other one a showgirl. These two women, as well as the other characters, are recognizable as members of the microcosms he has created through his general character development. They do not repeat themselves; they deepen their human condition whether living in the Americas or in Europe.

The stories "The Ghosts of August," "Tramontana," "Miss Forbes's Summer of Happiness," and "Light Is Like Water" share a most commonplace cast of characters that ties them together: a husband, his wife, and two children separated by a two-year difference. This is not a mere narrative technique to create the plot, but an autobiographical touch. We will elaborate more fully, farther down, on the factual aspects of Gabriel García Márquez's first trip to Europe that are identifiable in the stories of *Strange Pilgrims*. For the Gabriel García Márquez connoisseur all twelve stories are distinguishable by the "Marquezian" writing style of plot development, and the handling of thematic issues, with the exception of "Light Is Like Water." This latter story does not seem interconnected with the contents of *Strange Pilgrims* or with any other piece that García Márquez published. One may consider it as García Márquez's only attempt at science fiction for its futuristic content. But the veracity needed for a true sci-fi story falls short: the premise of the plot does not lend itself to a sci-fi storyline where the action needs to be partially true to the laws or theories of science.

All of the short stories in *Strange Pilgrims*, as is the case with all those he wrote, begin with a character or scene in *medias res*. In spite of this, unlike the three previous books, the omniscient narrator, the implied narrator, in some of the *Strange Pilgrims* stories is identifiable as García Márquez's voice. *Strange Pilgrims* can be read as a personal account, a travel catalogue of his days in Europe—the wandering years, indeed, as he put it, when he published *Cuando era feliz e indocumentado* (1973; When I Was Happy and Undocumented). The story "The Saint" draws on his first trip to Europe in 1955. The magical realist story of Margarito Duarte, the village clerk, as "the saint," rather than his disinterred daughter, is literally told as a personal account, a combination of the real and the fictionalization of the tale. García Márquez writes "it was my first visit to Rome, where I was studying at the Experimental Film Center, and I lived his Calvary [Margarito Duarte's] with unforgettable intensity" (41). In real-life history García Márquez was indeed studying cinematography, in Rome, at the Centro Sperimentale di Cinematografia.[11] This autobiographical approach to writing is similar to Borges' short story "The Other" from *The Book of Sand*.

The prologue to *Strange Pilgrims* elucidates for its readers why death inhabits the short stories and why in English we can call them, after Edith Grossman, *Strange Pilgrims*. They are pilgrims because of the "pilgrimage" the characters have made to Europe, where the stories take place: Switzerland, Italy, France, Austria, and Spain. They are pilgrim-stories, because García Márquez conceived them as he went on living in Europe, though he wrote them many years after those days of pilgrimage. The stories were written from 1976 to 1982. By 1976 García Márquez was living again in Mexico City after a long stay in Barcelona. The setting of the pieces is European, the main characters are Latin Americans, but it should be pointed out that the "problems" experienced in the narrative structure are not peculiar to Latin Americans. Take for example the violence against women in "The Ghosts of August" and "I Only Came to Use the Phone." In the latter, a Mexican emigrant is forced to undergo limitless physical and mental abuse in a Spanish insane asylum. In the former, an Italian renaissance nobleman has killed his beloved in bed after their having made love.

Reminiscent of Big Mama's limitless power over the townspeople of Macondo, "Miss Forbes's Summer of Happiness" displays the unbounded rigid discipline of a German governess over two absolutely powerless children. The humor and satire of both of these two stories outwardly disguise what the stories seem to denounce. One reads like a folktale, the other emphasizes the absurdity of such stereotyped German discipline.

The economic disparity "typical" of Latin America is observed in "Seventeen Poisoned Englishmen" as much as superstition is present in "Tramontana." In the latter we see that both the Latin American and the Italian characters are victims of their own delusions and not necessarily of the supernatural weather. In the former, a Yugoslav priest has to hassle people for a cup of coffee. Then there is the bureaucracy of the Catholic Church at its best: The Vatican—in "The Saint." This problem, the bureaucracy of the Catholic Church, well observed in earlier stories by García Márquez—think of "A Very Old Man with Enormous Wings"—is indeed universal. If the naïve reader of his early stories thought that what happens to the characters only happens to Latin Americans, *Strange Pilgrims* has perfectly crafted European settings in Barcelona, Geneva, Rome, Arezzo, and Paris.

Strange Pilgrims depicts human conditions. "Bon Voyage, Mr. President" inverts the long-standing idea of the Latin American president who cannot return to his country of origin because he has illicitly enriched himself. The story portrays an impoverished, dying, 73-year old Caribbean president, seeking medical attention in Geneva, who wants to return to his country. One may think he wishes to return to the French-speaking island of Martinique, but the narrative leads us to believe that his home is possibly elsewhere, some place named Puerto Santo. His ideals are altruistic; he believes he can start a new reform group with the help of the renowned and respected author Aimé Césaire[12] and friends. Who he might be is uncertain, but what is certain is that he is a Latin American ex-president. The will to craft the short story, the art of telling, is most apparent. García Márquez manages to present the reader not with an illegally enriched president, but a flesh-and-blood old man whose desire to live is stronger than his possibilities of dying. The reader feels empathy for the character. If only in fictional reality, his fellow townspeople, seen through Homero and Lázara, feel compassion and the desire to believe in their rulers. Of all the stories in *Strange Pilgrims* this is the only one in which love triumphs without the horrors of death. This opening story, along with "Maria dos Prazeres," and "The Trail of Your Blood in the Snow" can be considered among the best. But closely rivaling these three accounts is "Miss Forbes's Summer of Happiness" for its great appeal as a detective story, its experience of love denied, and its unending suspense.

The thematic issues in *Strange Pilgrims* are plentiful, the humor is exuberant, and the subversions are worth mentioning. The stereotypical ideas that women of color, in general, are subservient to men, often unmarried, frequently given the prostitute role, and cannot find love, are here put to the test. "Bon Voyage, Mr. President" contradicts every entry. Unlike Homero's last name (ironically King of the House), his colored wife runs the household, is not at all submissive, and enjoys the love of her husband and two children. How telling that the couple has a pair of kids, with a two-year age difference in age, but here we have a boy and a girl rather than two boys, as seen in the rest of the stories in which children appear as characters. The theme of death is at the center of the story, yet the narrative makes it look as if it were just an additional topic, like the love shared by Homero and Lázara. The character scene that starts the story reads "He [the President] sat on a wooden bench under the yellow leaves in the deserted park, contemplating the dusty swans with both his hands resting on the silver handle of his cane, and thinking about death" (3). There is death and there are the pride and morality of the poor, superstition, the obsession and power of dreams, the importance of the phallus, and the insistence on the passage of time.

Love and death, however, the two themes that frame this piece, are present in all the stories in *Strange Pilgrims* and in the previous three books. Both themes are intertwined through humor and inventiveness in nearly all the stories of García Márquez's total *oeuvre*. While the president is thinking about his own death in the opening sentence, before the story ends he goes on to do as he pleases. Going against doctor's orders, he decides to enjoy life as an old man by doing what he has always loved. If living is dying, then his life can be seen as the other side of death.

In "Maria dos Prazeres" the seventh story in the collection, death is also the axis of the narrative. However, death as theme is brought up by dreaming, yet another topic that permeates the author's *oeuvre*. Here a 76-year old prostitute has dreamed her death, much like, as García Márquez says in the prologue to *Strange Pilgrims*, he had dreamed his own: "I dreamed I was attending my own funeral, walking with a group of friends dressed in solemn mourning but in a festive mood [...] I thought this was a good point of departure for writing about the strange things that happen to Latin Americans in Europe" (viii).

Strange Pilgrims is fundamentally autobiographical. Other than the age difference between his sons Rodrigo and Gonzalo who serve as models for the children in some of the stories, he brings in his own experiences, as well as some of his friends as characters or references. In "I Sell my Dreams" Pablo Neruda and the omniscient narrator talk about dreaming—dreaming of being dreamed—and then cleverly argue that this is something Borges would have already written or soon would write as one of his labyrinths. Even Neruda's third wife, Matilde, is part of the witty storytelling. In "The Ghosts of August" we find the narrator, his wife, and two sons visiting not an imagined, but a real-life character: the Venezuelan writer Miguel Otero Silva, who in fact had a palazzo in Tuscany, where the mini-story takes place. This is the shortest of all stories in the collection and the one showing the most horrid depiction of death. The gruesome tale is a disturbing love tragedy in which the male has killed the female, thereby inverting the myth of the spider wherein the female kills the male. However, in this piece the male too dies for sex; it is hard to argue that it was for love. "I Sell my Dreams," on the other hand, in which dreams are at the core of the narrative, ingeniously takes place in Vienna, the city where Freud published his seminal text *The Interpretation of Dreams*. This story carries the sign of an atrocious death, that of Frau Frida whose body "was found secured behind the steering wheel by a seat belt. The blow had been so brutal that not a single one of her bones was left whole. Her face was destroyed, her boots had been ripped apart, and her clothes were in shreds" (63) but the humor in the tale is rampant. We can only imagine the great Neruda at a secondhand bookstore in Barcelona "moving through the crowd like an invalid elephant, with a child's curiosity in the inner workings of each thing he saw, for the world appeared to him as an immense wind-up toy with which life invented itself" (67). The story is greatly ironic regarding the authorship of "a dream within a dream," that is, dreaming that one is being dreamed, when Neruda says "I dreamed she was dreaming about me"—and the narrative voice tells him "That's right out of Borges" (69). The dialog is lively and unrestrained as a kind of gimmickry of literary criticism in the realm of *who said what* and *who said it first*. We know that the world of dreams that García Márquez came to write about, from the start of his career as a writer, was inspired by Kafka. Borges, who had translated Kafka, also wrote about dreams, and showed a fascination with dreams, hence the playfulness of the passage in the story makes perfect sense.

The spinster Frau Frida of "I Sell my Dreams" connects with Miss Forbes, the central character of "Miss Forbes's Summer of Happiness." But Miss Forbes's fate is worse than Frau Frida's. She ends up being killed by multiple stab wounds. Yet the two boys for whom she nannies had thought she would die from poisoning; after all, they had poisoned her bottle of wine. This turns the tale into a detective story and the reader has to decide who killed the nanny. These two single women, as if they were a character-type, connect the reader to Maria dos Prazeres, who unlike the other two bachelorettes, at least has a dog to keep her company. What we have here is a big bite of popular culture. The other two women do not have the proverbial "ni perro que les ladre," i.e., *they are all alone*. "Maria dos Prazeres," on the other hand, is somehow a projection of García Márquez's ideals. Maria, a refugee from Brazil living in Barcelona, sympathizes with the anarchist Catalonian leaders killed by the Franco regime. García Márquez, who identified with leftist ideals, lived in Barcelona during the Franco regime.

"Maria dos Prazeres," unlike Lázara Davis in "Bon Voyage, Mr. President," fits the stereotype of the mulata in some ways, but contradicts the typecasting in others. She has no motherly attributes, she is unmarried, and has been a prostitute all her life—part of the stereotype. Yet, unlike most prostitutes, she behaves as a subject and not as an object; she is the ruler of her sexuality and is proud of being a prostitute. She is deserving of respect and commands regard from men—an inversion of the type. Irony takes on an important role in this story, as it does in all the stories García Márquez wrote. Her own identity, her name—*dos Prazeres*—is Portuguese for "of *the* pleasures." Her self is precisely bound up with her sexuality. Her only connection with men is through sex, and the same can be said of her possessions. But underneath it all, old and immensely forlorn, she feels she is the ruler of her life; she is subservient to no one. She is supremely independent and does with her body only as she pleases. Furthermore, she displays a social and political social consciousness well beyond her abusive and cruel upbringing: "Her mother sold her in the port of Manaus when she was fourteen years old. The first mate of a Turkish ship used her without mercy during the Atlantic crossing, and then abandoned her, with no money, no language, and no name" (109). Hers is a forced and economically coerced prostitution that evolves from object of desire to desiring subject. Her political ideals sustain her amidst her solitude and lack of love. The end of her "friendship" with Count Cardona, her sexual benefactor, comes when the aristocrat tells her that Francisco Franco is a *"just man."* She thereupon responds that she is a *just prostitute* and ends the friendship. How telling it is that their relationship breaks up on the basis of an ideological dispute over Francisco Franco. While death and the lack of love can be seen at center stage, brought up by a dream that she has about her death, what "Maria dos Prazeres" portrays is prostitution as theme. Prostitution is indeed a recurring topic in García Márquez's fiction, and is at the forefront of "Maria dos Prazeres."

This leads us once again to "The Incredible and Sad Tale of Innocent Eréndira and Her Heartless Grandmother." There are different possible viewpoints to the story, but the one depicting child exploitation through prostitution cannot escape the reader. As Bell-Villada points out, "The basic plot, ironically, is as sad as the title indicates: a fourteen-year-old innocent is prostituted [...] by her grandmother."[13] Both characters—Eréndira and Maria dos Prazeres—share the same age when they start out; one is a white girl, the other a woman of color, but both share the same fate. What is the reader supposed to assume when reading these two stories? Is it a Caribbean convention, a cultural custom, a human vice the writer is trying to denounce or simply describe? Selling a fourteen-year-old as merchandise, as an object of consumerism, is a crime against women. But García Márquez is not a legislator, and the stories we read are not texts of jurisprudence either. The character Maria dos Prazeres is believable, well-rounded. Her character development defies the stereotypes we hold true in a patriarchal world, that is, the role of men to exercise power and control over women, particularly women of color. The story "Maria dos Prazeres" does not try to excuse prostitution nor censure it. The story unveils a hidden fact: desire. At age 76, Maria is still driven by desire. That flame within her still burns. She comes to understand, in the end, that as long as she desires, there is a reason to live. The final dream she experiences is not about death, as she thought it was, but about her lack of desire. "'My God,' she said to herself in astonishment at the prospect of lying in bed, one more time, with a young man. So it wasn't death" (114). How paradoxical that this theme was to be at the center of Gabriel García Márquez's last publication, *Memoria de mis putas tristes* (2004; *Memories of My Melancholy Whores*).

And now for a look at the collection of juvenilia, *Eyes of a Blue Dog*, gathered only in 1984, when the author had attained world fame. The ambiguity expected of the modern short story in Gabriel García Márquez is ever present, from "The Third Resignation," and "Eva Is inside Her Cat," his first two stories, to the controversial and shocking *Memories of My Melancholy Whores*. The ambiguity starts with the titles he selects. Readers of "Eyes of a Blue Dog" are left wondering whether this is a dog with blue eyes (perhaps a Great Dane, a Samoyed, a Weimaraner or an Akita). Or is it simply a blue dog, as if in a surrealist painting? The story, we find out, has nothing to do with a dog, but with a phrase that serves as the axis for a loveless story of boy-meets-girl connected through dreams (they only meet in their dreams), an unequivocal sign of the surrealist movement that influenced Europeans and American artists, but above all writers and painters who set out to depict a dream-like world.

From "Eyes of a Blue Dog" we can draw comparisons with Picasso's monochromatic Blue Period, when the Andalusian-born painter painted images exclusively in blue and blue-green. Picasso, indeed, has a painting titled *Blue Dog* and several portraits with dogs. Art lovers, however, may pick up on the analogy and connect the title with the work of American artist George Rodrigue (sic) who painted "only" blue dogs by the start of the 1990s.

Absurdity as technique in the volume *Eyes of a Blue Dog* adds to the ambiguity of García Márquez's writing. "Dialogue with the Mirror" (1949), for example, is actually a monologue; the narrative voice gives "life" to the man in the mirror and thus the monologue indeed becomes a dialogue with his own reflection. The collection *Eyes of a Blue Dog* shows a young writer experimenting with both forms and content influenced by Kafka, Woolf, and Faulkner. The maturity of these three writers was precisely what García Márquez wanted for himself. All three authors were influential in their use of interior monologue, psychological time, sexuality, ambiguity, satire, irony, the absurd, and language experimentation. The experimentation in *Eyes of a Blue Dog* was almost superior to the will to tell a story. This makes some of the plots in the book difficult to follow. However, from this collection, the stories "The Woman Who Arrived at Six O'clock" and "Monologue of Isabel Watching it Rain in Macondo" captivated the attention of critics and the reading public. The former is a crime story about a prostitute who is presumed to have committed a homicide in self-defense. The latter tale, also marked by death, depicts a lack of love. *Eyes of a Blue Dog* is a book without love or at best tinged by imaginary love.

In the following collection, *Los funerales de la Mamá Grande* (1962), translated as *Big Mama's Funeral*, the ambiguity of the story "Tuesday Siesta" is magnified by alluding to an oral tradition known as folk literature. The title piece, "Big Mama's Funeral" is truly a matrix of humor, irony and satire, and definitely the prototype for the theme of exploitation, the use of hyperbole and of the absolute superlative. The careful use of gigantism and carnival in this extravaganza strongly influenced by Rabelais, will later show up in *One Hundred Years of Solitude*. His *magnum opus* owes to it its narrative technique, narrative voice, plus the underlying social and historical criticism that also appear in the short stories, and in all his fictional works published thereafter.

The second book of short stories was *La increíble y triste historia de la cándida Eréndira y de su abuela desalmada* (1972; *Innocent Eréndira and Other Stories*, 1978). Six of the seven stories appeared independently in journals in 1968, the year after *One Hundred Years of Solitude* was published, but all seven show the influence of the magical realism of his masterpiece. The experimentalism of a now-established writer gave García Márquez the poetic freedom to tell the entire story of "The Last Voyage of the Ghost Ship" in one single sentence. The piece also experiments with the omniscient narrative voice and that of the character, mixing them in a fashion so that the reader will feel confused and contest the act of reading. The plot development appears to diffuse itself in the writing, making the plot unclear. This type of experimentation leads the reader to make neither head nor tail of the story. Yet we know that that is the intention of the structuring. The purpose of the plot is to prove that the ghost ship is not a product of the imagination. The tales "The Handsomest Drowned Man in the World" and "A Very Old Man with Enormous Wings" are supposed to be children's stories, and so they are, if the reader sticks to the plot line. But the "treatment" of the angel when it was turned into a film by Argentine director Fernando Birri in 1988 lost the children's approach and gave way to some raw sexuality verging on hardcore.

The Eros-and-Thanatos combination of "Death Constant Beyond Love" reaches the highest poetic form and shows that García Márquez had indeed undergone a strong Hispanic influence. García Márquez takes a seventeenth-century Spanish baroque sonnet and subverts the role of Eros in favor of Thanatos to create his tale. Francisco de Quevedo's sonnet is entitled "Amor constante más allá de la muerte," that is, *love* constant beyond death; for Quevedo, love will survive death. The great Spanish poet enjoyed wordplay; he delighted in the use of contrasting words in a witty manner to make contradictions; it is a good portion of what we now know as *Conceptismo*.[14]

These plays on words and contradictions of the Spanish baroque in García Márquez surface as the absurd and increased use of satire. The eternal love of Quevedo's sonnet "Love Constant Beyond Death" is inverted, and subverted to "Death Constant Beyond Love." The inversion of the nouns *love* vs. *death* brings together the contrasting contradictions of the baroque and the absurdity of modern times. In either instance, whether Quevedo's sonnet or Garcia Marquez's tale, what we have is a song to love while dancing with death. Time equals death, and time will take us all—sooner or later. While García Márquez made the connection with Quevedo, we can see Eros and Thanatos connected by *time* through the paintings of Peter Paul Rubens and Francisco de Goya known as "Saturn Devouring His Son."[15] The Romans equated the Greek god Cronos with Saturn. Goya's painting, horrid in its depiction of death, shows clearly how time, Saturn, devours his offspring. Goya, in turn, was inspired by Rubens' earlier depiction of the same subject matter.

The last story in the volume shares the title with the book itself, *The Incredible and Sad Tale of Innocent Erendira and Her Heartless Grandmother*. The tale is as long as the title suggests. The text and context are the most disturbing of all of García Márquez forty-one stories. There is a layer of love observed between Eréndira and Ulises, but the sexual exploitation of Eréndira by her own grandmother blurs it all. The subject of child prostitution is an alarming one. However, if we can read the tale as an allegory, we may see the three hundred years of exploitation of the Spanish Americas. By juxtaposing the colonial period to the plot we can see clearly that Eréndira's exploitation is the abuse that the newly colonized territories of the Americas experienced under the command of Spain, Portugal, and later on, France. (Not to mention the exploitation and almost total extermination of Native Americans in English-speaking America.) The juxtaposition allows for a briefing on the exploitation of the New World. We believe that the history of Latin America is a myriad of legislative, political, financial, and ethnic exploitations at all levels. The juxtaposition shows, above all, human exploitation: the abuse of one human being by another. But these interpretations are left up to the reader. In any case, that is a vertical reading (reading the text critically) as oppose to a horizontal reading—the reading of the anecdote alone.

If no juxtaposition is made, and no vertical reading attempted, the reader is yet faced with one typical García Márquez subversion. Eréndira's exploitation subverts the traditional patriarchal exploitation of women and does it through a matriarch. What we have in the tale are the abuses of matriarchy. The reader can keep the plot with the images of an older, big white woman, with no ethical or moral consideration for her granddaughter, a pedophile matriarch without any scruples.

Going back to *Strange Pilgrims*, the voyage of the president, adding to ambiguity, irony, and satire, is a journey toward death, yet "his trip to Geneva had been providential" (35). Literally heaven-sent. The cure he needed was for the mind, and not so much for his aches and pains. But ambiguity, irony, and satire are best represented in "Miss Forbes's Summer of Happiness." What a horrid way to *enjoy* her summer of happiness by getting brutally killed. The vagueness of the language in the title—for happiness is in itself illusory, and hard to grasp—oftentimes considered an error in reasoning, enriches the story and leads to the irony of the plot. Of the twelve short stories comprising this collection, only three do not portray death itself. On the other hand, the total death toll from the rest of the stories in the book adds up to sixty-seven people. Some casualties are worse than others, yet none as sad, and slow, and lonely as is Nena Daconte's in "The Trail of Your Blood in the Snow." "Light Is Like Water" holds the record with thirty-nine dead, followed by "Seventeen Poisoned Englishmen" where the total is actually eighteen —the seventeen college students from Trinity College, plus a bald, mature drowned man in the waters of the Mediterranean. Thanatos, the Greek god of death, is seen almost everywhere. However, his counterpart, Eros, is not easily found. Love, unlike death, is much harder to find in *Strange Pilgrims* than in all the other collections.

Of all the stories in *Strange Pilgrims*, "The Trail of Your Blood in the Snow" is the one that best frames the combined magic of love and horrors of death announced in the title of this chapter. On the other hand, it also grants a substantial opportunity to prove that this collection is more autobiographical than the first three. "The Trail of Your Blood in the Snow" foreshadows, in Kafkaesque-Marquezian style, something tragic to come from the opening sentence: "At nightfall, when they reached the frontier, Nena Daconte realized that her finger with the wedding band on it was still bleeding" (162).

Nena is beautiful and her husband Billy is described as handsome as well. They are young, gorgeous, wealthy, members of the Colombian aristocracy, and are about to celebrate their honeymoon in Paris. The irony, however, is that Nena is two months pregnant, although married only three days. Their wedding, to a certain extent, reflects the marrying of the couple in *Love in the Time of Cholera*: they marry in Cartagena "to the astonishment of his parents and the disillusionment of hers, and with the personal blessing of the archbishop" (165). But their young love and their wedding vows were not meant to last. The combination of the absurd, the language limitation for Billy, and the strict regulations of a French hospital lead Nena Daconte to death, sixty hours after being admitted to the hospital's intensive care unit from her having pinched her ring finger on a rose thorn. Billy's solitude is complete isolation and frustration for not understanding the French language or its culture, a projection of García Márquez, whose linguistic skill in French, at the time, was limited.

We know that the best way to know a writer, to a certain extent, is through his or her writing. Gabriel García Márquez, on occasion, said that one has three lives: a public life, a private life, and a secret life. We have learned through *Strange Pilgrims* of the age difference of his two sons, of his friendships, of his European travels, of his passion for music, and art. But what we could not have decoded on our own as ordinary readers is that "The Trail of Your Blood in the Snow" is somewhat autobiographical.

In Gerald Martin's *Gabriel García Márquez: A Life* (2008), the reader finds the chapter "Hungry in Paris: La Bohème, 1956–1957" where the biographical connection with the short story is made. By association, Nena Daconte is fictionalized after a Spanish girl named Tachia (María Concepción Quintana) with whom García Márquez had a romantic interlude and with whom he shared his life at the time. The drama at the hospital in "The Trail of Your Blood in the Snow" correlates with Tachia's abortion at Maternité Port Royal where she spent eight days. She was four and half months pregnant. It was she, she tells the biographer, who wanted the abortion.[16] She lived to tell the tale and relayed it to Gerald Martin. The death of Nena Daconte, on the other hand, is symbolic. She dies in the fiction, as did the relationship that García Márquez had had with Tachia in real life. "Tachia was a woman [like Nena Daconte] who was brave, lucky, determined, adventurous, foolish or intelligent enough to lead a completely independent life long before this became a woman's right." (Martin, 203).

In closing, it bears mention that Gabriel García Márquez the storyteller was also well-known as a journalist and screenwriter. He is a global writer of unimaginable mythical proportions. The value of his writing goes far beyond literary impact. First editions of his works are objects of consumerism and are subject to thievery—as was the case during the recent Bogotá, Colombia, book fair. In 2015, during the event meant to honor García Márquez on the first anniversary of his death, a signed copy of the first edition of *One Hundred Years of Solitude* was stolen. The BBC and the national Hispanic newspapers reported the case as they might have reported the theft of a Picasso, a Matisse or a Van Gogh. The book was later found with the help of Colombia's National Police force. Today, a copy of the first eight thousand original copies published by Editorial Sudamericana in 1967 can sell for as much as US $23,000 online.

On August 1, 2015, according to *Prensa Latina*, the village of Perdasdefogu, in the Italian region of Sardinia, named a square "One Hundred Years of Solitude." Korean pansori singer Lee Ja-ram, on the other hand, has adapted "Bon Voyage Mr. President," from the short story collection *Strange Pilgrims* to her pansori singing presentations. "Pansori is a traditional Korean narrative music, an artistic form that is often associated only with centuries-old materials such as *Chunhyang-ga* and *Simcheong-ga*."[17]

The master of magical realism died on April 17, 2014. But his spellbinding narrative will live on, as will the traces of his private/public life, which are as fascinating as his fiction. His career as writer and storyteller belongs to the ages. Dictionaries one day will register the adjective "Marquezian" to describe his characters and their temperament, as when we write in Spanish "Quevedesco" or "Quijotesco," and "Dantesco." In English we have "Kafkaesque," "Dickensian," and "Shakespearian" to refer to their writing style or the characterization in their writings. In the not too distant future, in addition to Marquezian, we will also have "Marquezianize," as analogous to Shakespeareanize, when treating characters in the manner of García Márquez.

NOTES

1. Yasunari Kawabata, *The House of the Sleeping Beauties and Other Stories*. Trans. from the Japanese by Edwrad G. Seidensticker. Tokio: Palo Alto Kodansha International, 1969.

2. Of these titles, only *Doce cuentos peregrinos* appeared in English as a self-contained book: *Strange Pilgrims*. Trans. Edith Grossman. New York: Knopf, 1993. All others were published separately in three volumes under the following titles: *Leaf Storm and Other Stories*. Trans. Gregory Rabassa. New York: Harper & Row, 1972; *No One Writes to the Colonel and Other Stories*. Trans. J.S. Bernstein. New York: Harper and Row, 1968; *Innocent Eréndira, and Other Stories*. Trans. Gregory Rabassa. New York: Harper and Row, 1978. Subsequently, all the stories published in these three volumes appeared in English *as Collected Stories*. Trans. Gregory Rabassa and J.S. Bernstein. New York: Harper-Collins, 1984.

3. Gerald Martin, quoting a journalist for the Argentine newspaper "La Nación," Osvaldo Quiroga: "It is difficult to recognize the author of *One Hundred Years of Solitude* in this long monologue by a woman tired of being happy without love…. It shows his complete ignorance of dramatic language. It cannot be denied that *Diatribe* is a superficial, repetitive and tedious melodrama." See Martin Gerald, *Gabriel Garcia Marquez: a Life*. New York: Alfred A. Knopt, 2009 (p. 455).

4. Roberto González Echevarría, edit. *The Oxford Book of Latin American Short Stories*. New York: Oxford University Press, 1997 (p. 3).

5. Interview: "Hallucinatory realism" of China's Mo Yan springs from LatAm's magic realism. http://news.xinhuanet.com/english2015-07/27/c_134450876.htm

6. Gabriel García Márquez, *Strange Pilgrims*. Trans. Edith Grossman. New York: Vintage International, 2006. All quotations from *Strange Pilgrims* in this essay are from this edition.

7. Jorge Luis Borges, El *libro de arena*. Madrid: Alianza Editorial, 1986.

8. It's hard to know whether the eventual publication of the short stories in book form was his idea or that of the publishing industry, i.e., his literary agent and friend Carmen Balcells, one of the most powerful personalities in the Spanish-speaking book world. While it is commonplace to talk about the writers of the Latin American Boom, not many realize that Balcells (1930–2015) was their main supporter.

9. Gene H. Bell-Villada, *García Márquez: The Man and His Work*. Chapel Hill: University of North Carolina Press, 1990 (p. 119).

10. Michiko Kakutani, "Books of the Times; Gabriel García Márquez, Short Form." *The New York Times*, October 15, 1993. http://www.nytimes.com/1993/10/15books/books-of-the-times-gabriel-garcia-marquez-short-form-html

11. The story of "The Saint" brings out García Márquez's age-old desire to make films. By 1955, the time when he went to Europe for the first time, he had already made his first film, the short subject "La langosta azul" (1954). His tribulations of later years, trying to take his stories to film, are brought forth in this story where Cesare Zavattini plays merely a "reference role." In reality, however, Zavattini was one of the leading figures of the proponents of the Neorealist film movement that influenced García Márquez.

12. Aimé Césaire, French-speaking Martiniquais poet and playwright, cofounder with Léopold Senghor and León Damas of *negritude*, an influential movement to restore the cultural identity of black Africans. A member of the Communist Party, he later discarded *negritude* for black militancy, and lashed out against the French oppressors. See Merriam-Webster's, *Encyclopedia of Literature*. Springfield, MA: Merriam-Webster, Inc., 1995 (p. 224).

13. Bell-Villada (p. 177).

14. *Conceptismo*, a term derived from *concepto*, concept, conceit, ingenious expression in Spanish literature. Concerned primarily with the stripping off of appearances, *Conceptismo* found its chief exponent in Quevedo, considered the master satirist of his age. See Merriam-Webster's, *Encyclopedia of Literature*. Springfield, MA: Merriam-Webster, Inc., 1995 (p. 264).

15. Saturn was the name that the Romans gave to the Greek God Cronos. According to mythology, Cronos swallowed his newborn children in fear that one of them would overthrow him.

16. Martin (pp. 189–210).

17. Kwon Mee-yoo. "Pansori Singer Tackles Gabriel García Márquez." http://m.koreatimes.co.kr/phone/news/view.jsp?req_newsidx=179695

WORKS CITED

Bell-Villada, Gene H. *García Márquez: The Man and His Work*. Chapel Hill: University of North Carolina Press, 1990.

Borges, Jorge Luis. *El libro de arena*. Madrid: Alianza Editorial, 1986.

García Márquez, Gabriel. *Collected Stories* (an anthology containing stories from Eyes of a *Blue Dog*, *Big Mama's Funeral*, and *The Incredible and Sad Tale of Innocent Eréndira and Her Heartless Grandmother*). Trans. Gregory Rabassa and J.S. Bernstein. New York: Harper and Row, 1984.

———. *Cuando era feliz e indocumentado*. Caracas: El Ojo del Camello, 1973.

———. *Diatriba de amor contra un hombre sentado*. Barcelona: Grijalbo Mondadori, 1995.

———. *Innocent Eréndira and Other Stories*. Trans. Gregory Rabassa. New York: Harper and Row, 1978.
———. *Memories of My Melancholy Whores*. Trans. Edith Grossman. New York: Knopf, 2005.
———. *One Hundred Years of Solitude*. Trans. Gregory Rabassa. New York: Harper Perennial Classics, 1998.
———. *Strange Pilgrims*. Trans. Edith Grossman. New York: Vintage International, 2006.
———. *The Autumn of the Patriarch*. Trans. Gregory Rabassa. New York: Harper Perennial, 1991.
González Echevarría, Roberto, ed. *The Oxford Book of Latin American Short Stories*. New York: Oxford University Press, 1997.
Kakutani, Michiko, "Books of the Times; Gabriel García Márquez, Short Form." *The New York Times*, October 15, 1993. http://www.nytimes.com/1993/10/15books/books-of-the-times-gabriel-garcia-marquez-short-form-html
Kawabata, Yasunari. *The House of the Sleeping Beauties and Other Stories*. Trans. from the Japanese by Edwrad G. Seidensticker. Tokio: Palo Alto Kodansha International, 1969.
Kwon, Mee-yoo. "Pansori Singer Tackles Gabriel García Márquez." http://m.koreatimes.co.kr/phone/news/view.jsp?req_newsidx=179695
Martin, Gerald. *Gabriel García Márquez: A Life*. New York: Alfred A. Knopt, 2009.
Menton, Seymour. *El cuento hispanoamericano*. México: Fondo de Cultura Económica, 1976.

Chapter 11

Gabriel García Márquez
Pilgrimage and Gastronomy
Fernando Valerio-Holguín

In Gabriel García Márquez's *Strange Pilgrims*, references abound to the dishes of Latin American and international cuisine, as well as to restaurants, situations, and characters that connect gastronomy with the Pleasure of the Text. In his "Prologue," García Márquez draws a parallel between cuisine and the writing process: "In the way the *cook* knows when the *soup* is ready, this is a trade secret that does not obey the laws of reason but the magic of instinct" (xiii. My emphasis).[1] Moreover, it is not only the *knowledge* of the craft that is at stake, but also the pleasure that arises from both activities: "All the rest is the *pleasure* of writing, the most intimate, solitary pleasure one can imagine..." ("Prologue," ix. My emphasis).[2] He also states: "Then the writing became so fluid that I sometimes felt as if I were writing for the sheer *pleasure* of telling a story..." ("Prologue," xii. My emphasis).[3] The pleasure of narrating, of cooking, of living leads to an addiction. On this score, the Colombian writer exclaims, "... how insatiable and abrasive the writing habit can be" (vii).[4] If graphomania and gluttony are vices, living too can grow into an addiction.[5] The writer thus becomes—like the character Cesare Zavattini in the story "The Saint"—someone who is "greedy for life" (48).[6] And if not gifted with a sweet tooth or fine culinary skills, the writer is, therefore, a *gourmand* as remarked in "The Ghosts of August:" "Miguel Otero Silva, who was a splendid host and a refined gourmet as well as a good writer, has an unforgettable lunch waiting for us" (93).[7]

Savor and *savoir*, which converge in García Márquez's writing of *Strange Pilgrims*, are produced in the paradoxical or paratopic spaces of migration. Food has as its objective, on one hand, to define the personality, social status, and cultural identity of the characters, and, on the other, to establish a relational poetics in the social space in which those characters develop. My purpose in this chapter will consist in analyzing the references that are intrinsically bound up with the paratopia of certain individuals in the construction of a cultural identity, through their bodies in connection with paradoxical social spaces.

PEREGRINATIONS: PARATOPIC DISPLACEMENTS, NONPLACES, AND STRANGENESS

In this book of short fictions, the characters are pilgrims, as also are the dishes of gastronomy. In the etymology of the word "pilgrim" there exists the sense of "foreign travel" as well as "visiting holy places," which suggests that the Latin American characters of these stories visit the "sacralized" places of European culture: Paris, Rome, Geneva, Barcelona, and Madrid.[8]

If, in the original Spanish title, the stories are "pilgrims" as well as the author—who, on occasion, becomes involved via first-person singular or plural, thereby creating a partial autobiographical pact[9]—the writing and the literary genre also qualify as "pilgrims." At some point, García Márquez had thought he might write a novel on these subjects, but it was not until 1974 that he realized he would adopt the short-story genre. Hence we have the peregrinations of these texts through different countries, literary genres, and artistic media over a period of eighteen years. The languages spoken by the characters who roam through European cities also signal a displacement. His narrators emphasize the accents, intonations, and difficulties of the foreign speakers. The Latin American characters undergo an estrangement in Europe's languages, thus having to negotiate their identity in these disruptions of meaning.[10]

The paratopic dimension of the characters generates an estrangement that affects the meaning of the narrative contents. *Paratopia* (peregrination, displacement, exile) is a concept that embraces not only the stories and the process of writing them, but also all the activities surrounding the food, its ingestion, and the characters who consume it. Concerning "paratopia," Kristine Vanden Berghe explains:

> A fundamental implication of the paradoxical position—or paratopia—is that the writer constantly exploits the fissures that come open in society. He thus presents himself as a bohemian, a loner, an artist, or, simply, *different* in some way from others: Maingueneau defines it as *he who is not in the place where he is*, who *moves around from place to place without becoming rooted* in some more or less definitive way, he who *doesn't find his place*, who *doesn't fit in*. (87. My emphasis)

As an example of the paratopia of these characters, in "*Bon Voyage, Mr. President*," an ex-President finds himself exiled in Martinique and later on a medical visit to Geneva, living in poverty after having been deposed in his country of origin. Likewise, in "The Saint," Margarito Duarte takes the dead body of his young daughter to Rome in order to have her canonized by the Pope in the Vatican. In "I Sell My Dreams," the narrator, the protagonist Frau Frieda, and the poet Neruda all coincide accidentally in several European cities. Finally, Maria dos Prazeres, a retired prostitute who lives in Barcelona, readies herself for death.

If these characters find themselves in a paratopical position in European cities, some spaces within those settings constitute what Marc Augé calls "non-places." In his book *Non-Places*, Augé designates by that term those spaces to which a person cannot relate either affectively or cognitively. Some of these spaces include airports, highways, supermarkets, and hotels. Although Augé is much more interested in the spaces than in the persons who inhabit them, one could also designate as "nonindividuals" (or dehumanized individuals) those with whom it is difficult to relate affectively or cognitively. The impossibility of recognizing a place (or an individual) as such, or of identifying with same, is the product of an "uncanny strangeness." According to Freud, the *uncanny*, or "disturbing or disquieting strangeness," as it would be preferable to translate the German term *unheimlich*, consists in the discomfort of an experience that borders on anguish and becomes initially present through the repetition of a banal fact: "The uncanny would be that type of horror attached to things long since known, and always familiar" (Freud quoted by Clancier 48).[11]

In *Strange Pilgrims*, not only do the characters have to "negotiate" the discomfort of living in exile, but they also find themselves "dehumanized" in hotels, insane asylums, hospitals, castles, rooming houses, cafés, and seedy restaurants. In "I Only Came to Use the Phone," María de la Luz finds herself confined by mistake in a psychiatric hospital, separated from her boy friend and then left abandoned there by him. In "*Bon Voyage*, Mr. President," the ex-president stays at "a fourth-class hotel," has lunch at "cheap restaurants," and later is admitted to a hospital for surgery; alone, without relatives or friends, and in a foreign (strange) city, the former president will have to confront his destiny. In "Seventeen Poisoned Englishmen," Prudencia Linero takes a room in a complex set of cheap hotels. The estrangement is evidenced in the description of the elevator: "a chicken cage rising slowly through the center of an echoing marble staircase... On the third floor the elevator jolted to a halt... and then the porter... opened the sliding rhomboids of the door ..." (122–123).[12]

In these spaces of Europe's cities, the foreign characters perceive reality with a sense of "defamiliarization."[13] García Márquez himself, in his "Prologue," accounts for the sensation of strangeness in the process of creating these texts and his characters: "This has been a *strange* creative experience that should be explained..." (vii. My emphasis).[14] Or again: "I thought this was a point of departure for writing about the *strange things* that happen to Latin Americans in Europe" (vii. My emphasis).[15] In a word, the discomfort of life in foreign (strange) lands becomes *uncanny*, literally "outside of home" (*unheimlich*).[16]

It is in these kinds of spaces that the preparation of foods and their intake occur. In this way, we are confronted with what I shall call a gastronomical pilgrimage, or the paratopia of dinner guests. Paratopia, as a temporal and spatial displacement, has a certain relevance regarding the food consumed, which may or may not be native to the country in which the characters find themselves exiled, but is connected, in some way, with the national culture of origin. All of the foregoing poses also a paratopia of the body that ingests the food. In "I Sell My Dreams," Neruda, the Chilean poet, happens to be in Barcelona.[17] In "Miss Forbes's Summer of Happiness," the German governess and the Colombian boys are in the island of Pantelleria, which belongs to Italy. In "Maria dos Prazeres," a Brazilian prostitute ends up retired in Barcelona. Food, then, serves as a mediator between the characters and their bodies, which "express" themselves through food, and are constructed as transnational subjects through food. García Márquez himself wrote these stories over a period of eighteen years in a lengthy pilgrimage through different countries. As exiles, the characters in his stories reflect the uncomfortable situations in which the writer found himself, displaced from his native land.

NOSTALGIA, CULTURAL IDENTITY, AND LIMINALITY OF THE BODY

What is the function of gastronomy in these uncomfortable spaces of exile? Mediating estrangement? Connecting with the native soil? Recovering a threatened identity? In *Strange Pilgrims*, food and its intake constitute not only nostalgemes[18] as cultural signs, but also social acts that put into contact two or more people who mediate the significations between them (Yúdice 20). In stories such as "*Bon Voyage*, Mr. President," "Maria dos Prazeres," "I Sell My Dreams," and "Miss Forbes's Summer of Happiness," food is a symptom of the bodies that negotiate their place in the world in connection with others, starting from exile, nostalgia, loneliness, sadness, and deracination. Food thus constitutes an articulation of meaning in those texts.

If, for these characters, food and cultural identity are linked, the former must not be reduced to some essentialized nostalgia, even at times when this may well be the intent of the author (Nyman 282). In his essays, "Wine and Milk" and "Steak and Chips" from *Mythologies*, Roland Barthes sets forth the essentialism of French culture by proposing the "Frenchness" of those products, starting from a semiology of taste. Wine is French, just as milk is

American: "But milk remains an exotic substance; it is wine which is part of the nation" (61). Wine and beefsteak, both of them French, share "blood-kinship" (*saignant*—the French adjective for "rare"), but what is truly French is fried potatoes (not accidentally are they known in English as "French fries"). And in this respect Barthes cites an anecdote that appeared in the magazine *Paris Match* about one General de Castries, who, on his return from the Indochina war, ordered French fries: "'General de Castries, for his first meal, asked for chips' ... The General understood well our national symbolism; he knew that *la frite*, chips, are the alimentary sign of Frenchness" (63–64). Hence, every country seeks the essence of its culture in a particular food.

Food constitutes a major factor in the construction of a cultural identity, in social practices, but one must also take into account the "incorporation principle" that communicates the body with the external world through the mouth (Fischler 276–278). Fischler describes the incorporation of foodstuffs as "real" and "imaginary:" "We are what we eat" (278). He also states, "Incorporation is also the basis of collective identity and, by the same token, of otherness. Food and cuisine are a quite central component of a sense of collective belonging" (278). The incorporation of foods thus brings with it the essentialization of a particular culture.

In this sense, my line of argument follows the thinking of both Claude Fischler and George Yúdice. Unlike Baudrillard, for whom the body is an allegory of the microcosm, Yúdice in his article, "Feeding the Transcendent Body," states the following: "The body is not simply the screen on which the rampant exchange of information and images is captured, it is, rather, the battleground in which subjects are constituted, contradictorily desiring and rejecting prescribed representations" (81). In *Strange Pilgrims*, food and its ingestion constitute not only *nostalgemes* and cultural signs, but also a social act that puts two or more persons in contact and that is a mediator of meanings between them (Yúdice 20).

Food reflects personality as well as constructing a subjectivity in connection with social spaces. In his article, "Food, Self and Identity," Claude Fischler poses the "incorporation principle" as a key concept for understanding the nature of the incorporation of foodstuffs in relation to representations. The mouth is the fundamental organ for the incorporation of foods. Nevertheless, it is preceded by the nose, eyes, and fingers in regards to the sensorial perception of the food. If the mouth determines what is ingested or not, the skin is the largest organ and constitutes the limit of the body.[19] The skin is also the border between the inside and the outside. In some stories, this phenomenon is methaphorized via food: Lázara Davis in "*Bon Voyage...*" has "the color of cooked caramel" (15),[20] while the Sleeping Beauty has "soft skin the color of bread" (54).[21] Other parts of the body take on a meaning with regard to food. Sleeping Beauty has "eyes like green almonds" (54).[22] In the same story,

"Sleeping Beauty and the Airplane," the narrator employs a synechdoche that substitutes the abstract "beauty" for the concrete "scent:" "... and her skin exhaled a delicate breath that could only be the scent of her beauty" (59–60).[23] Later, the narrator likens the fragrance of Sleeping Beauty's "bread" to beauty itself. If we adhere to the "incorporation principle," it is as if we were to "eat up" the girl and thereby incorporate her beauty in our body.[24]

Smell is a major sensorial aspect regarding the manifestation of foods.[25] In some of the stories, food is manifested immaterially through smells. And although the foods that emit those fragrances are not incorporated into the body, the fragrances indeed are, through our nose. As with the foods, those smells can be "bad objects" and thus carry a negative semantic weight.[26] In "Seventeen Poisoned Englishmen," the waters of the port of Naples let off a stench of decay: "... Señora Prudencia Linero recognized from the backyard of her house as a foul breath of rotting crabs" (119).[27] Later on, when on ship, she feels "Dazed by the wild jubilation and the rancid onion smell of so many families in summer..." (120).[28] In this story, bread does not connote the appetizing skin of the Sleeping Beauty but rather, accompanied as it is by an onion, connotes poverty. The mixed odors of rotten shellfish and the onion announce the death by poisoning of the English tourists. In "The Ghosts of August," the fragrance of strawberries is the manifestation of the phantom of Ludovico, who murdered his lover shortly after having made love with her, and then committed suicide by having his own dogs tear him to pieces, in the Renaissance castle of Arezzo, Italy.[29] The strawberries, as a symbol of love, refer us back to the lover murdered in a fit of passion.[30] Says the narrator, "What affected me most, however, was the unexplainable scent of fresh strawberries that hung over the entire bedroom" (94).[31] And again, "Only then was I shaken by the scent of strawberries..." (95).[32] The fragrance of strawberries unleashes the magical event in which the narrator and his wife retire for the night in one bedroom and awaken in another: Ludovico's, and in the same bed in which his beautiful lover was murdered. The bodies of the modern couple are placed in the castle-space in a magical-gastronomical relation[33] with respect to the past and the present, and the here/there of peregrination, through the smell of strawberries.

The skin—as the limit of the body—and the other organs that allow the perception of the qualities of food, are relevant to the connection with external space. But the mouth has the greatest importance in terms of the incorporation of external foods into the anatomy of the body. In the sections that follow, I shall concentrate on four stories in which gastronomy plays a dominant role: "I Sell My Dreams," "Miss Forbes's Summer of Happiness," "*Bon Voyage*, Mr. President," and "Maria dos Prazeres." In addition, I will discuss in my end notes those aspects of gastronomy that, while marginal, carry a strong semantic weight.

PABLO NERUDA: "A GLUTTON FOR LIVING"

"I Sell My Dreams" tells the story of Frau Frieda, a mysterious woman who had been the housekeeper for the Portuguese ambassador to Havana, and who had the ability to foretell the future in her dreams, which she could do only before breakfast.[34] In a visit to Barcelona, the narrator tells of the encounter with Frau Frieda and Chilean poet Pablo Neruda, whom they have invited to dinner:

> I have never known anyone closer to the idea one has of a Renaissance pope: He was gluttonous and refined... Matilde, his wife, would put a bib around his neck that belonged in a barbershop rather than in a dining room ... That day at Carvalleiras was typical. He ate three whole lobsters, dissecting them with a surgeon's skill, and at the same time devoured everyone else's plate with his eyes and tasted a little from each with a delight that made the desire to eat contagious: clams from Galicia, mussels from Cantabria, prawns from Alicante, sea cucumbers from the Costa Brava. In the meantime, like the French, he spoke of nothing but other culinary delicacies, in particular the prehistoric shellfish of Chile, which he carried in his heart. All at once he stopped eating, tuned his lobster's antennae... (67).[35]

In this lengthy excerpt, the poet Pablo Neruda is characterized/caricatured. It is a sketch filled with jesting between two friends: García Márquez and Pablo Neruda. The humor comes forth in phrases such as, "Renaissance pope: gluttonous and refined," which harbors an apparent contradiction, inasmuch as a glutton is supposed to be gross and ill-mannered. The list of shellfish from the Spanish coasts serves as a reference to the "prehistoric shellfish of Chile" that he carries in his heart, thereby reinforcing the identity between the poet and his culture.

In his errancy through different countries, one of the forms in which the body of Neruda positions itself before the world resembles baroque excess, resembles our prolific poet, so "greedy of life: "El mundo/es una mesa/ rodeada por la miel y por el humo,/cubierta de manzanas o de sangre./ La mesa preparada/y ya sabemos cuando/nos llamaron" (Neruda, quoted by Daydí-Tolson 137).[36] ("The world/Is a table/Surrounded by honey and smoke,/Covered with apples or blood./The table being spread out/We now know/When we're being called." Translated by Gene H. Bell-Villada.) Besides bolting down the shellfish and all the food he can see, he devours with his eyes the world, in order to transform it into poetry. Similarly, the poet "infects" (as in a disease) others with the desire to eat. His gluttony for food and for life spreads to his readers. As a *gourmand*, Neruda wrote "Elementary Odes" dedicated to food: to the tomato, the onion, the potato, the artichoke, to French fries, salt, and conger chowder, among others.[37] In the story, Neruda writes with the same passion that he eats with: "... [He] sat down at an isolated table, and began to write fluid verses in the green ink he used from drawing flowers and fish and birds when he dedicated his books" (69).[37] If Neruda's relationship to the world, via food, is the "incorporating" of reality, that of Miss Forbes, in another story, consists of managing dishes as punishment/reward for the bodies she wishes to control, her own included.

MISS FORBES, OR THE SWEET DESIRE OF PASSION

In "Miss Forbes's Summer of Happiness," a German governess is charged with taking care of two boys, during a summer in which the parents are away traveling. Both Miss Forbes, from Dortmund, Germany, and the boys and their parents, from Guacamayal, Colombia, find themselves displaced, in transit, spending summer on the island of Pantelleria, in the Mediterranean. It bears noting that neither Dortmund nor Guacamayal are major urban centers, nor is the island. Miss Forbes talks to the kids in a "stony" English and, on other occasions, speaks in a "melodious" German and in Italian.

Communication between the governess and the boys takes places via food. Miss Forbes imposes strict rules of conduct, in accordance with the stereotypical discipline of German culture. Through a grading system, the kids have the right to a double portion of dessert on reaching fifty points: "... we never again tasted any desserts as delicious as those made by Miss Forbes" (143); "... her cream cakes, her vanilla tarts, her exquisite plum pastries the likes of which would not taste again for the rest of our lives" (146).[38]

Among the rules of etiquette was having to sit at table "...with our spines against the back of our chairs, chewing ten times on one side and ten times on the other" (144).[39] The boys strike up a love-hate relationship with the food. If on the one hand, they love the puddings, on the other they detest the soup: "... the eternal vermicelli soup of that abominable summer" (144).[40] "This worm water gives me a pain in the ass," (152)[41] one of the boys says. Another one comments that he did not like the "moray eel" that he was served for dinner, to which Miss Forbes responds with an elaborate historical and cultural explanation about that sea creature. On tasting the first mouthful, the boy vomits, his punishment being no dessert. In the end, the kids attempt to poison Miss Forbes, but she dies murdered by twenty-seven knife wounds.

Miss Forbes establishes with the two boys an abject relation through food, perhaps a phantasmagorical relation expressing the abjectness of the absent mother. The moray eel as a phallic symbol is present in the spinsterhood of Miss Forbes, who at the same time assumes a certain masculinity in her appearance ("combat boots," "hair cut like a man's under her felt hat" (148), "soldier's voice" (156),[42] as well as in her authoritarianism and discipline ("sargent from Dortmund") (148).[43] The moray eel that terrorizes the boys has, in turn, "people's eyes." If on one hand she wishes to oblige the kids to "eat up" the eel, on the other she regales herself with cakes and wine in the privacy of her bedroom. Miss Forbes gratifies herself via the food with which she punishes the boys. "[E]ating entire cakes and even drinking from the bottle of special wine that my father saved with so much devotion for memorable occasions" (150);[44] and also: "[W]e saw her... carrying half a chocolate cake and the bottle with more than four fingers of poisoned wine" (153).[45]

Unlike the Sleeping Beauty, whose skin "exhaled a delicate breath that could only be the scent of her beauty" (59–60),[46] Miss Forbes "smelled of monkey urine" (148).[47] The father says to the children: "That's how every European smells... It's the smell of civilization" (148).[48] The "color of bread" skin of the Sleeping Beauty, which exudes an aroma of loveliness, is an invitation to be "incorporated" to our bodies through the senses and, more specifically, through the mouth. To eat up the Sleeping Beauty, who is Latin American, is to assimilate her exquisite allure via a process of substantiation. By contrast, the skin of Miss Forbes imposes a strict limit of nonincorporation because of the smell of monkey urine. Metonymically, the disgust generated by Miss Forbes constitutes a rejection of European culture.

The "scrawny"[49] body of Miss Forbes expresses her relationship to the world—the gluttony and alcoholism of a body that nonetheless gains no weight, a body that is not made to be loved. The way in which Miss Forbes constructs meaning and her relation to others in the world, is through desserts and wine, which end up substituting the eroticism that is absent from her body. In the privacy of her bedroom, Miss Forbes watches pornographic films while eating tarts and imbibing wine. The skin of Miss Forbes, however, ends up perforated by knives, which implies that her body is in violent communication with the external world. Although the criminal act is omitted from the story, it is possible that Oreste was the culprit in this crime of passion. At the beginning of the narrative, when Miss Forbes sees Oreste, she is captivated by his good looks: "...it was impossible to imagine a more beautiful human being"(142).[50] Miss Forbes ends up a victim of her own passion for beauty.

"*BON VOYAGE*, MR. PRESIDENT," OR THE TIRED SKIN

In the story "*Bon Voyage*, Mr. President," an ex-president of a Caribbean nation, exiled in Martinique, is visiting Geneva for medical attention and surgery. The body of the (nameless) ex-president is a sick body. His pain is both physical and emotional (nostalgia). His organs are detailed in the narrative: "They looked for the pain in his liver, his kidneys, his pancreas, his prostate, wherever it was not [...] His pain was improbable and devious, and sometimes seemed to be in his ribs on the right side and sometimes in his lower abdomen, and often it caught him off guard with a sudden stab in his groin" (4–5).⁵¹ The body with diseased organs of the former president has its antithesis in the Saint, in the García Márquez story by the same name, whose body is weightless, a body without organs: "Most astonishing of all, however, was that her body had no weight" (38).⁵² The body with diseased organs is a body for death; the body of the Saint is incorruptible.

The ex-president runs into a compatriot who recognizes him; he invites him to lunch at the restaurant Le Boeuf Couronné, where the former chief of state orders, in addition to salad with olive oil, the house specialty: charcoal-broiled ribs of beef: "… and he saw the great roasted slabs edged in tender fat on the other tables" (10).⁵³ For the ex-president, who is living in poverty, this means an opportunity not only to allay his hunger but to taste a special dish. Eventually, Homero, the fellow countryman, invites him over to try out some shrimps with rice, his wife's specialty. The only thing is, the shrimps she prepares come out of a can. On entering the house, the former president "exclaimed with eyes closed and arms spread wide, 'Ah the smell of our ocean!'" (19).⁵⁴ Later on, the ex-president "took two helpings and showed no restraint in his praise, and he was delighted by the slices of fried ripe plantain and the avocado salad, although he did not share in their *nostalgia*" (19. My emphasis).⁵⁵ The broiled ribs as well as the shrimp, ripe plantains, and avocadoes are a nostalgic fallacy, since they are products that can be produced/acquired in other parts of the world, that are not unique nor exclusive to his country. His body, deprived of the pleasures of the table, through doctor's orders, and due to old age, tries to situate itself metonymically in relation to the nation from which he finds himself absent.

The food bans have to do with the incorporation of "good objects" such as coffee and alcohol, claimed by nostalgia. Coffee is not only a beverage of culture, but also an element of cognition. On various occasions, the ex-president reads the bottom of the cup's contents in order to know his future: "He drank it without sugar, in slow sips, and then turned the cup upside down on the saucer so that the coffee grounds, after so many years, would have time to write out his destiny […] Before removing his glasses he deciphered his destiny in the coffee grounds and felt an icy shudder: He saw uncertainty there" (7–8).⁵⁶ The drink in this case is a cipher of and a writing on the body. At his seventy-five years of age, the former president stops reading the coffee grounds, disregards doctor's orders and decides to eat everything and start smoking again, decides to "live his life as it came" (34).⁵⁷

"MARIA DOS PRAZERES" OR THE PLEASURE OF SEX

If in the story "The Ghosts of August" the fragrance of strawberries connotes magically the murder of Ludovico's lover, in "Maria dos Prazeres" the fragrance of smoked herring connotes, on one hand, the musty atmosphere of the apartment, and, on the other, the sex organ of the protagonist, an aging, retired prostitute.[58] The most significant gastronomical event in the piece is the dinner prepared by Maria. Count Cardona has been visiting her "on the last Friday of every month to have supper with her and make languid, after-dinner love" (103).[59] The dinner consists of local champagne (cava), filled truffles, canelloni au gratin, chicken au jus, fruit, and Port wine. The narrator points out the social class-status of this dinner: "the favorite dishes from the halcyon days of the fine old Catalonian families" (108).[60] Maria's relationship with the Count is contractual and owes its existence to an old habit between them: the Count used to leave her twenty-five pesetas in fee for her services. Hence the narrator again stresses the kind of relationship there is between these two characters: "After the unhurried supper and conversation, they made sedentary love from memory, which left both of them with a taste of disaster" (108).[61] Their *sobremesa*—the traditional term in Spanish for after-dinner chat—is used by them to have sex.

Being seventy-one years of age, Maria's is a body that is preparing for death. María, "with no Money, no language and no name..." (109),[62] "felt ugly and pitiful" (113).[63] A body that in the past was made for the pleasures (hence her surname) of sex and food, is now a body headed for death, foreseen by her in a dream. It is why she purchases in advance her tomb at Mont Juic cemetery and teaches her only companion, her dog Noi, how to take the bus so that he may visit her gravesite after she has died. Is it a nonplace, the cemetery? It is a place where we can connect affectively with relatives and friends who've passed away and are buried there. The only strange thing in this case is that the dog is the only one that, by his own free will, might go visit her.

CONCLUSION

In *Strange Pilgrims* by Gabriel García Márquez, food has the function, on one hand, of establishing the personality, social status, and cultural identity of the characters, and, on the other, establishing a relational poetics within the social space in which those characters are developed. The culinary references in these stories, aside from being bound up with the culture of the countries to which those characters belong, constitute a displacement or a paratopia of the bodies with respect to the national origins of the characters.

García Márquez transforms the process of pilgrimage, starting from his eighteen years' errancy, into a poetics that governs the pieces in this collection. Such a poetics expresses itself through the strangeness and defamiliarization experienced by these characters, displaced as they are in European cities. Gastronomy plays a dominant role in the construction of these characters' subjectivity. Although culinary references abound in other works by the Colombian author, *Strange Pilgrims* stands as a unique book in its articulation of food with the bodies that seek to express themselves.

Translated by Gene H. Bell-Villada

NOTES

1. "Es un secreto del oficio que no obedece a las leyes de la inteligencia sino a la magia de los instintos, como sabe la *cocinera* cuando está la *sopa*" (19. My emphasis).

2. "Lo demás es el *placer* de escribir, el más íntimo y solitario que pueda imaginarse…" ("Prólogo," 15. My emphasis).

3. "La escritura se me hizo entonces tan fluida que a ratos me sentía escribiendo por el puro *placer* de narrar…" ("Prólogo," 18).

4. "…qué insaciable y abrasivo es el vicio de escribir" (13).

5. "Graphomania" can be defined as the compulsion that leads a writer to write permanently. The need to write can be compared to the constant ingestion of foods. Gluttony and writing are thus likened.

6. "[G]oloso de la vida" (72). Even though "goloso" is translated as greedy, the former does not have the connotation of gluttony.

7. "Miguel Otero Silva, que además de buen escritor era un anfitrión espléndido y un comedor refinado, nos esperaba con un almuerzo de nunca olvidar" (130).

8. The Spanish word "peregrino," from the Latin *peregrinus*, signifies "traveler" or "he who goes abroad." During his eighteen years of peregrination through Europe and Latin America, García Márquez managed to accumulate sixty-four written-down subjects for stories, which he lost in Mexico around 1978 ("Prologue," x). Of these, only thirty were rewritten and eighteen survived his scrutiny, until he ended up polishing them into the twelve stories we know in their current form. Similarly, this material went through various avatars with respect to literary genre. Some of these pieces first saw the light as journalistic accouns, film scripts, and TV series.

9. Philippe Lejeune designates "autobiographical pact" as the identity between writer, narrator, and character. In the case of the stories in *Strange Pilgrims*, the narrator, who appears in first-person singular and plural, mentions biographical data that could identify Gabriel García Márquez in his travels through Europe.

10. Other references to foreign languages include the following: In "I Sell My Dreams," the students invent for Frau Frieda a "Germanic tongue twister" (64). Maria dos Prazeres, a Brazilian immigrant from Manaos, residing in Barcelona, dictates her last will and testament in "medieval Catalan" (104). In the same piece, the young man who gives her a ride in the the car speaks in "awkward Catalan," which is why he continues the conversation in "Castilian" (112). In the story, "The Trail of Your Blood in the Snow," we read that the hospital guard "shit on [Billy's] mother in French" (182). In "Miss Forbes's Summer of Happiness," a group of women are "praying in dialect" (155) in front of the Miss Forbes's lying body-in-state.

11. It is important to bring out the ambivalence of the German word *heimlich*, among whose several meanings is "that which coincides with its opposite, *unheimlich* (48). Perceiving the absurd is nothing more than another way of naming this "disturbing strangeness." The term *unheimlich* refers us to the English neologism "unhomely" ("uncanny"), which designates something that belongs in the home yet that, even as a familiar object, arouses a sense of strangeness.

12. "una jaula de gallina que subía muy despacio por el centro de una escalera... En el tercer piso el ascensor se detuvo... y entonces el maletero... abrió la puerta de rombos plegadizos..." (166).

13. For the Russian Formalists, "defamiliarization" consists in the phenomenon of depicting familiar objects and situations as strange in art.

14. "Ha sido una *rara* experiencia creativa que merece ser explicada..." (13. My emphasis).

15. "... y pensé que era un buen punto de partida para escribir sobre las *cosas extrañas* que les suceden a los latinoamericanos en Europa" (14. My emphasis).

16. The Spanish word "extranjero" comes from the Old French *strangier*, which in turn comes from *strange*. It is not odd, then, that these foreign characters feel "extrañamiento" ("surprise" or "estrangement") while in Europe.

17. Frau Frieda, a woman of Colombian birth and origin, came to Austria as a young girl and has since lived in several cities. Neruda runs into the narrator and Frau Frieda in Barcelona, on board a ship sailing for Valparaíso. The trait shared by these three characters is errancy. The three are in transit heading somewhere. Meaning also migrates in different languages: Frau Frieda speaks German, is housekeeper to the Portuguese ambassador and is in Barcelona and Havana.

18. I employ *nostalgeme* to designate the smallest unit of meaning that provokes nostalgia. The word "nostalgia" comes from the Greek *nostos* ("I return") and *algia* ("pain"). Hence, a person who feels nostalgia returns to the past, to things. In *"Bon Voyage*, Mr. President," the shrimp cooked by Lázara constitute a nostalgeme. When the ex-President breathes in the aroma of the shrimps, he exclaims, "Ah, the smell of our ocean!" (19).

19. The skin is considered an organ because an organ is a complex of tissues that fulfill certain specific functions. Skin can incorporate and secrete substances through its pores. In fact, the ingestion of certain foods becomes manifest through the odor of transpiration.

20. "el color del caramelo en reposo" (35).

21. "una piel tierna del color del pan" (81). In *"Bon Voyage*, Mr. President," "Only the weariness of his skin betrayed the state of his health" (4). The "weary" skin connotes not only his illness but also his age. His skin is tired from rubbing against the external world during so many years.

22. "los ojos de almendra verde" (81).

23. ".... y su piel exhalaba un hálito tenue que sólo podía ser el olor propio de su belleza" (87).

24. In Spanish, the verb "comer" ("to eat") is often employed metaphorically with regard to sexual orality. "Comerse a una persona a besos" ("To devour/eat someone up with kisses"), or simply "comérsela" ("to eat her up"), expresses a strong erotic desire

through orality. It is a kind of metaphorized sexual cannibalism, as if the speaker wished to achieve a transubstantiation of the body of the love object.

25. Olfactory metaphors are among the most difficult in Spanish. Similarly, the verb "oler" ("to smell") necessarily takes the preposition "a" ("to"): "oler a + the name of the object" (in English, "to smell of + the name of the object"). The perception of food is expressed through synesthesia. The sense of smell is related first with sight and then with taste. In a subject faced with the olfactory stimulus of a food, there first arises an image of the food itself, and the papillae secrete saliva. The aforementioned quotation expresses that relation: In "*Bon Voyage*, Mr. President," the ex-President breathes in the smell of the shrimps and there immediately bursts into his mind the image of the Caribbean. See note 18.

26. The foods that provoke a rejection of incorporation refer us to the "bad objects" of Melanie Klein. Although García Márquez compares the process of writing to the cooking of a soup ("Prologue," xiii), in several stories the incorporation of soup is negative. In "Miss Forbes's Summer of Happiness," the boys hate the noodle soup, which they compare to worms, and one of the kids vomits on tasting a moray eel. In "Maria dos Prazeres," the protagonist of that name threatens the Count with poisoning his soup. On the other hand, in "Seventeen Poisoned Englishmen," Prudencia Linero prefers having a bowl of noodle soup over eating "little songbirds" (127).

27. "…una tufada insoportable que la señora Prudencia Linero reconoció como el aliento a cangrejos podridos del patio de su casa" (162).

28. "Aturdida por el júbilo y el tufo a cebollas rancias de tantas familias en verano" (163). This smell emigrates semantically to a priest "*que comía cebollas con pan en un lugar apartado*" (169. My emphasis).

29. In Greek mythology, the famous hunter Actaeon was transformed into a deer by Artemisa (Diana the huntress) in punishment for his having seen her naked. Actaeon was devoured by his own dogs. This devouring can be translated as an erotic act.

30. Strawberries connote love because of their color red and their shape in the form of a heart. The Spanish word "fresa" comes from Latin *fraga*, "fragrant," from the strong aroma emitted by this fruit. Strawberries are a symbol of Venus, the Roman goddess of sex, love, beauty, and fertility.

31. "Sin embargo, lo que más me impresionó fue el olor de fresas recientes que permanecía estancado sin explicación posible en el ámbito del dormitorio" (131).

32. "Sólo entonces me estremeció el olor de fresas recién cortadas…" (133).

33. Another instance of what I call "magical-gastronomical realism" can be seen in the trail of blood left behind by Nena Daconte in the story "The Trail of Your Blood in the Snow." Although the connection may seem remote, the drops of blood from Nena Daconte, who will bleed to death in the course of many miles of travel, have their correlation in the filet eaten by Billy Sánchez in a Parisian café: "[A]s he was trying to set his head to rights, he ordered a veal filet with fried potatoes and a bottle of wine" (181). Here we find together the three foods that, according to Barthes, connote "Frenchness." Both the filet and the wine share in a "blood-kinship." In some way, there is a magical connection between Nena Daconte's bleeding to death, and the *saignant* ("rare") filet that he consumes the following day.

34. It's interesting to note that Frau Frieda reveals her dreams before having breakfast, during the absence of ingested food. Quite the contrary to Neruda—whom we see connoted as a *gourmand*.

35. "No he conocido a nadie más parecido a la idea que uno tiene de un Papa renacentista: glotón y refinado ... Matilde, su esposa, le ponía un babero que parecía más de peluquería que de comedor ... Aquel día en Carvalleiras fue ejemplar. Se comió tres langostas enteras descuartizándolas con una maestría de cirujano, y al mismo tiempo devoraba con la vista los platos de todos, e iba picando un poco de cada uno, con un deleite que contagiaba las ganas de comer: las almejas de Galicia, los percebes del Cantábrico, las cigalas de Alicante, las espardenyas de la Costa Brava. Mientras tanto, como los franceses, sólo hablaba de otras exquisiteces de cocina, y en especial de los mariscos prehistóricos de Chile que llevaba en el corazón. De pronto dejó de comer, afinó sus antenas de bogavante ..." (98–99).

36. See the excellent essay, "Imagen y palabra: el arte del bodegón y la poesía nerudiana," in which Santiago Daydí-Tolson analyzes food in the Nerudian *oeuvre*.

37. "... [S]e sentó en una mesa apartada, y empezó a escribir versos fluidos con la pluma de tinta verde con que dibujaba flores y peces y pájaros en las dedicatorias de sus libros" (101).

38. "[N]unca volvimos a encontrar unos budines más deliciosos que los de la señora Forbes" (191); "sus pasteles de crema, sus tartas de vainilla, sus exquisitos bizcochos de ciruelas, como no habíamos de conocer otros en el resto de nuestras vidas" (194).

39. "...con la espina dorsal apoyada en la silla, masticando diez veces con un carrillo y diez veces con el otro" (192).

40. "la eterna sopa de fideos de aquel verano aborrecible" (192).

41. "—Estoy hasta los cojones de esta agua de lombrices" (201).

42. ("botas de miliciano," "el pelo cortado como el de un hombre bajo el sombrero de fieltro," "voz de soldado") (196–197).

43. ("sargenta de Dortmund") (196).

44. "[M]ientras comía tratas enteras y se bebía hasta una botella de vino especial que mi padre guardaba con tanto celo para las ocasiones memorables" (199).

45. "la vimos ... llevando para el dormitorio medio pastel de chocolate y la botella con más de cuatro dedos del vino envenenado" (202).

46. "exhalaba un hálito tenue que sólo podía ser el olor propio de su belleza" (87).

47. "Olía a orines de mico" (197).

48. "Así huelen todos los europeos, sobre todo en verano... Es el olor de la civilización" (197).

49. "escuálido." This Spanish word is etymologically related to "escualos" = "sharks." The body of Mrs. Forbes has the shape of a fish or shark.

50. "....era imposible concebir un ser humano más hermoso" (190).

51. "Buscaban el dolor en el hígado, en el riñón, en el páncreas, en la próstata, donde menos estaba (....) Su dolor era improbable y escurridizo, y a veces parecía estar en el costillar derecho y a veces en el bajo vientre, y a menudo lo sorprendía con una punzada instantánea en la ingle" (24).

52. "Lo más asombroso, sin embargo, era que el cuerpo carecía de peso" (61).

53. "…y vieron en las otras mesas los grandes trozo asados con un borde de grasa tierna" (30).

54. "exclamó con los ojos cerrados y los brazos abiertos: 'Ah, el olor de nuestro mar'" (39).

55. "se sirvió dos veces sin medirse en los elogios, y le encantaron las tajadas fritas de plátano maduro y la ensalada de aguacate, aunque no compartió las *nostalgias*" (40. My emphasis).

56. "Se lo tomó sin azúcar, a sorbos lentos, y después puso la taza bocabajo en el plato para que el sedimento del café, después de tantos años, tuviera tiempo de escribir su destino (….) Antes de quitarse los lentes descifró su destino en el asiento del café, y sintió un estremecimiento glacial: allí estaba la incertidumbre" (27).

57. "vivir la vida como viniera" (55).

58. The odor of fish or specifically of herring as connoting the odor of the female sex organ is a common notion within Latin American popular culture.

59. "el último viernes de cada mes para cenar con ella y hacer un lánguido amor de sobremesa" (144).

60. "que eran los platos favoritos de los catalanes de alcurnia de los buenos tiempos" (149).

61. "Después de la cena, larga y bien conversada, hacían de memoria un amor sedentario que les dejaba a ambos un sedimento de desastre" (149).

62. "abandonada sin dinero, sin idioma y sin nombre…" (150).

63. "….Se sintió fea y compadecida" (154).

WORKS CITED

Augé, Marc. *Non-places: Introduction to an Anthropology of Supermodernity*. Trans. John Howe. London & New York: Verso, 1995.

Barthes, Roland. *Mythologies*. Trans. Annette Lavers. New York: The Noonday Press, 1991.

Clancier, Anne. *Psicoanálisis, Literatura, Crítica*. Madrid: Cátedra, 1979.

Daydí-Tolson, Santiago. "Imagen y palabra: el arte del bodegón y la poesía nerudiana." *Cincinnati Romance Review* 33 (2012): 133–144.

Fischler, Claude. "Food, Self and Identity." *Social Sciences Information* 27 (1998): 275–293.

García Márquez, Gabriel. *Doce cuentos peregrinos*. Madrid: Mondadori, 1992.

———. "Prólogo." *Doce cuentos peregrinos*. Madrid: Mondadori, 1992. 11–19.

———. *Strange Pilgrims*. Trans. Edith Grossman. New York: Alfred A. Knopf, 1993.

———. "Prologue." Strange Pilgrims. Trans. Edith Grossman. New York: Alfred A. Knopf, 1993. vii–xiii.

Lejeune, Philippe. *Le pacte autobiographique*. París: Éditions du Seuil, 1996.

Nyman, Jopi. "Cultural Contact and the Contemporary Culinary Memoir: Home, Memory and Identity in Madhur Jaffrey and Diana Abu-Jaber." *Autobiographical Studies* 24:2 (2009): 282–298.

Pugh Briceño, Karina. "Los Strange Pilgrims gastronómicos de Gabriel García Márquez." *Afuegolento.com*. http://www.afuegolento.com/noticias/44/firmas/karina/1826/los-doce-cuentos-peregrinos-y-gastronomicos-de-gabriel-garcia-marquez. Web. Access on June 29, 2015.

Vanden Berghe, Kristine. "Los *Doce cuentos peregrinos* de García Márquez. ¿O son trece? Paratopía, parodia, e intertextualidad en *Doce cuentos peregrinos*." *Bulletin of Hispanic Studies* LXXXVI (2001): 85–98.

Yúdice. George. "Feeding the Trascendent Body." In *Essays in Post-Modern Culture*, eds. Eyal Amiran and John Unsworth. New York: Oxford University Press, 1993. 14–36.

Chapter 12

Reading Illness in Gabriel García Márquez's *Of Love and Other Demons*

Olivia Vázquez-Medina

> Love, [...] if it rage, it is no more love, but burning lust, a disease, frenzy, madness, hell. *Est orcus ille, vis est immedicabilis, est rabies insana.* (Plutarch, *Amator lib.*)
>
> Robert Burton, The Anatomy of Melancholy[1]

An important concept in the tradition of hermeneutics, particularly in the work of Hans-Georg Gadamer, is that of situated reason: reason understood as an interpretive process that involves the social and historical location of the subject (Alcoff 95). Given that a situation "represents a standpoint that limits the possibility of vision," fundamental to the concept of situation is that of horizon, a concept that Gadamer traces back to Nietzsche and Husserl, and which he defines as "the range of vision that includes everything that can be seen from a particular vantage point" (Gadamer 302). The horizon, as Linda Martín Alcoff explains,

> is not a mere instrument of vision, but the condition in which vision occurs. [...] The horizon is a substantive perspectival location from which the interpreter looks out at the world, a perspective that is always present but that is open and dynamic, with a temporal as well as physical dimension, moving into the future and into new spaces as the subject moves. (95)

Readers of Gabriel García Márquez would agree that the notions of vision, perspective and interpretive horizon are of crucial importance in the writings of the Colombian author. García Márquez's fictions are characterized by the interweaving of perspectives (in both the narrative and the hermeneutic senses) and by the seemingly unproblematical textualization of diverse cultural traditions. Arguably, much of García Márquez's production explores the epistemological implications of the concept of horizon as "the background, framing assumptions we bring with us to perception and understanding, the congealed experiences that become premises by which we strive to make sense of the world, the range of concepts and categories of description that we have at our disposal" (Alcoff 95). This chapter focuses on *Of Love and Other Demons* (1994), arguing that questions concerning vision, perception and interpretation at the core of this novel are explored in the narrative through the theme of illness—a ubiquitous and multilayered topic in García Márquez's writings.

Representations of individual and collective disease span across García Márquez's fiction: from the insomnia plague in *One Hundred Years of Solitude* (1967) to Simón Bolívar's slow decline in *The General in His Labyrinth* (1989), to mention just two examples. The metaphor of love as a disease underpins *Love in the Time of Cholera* (1985); plagues are recurrent motifs, typically portrayed in line with a Western tradition dating from Antiquity that links them to social dissolution and generalized chaos.[2] Moreover, illness in García Márquez's novels often has implications that go beyond the metaphorical, for it plays a part in the textualization of the narratives and in the interpellation of the reader. In *Of Love*, illness serves to articulate the key issues of racial conflict and religious intolerance, while also being central to characterization and narrative development. More importantly, the allegedly diseased body of the protagonist, Sierva María de Todos los Ángeles, is a site of conflicting readings within the novel. Presented as a riddle, it invites interpretation; subject to the medical gaze, it is offered to the reader as a site where anxieties, desires and discourses of power are inscribed. By making illness and the body the sites of ambiguous and equivocal meanings, the novel ultimately invites the reader to question her own act of reading and, in turn, to reflect on her own horizon of understanding and interpretation.[3]

READING DISEASE

Set in the late eighteenth century in Cartagena de Indias, the novel tells the story of Sierva María de Todos los Ángeles, the twelve year-old daughter of Ygnacio, Marquis de Casalduero, and his wife Bernarda. Sierva María is neglected by her parents from an early age, and raised by the African slaves in the courtyard of her parents' house. Although her physical features clearly identify her as belonging to the *criollo* community, the girl learns the customs and languages of the slaves, and chooses for herself the name María Mandinga. When she is bitten by a rabid dog, Sierva María is first thought to have contracted rabies (although this diagnosis is never confirmed by the doctors) and later suspected of possession by demons. By order of the bishop, she is locked up in the Convent of Santa Clara, and the thirty-six year old priest Cayetano Delaura is appointed as her exorcist. Shortly after having met Sierva María, Cayetano falls in love with her, and a secret relationship between them ensues, abruptly interrupted when Cayetano is forcefully prevented from seeing her. The priest is condemned to serve as a nurse in the local leprosarium, and the girl dies after five sessions of exorcisms performed by the bishop, unaware of why Cayetano never came back to her.

As some scholars have noted, illness is crucial in constructing the novel's atmosphere.[4] Illness adds to the material decline of the city, which is in turn linked to an oppressive moral climate. Several characters suffer from some form of physical or mental illness, which becomes their defining trait: Bernarda (bile complaints and addiction to cocoa), Dulce Olivia (madness), the bishop (asthma), and the Marquis ("undeniable signs of mental retardation" [García Márquez, *Of Love and Other Demons* 34]).[5] Even lesser characters such as Sierva María's paternal grandmother are said to have been "crippled by rheumatism" (34).[6] The collective fear of "some African plague" threatening the town is mentioned from the first lines of the novel, although later dismissed as a false alarm (5). The repeated references to lepers around the convent and the cathedral become all the more significant when we learn of Cayetano's fate: morally polluted in the eyes of the bishop, Cayetano is literally put away and metaphorically dead for society, reminiscent of the "putting out of the world" of the leper by the Church.[7] The inclusion of this broad spectrum of disease in *Of Love* relies on the semantic power of illness in the cultural imagination of the West. For the modern reader, illnesses such as the plague and leprosy would evoke a time in the distant past, and a certain idea of disease, better explained by what Herzlich and Pierret have termed the "ancien régime of disease": "a régime—one that essentially no longer exists [in the West]—in which illness was marked by three characteristics: numbers, impotence and death, and exclusion" (3).

However, it is Sierva María's presumed illness that constitutes the core of the novel. From the moment when she is bitten by the dog, at the beginning of the first chapter, her body becomes a surface to be scrutinized for symptoms of rabies, and rabies itself is given a number of meanings by the characters. A dual act of reading, then, is involved in the understanding of illness inside the narrative. Firstly, a medical gaze (in which the reader is made complicit) performs the reading of the girl's body: we follow the detailed description of any changes in the wound left by the dog in Sierva María's ankle, as it is seen, successively among others, by the slave that accompanies her to the market (6), by Bernarda (11), by Abrenuncio (31), by other doctors (52), and by Cayetano (88). Worth noting from the outset is the careful manipulation of perspective and voice in *Of Love*: often, the seeing consciousness (a given character) is not the same as the voice that tells (the narrator).

A second form of reading illness performed by the characters is the act of giving meaning to disease. The following conversation between Sagunta, an Indian healer, and the Marquis, is one of the earliest examples:

> 'We are threatened by a plague of rabies', said Sagunta, 'and I am the only one who has the keys of Saint Hubert, protector of hunters and healer of the rabid'. 'I see no reason for a plague', said the Marquis. 'As far as I know, no comets or eclipses have been forecast, and our sins are not great enough for God to be concerned with us.' (13–14)[8]

Through the words *plague* and *sins*—as well as *mal* in the original Spanish, meaning both illness and evil—this passage highlights a link between rabies and collective punishment, fitting squarely within Herzlich and Pierret's "ancien régime of disease," of which the plague is the prime example. The conversation between Sagunta and the Marquis also explains for the reader the codes according to which the characters in the novel read disease, wherein illness forms part of a grammar that goes beyond the individual and includes her society, the religious sphere and even the cosmos, as the allusion to comets and eclipses makes explicit.[9] As Sander Gilman argues in another context, "Like any complex text, the signs of illness are read within the conventions of an interpretive community that comprehends them in the light of earlier, powerful readings of what are understood to be similar or parallel texts" (*Disease and Representation* 7). From the reader's point of view, the spelling out of the characters' interpretive horizon vis-à-vis rabies serves a purpose of distance and differentiation: we become aware of our own modern—or postmodern—perspective, whereby rabies has no links whatsoever with sins, saints, collective punishment or comets. In Gadamer's idiom, by being presented with another's understanding, we become aware of the horizon that defines our hermeneutical situation; we discover ourselves to be defined by our own historicity (301). Through our cognitive and temporal vantage point, we read Sierva María's tale as belonging to an exotic and distant fictionalized past, riddled with superstition. Yet it is worth asking if this is indeed what the narrative is suggesting. Sagunta, after all, informs the Marquis accurately that Sierva María has been bitten by the rabid dog—a fact of which he was unaware—as well as giving him precise details about the other people who had been bitten and, more importantly, foretelling an eclipse that does take place later in the novel (95–96). There is a tendency in the narrative, therefore, toward granting some degree of validity to certain interpretive horizons that do not necessarily correspond to that of the modern reader.

Later on in the novel, the single most important act of reading disease is performed by the bishop: "'No matter what the physicians may claim,' he said, 'rabies in humans is often one of the many snares of the Enemy'" (59).[10] This reading of disease seals Sierva María's fate. The transformation of Sierva María's suspected diagnosis from rabies to possession, via madness, had just been suggested by the doctors, and the confusion between these notions determines the generalized perception of Sierva María by many other characters from this moment onwards:

> A young physician from Salamanca opened Sierva María's closed wound and applied caustic poultices [...]. Another attempted to achieve the same end with leeches on her back [...]. At the end of two weeks, she had been subjected to two herbal baths and two emollient enemas a day and was brought to the brink of death with potions of natural antimony and other fatal concoctions. [...] Sierva María felt as if she were dying. [....] She had suffered everything: vertigo, convulsions, spasms, deliriums, looseness of the bowels and bladder; and she rolled on the floor howling in pain and fury. Even the boldest healers left her to her fate, convinced she was mad or possessed by demons. (52–53)[11]

The wound is a sign to be read in Sierva María's body, but since the expected signified (rabies) is not conclusively denoted by the *closed wound*, the latter is re-opened: the body is literally a surface where others' anxieties are inscribed, becoming in turn for the reader indicative of Sierva's vulnerability and suffering. The presumably diseased body is here a space for violence and control by doctors and healers. Paradoxically, and ironically, what should be an instance of healing becomes one of torture: Sierva María is powerless at the hands of the healers, and later the bishop, for the sessions of exorcism are characterized by a similar degree of cruelty.

The narrator suggests elsewhere that it is highly unlikely that Sierva María has contracted rabies, although he never offers his own diagnosis but limits himself to quoting the lack of conclusiveness of the symptoms: "It was in the farthest cell of this forgotten corner where they would lock up Sierva María ninety-three days after she was bitten by the dog and showed no symptoms of rabies" (66).[12] By the time Sierva María is examined by the Viceroy's doctors, "They confirmed that she showed no symptom of rabies and they agreed with Abrenuncio that it was improbable she could contract the disease now. But no one believed himself authorized to doubt she was possessed by the demon" (106).[13] It is clear, as Ortega has suggested, that Sierva María's ordeal is very much the product of a difference in the authority of the readings (14): because of its place in the hierarchy, the demonic reading by the bishop of the girl's alleged disease prevails over and against any other readings (such as that of Cayetano or Abrenuncio).

Scholarship on the subject suggests that a demonological conception of rabies may have been developed since early Christianity. Andrea Nicolotti notes that some symptoms of rabies could have been mistaken for possession:

"restlessness, violence, yelling, feeling of suffocation, and physical exhaustion" (530). Clearly, Sierva María's restlessness, violence and yelling are more often than not a response to the pain inflicted on her and to the widespread aggression of which she is a victim. Other typical symptoms of demonic possession that she presents—such as the "wild and painful contortions of the body"—are attributable to the same cause, whereas the allegation that she exhibits a further symptom, super-normal strength, is dismissed by Cayetano (125).[14] The fixed meaning ascribed by the ecclesiastical reading thus contrasts with the equivocality of the symptoms.

The slippage between rabies, madness and possession as suggested by the healers is not unexpected. The connection between madness and rabies had been indicated in the Marquis's first visit to the Amor de Dios Hospital: "In the pavilion that housed raving lunatics he found the rabies victim tied to a pillar" (16).[15] If the historical link between rabies and madness is implicit since the earliest conceptions of the disease—according to Wilkinson, "the 'mad dog' was mentioned [...] in the legal documents of Mesopotamia in the 23rd century B.C." (1)—the broad association between madness and demonic possession is also clearly not particular to García Márquez's novel: "Throughout the fifteenth and sixteenth centuries in Europe, influenced by the notorious *Malleus Maleficarum*, written for Pope Innocent VIII in 1485, an equation was widely made between sin, mental disorder, witchcraft, and demonic influence" (Radden 96). Abrenuncio is therefore right when he informs Cayetano that rabies "had always been confused with demonic possession, as had certain forms of madness and other disturbances of the spirit" (124).[16] The relation of contiguity between rabies, madness and demonic possession thus brings the narrative forward; provides the framework in which Sierva María's story is to be understood; and reinforces the effect of distance and differentiation on the part of the reader.

Of Love is a story about how an idea of illness "is constructed on the basis of specific ideological needs and structured along the categories of representation accepted within that ideology" (Gilman, *Disease* 2). According to the dominant ideology in her society, Sierva María's presumed illness (whether understood as rabies, madness or demonic possession) derives largely from the fact that the habits and languages of the black slaves in which she partakes are perceived in themselves as demonic. The bishop enunciates this clearly: "'It is an open secret that your poor child rolls on the floor in obscene convulsions, howling the gibberish of idolaters. Are these not the unequivocal symptoms of demonic possession?'" (57).[17] In contrast, Cayetano explains what is presumably the reader's own conclusion: "'I believe, however,' said Delaura, 'that what seems demonic to us are the customs of the blacks, learned by the girl as a consequence of the neglected condition in which her parents kept her'" (97).[18] Sierva María's link to blackness as a marker of difference opens up the question of the relationship between identity and visibility, as explored in the following section of this chapter.

DIFFERENCE AND VISIBILITY

Sander Gilman documents the extent to which the conceptualization and representation of disease fulfil a function of *othering*. Drawing on illness, sexuality and race as categories of difference, Gilman refers to the analogies between "the ill and the perverse" and expands on Fanon's denunciation of the satanic image of the black in the West, as well as exploring the "historical relationship between madness and blackness in Western culture" (*Difference* 25, 134). In the case of Sierva María, the connection between rabies, madness and possession occurs within this framework of the representation and understanding of illness as a form of *othering*. Although it is never proven that Sierva María has contracted rabies, the suspicion that looms over her is very much dependent upon her marginal status. However, the reasons for her marginality are more complex than scholarship on the novel has suggested thus far. Margaret Olsen notes that the episode of Sierva María's bite by the dog is inscribed in a context associated with the black Africans, and that the other three people bitten are African slaves, which reinforces the girl's belonging to this group (1072–73). Olsen argues convincingly that the novel draws upon the link between blackness and pathology that scholars such as Gilman have explored. Her thesis, however, rests upon the premise that Sierva María's racial identity is self-defined as black (1075). Although I agree with Olsen's exploration of the links between pathology and Africanness in the novel, her understanding of identity does not take into account the problems arising from defining Sierva María simply as black African, nor the far more complex construction of the character offered by the novel.

It has to be noted that Sierva María is marginal not only because of her links with the slaves, but also because of her age and gender. Much has been written about the "medicalization of femininity" within patriarchal configurations, whereby the woman's body is inscribed as full of disease (Doane 39). Referring to a number of mainstream films from the mid-twentieth century, Mary Ann Doane argues that the female protagonist is presented "quite literally [as] the object of knowledge, her body the site of continual examination of symptoms" (134). In this respect, Sierva María's body is even more susceptible of objectification on account of her age, which locates her in a far more ambiguous and marginal place than an adult woman's.[19] And yet the novel avoids giving a univocal definition of the character: Sierva María is an ambiguous and liminal figure, who crosses the boundaries between child and woman, black and white, and renders problematical the distinctions between health and disease; madness, wickedness, demonic possession, martyrdom and sanctity.[20] Cayetano reminds the reader that some signs of possession and sanctity can sometimes be confused (125), and indeed the slippage between the demonic and the sacred is crucial in the novel. Not only is the narrative sympathetic to Sierva María to the extent that we read her ordeal as martyrdom, but the legend to which the author refers in the prologue states that the "twelve-year old marquise" who allegedly inspires the novel was "venerated [...] for the many miracles she had performed" (3). As perceptively noted by Palencia-Roth, moreover, it is inexplicable that Sierva María is buried in a "niche of the high altar, on the side where the Gospels were kept" (*Of Love* 2), given that she dies during the sessions of exorcism, suspected of possession by demons, and treated more precisely as a suspect of *hechicería* by the bishop (Palencia-Roth para. 16 and 17). A further ambiguous sign is the powerful smell of flowers that accompanies Cayetano's vision of Sierva María in his library (94), and which could be read as an oblique allusion to the odor of sanctity. Different sides of this polyvalent representation are stressed at different moments in the narrative, thus inviting the reader into the quest for interpreting Sierva María, which runs parallel to the quest inside the novel for diagnosing her condition: is she rabid, mad, possessed?

If the narrative suggests that Sierva María never contracts rabies, the verdict is at times far less conclusive with regard to possession, as in the following examples: "Then Delaura witnessed the fearful spectacle of one truly possessed. Sierva María's hair coiled with as life of its own, like the serpents of Medusa, and green spittle and a string of obscenities in idolatrous languages poured from her mouth" (127); "On the second day [of her exorcism] the immense bellowing of maddened cattle could be heard, the earth trembled and it was no longer possible to think that Sierva María was not at the mercy of all the demons of hell" (159–60).[21] As suggested earlier, a multiplicity of perspectives is filtered through the narrator's voice—Cayetano's in the former example and the general, collective opinion in the latter, which further adds to the ambiguity. It should also be noted that the girl's chosen "African" name—"María Mandinga"—is used only once in the narrative and that the narrator never refers to her by this name, endorsing instead "Sierva María" throughout. The Marian component of both names is evident, although the possible demonic connotations of the word "Mandinga" are abandoned in favor of the more ambiguous "Sierva," which links the girl to the group of the slaves but also to Mary's self-definition as *ancilla domini*, "the handmaid of the Lord" (Luke 1. 38).[22]

From the reader's point of view, grasping the character's identity is further complicated by the fact that for most parts of the narrative we do not have access to Sierva María's subjectivity; we witness her being read by other characters, but only on limited occasions is she granted a voice (and when she is, we are often reminded of her proclivity to lying).[23] To exemplify the extent to which the narrative eludes a univocal definition of the character, we can compare her earliest descriptions:

> The girl displayed just who she was. She could dance with more grace and fire than the Africans, sing in voices different from her own in the various languages of Africa, agitate the birds and animals when she imitated their voices. By order of Dominga de Adviento, the younger slave girls would blacken her face with soot. They hung Santería necklaces over the baptism scapular and looked after her hair [...]. She had her father's thin body, however, and his irremediable shyness, pale skin, eyes of taciturn blue and the pure copper of her radiant hair. Her movements were so stealthy that she seemed an invisible creature. Frightened by her strange nature, her mother had hung a cowbell around the girl's wrist so she would not lose track of her in the shadows of the house. (10–11)[24]

The opening line quoted above suggests some narratorial omniscience that any reader of García Márquez would take with caution: "displayed just who she was" puts forward a link between visibility and truth that is challenged elsewhere in the narrative. In the first part of the above quotation, we see Sierva's black identity as theatricality and performance, and as alterity in itself. Her voice is "different from her own," which makes her disconcerting even for the group that embodies otherness in the novel—and, more interestingly, constitutes a well-known symptom of demonic possession. The voices of birds and animals suggest a link between Sierva María and animality, which is a key thread in the narrative, also hinted at by the cowbell. "The fear of the Other's wildness and potential destructiveness is a common feature of the nexus between blackness and madness," Gilman argues (*Difference* 136), and for large parts of the narrative Sierva María is presented as wild and potentially destructive.

In the second part of the above quotation, however, we are presented with a radically different, and even contradictory, description of Sierva María: the strong bodily presence mentioned before, defined by expressiveness and vitality, gives way to a silent and invisible, ethereal creature, whose "nature" cannot be further away from what has just been described. What both descriptions have in common is that they provide no access to the girl's subjectivity: they present Sierva María as observed by others, by the African slaves in the first paragraph, and by her mother in the second. In fact, throughout the narrative we are told of the effects that the sight of Sierva has on other characters, and quite often what she inspires is puzzlement and fear, particularly in her own mother:

> [Bernarda] had lived with her heart in her mouth ever since she discovered a certain phantasmal quality in her daughter. She trembled at the mere memory of the times she would turn around and find herself face to face with the inscrutable

eyes of the languid creature [...]. 'Girl!', she would shout. 'I forbid you to look at me that way!' When she was most involved in her business affairs, she would feel on the back of her neck the sibilant breath of a snake lying in ambush and recoil in terror. (45)[25]

Much could be said about Bernarda's fear of Sierva María's gaze, for it is only on very few occasions that the girl is indeed the holder and not the object of the gaze (when she looks at Bernarda and when she looks at the bishop during the exorcism).[26]

Given her fair skin, blue eyes and dazzling copper-colored hair, Sierva María's racial identity can only problematically be defined simply as black. "Race and gender," suggests Alcoff, "are forms of social identity that share at least two features: they are fundamental rather than peripheral to the self [...] and they operate through visual markers on the body" (6). For most characters in the novel, Sierva María's cultural blackness is incongruous with her visible racial identity (and social class). This mismatch is precisely what enhances her marginality and her perceived pathology. The fact that some readers, such as Olsen, consider Sierva María as black in direct opposition to her visible racial markers shows the extent to which, in García Márquez's fiction, we are asked to suspend our belief that only the visible is true, and to engage with a narrative that suggests one truth at one level, only to render it very problematical at some other level.

THE SECRET WOUND OF LOVE

A further tension between visibility and invisibility and their respective links to truth is suggested in the novel through the association between Sierva María and the rabid dog. Let us consider the opening lines of the novel in juxtaposition with the description of Sierva María's entry into the convent:

> An ash-gray dog with a white blaze on its forehead burst onto the rough terrain of the market on the first Sunday in December, knocked down tables of fried food, over-turned Indians' stalls and lottery kiosks and bit four people who happened to cross its path. (5) In the end they took her by force, kicking and snapping at the air like a dog [...] Sierva María [...] climbed onto the table, and ran from one end to the other in a rampage of destruction, shrieking as if truly possessed. She broke everything in her path, then leapt through the window and wrecked the arbors in the courtyard, upset the beehives and knocked over the railings in the stables and the fences around the corrals. The bees flew away, and the animals, bellowing with panic, stamped as far as the cloistered sleeping quarters. (71–73)[27]

Both Sierva María and the dog are agents of chaos; they are both thought to be agents of disease; they both instil fear; and, ultimately, they both die in the novel.[28] The narrator refers repeatedly to the popular belief that rabies transforms its sufferers into dogs—a belief dating from the Middle Ages, according to Herzlich and Pierret (130). On the one hand, this superstition is dismissed by Abrenuncio (51), whose opinions on various matters are likely to be shared by the reader. Yet the novel does revive the parallels between Sierva María and the dog on various occasions, as if to threaten subtly the pact between the reader and the narrator: a reading pact that would establish that Sierva María's illness and her story are to be read according to the contemporary reader's interpretive horizon.

The most important characterization of Sierva María's behavior as "doglike" occurs during an early meeting with Cayetano:

> Then [Sierva María] looked at Delaura for the first time, weighed and measured him and attacked with the well-aimed pounce of a hunted animal. […] 'I was bitten by a little rabid dog with a tail more than a meter long.' Sierva María wanted to see the wound. Delaura removed the bandage, and with her index finger she touched the crimson halo of swelling as if it were a burning coal, and laughed for the first time. 'I'm worse than the plague,' she said. Delaura responded not with the Gospels but with Garcilaso: '*Well may you do this to one who can endure it.*' (90, 93)[29]

We have seen how the slippage from rabies to madness and demonic possession propels the narrative forward. This is a "visible" semantic link, which structures the bishop's and others' understanding of Sierva María's presumed illness. Nevertheless, a further connection is suggested, which is far less obvious. If the symptoms of rabies were ever confused with demonic possession, one further link between rabies and possession is lycanthropy. Although I am in no way suggesting that Sierva María suffers from lycanthropy, it is intriguing that the passage just quoted (and many others) furthers the parallel between Sierva María and the dog, as when she is described as *aullando* (howling) or *ladrando* (barking).

More importantly, the passage quoted above suggests an unusual causality between Cayetano being bitten by Sierva María and his falling in love. Ultimately, another illness is central to *Of Love*—lovesickness—but its status as a disease is far less discernible from our interpretive horizon. Aníbal González notes that Cayetano falls in love with Sierva María after being bitten by her (88) and posits rabies as a metaphor for lovesickness and unleashed passion more broadly (96), but the full significance of lovesickness in the novel is underexplored in his perceptive study.[30] A recent medical text on rabies notes that Plato "used the word Lyssa to describe erotic passion" (Baer 1), and of course *lyssa* is visible in the genus *Lyssavirus* (from the Greek *lussa* meaning madness or rage) of which the rabies virus is the prototype (Wunner 23). Narrative tension in *Of Love* rests upon the idea of disease, and the transition from rabies to lovesickness suggests that the latter is as real a disease as the former. Lovesickness is the *rabies insana* of Burton's Plutarch quotation in the epigraph above, and the "rage" (*furor*) from medieval and early modern medical discourses of love. We should also note that within an early modern horizon, both lovesickness and lycanthropy would be marked by melancholia—or rather, would be considered a type of melancholia.[31] Interestingly, in his famous *Anatomy of Melancholy*, Robert Burton brings together "Dotage, Phrensie, Madnesse, Hydrophobia, Lycanthropia; Chorus sancti Vitii, [and] Exstasis [demonic possession]," suggesting links between them (132). Moreover, Burton writes in the same section, other authors "adde to these another Fury that proceeds from *Love*, and another from *Study*, [and] another Divine or *religious Fury*" (136); three "furies" that thoroughly afflict Cayetano Delaura.

There is a correspondence between Sierva María's wound on the ankle and Cayetano's wound on the hand, perhaps a visible signifier of "the secret wound of love," the image that organizes Marion Wells's study of love-melancholy.[32] According to Wells, in sixteenth- and seventeenth-century medical texts, "intense unfulfilled erotic desire is classified as a species of melancholy, with mental and physiological etiologies and cures. Rather than dismiss lovesickness as a literary trope and decode its symptoms as an artificial display of exaggerated despair, early modern medical authors held erotic obsession to be a real and virulent disease" (1–2). The following is an extract on "amorous melancholie" from the physician André Du Lauren's *Discourse of the Preservation of Sight* (1597):

> [T]he man is quite undone and cast away, the sences are wandring to and fro, up and downe, reason is confounded, the imagination is corrupted, the talk fond and senceless; the sillie loving worme cannot any more look upon any thing but his idol: all the functions of the bodie are likewise perverted, he becommeth pale, leane, swouning … hollow and sunke eyed… You shall finde him weeping, sobbing, sighing and redoubling his sighs, and in continual restlessness avoyding company, loving solitariness, the better to feed and follow his foolish imaginations. (Quoted in Wells 1)

Cayetano's behavior in the last chapters of the novel would fit this medical description of the malady of love (the so-called *amor hereos*): his pallor, sighing and restlessness are completed with "tears of burning oil that seared him deep inside" (127), and a constant "yearning in his heart" (136).[33] More importantly, the reader witnesses a progressive damage to Cayetano's "estimative faculty"—his reasoning "corrupted," his behavior irrational in stark contrast to his previous temperance—with the characteristic "perseverative focus on the image (or more technically the 'phantasm') of the beloved that becomes the constitutive feature of the disease" (Wells 2). The latter is symbolized by the mark left by the eclipse in Cayetano's retina, the image of the sun (Sierva María) engraved in her lover's eye: "'Now when I close my eyes I see a hair like a river of gold'" (134).[34] Even Abrenuncio is perplexed at Cayetano's transformation: "I would have imagined anything about you except these extremes of lunacy" (157).[35]

According to Jacalyn Duffin, it is not until the eighteenth century that love-sickness disappears from medical discourses as a full-blown disease (60–61). Could it be that, in *Of Love*, we are meant to read love as a disease—not metaphorically, but literally? This would seem an implausible suggestion, were it not reinforced by the last words in the novel. The last pages recount Sierva María's exorcisms performed by the bishop, and some readers attribute the girl's death to the violence of the process. Although the novel does lend itself to this explanation, there is also mention of the fact that Sierva María is devastated by the loss of Cayetano: "The warder who came in to prepare her for the sixth session of exorcism found her *dead of love* in her bed, her eyes radiant and her skin like that of a newborn baby. Strands of hair gushed like bubbles as they grew back on her shaved head" (160, emphasis added).[36]

The narrator tells us—this time firmly and unambiguously—that Sierva María dies from love.[37] This can be read in ironical terms: given the violence exerted over Sierva María, it is not love but its opposite that kills her. However, another reading would see this death as literally enacting some of the lines by Garcilaso de la Vega that feed Cayetano and Sierva María's "furor:" *"For you was I born, for you do I have life, for you will I die, for you now I am dying"* (94).[38] As González has persuasively suggested, in *Of Love*, the "force of writing as eros is too overpowering and, like rabies, it is incurable" (100). Paradoxically, this death by love actually erases the confused symptoms of rabies, madness or possession from Sierva María's body: her radiant eyes and skin suggest bliss as we never see her experience before, recovery and rebirth. Chronologically, after this death by love she will reappear by the high altar (2), in the territory of the sacred.

Metaphors (including bodily metaphors) that become literal appear in García Márquez's fiction. In this case, whether we take *dead of love* at face value or not, the way the novel ends concretizes the demand for the reader to elucidate her hermeneutical situation, that is, "the situation in which we find ourselves with regard to the tradition that we are trying to understand" (Gadamer 301–2). Although for Gadamer the task of shedding light on our own situation can never be fully completed (because being *in* a situation means that we cannot step outside it and see it objectively), "working out the hermeneutical situation means acquiring the right horizon of inquiry for the questions evoked by the encounter with tradition" (302). Through its profuse use of conflicting perspectives and its reliance on ambiguity; through the multiplicity of traditions that it evokes; and through its cautionary tale of characters blinded by a narrow interpretive horizon, the novel presents the reader with this type of interpellation.

An earlier version of this essay was originally published in the Modern Language Review 108.1 (2013): 162–179. I am grateful to the editors for permission to reprint it, and to Timothy Chesters, Arantza Mayo, Robin Fiddian and Christopher Pownall for their valuable feedback on the original version.

NOTES

1. Plutarch (*Amatorius*, 757 A) is quoting from a lost play of Sophocles (fragment 941): "It is hell, an incurable force, an insane madness."
2. René Girard's theorization of the plague in Western literature is useful to approach García Márquez's treatment of the topic; his fascination with some of the texts considered by Girard (136–154) is widely acknowledged.
3. Although he does not treat the themes of illness or the body, Julio Ortega has argued that, in *Of Love*, everything is subject to interpretation, highlighting Sierva María's status as a hybrid and ambiguous sign (12–13).
4. See, inter alia, Conrado Zuloaga, Isabel Rodríguez-Vergara, and Margaret M. Olsen.
5. All quotations in English are taken from the published translation and indicated in brackets in the text. "[C]iertos signos de retraso mental" (García Márquez, *Del amor y otros demonios* 45).
6. "Baldada por el reumatismo" (*Del amor* 34).
7. In the Middle Ages, "the 'denunciation' of the leper, his 'separation' or 'putting out of the world', was carried out according to strange rituals in which the Church played a major role and which always symbolized death" (Herzlich and Pierret 5).
8. "'Estamos amenazados por una peste de mal de rabia,' dijo Sagunta, 'y yo soy la única que tengo las llaves de San Huberto, patrono de los cazadores y sanador de los arrabiados.' 'No veo el porqué de una peste,' dijo el marqués. 'No hay anuncios de cometas ni eclipses, que yo sepa, ni tenemos culpas tan grandes como para que Dios se ocupe de nosotros'" (*Del amor* 23–24).
9. The devotion to Saint Hubert, "most known because he was 'patron of the hunters' and protector against rabies" dates from the eighth century, according to George M. Baer (2).
10. "'Digan lo que digan los médicos,' dijo, 'la rabia en los humanos suele ser una de las tantas artimañas del Enemigo'" (*Del amor* 60).
11. "Un médico joven de Salamanca le abrió a Sierva María la herida sellada y le puso unas cataplasmas cáusticas para extraer los humores rancios. Otro intentó lo mismo con sanguijuelas en la espalda. [...] Al cabo de dos semanas había soportado

dos baños de hierbas y dos lavativas emolientes por día, y la habían llevado al borde de la agonía con pócimas de estibio natural y otros filtros mortales. [...] Sierva María se sentía morir. [...] Había pasado por todo: vértigos, convulsiones, espasmos, delirios, solturas de vientre y de vejiga, y se revolcaba por los suelos aullando de dolor y de furia. Hasta los curanderos más audaces la abandonaron a su suerte, convencidos de que estaba loca, o poseída por los demonios" (*Del amor* 62–63).

12. "Fue en la última celda de ese rincón de olvido donde encerraron a Sierva María, a los noventa y tres días de ser mordida por el perro y sin ningún síntoma de la rabia" (*Del amor* 77).

13. "Éstos confirmaron que no tenía ningún síntoma de la rabia, y coincidieron con Abrenuncio en que ya no era posible que la contrajera. Sin embargo, nadie se creyó autorizado para dudar de que estuviera poseída por el demonio" (*Del amor* 115–116).

14. These two symptoms of possession are mentioned by Adrian Schober (25).

15. "En el pabellón de los furiosos continuos, amarrado a un poste, estaba el arrabiado" (*Del amor* 26).

16. "Dio ejemplos lamentables de cómo se la había confundido desde siempre con la posesión demoníaca, igual que ciertas formas de locura y otros trastornos del espíritu" (*Del amor* 133).

17. "'Es un secreto a gritos que tu pobre niña rueda por los suelos presa de convulsiones obscenas y ladrando en jerga de idólatras. ¿No son síntomas inequívocos de una posesión demoníaca?'" (*Del amor* 68). The choice of the word *ladrando*—barking, just like the previously quoted *aullando* [howling]—is highly significant, and its repercusiones are discussed later in this essay.

18. "'[C]reo que lo que nos parece demoníaco son las costumbres de los negros, que la niña ha aprendido por el abandono en que la tuvieron sus padres'" (*Del amor* 107–108).

19. Referring to "the child as Other" as a leitmotiv in the genre of horror film, Andrew Scahill cites Robin Wood's suggestion that "children are one of many oppressed groups that bring the eruption of chaos into a tenuous space of social order" (39).

20. This has been noted also by Rodríguez-Vergara [para. 3 and passim].

21. "Entonces Delaura asistió al espectáculo pavoroso de una verdadera energúmena. La cabellera de Sierva María se encrespó con vida propia como las serpientes de la Medusa, y de la boca salió una baba verde y un sartal de improperios en lenguas de idólatras"; "[e]l segundo día se sintió un bramido inmenso de ganados embravecidos, la tierra tembló, y ya no fue posible pensar que Sierva María no estuviera a merced de todos los demonios del averno" (*Del amor* 136, 169). There is no space here to comment in detail on the numerous passages where possession is dismissed —for instance when Sierva María's pretended communication with demons is treated as "deception" on her part (74, 130)—"picardías" in Spanish (*Del amor* 84, 140)—in contrast to those others where it is more ambiguously suggested.

22. Significantly, early modern European witches are referred to as servants of Satan. See Joseph Klaits (1985).

23. This changes gradually as the narrative progresses: Sierva María's subjectivity is rendered more directly after she falls in love with Cayetano.

24. "La niña se mostraba como era. Bailaba con más gracia y más brío que los africanos de nación, cantaba con voces distintas de la suya en las diversas lenguas de África, o con voces de pájaros y animales, que los desconcertaban a ellos mismos. Por orden de Dominga de Adviento las esclavas más jóvenes le pintaban la cara con negro de humo, le colgaron collares de santería sobre el escapulario del bautismo y le cuidaban la cabellera que nunca le cortaron [...]. Del padre, en cambio, tenía el cuerpo escuálido, la timidez irredimible, la piel lívida, los ojos de un azul taciturno, y el cobre puro de la cabellera radiante. Su modo de ser era tan sigiloso que parecía una criatura invisible. Asustada con tan extraña condición, la madre le colgaba un cencerro en el puño para no perder su rumbo en la penumbra de la casa" (*Del amor* 20–21).

25. "[Bernarda] vivía con el alma en un hilo desde que creyó descubrir en la hija una cierta condición fantasmal. Temblaba sólo de pensar en el instante en que miraba hacia atrás y se encontraba con los ojos inescrutables de la criatura lánguida [...]. '¡Niña!', le gritaba, '¡te prohíbo que me mires así!'. Cuando más concentrada estaba en sus negocios, sentía en la nuca el aliento sibilante de serpiente en acecho, y daba un salto de pavor" (*Del amor* 56).

26. Bernarda's anxiety is one among many elements reminiscent of Nathaniel Hawthorne's *The Scarlet Letter* (1850) in García Márquez's novel. Bernarda's feelings are comparable to Hester's puzzlement at Pearl's way of looking at her, as discussed by Adrian Schober (48).

27. "Un perro cenizo con un lucero en la frente irrumpió en los vericuetos del mercado el primer domingo de diciembre, revolcó mesas de fritangas, desbarató tenderetes de indios y toldos de lotería, y de paso mordió a cuatro personas que se le atravesaron en el camino" (*Del amor* 15–16); "[t]erminaron por llevarla a la fuerza, pataleando y tirando al aire dentelladas de perro [...]. Sierva María [...] se subió a la mesa, corrió de un extremo a otro gritando como una poseída verdadera en zafarrancho de abordaje. Rompió cuanto encontró a su paso, saltó por la ventana y desbarató las pérgolas del patio, alborotó las colmenas y las cercas de los corrales. Las abejas se dispersaron y los animales en estampida irrumpieron aullando de pánico hasta en los dormitorios de la clausura" (*Del amor* 81–83).

28. Towards the end of the novel, a second dead rabid dog is mentioned in the same area of town where Sierva María was bitten, around the barrio of Getsemaní (145). The circularity and dissonance could be read as an anticipation of Sierva María's forthcoming death (169). The smell of roses is striking; it precedes more directly the death of Father Tomás de Aquino and could again be suggested as a signifier for sanctity.

29. "Entonces [Sierva María] miró a Delaura por primera vez, lo pesó, lo midió y se le fue encima con un salto certero de animal de presa. [...] 'Me mordió una perrita rabiosa con una cola de más de un metro', dijo Delaura'. Sierva María quiso ver la herida. Delaura se quitó la venda, y ella tocó apenas con el índice el halo solferino de la inflamación, como si fuera una brasa, y se rió por primera vez. 'Soy más mala que la peste', dijo. Delaura no le contestó con los Evangelios sino con Garcilaso: '*Bien puedes hacer esto con quien pueda sufrirlo*'" (*Del amor* 100–102).

30. Palencia-Roth also interprets the dog's bite as a symbol of the awakening of erotic passion (para. 17).

31. See Summers (39). Moreover, melancholia itself could have also been perceived as being of diabolic origin (Radden 104).

32. After Ficino, the wound would refer to "an internal wound of the heart caused by the blood-borne 'infection' passing through the lover's eyes" (Wells 282, note 24). The specific bodily location of Cayetano and Sierva's wounds is also evocative of stigmata.

33. "lágrimas de aceite hirviente que le abrasaron las entrañas" (*Del amor* 136); "zozobra del corazón" (*Del amor* 146).

34. "'Ahora cierro los ojos y veo una cabellera como un río de oro'" (*Del amor* 144).

35. "Me hubiera imaginado cualquier cosa de usted, menos estos extremos de demencia" (*Del amor* 166). Space prohibits fuller discussion of the transformation suffered by Cayetano. It is interesting to note that his first name might be an allusion to the theologian, philosopher and exegete Tommaso de Vio Gaetani, known as Cajetan (1469–1534).

36. "La guardiana que entró a prepararla para la sexta sesión de exorcismos la encontró *muerta de amor* en la cama con los ojos radiantes y la piel de recién nacida. Los troncos de los cabellos brotaban como burbujas en el cráneo rapado, y se les veía crecer" (*Del amor* 169, emphasis added).

37. We are told that, in her despair, Sierva María had stopped eating (160). This behavior would correspond to the early modern medical conceptions of lovesickness, which stress that if left untreated, this disease could "degenerate into mania, marasmus and death by suicide" (Duffin 55).

38. "*Por vos nací, por vos tengo la vida, por vos he de morir, y por vos muero*" (*Del amor* 103).

WORKS CITED

Alcoff, Linda Martín. *Visible Identities: Race, Gender and the Self*. New York: Oxford UP, 2006. Print.

Baer, George M. "The History of Rabies." Cf. Jackson and Wunner. 1–22.

Burton, Robert. *The Anatomy of Melancholy*. Ed. Thomas C. Faulkner et al. 3 Vols. Oxford: Clarendon P, 1989–1994. Print.

Doane, Mary Anne. *The Desire to Desire: The Woman's Film of the 1940s*. Bloomington: Indiana UP, 1987. Print.

Duffin, Jacalyn. *Lovers and Livers. Disease Concepts in History*. Toronto: U of Toronto P, 2005. Print.

Gadamer, Hans-Georg. *Truth and Method*. Trans. Joel Weinsheimer and Donald G. Marshall. 2nd rev. ed. London: Sheed & Ward, 1989. Print.

García Márquez, Gabriel. *Del amor y otros demonios*. Barcelona: Random House Mondadori, 2009. Print.

———. *Of Love and Other Demons*. Trans. Edith Grossman. London: Penguin, 1995. Print.

Gilman, Sander. *Difference and Pathology: Stereotypes of Sexuality, Race, and Madness*. Ithaca: Cornell UP, 1985. Print.

———. *Disease and Representation. Images of Illness from Madness to AIDS*. Ithaca: Cornell UP, 1988. Print.
Girard, René. "The Plague in Literature and Myth." *'To double business bound': Essays on Literature, Mimesis, and Anthropology*. London: Athlone, 1998. 136–154. Print.
González, Aníbal. *Love and Politics in the Contemporary Spanish American Novel*. Austin: U of Texas P, 2010. Print.
Herzlich, Claudine and Janine Pierret. *Illness and Self in Society*. Trans. Elborg Forster. Baltimore and London: Johns Hopkins UP, 1987. Print.
Jackson, Alan C and William H. Wunner. *Rabies*. 2nd ed. London: Elsevier-Academic Press, 2007. Print.
Klaits, Joseph. *Servants of Satan: The Age of the Witch Hunts*. Bloomington: Indiana UP, 1985. Print.
Kline, Carmenza, comp. *Apuntes sobre literatura colombiana*. Web. 29 January 2016.
Nicolotti, Andrea. "A Cure for Rabies or a Remedy for Concupiscence? A Baptism of the Elchasaites." *Journal of Early Christian Studies* 16.4 (2008): 513–534. Web. 29 January 2016.
Olsen, Margaret M. "La patología de la africanía en *Del amor y otros demonios* de García Márquez." *Revista Iberoamericana* 68.201 (2002): 1067–1080. Web. 29 January 2016.
Ortega, Julio. "García Márquez posmoderno o el relativismo de la verdad." *Ínsula* 723 (2007): 12–15. Print.
Palencia-Roth, Michael. "Del amor y otros demonios: tragedia inquisitorial, beatificación Africana." Cf. Kline. Web. 29 January 2016.
Radden, Jennifer, ed. *The Nature of Melancholy: From Aristotle to Kristeva*. New York: Oxford UP, 2000.
Rodríguez-Vergara, Isabel. "*Del amor y otros demonios*: incinerando la colonia." Kline. Web. 29 January 2016.
Scahill, Andrew. "Demons are a Girl's Best Friend: Queering the Revolting Child in *The Exorcist*." *Red Feather Journal* 1 (2010): 39–55. Web. 31 January 2016.
Schober, Adrian. *Possessed Child Narratives in Literature and Film*. New York: Palgrave MacMillan, 2004. Print.
Summers, Montague. *The Werewolf*. London: K. Paul, Trench, Trubiner, 1933. Print.
Wells, Marion A. *The Secret Wound. Love-Melancholy and Early Modern Romance*. Stanford: Stanford UP, 2007. Print.
Wilkinson, Lise. "Understanding the Nature of Rabies: A Historical Perspective." *Rabies*. Ed. J.B. Campbell and K.M Charlton. Boston: Kluwer, 1988. 1–23. Print.
Wunner, William H. "Rabies Virus." Cf. Jackson and Wunner. 23–68.
Zuloaga, Conrado. "*Del amor y otros demonios*, incluido el amor." Cf. Kline. Web. 29 January 2016.

Chapter 13

Translation, Unreliable Narrators, and the Comical Use of (Pseudo-)Magical Realism in *Of Love and Other Demons*

Ignacio López-Calvo

Most critics who have theorized magical realism, including Wendy Faris, Maggie Ann Bowers, Lois Parkinson Zamora, Alberto Moreiras and Erik Camayd-Freixas, have disregarded, for the most part, its potential for the creation of comedy and humor. Regarding Gabriel García Márquez's original use of magical realism in *Del amor y otros demonios* (1994; trans. *Of Love and Other Demons*) specifically, only a few of his critics have paid fleeting attention to the function of comedy or even the comic tone of his novel, perhaps because, as will be seen, many of the virtually untranslatable puns and jokes are lost in Edith Grossman's translation. Among these few, Gene Bell-Villada mentions: "An unusually serious and tragic work, it nonetheless offers many smiling specimens of the author's signature irony and humor, notably in the exaggerated portraits of its less-lovable characters" (257). Yet, in my view, García Márquez—and this novel in particular—has not received the praise he deserves for his key contribution to Spanish-language humorous fiction. In fact, in most cases *Of Love* has not even perceived as a comedy at all, presumably because of the tragic end to the love story and to the life of the first neglected and then abused child. From this perspective, while Bell-Villada describes this work as one of García Márquez's saddest and most beautiful novels (*García Márquez: The Man...* 258), as well as "among the Colombian author's most masterfully conceived and constructed works" ("Gabriel García Márquez: life" 20), in the following paragraphs I shall maintain that it is perhaps the funniest. After all, the love story per se only occupies a few pages toward the end of the novel and, as Raymond L. Williams points out, it is "not the central focus of the entire novel ... The main focus is on a young girl" (131).

Following in the footsteps of an impressive tradition of literary comedy by Spanish masters, including the authors of picaresque novels, as well as Fernando de Rojas, Miguel de Cervantes, and Francisco de Quevedo, numerous Latin American writers have also practiced different humorous styles. Paul McAleer identifies the beginnings of humorous writing in Latin America "in the lampooning genre of journalistic editorials of the nineteenth century, which developed into the short satirical portraits and novels of the *costumbrismo* tradition" (McAleer 1). One could go as far back as Joaquín Fernández de Lizardi's satirical novel *El Periquillo Sarniento*, first published in 1816. Among contemporary writers, McAleer lists Miguel Ángel Asturias, Enrique Araya, Genaro Prieto, Macedonio Fernández, Leopoldo Marechal, Jorge Luis Borges, Gabriel García Márquez, Ernesto Sábato, Mario Vargas Llosa, Alejo Carpentier, Guillermo Cabrera Infante, Julio Cortázar, José Donoso, Antonio Skármeta, Alfredo Bryce Echenique, and Jaime Bayly (McAleer 1). One could easily add to this list Rosario Castellanos, Ana Lydia Vega, Griselda Gámbaro, Luisa Valenzuela, Rosario Ferré, Roberto Bolaño, and Fernando Iwasaki, among many others. At any rate, in my view, García Márquez is among the brightest stars in Hispanic comedic writing.

In this essay, I argue that the Colombian author's use of both true magical realism and what I call pseudo-magical realism (the case when an unreliable narrator presents a case of apparent magical realism only to unmask it later as mere ignorance, superstition, or fanaticism) should not be separated from his talent to elicit laughter from his readers, a facet of magical realism that critics tend to ignore. I likewise contend that he resorts to both magical realism and pseudo-magical realism as sources of dramatic relief in what would otherwise be just the sad story of an innocent girl neglected by her roguish and resentful parents, possibly taken advantage of by an exorcist, and brutalized to death by a fanatically blind Inquisition. With this goal in mind, I explore the motivations for choosing the comedic genre and its implications, as well as a potential allegorical message in relation to national and/or regional cultural identity.

The novel's occasional incongruity and lack of verisimilitude, together with a flowery and atavistic language that is sometimes reminiscent of the chronicles of the Spanish conquest of the Americas or of tales of chivalry (tellingly, the physician owns a copy of the novel of chivalry *Amadís de Gaula*), may bring to mind—like other works by García Márquez—the usual criticism about an alienating exoticism that tropicalizes Latin America and its cultures. On the other hand, Rudyard J. Alcocer contends that the mixed reviews received by *Of Love* respond to its problematical relationship with the magical realist style. According to him, instead of creating a "coherent" magical realist world, in this (in his opinion) flawed novel, García Márquez limits himself to isolated instances of the style that end up seeming forced and misplaced:

> For a narrative of this genre to be successful (in terms of Khair's internal coherence but also, perhaps, in terms of critical reception and sales), it has to be fully committed to the genre, that is, to the development of an internally coherent magical realist world. Similarly, an effective magical realist text probably needs a critical mass of magical realist occurrences for the illusion of internal coherence to be attained. The case of *Of Love and Other Demons* may suggest that even in a shorter novel, more than just a couple of magical realist events are necessary to keep these events from seeming random and unnecessary. (80)

In other words, García Márquez's incorporation of magical realist techniques in this type of novel is problematical according to this critic.

While I see the merit in Alcocer's assessment of García Márquez's use of magical realism in *Of Love*, I argue that magical realism and its latter-day offshoot, pseudo-magical realism, which is much more commonly used in this novel, do work as comic relief and as a tool for corrective comedy, even if it hurts the story's verisimilitude. In other words, for the most part the use of these literary modes in *Of Love* is quite different from the ones seen in more totalizing or ambitious novels, such as *Cien años de soledad* (*One Hundred Years of Solitude*) or what, is in my view, García Márquez's crowning achievement, *El otoño del patriarca* (*The Autumn of the Patriarch*). While still challenging—and more than ever before—the Eurocentric gaze and rationalist worldviews through the incorporation of alternative non-Western subjectivities (the African and indigenous ways of being in the world), here (pseudo-)magical realism often becomes a more humble tool for mockery of intolerance, ignorant superstition and religious fanaticism, as well as for the creation of exuberant and transgressive comedy, a literary genre that is not always well received by critics. Along these lines, the archaic language in the novel, besides re-creating the world of eighteenth-century Cartagena de Indias, is often used as another tool for humor and mockery.

Therefore, I conceive of *Of Love* as a novel in which, twelve years after being awarded the Nobel Prize for literature, the world-renowned author of *One Hundred Years of Solitude* decides that he can afford writing a fun and humorous novel without the totalizing scope or trailblazing ambitions of his masterpieces. Already in the 1980s, the Colombian author began to distance himself from magical realism, as critics' respect for this literary mode was beginning to dwindle and more readers began to see it as a tired and commodified cliché or market strategy. Indeed, perhaps by this time tired of being labeled as a magical realist and disappointed with the path taken by his epigones, throughout the plot of *Of Love*, García Márquez toys with his readers, challenging them to discern in which passages he is truly resorting to his famous brand of magical realism and in which ones he is just mocking ignorant superstition or religious fanaticism through pseudo-magical realism. He creates this confusion through an unreliable narrator that initially seems to be presenting an instance of the magical realism García Márquez popularized worldwide, only to end up clarifying, later in the plot, that what readers are witnessing are the outcomes of ignorant superstition, unfounded rumors, and religious fanaticism. Fernando Reati coincides with his assessment of *Of Love* as a novel in which the Colombian master is trying to separate himself from newer tropicalizing literary trends:

> Aware that the magical realism of the sixties and seventies has become a caricature of the continent, and that some of its more recent manifestations–certain novels by Isabel Allende and Laura Esquivel, for example–contribute to the fossilization of a stereotyped image and *for export* of the continent, the author labors now to dismantle what Adriana Bergero terms the "holiday or tourist aesthetic of Latin America" practiced by some proponents of magical realism. (91; qtd Alcocer 73)[1]

Yet, to deepen the confusion even further, in a few passages the *trompe-l'oeil* works the other way around: something that is initially denounced as ignorant superstition ends up being reframed as a strange reality in the literary mode of traditional magical realism. Thus, whereas at one point father Cayetano Delaura, the seemingly progressive exorcist who is examining the protagonist, Sierva María de Todos los Ángeles, assesses that rather than being possessed by demons, she is only terrorized by credulous nuns in the convent, he later comes to the conclusion that the girl is indeed possessed by a demon when he sees her hair come to life like Medusa while she yells in other languages. This confusing and ambiguously magical atmosphere is enhanced by a preliminary note to the novel where the author explains how his grandmother would tell him, as a child, about the legend of a marquise's twelve-year-old daughter with extremely long hair, who had died of rabies and been venerated in several Caribbean towns. When her cadaver was unearthed, García Márquez explains in the note, her hair was more than twenty-two meters long.

As stated, with only two or three exceptions, in all the other instances the Colombian author makes the reader of *Of Love* speculate with possible cases of magical realism or of supernatural, otherworldly events, only to end up unveiling them as mere rumors, tricks, or jokes by the characters. For instance, from the beginning we learn that Sierva María, the only daughter of Don Ygnacio de Alfaro y Dueñas, the second Marquis de Casualdero, is able to speak three African languages and believes in Yoruba orishas simply because she was raised by African slaves after being rejected by her parents. It is even suggested that it was an African remedy that prevented her from getting rabies, even though she was bitten by the same rabid dog that killed four slaves. Yet the reasons the protagonist sings in voices different from her own or emulates the sounds of animals, satanic ghosts, and the dead are at best unclear. Some readers could interpret these scenes as instances of Santería trance-possession, in which, once the girl enters a state of altered consciousness, an Orisha "mounts" (possesses) her body and speaks through her. However, according to the narrator, Sierva María's voices and sounds would shock the slaves themselves. Surprisingly, Edith Grossman left the phrase in the original Spanish version ("que los desconcertaban a ellos mismos" [19–20]) untranslated in the English version. Later, however, the narrator reveals these seemingly otherworldly voices and sounds as mere mischievousness through which the girl is trying to scare the nuns.

Likewise, in another potentially metaphysical scene, we learn that Sierva María seemed invisible when she walks in such a stealthy manner that her mother Bernarda has to hang a bell around the girl's neck in order to be able to locate her in the house. The narrator later clarifies, however, that she had *learned* (it is, therefore, another of her mischievous tricks) to walk by people without being seen as if she were incorporeal. Whereas at this point, we are only told that she *seemed* invisible, the exorcist Delaura later affirms the girl had made herself invisible only to the Abbess's eyes. But again, this could also be understood as another case in which the girl uses her slyness to avoid unpleasant situations or punishment.

Other passages, however, seem closer to the type of magical realism that García Márquez popularized in some of his previous works. We learn, for example, that Sierva María's radiant red hair grows so rapidly that it could have impaired her walking had it not been for the slaves braiding her hair every day. This miraculous hair growth continues after her death, as one can see it grow rapidly from her shaved head. As Bell-Villada explains, this type of post-mortem hair growth is "medically impossible" (254). A last example of magical realism in which there is no attempt at verisimilitude or logical explanation by the author takes place when origami birds fall from the sky while the marquis, Sierva María's father, is returning from the cemetery: "he was surprised by a storm of little paper birds falling like snow on the orange trees in the orchard. He caught one of them, unfolded it, and read: That lightning bolt was mine" (38).[2]

By contrast, there are strange phenomena taking place that are not clear-cut cases of magical realism, such as the devilish, rabid monkeys that attack animals in town and people in the cathedral; or a black man, Judas Iscariote, who fights a bull with no weapons or protection. In this same category, a servant named Dominga de Adviento dies without finding out why corridors were cleaner in the morning than before she went to bed or why objects moved around at night. Other strange or unexplained occurrences attributed to Sierva María's possession seem to be mere superstition or rumors: according to some nuns, a pig has spoken, bees and enraged cattle escape, and hens fly away to the sea.[3] They also claim that she flies with transparent wings and blame her for earth tremors, pigs being poisoned, and water causing prophetic visions. And Sierva María is not the only object of strange rumors: the Jewish Portuguese physician, Abrenuncio, is said to have resurrected a dead tailor. In the same ambivalently magical category, Cayetano dreams of Sierva María looking at the winter in Salamanca before meeting her, and Sierva María has the same dream, even though she has never visited Salamanca.

In a passage reminiscent of the magical realism in *One Hundred Years of Solitude* (perhaps an ironic wink to his long-time readers), the Jewish physician, Abrenuncio de Sa Pereira Cao, assures the marquis (who hopes that this doctor can cure his daughter) that his horse is one hundred years old; later, however, the marquis admits that it was just a private joke. Among other suspicious events in the novel, a nun falls down the stairs and breaks her skull right after trying to take Sierva María's African necklaces away from her. A possible explanation to some of these events and phenomena could be that, as the exorcist Delaura explains, the clerics confuse Sierva María's African worldview, behavior, and customs with devilish possession. Indeed, along with African bodies of knowledge, the novel includes indigenous ones that also contest Eurocentric rationalism, such as that of an indigenous woman called Sagunta, who is said to perform abortions and restore virginity, and who claims to be the only one with the healing powers to combat the rabies plague. At one point, Sagunta tries to heal (the perfectly healthy) Sierva María by spreading ointment onto her own naked body and then rubbing their two bodies together.

But aside from all of its possible literary merits or flaws, *Of Love* is an entertaining and funny novel (funnier in the original Spanish than in the English translation) that often uses corrective humor and satire to mock ignorant superstition or the sordid fanaticism of the omnipotent Catholic Church at the time. Some of these superstitions provoke hilarity throughout the plot. For instance, Sierva María's father, a symbol of a decrepit *criollo* aristocracy, believes that there could not possibly be a plague in town because there had been no sightings of comets or eclipses. He also boasts publicly: "En mi casa se hace lo que yo obedezco" (36), a funny contradiction that is unfortunately lost in Grossman's translation: "In my house I do not say, I obey" (25).[4] Similarly, his proud conclusion after retelling the numerous lies that his daughter constantly says is that "Perhaps she will be a poet" (31).[5] And when the servant Dominga de Adviento concludes that the newborn Sierva María is going to be a saint because she cries after hearing her promise to her saints (that, if the girl survives, she will not get her hair cut until her wedding), the marquis disagrees, stating that she will be a prostitute, provided that she survives. Along these lines, when Abrenuncio tells the marquis that his hated wife will be dead by September 15, the latter's only reaction is to lament that there is so much time left until that day.

The physician, Abrenuncio de Sa Pereira Cao, who is comically described as "Identical to the king of clubs" (18)[6] and wants to bury his horse in a cemetery, is also a funny character. As an enlightened intellectual who reads Voltaire in Latin, he represents the voice of the new reason against the anachronistic blindness of the Church. Yet the unorthodox and eccentric ways in which he makes medical diagnoses for his patients often elicit laughter. For instance, perhaps in mockery of some of the outrageous medical beliefs at the time, Abrenuncio claims that Sierva María's very heart, which he describes as a little caged frog, has told him that she is aware that the dog that had bit her was rabid. Later, he claims to know that the marquis's wife has a liver disease because she is complaining with her mouth open.

There are also plenty of sexual and scatological humorous scenes, most of them dealing with Sierva María's mother, the *mestiza* Bernarda Cabrera, who is comically described as a sort of nymphomaniac "with a hunger in her womb that could have satisfied an entire barracks" (8).[7] The hyperbolic tone assumed by the narrator in describing the grotesque and carnivalesque ways whereby Bernarda tries to retain her lover Judas Iscariote through the use of costumes, or the scene in which she jumps onto the marquis's hammock and sexually assaults him, all add to the irreverent humor that pervades the novel: "The madwomen encouraged them from the terraces with indecent songs, and celebrated their triumphs with stadium ovations" (41).[8] Still challenging accepted societal norms, another source of comedy is the vulgarity of Bernarda Cabrera's coarse vocabulary, which transgresses dominant codes and values: "And no woman, white or black, is worth one hundred twenty pounds of gold, unless she shits diamonds" (9).[9] Even the mean, disparaging remarks she makes about her own daughter, Sierva María, are quite comical: "Not a bad little business: You could breed American-born marquises with chicken feet and sell them to the circus" (26).[10] Like Bernarda, the black servant Dominga de Adviento elicits laughter through her unrefined colloquial expressions: "Dominga de Adviento lo dijo mejor: 'El culo no le cabía en el cuerpo'" (62), which is translated by Edith Grossman as: "Dominga de Adviento said it best: 'Her ass was too big for her body'" (44).

But perhaps the funniest voice in the novel is that of the narrator. For instance, he assesses that the marquis is acting "with all the clumsiness of a borrowed father" (58)[11] when, following years of utter neglect, he attempts to help and care for his daughter. Earlier on, in a dialogue in which the marquis confesses that he does not know Latin, the narrator ironically explains Abrenuncio's reaction in the following way: "'There is no reason you should!' said Abrenuncio. And he said it in Latin, of course" (20).[12] Similarly, when the marquis is trying to steer his daughter Sierva María away from African culture (the conflict of identities is emblematized by the fact that she even gives herself an African-sounding name, María Mandinga), the narrator states that he "Trató de enseñarla a ser blanca de ley" (66), making a pun with the expression "oro de ley" (fine gold). Once again, because it is so difficult to translate such jokes, the humor is unfortunately lost in Edith Grossman's English-language version: "He tried to teach her to be a real white" (47). These passages prove that sarcastic and grotesque humor, which elicits laughter through comical exaggerations and scatological transgressions to society's accepted norms, is central to García Márquez's recreation of the colonial world in Latin America (and particularly in eighteenth-century Cartagena) in this work, making it one of his funniest. This approach, however, does not prevent the author from including a parody of Eurocentrism as well as some harsh criticism of the colonial Catholic Church, two aspects of coloniality (to use Aníbal Quijano's term) that are still relevant in contemporary Latin America. This use of subversive humor to denounce historical abuses and to mock anachronistic beliefs fits right in with the traditionally corrosive attributes of comic literature in Latin America that have been pointed out by numerous critics.

One of the main vehicles for this anti-clerical criticism is the Jewish physician Abrenuncio, who sarcastically describes the port city of Cartagena de Indias, in what used to be Nueva Granada and is now a Caribbean city in Colombia, as "an outpost of the world intimidated by the Holy Office" (47).[13] He suspects that Sierva María may not have been infected with rabies, criticizes the marquis's decision to bury his own daughter alive in a cloister convent, and even questions openly (thus risking his own life) the credibility of exorcisms and autos da fe. On the other side of the spectrum, we have the bishop of Cartagena, don Toribio de Cáceres y Virtudes, who is convinced that Sierva María's body is condemned by demonic possession, but that her soul can still be saved through exorcism. The bishop mistrusts the enlightened Abrenuncio for several reasons: the latter is said to have resurrected a tailor, was once persecuted by the Inquisition, and his Portuguese surname, Cao (*cão*), means "dog" at a time when there is a rabies epidemic in town. The ridiculed bishop also disapproves of the physician's libertine, Enlightenment readings and suspects that he may be a pederast when, in fact, the real pederast (at least by today's standards) turns out to be the priest sent by the bishop himself to exorcize Sierva María. But the bishop's most disgraceful acts are his orders to have the innocent girl exorcized several times and then interned—ninety-three days after her being bitten on her ankle by a rabid dog and with no real symptoms of having rabies—in the convent of Santa Clara, where she dies shortly afterward. To make his image even more despicable, García Márquez depicts the overweight bishop arriving at the first exorcism in rich ceremonial garments and being carried by four slaves.

A more enlightened and tolerant voice from the Church is the thirty-six-year-old exorcist Cayetano Delaura, who is unfairly rumored to be the bishop's son or lover. Initially, Delaura tries to convince the bishop that Sierva María is not possessed; he argues, instead, that the rancorous and narrow-minded abbess, Josefa Miranda, is the one with psychological problems.[14] Although Delaura may be perceived by contemporary readers as a lecherous pervert who feels pleasure when the pre-adolescent Sierva María bites and scratches him, García Márquez, in the spirit of the novel, does not describe the priest in a negative light: turning the male nightmare of the possessed witch into the male fantasy of the (very) young lover, Cayetano falls madly in love with the thirteen-year-old girl and looks forward to marrying her. Eventually she reciprocates and looks forward to his secretive, nocturnal visits to her convent cell. Even though he is not described with an accusatory tone as a pederast in the novel, Delaura ultimately takes advantage, as an exorcist, of a thirteen-year-old whom he finds in the malodorous convent cell, she laying on a stone bed without a mattress and with her hands and feet tied. Yet they never consummate their relationship, limiting themselves instead to kissing and hugging each other, between literacy lessons and declamations of Garcilaso de la Vega's love poetry. Delaura even dreams about escaping with her and marrying her one day. Again playing with a possible instance of magical realism, one night the guardian enters Sierva María's cell yet never sees the exorcist there. Tellingly, Delaura jokes about the purported invisibility of his beloved Sierva María: "'Lucifer is quite a villain,' he mocked when he could breathe again. 'He has made me invisible too'" (126).[15] When their secret romance is discovered, Sierva María is locked away in a cell and Delaura is never allowed to meet with her again. After confessing his love for the marquis's daughter, the exorcist-priest is condemned by the Inquisition as a heretic, although he is later allowed to work at a leper hospital. In the end, Sierva María goes on a three-day hunger strike, before "dying of love" in her cell.

To return to the function of comedy in this novel, McAleer argues broadly that "there is an intrinsic relationship between all comic expressions, including generic ones, and the very human desire to affirm one's identity, both individual and social. Whether transgressive or prescriptive, comic laughter always relies on the pre-existence and internalisation of social norms and rules. Consequently it is deeply related to articulations of individual, social and cultural narratives of identity" (4). Indeed, García Márquez's satirizing of colonial Latin American society, with all the different brands of intolerance, superstition, and closemindedness that an ideal reader can still partially recognize in today's society, can be framed within McAleer's parameters for narratives of identity affirmation and social reconciliation. García Márquez's focus on such aspects as the African and indigenous cultures in the Caribbean region of Colombia, the history of black slavery, class antagonisms, the degeneration of Criollo aristocracy and the presence of the omnipotent Church, serves to highlight key ingredients in the Colombian national identity of yesterday and today. And it is precisely the use of a corrosive humor in all these social critiques that prevents the novel from appearing too moralizing or sententious.

McAleer also maintains that "from the very beginning of its inception into prose, comedy has been fascinated with the bawdy and exuberant tale of youthful progression and maturation" (14). *Of Love* also corroborates that assertion through the character of Sierva María, who chooses to become the Africanized María Mandinga and never gives up her agency, in spite of Criollo society's absurd association of African languages, dances, and culture in general with the realm of the demonic. Since the action takes place over little more than three months, the novel is not a *Bildungsroman*. Yet the individual struggle of this indomitable girl to affirm her own adopted African identity against the Eurocentric impositions of both her father and the Church, ultimately functions as an allegory of Colombian and Latin American identity struggles. The lack of a happy ending and the failure of her romantic relationship with a member of the antagonistic Church signals the end of a potential utopian impulse and points to a pessimistic, allegorical view of social reconciliation in a dystopian country. The only character who truly understands Sierva María's rejection of Eurocentrism and Catholic dogma from the outset is Abrenuncio, who is an outsider himself on account of his Portuguese nationality and Jewish background. The physician, who feels the oppression of being a desired target of the Holy Office, is also the only one who suspects, from the beginning, that there is nothing wrong—either physically or mentally—with the girl.

In conclusion, because of the difficulty of translating Spanish-language jokes and puns into English, the novel is not as funny in translation as it is in the original version. Still, *Of Love* is, in my opinion, a comedy, one of the funniest texts by García Márquez, if not the funniest, even if there is a short, tragic, unfulfilled love story toward the end of the plot and an innocent girl is unfairly punished by the absurdity of religious fanaticism. The comedy itself, together with the evolution of most of the potentially magical-realist scenes into what I call pseudo-magical realism, are plausible devices to mock his latter-day epigones' commercial use of magical realism. More so than in any of his previous novels, *Of Love* challenges Eurocentric rationalism and positivism from the post-colonial Latin American periphery through the incorporation of subaltern and racialized African and indigenous thought systems. It also engages in an identity quest that problematizes—and ultimately rejects—the European modernity historically imposed in both Colombia and Latin America. As a result, the novel announces the essence of a future Colombian national identity that is the final outcome of transculturation: a palimpsest formed by the clash of different ethnocultural identities, mostly European, African, and indigenous, but also, on a smaller scale, Jewish identities.

NOTES

1. "Consciente al parecer de que el realismo mágico de los años 60 y 70 ha terminado por convertirse en una caricatura del continente, y de que algunos de sus productores más recientes—ciertas novelas de Isabel Allende y de Laura Esquivel, por ejemplo—contribuyen a fosilizar una imagen estereotípica y *for export* del continente, el autor colabora ahora en desmontar lo que Adriana Bergero denomina la 'estética vacacional o turística de América Latina' que practican algunos cultores del realismo mágico.'"

2. "Lo sorprendió una nevada de palomitas de papel sobre los naranjos del huerto. Atrapóuna al azar, la deshizo, y leyó: *Ese rayo era mío*" (54).

3. In another comical scene, the nuns, seeing that Sierva María does not speak, wonder whether she is deaf and mute or just German. This joke is reminiscent of his short story "Un hombre muy viejo con unas alas enormes," where the neighbors wonder whether the angel is a Norwegian with wings.

4. "En mi casa se hace lo que yo obedezco" (36).

5. "Quizás vaya a ser poeta" (45).

6. "Idéntico al rey de bastos" (27).

7. "con una avidez de vientre para saciar un cuartel" (15).

8. "Las locas los alentaban con canciones procaces desde las terrazas, y celebraban sus triunfos con aplausos de estadio" (58).

9. "'Y no hay mujer ni negra ni blanca que valga ciento veinte libras de oro, a no ser que cague diamantes'" (16).

10. "No sería un mal negocio parir marquesitas criollas con patas de gallina para venderlas a los circos" (38).

11. "Con una torpeza de papá prestado" (81).

12. "'¡Ni falta que le hace!', dijo Abrenuncio. Y lo dijo en latín, por supuesto" (31).

13. "Un suburbio del mundo intimidado por el Santo Oficio" (66).

14. The narrator also describes the abbess, Josefa Miranda, in negative terms: "She had been brought up in Burgos, in the shadow of the Holy Office, but her talent for command and the rigor of her prejudices came from within and had always been hers" (65). ("Se había formado en Burgos, a la sombra del Santo Oficio, pero el don de mando y el rigor de sus prejuicios eran de dentro y de siempre" [91]).

15. "Lucifer es un bicho', se burló él cuando recobró el aire. 'También a mí me ha vuelto invisible'" (173).

WORKS CITED

Alcocer, Rudyard J. "When Magical Realism Loses Its Spell: Revisiting *Of Love and Other Demons*, by Gabriel García Márquez." *Critical Insights: Magical Realism*. Ed. Ignacio López-Calvo. Ipswich, Massachusetts: Salem Press, 2014. 67–83. Print.

Bell-Villada, Gene. "Gabriel García Márquez: Life and Times." *The Cambridge Companion to Gabriel García Márquez*. Ed. Philip Swanson. Cambridge: Cambridge University Press, 2010. 7–24. Print.

———. *García Márquez: The Man and His Work*. Chapel Hill: University of North Carolina Press, 2010. Print.

Bowers, Maggie Ann. *Magic(al) Realism*. New York: Routledge, 2004. Print.

Camayd-Freixas, Erik. "Reflections on *Magical Realism*: A Return to Legitimacy, the Legitimacy of Return." *Canadian Review of Comparative Literature/Revue Canadienne de Littérature Comparée* 23.2 (Jan. 1996). 580–89. Print.

Faris, Wendy B. *Ordinary Enchantments: Magical Realism and the Remystification of Narrative*. New York: Vanderbil University Press, 2004. Print.

García Márquez, Gabriel. *The Autumn of the Patriarch*. Trans. Gregory Rabassa. New York: Harper & Row, 1976. Print.

———. *Cien años de soledad*. New York: Vintage Español, 2009. Print.

———. *Del amor y otros demonios*. Mexico City: Diana, 1994. Print.

———. *Of Love and Other Demons*. Trans. Edith Grossman. New York: Alfred A. Knopf, 1995. Print.

———. *One Hundred Years of Solitude*. Trans. Gregory Rabassa. New York: Perennial Classics, 1998. Print.

———. *El otoño del Patriarca*. Buenos Aires: Sudamericana, 1998. Print.

McAleer, Paul R. *Hybrid Identity and the Utopian Impulse in the Postmodern Spanish-American Comic Novel*. New York: Támesis, 2015. Print.

Moreiras, Alberto. "The End of Magical Realism: José María Arguedas's Passionate Signifier (*El zorro de arriba y el zorro de abajo*)." *The Journal of Narrative Technique* 27.1 (Winter 1997): 84–112. Print.

Parkinson Zamora, Lois and Wendy B. Faris, eds. *Magical Realism: Theory, History, Community*. Durham, North Carolina: Duke University Press, 1995. Print.

Reati, Fernando. "Andes españoles, costa africana: Multiculturalismo e identidad en *Del amor y otros demonios* de García Márquez." *Proceedings of 1998 Jornadas Andinas de Literatura Latinoamericana (JALLA)*. Quito, Ecuador: Universidad Andina Simón Bolívar, 1998. 91–96. Print.

Williams, Raymond L. *A Companion to Gabriel García Márquez*. New York: Tamesis, 2010. Print.

Part IV

OTHER GENRES, OTHER MEDIA

Chapter 14

Felt History and the Permutations of the Fictional, Real, and Autobiographical "I" in Gabriel García Márquez's *Chronicle of a Death Foretold* and *Living to Tell the Tale*

Robert L. Sims

As Camilla Segura Bonnett states: "When we deal with an autobiographical text, we immediately think that we are going to read the 'whole truth' about the life of the person who wrote it. Upon reading a work in which a referential world is articulated where a real person is creating a retrospective account of his own like, the literary critic is confronted with problems such as the literary genre, subject, memory, truth, representation, referentiality, history and language, among others" (Segura Bonnett 113. Translation is mine).[1]

The following definitions will serve as a context for our study of the permutations and evolution of the fictional, real and autobiographical "I" in García Márquez's work, the latter of which culminates with his memoir/autobiography *Living to Tell the Tale*. It should also be mentioned that an unpublished manuscript has come to light entitled *En agosto nos vemos*.[2] Philippe Lejeune defines autobiography as "a retrospective prose narrative written by a real person concerning his own existence, where the focus is his individual life, in particular the history of his personality" (Smith and Watson 4). Sidonie Smith and Julia Watson offer a more extensive definition: "Our working definition of *self life writing* assumes that it is not a single unitary genre or form, 'autobiography.' Rather, the historically situated practices of self-representation may take many guises as narrators selectively engage their lived experience and situate their social identities through personal storytelling" (18). The form of autobiography García Márquez uses is what Jens Brockmeier calls the fragmentary model:

> In cultural analysis, identity is today generally imagined as discontinuous, shifting, and polycentric. As in most avant-garde discourse, individual or personal identity is referred to, if at all, only in terms of irony and parody, as an essentially fictitious construction. And we find, on the level of larger narrative units, alternative versions that are told simultaneously, mingling real, possible, imagined and anticipated life courses like equal story lines. Instead of the traditional autobiographical "I", the "first voice" narrative, we find two, three or more voices in dialogic or multivoiced discourse, creating a mosaic composition of identity. Accordingly, the visions of time, both individual and historical, inherent in these life stories display a likewise fragmentary layout. (Brockmeier 69)

Chronicle of a Death Foretold (1981) and *Living to Tell the Tale* (2002) form an interconnected diptych because of the unconventional use of the first person narrator, the merging of real and fictional components, and the displacement of chronology and official event history in favor of felt history which can be defined as follows:

> Felt history must be distinguished from official history with its attention to leaders, its overview of events, or its analysis of underlying trends. And it should also be distinguished from emotions or feelings, since history's psychological effects are usually less dramatic and revealing than its immediate feel, its physical impact on the body and the senses. In essence, then, felt history refers to the eloquent gestures and images with which a character or lyric persona registers the direct pressure of events, whether enlarging and buoyant or limiting and harsh. In this broad sense, of course, any critic who is sufficiently judicious in defining the historical context of a work could interpret most literature as felt history. (Foster 273)

As Sidonie Smith and Julia Watson state: "Of course, the boundary between the autobiographical and the novelistic is, like the boundary between biography and life narrative, sometimes exceedingly hard to fix. Many life writers take liberties with the novelistic mode in order to negotiate their own struggles with the past and with the complexities of identities forged in the present" (12).

The epigraph to *Living to Tell the Tale* ("Life is not what one lived, but what one remembers and how one remembers it in order to recount it") reveals three different "I" narrators: the "real" or historical "I," the narrating "I," and the narrated "I" (Smith and Watson 72). García Márquez eschews the historical "I" immediately ("Life is not what one lived") and replaces it with the narrating "I" ("but what one remembers") and the narrated "I" ("and how one remembers it in order to recount it). The epigraph clearly distinguishes between story and discourse and implies a selection of memories and the order in which they will be narrated.

A crucial change that García Márquez did in the Spanish title of the autobiography shifts the initial focus from the memories his life lived/remembered as a totality, to those related to his life of becoming a writer: "At the last moment '*Vivir para contarlo*' (living to tell 'it,' masculine, living to tell the act of living itself) changed to '*Vivir para contarla*' (living to tell 'it,' feminine, living to tell 'la vida,' life, the contemplation of life" (Martin 522). What distinguishes the first-person narrator in García Márquez's works is that, unlike the traditional "omniscient" narrating "I," his narrating "I" more closely resembles the unreliable narrator who is more vulnerable and does not know or say more than other characters. This crucial modification of the first-person narrator goes back to his work as an investigative reporter for *El Espectador* in 1954–1955 during which he wrote a series of *refritos*[3] or follow-up stories to the "official" versions of the events.

According to biographer Gerald Martin, García Márquez "had been talking about his memoirs ever since the publication of his great novel about Macondo. That should have given his readers the clue to his deepest motivation as a writer. Going back was all he ever wanted, writing about himself was all he ever wanted; Narcissus wanted to return to his own original face but even his face, lost in time, lost in all the times, was constantly changing, never the same, so even if he had found that original—eternal, oracular—face he would have seen it differently each time it appeared to him" (523). The fact that García Márquez was already talking about his memoirs in 1967 in which he would write about *himself* in the first person seems to contrast sharply with the unknowable narrator in *One Hundred Years of Solitude*: "In magical realism, the focalization—the perspective from which events are presented—is indeterminate; the kinds of perceptions it presents are indefinable and the origins of those perceptions are unlocatable. I have coined the term *defocalization* to take account of the special narrative situation that seems to me to characterize magical realism as a genre" (Faris 41). With the publication of his signature novel, unlike its ubiquitous unidentifiable narrator(s), not only will he be vaulted to fame with his public visage on display, but he will henceforth, like Albert Camus and his first novel, *The Stranger*, be unremittingly associated with it for the rest of his life. His literary identity will be the world famous "magical-realist writer." This narrative chiaroscuro identity will also affect the narrative identity of future works, especially *Chronicle of a Death Foretold*. It is no less certain, however, that García Márquez wrote about himself in *One Hundred Years of Solitude* in the indirect personalization of historical events that parallel Colombian history.

García Márquez has stated that "everyone has three lives: a public life, a private life, and a secret life" (Martin 198). Obviously the narrating "I" can write about one of these lives, or about two or even all three of them. The major factor in narrative, in Genettian terms, consists of controlling of the flow of information. To that end Genette presents three degrees of information (paralepsis or giving an overabundance of information; paralipsis, or providing information characterized by partial or lateral omissions; and ellipsis, or a complete omission of information). In traditional autobiography "telling one's life is closely intertwined with autobiographical remembering, the retrospective reconstruction of one's life history" (Brockmeier 52). In many cases the autonomous "I" (associated with an "omniscient" narrator) narrates his life in a chronological order with dates and creates the illusion of a seamless linear flow without gaps. Since the two works by García Márquez can be considered "autobiographical novels" or "novelized autobiographies," and they eschew chronology as well as the privileges of the first-person autonomous narrator, "if it comes to the oscillating and multi-layered scenarios of autobiographical time, chronology seems to be inappropriate. Because chronological operators of time always remain tied to the notion of a sequence (a sequence of 'nows,' that is), they simply are not appropriately complex if faced with the much more sophisticated fabric of narrative time construction" (54).

The openings of the two works under study not only illustrate the relinquishment and indeed, rejection of the traditional prerogatives of the narrating "I" but also underscore the idea that "the autobiographical process overlaps with the process of identity construction: both are processes of understanding one's self in time… Looking closer at autobiographical narratives we find, moreover, that these constructions are not so much about time but about *times*. They encompass and evoke a number of different forms and orders of time, creating a multi-layered weave of human temporality" (55–56). Within these new spatiotemporal moments of felt history/memories, a new set of elements comes into play:

> First, adhering to the principle of *multi-focalization*, the geocritic is required to engage with many different points of view on the grounds that a variety of perspectives are necessary to establish the contours of literary space and to ensure that its representation is not limited by individual bias or stereotyping. Second, the geocritic is required to embrace *polysensoriality*, inasmuch as the space under consideration may not be perceived by vision alone, but also by smell, or sound. Third, Westphal argues that geocritics must maintain a *stratigraphic vision*, in which the *topos* is understood to comprise multiple layers of meaning, deterritorialized and reterritorialized. Finally, geocritics must keep *intertextuality* to the fore in their research, noting that all textual spaces necessarily encompass "interface" with, or relate in other ways to other spaces in literature and in reality. (Tally 142)

Chronicle of a Death Foretold opens at the end of the story: "On the day they were going to kill him, Santiago Nasar got up at five-thirty in the morning to wait for the boat the bishop was coming on. 'He was always dreaming about trees,' Plácida Linero, his mother, told me twenty-seven years later, recalling the details of that distressing Monday" (García Márquez 2003, 3).[4] Several pages later, the narrating "I" initiates the reconstruction of the crime of this semiautobiographical novel: "She had watched him from the same hammock in which I found her prostrated by the last lights of old age when I returned to this forgotten village, trying to put the broken mirror of memory back together from so many scattered shards" (6). As Gerald Martin states:

> The postmodern *Chronicle of a Death Foretold* makes its autobiographical dimension explicit: its narrator is Gabriel García Márquez, who is not named but we know it is he because he has a wife called Mercedes (and seems to expect us to know who she is), a mother called Luisa Santiaga, brothers called Luis Enrique and Jaime, a sister called Margot, another, unnamed, who is a nun, and even, for the first time, a father, who is also unnamed. (395)

In García Márquez's investigative reporting for *El Espectador* in 1954–1955, his articles consisted of writing follow-up stories to the already transpired and recorded official version of the event. This method enabled him to shift his focus to *how* the event occurred and in the process subvert the official version. García Márquez dispatches the primary event in the first sentence of the novel so that his unnamed narrator can concentrate on the how the crime was committed. This unnamed narrator who returns twenty-seven years later must reconstruct the crime whose official version is riddled with gaps just like the memories of those who were involved in the crime. Chronology quickly gives way to a "broken-line" narrative that "connects" the scattered shards. The alternating overt (because of his references to his family which identifies him as García Márquez) and covert unnamed narrator uses a number of journalistic techniques (interviews, rumors, recording specific details, background information, comparisons of different versions, searching for documented evidence) to "reconstruct" not the event structure but its felt history.

For the most part, the narrator vacillates between the present autodiegetic narrator who narrates a story in which he is the main protagonist (his autobiographical self surfaces intermittently) and a past homodiegetic narrator who tells a story in which he is a character. *Chronicle of a Death Foretold* corresponds to the epigraph in his autobiography because the lived event is at first reduced to one sentence and is immediately replaced by a dream of Santiago Nasar that the homodiegectic narrator remembers.

While the autodiegetic narrating "I" reconstructs the crime by remembering through others via a reinvestigating of the past and a setting in motion of the heteroglossia or the many discourses surrounding the crime, he also constitutes a narrated "I" acting as a homodiegetic narrator. The binary differentiation between the narrating "I" and the narrated "I" is more complicated when we read an autobiographical work:

The narrating "I" is in effect composed of multiple voices, a heteroglossia attached to multiple and mobile subject positions, because the narrating "I" is neither unified nor stable. It is split, fragmented, provisional, and multiple, a subject always in the process of coming together and of dispersing. We can read or "hear," this fragmentation in the multiple voices through which the narrator speaks in the text. Thus the narrating "I" is a composite of speaking voices. The "I" can be seen as a sign marking the site of multiple voices that can be disentangled to a greater or lesser degree, rather than a single, unified monolithic "I." (Smith and Watson 74)

Chronicle of a Death Foretold constitutes on one level an experiment in autobiography to the extent that the narrator is deciding whether he will give more exposure to his public, private or secret life through the filter of memory. We detect the presence of a memory-chronotope constituted by the presence of autodiegetic and homodiegetic narrators in the novel: "Chronotope, like most of the terms characteristic of dialogism, must be treated 'bifocally,' as it were: invoking it in any particular case, one must be careful to discriminate between its use as a lens for close-up work and its ability to serve as an optic for seeing in the distance" (Holquist 113).

Although some of García Márquez's family members were in Sucre on the day of the murder, he himself was not (Martin 395). The fact that he was not an eyewitness to the crime inevitably meant that he would have to combine autobiographical and fictional elements. Essentially, then, he would shift the focus from *what* happened to *how* it happened. The first sentence establishes the framework for the narrator's reconstruction of the crime and offers the reader the illusion of an "exact chronology" of the sequence of events. If it is true that, as the saying goes, a writer only writes one work with different titles, and his autobiography follows a parallel but more fragmentary course, then *Chronicle of a Death Foretold* not only continues that trend but it also marks an important shift in the developing autobiography:

> *Living to Tell a Tale* can confirm it, since there we can find all his books forming part of a single work, recasting itself and explaining itself while his life continues unfolding. This unique work is nothing more than his literaturized reality or rather his literary world which is nurtured, or must be nurtured, only from reality. There are innumerable passages in *Living to Tell the Tale* that can illustrate this lack of division between reality and fiction. (Lergo Martín 265. Translation is mine)[5]

Many times fiction allows a writer to discuss certain problems that he cannot do effectively in other contexts, and here the question centers on autobiographical truth. Just as a split develops in the novel between fiction and reality, the unnamed "autobiofictional" narrator also splits in accordance with the division between the illusionary official history/chronology and felt history/broken-line reconstruction of the crime: "Any utterance in an autobiographical text, even if inaccurate or distorted, is a characterization of its writer. Thus, when one is both the narrator and the protagonist of the narrative, as in life writing, the truth becomes undecidable; it can be neither fully verified nor fully discredited. We need, then, to adjust our expectations of the truth told in self-referential writing" (Smith and Watson 15–16). The autodiegetic narrator becomes as it were a *voyeur voyant*: "The peculiarity that Francisco Rico sees in the biographer, to be able to construct himself as he continues narrating, that 'fascination of objectifying the *self* and recognizing him as *other*' (Villanueva 21), stands out in *Living to Tell the Tale* with particular intensity" (Lergo Martín 262. Translation is mine).[6]

We see this process of constructing his autobiographical self as García Márquez narrates and his narrated "I" is objectified and he envisages him as other as in *Chronicle of a Death Foretold*. The evolving narrating "I" combines fictional and "factual" details that belong to felt history and in turn will dominate his autobiography because what interests him is not the description of the event but the subjective impression it made on him and how he looked at it and lived it: "Thus autobiographical truth resides in the intersubjective exchange between the narrator and reader aimed at producing a shared understanding of the meaning of life. Susanna Egan's concept of 'mirror talk' captures the refractive interplay of such dialogic exchange between life narrator and reader (or viewer). The multifacetedness inherent in autobiographic writing produces a polyphonic site of indeterminacy rather than a single, stable truth" (Smith and Watson 16).

On another occasion the retrospective "I" narrator expresses disbelief that his sister Margot did not know that the Vicario twins were going to kill Santiago Nasar, but even more so concerning his mother:

> It was even stranger that my mother didn't know either, because she knew about everything before anyone else in the house, in spite of the fact that she had not gone out into the street in years, not even to attend mass. I had become aware of that quality of hers ever since I began to get up early for school. She seemed to have secret threads of communication with the other people in town, especially those her age, and sometimes she would surprise us with news so ahead of its time that she could only have known it through powers of divination. That morning, however, she didn't feel the throb of the tragedy that had been gestating since three o'clock. (*Chronicle* 20)

Since autobiographical time presents a plurality of temporalities, either closed (chronological and linear) or open (presenting patterns and combinations of temporalities open to new configurations), *Chronicle of a Death*

Foretold is structured according to open pluralities of temporalities. One of the characteristics of open temporalities is sideshadowing:

> Within the plurality of temporalities, I advocate a particular conception of open time that I call *sideshadowing*. I do not want to deny that closed temporalities frequently have value, but I suspect that they are often adopted by default, without a deep appreciation of more open alternatives. Sideshadowing admits, in addition to actualities and impossibilities, a *middle realm* of real possibilities which could have happened even if they did not. By focusing on the middle realm of possibilities, by exploring its relation to actual events, and by attending to that fact that things could have been different, sideshadowing deepens our sense of the openness of time. (Morson 5–6)

In the aforementioned quotation from *Chronicle*, then, history, sideshadowing and several characteristics of geocriticism come into play.

Since neither García Márquez nor the retrospective narrator/protagonist actually witnesses the crime, his "version" has nothing to do with event history but with the images, feelings, and the impact of the event on all those involved, both directly and indirectly. We see felt history when the narrator says: "I had become aware of that quality of hers ever since I began to get up early for school" (*Chronicle of a Death Foretold* 20). The narrator also sideshadows the event by focusing on a middle realm in which a different pattern of discovering that Santiago Nasar was going to be killed might have emerged if his sister Margot and his mother had known about it. Since his mother's powers of divination inexplicably fail, sideshadowing opens the door to questioning the supposedly impregnable official version when the realm of possibilities expands and suggests that other possible but unaccounted-for witnesses may have observed the crime. Felt history enables the autodiegetic narrator to establish an emotional bond between himself as the retrospective narrator and the auto-homodiegetic protagonist/character since he shows different degrees of participation in the narration. This quote is also multifocalized because not only do we see and feel the event from the perspective of the retrospective narrator ("it was even stranger that my mother didn't know either"), but also from that of the narrator/protagonist, that of the narrator as just a character in the novel ("and sometimes she would surprise us"—20) and also indirectly from the point of view of his mother ("That morning, however, she didn't feel the throb of the tragedy that had been gestating since three o'clock"—20). What these gradations of focalization reveal is the failure of the characters to register "the direct pressure of events, whether enlarging and buoyant or limiting and harsh" (Foster 273).

Multifocalization is also coupled with a stratigraphic vision. The absence of an eye witness in this passage creates a deterritorialized space which is then reterritorialized by layers of possible meanings which serve to dismantle the framework of the official version of the event (the Vicario twins killed Santiago Nasar in defense of their family's honor) and introduce other voices that either heard different versions, spread rumors, actually witnessed the event, or that provide information which contradicts other versions or proves to be extraneous (whether it rained or not on the day the crime). First, each successive interview or inquiry spawns more perspectives that agree with, disagree with or contradict each other so that the reader must sift through all the information to decide for him/herself. Since the retrospective first-person narrator's reconstruction of the crime is filled with gaps and unanswered questions, the reader is thus able to accompany him on his journey through the past without arriving at any definitive answers. All these voices cast sideshadows over the narrative and disrupt the chronocentrism marked out in the precise time references and create a polyphonic narration in which there are multiple plots possible and a dialogic narrative filled with the multiple voices, thus creating new possibilities and establishing a plurality of open temporalities.

Chronicle of a Death Foretold also intertextualizes with García Márquez's (future) autobiography in the sense that his fiction and life intertwine from the beginning. The "invisible" ubiquitous narrator of *One Hundred Years of Solitude* divides into a primarily foregrounded fictional narrator and an adumbrated backgrounded narrator, both of whom then seem to merge into a hybrid autobiofictional narrator who speaks in the first person. García Márquez sprinkles details of his personal life throughout the novel, yet the embryonic autobiographical "I" yields to the stronger presence of the narrated "I," most likely because he did not witness the actual murder. Even though he had started to gather evidence so he could write a report of the crime, in his own words he "found all kinds of impediments. What interested me was no longer the crime itself but the literary theme of collective responsibility" (*Living to Tell the Tale* 421–422). Already the permutations of the event had passed from reality to fiction, yet his mother convinced him not to write it out of respect for others: "But after that not a day went by that I was not hounded by the desire to write the story" (421).

The hybrid narrator of the novel alternates between the autobiographical and fictional narrators who never say or know more than any other character and thereby becomes vulnerable and accessible to the reader. The traditional autobiographical "I," the first voice, gives way to the fictional "I" that intermingles with other voices in a dialogical dance of identity that in turn blur generic boundaries between autobiography and fiction in García Márquez's own hybrid autobiography, in which his public, private and secret selves come into play to different degrees.

Living to Tell the Tale opens in medias res: "My mother asked me to go with her to sell the house. She had come that morning from the distant town where the family lived and she had no idea how to find me" (3). Several pages later, as if to initiate the construction of his identity as a writer, García Márquez states:

> Neither my mother nor I, of course, could even have imagined that this simple two-day trip would be so decisive that the longest and most diligent of lives would not be enough for me to finish recounting it. Now, with more than seventy-five years behind me, I know it was the most important of the all decisions I had to make in my career as a writer. That is to say, in my entire life. Before adolescence, memory is more interested in the future than in the past, and so my recollections of the town were not yet idealized by nostalgia. (5)

García Márquez does not return to the "beginning" of his autobiography until page 37 and he associates his early childhood memories with becoming a writer. For García Márquez, his house represents the repository of his dreams and memories, and from the outset his public self as a writer receives the most attention. The importance of the house appears earlier in one of the columns he called "La Jirafa" that bore the title "Self-Critique." Besides discussing a short story that he wants to get published, he also mentions his return from Aracataca, which resembles towns in the Deep South and the works of William Faulkner: "I have just returned from Aracataca. It continues to be a dusty little town, full of silence and dead people," (*Obra Periodística* 725. Translation is mine).[7] At the very end of the column he mentions his reaction to his trip: "I had intended to write a chronicle about the trip. But now I have decided to save the material for *The House*, a big seven hundred page novel I plan to finish within two years" (726. Translation is mine).[8]

Before considering in depth the connection between memories and García Márquez's central theme of becoming a writer and preserving his public image, we must consider his version of the Proustian madeleine moment. First comes the famous passage in Proust:

> No sooner had the warm liquid mixed with the crumbs touched my palate than a shiver ran through me and I stopped, intent upon the extraordinary thing that was happening to me. An exquisite pleasure had invaded my senses, something isolated, detached, with no suggestion of its origin. And at once the vicissitudes of life had become indifferent to me, its disasters innocuous, its brevity illusory—this new sensation having the effect, which love has, of filling me with a precious essence; or rather this essence was not in me, it *was* me. (*In Search of Lost Time* 60)

This scintillating moment of involuntary spontaneous memory first produces a feeling of felt history after which the narrator Marcel engages in deep introspection and repeated attempts to recuperate his past: "I can feel it mounting slowly; I can measure the resistance, I can hear the echo of great spaces traversed." (62). Finally, he recovers the village of Combray and his childhood through the arduous process of voluntary memory.

García Márquez's Proustian moment differs considerably: "And so we shared with them a local meal whose simplicity had nothing to do with poverty but with a regimen of sobriety that he [the local doctor] practiced and advocated not only for the table but for all life's activities. From the moment I tasted the soup I had the sensation that an entire sleeping world was waking in my memory. Tastes that had been mine in childhood and that I had lost when I left the town reappeared intact with each spoonful, and they gripped my heart" (*Living to Tell the Tale* 31). His version constitutes a variation of the initial moment of Marcel's spontaneous realization that "this essence was not in me, it *was* me." García Márquez's memory also flows from felt history but one taste of the soup generates a transtemporal olfactory experience that quickly passes from a sensation to encompassing an entire world. The tastes multiply and everything reemerges intact.

The difference between these two experiences is that Proust's profound personal self (identity), which is indissolubly linked to his "more public" identity as a writer, materializes instantaneously, and then he struggles to reconstruct the world in which he would become a writer. Proust's primary mission consists of an epistemological search for meaning in a stable world, so he does not engage in the process of *how he became a writer*. In García Márquez's case, his Proustian moment has little to do with reconstructing his past in order to discover his true self. His primary mission will be to reconstruct the past that centers mainly not on *how he became a writer but how he came to be a writer*. Becoming a writer is too banal and implies a linear sequence. He preferred *came* in the sense of revelation and *to*, that is, he started writing and, finally, *be* or the arduous process of creating his public self as a writer.

García Márquez can live twice by writing his autobiography because his invented self has already appeared directly and indirectly in his fiction. Nevertheless, *Living to Tell the Tale* presents a problematical conundrum. As his biographer states: "There are no real intimacies or confessions. The book contains his public life and his 'false,' invented life, but it does not contain much of his 'private' life and little indeed of his 'secret' life" (Martin 524). It seems that García Márquez had decided that in order to preserve intact his public image, and since Gerald Martin had been interviewing him for the "official" biography of his life, he would simply not finish the last two projected volumes and replace them with his biography written by Gerald Martin.

Several other key statements can shed some light on García Márquez's public self as a writer. Elsewhere he declares his complete commitment to writing and his as identity as a writer overarches everything: "In other words: the years were flying by and I did not have the slightest idea what I was going to do with my life, for much more time would still have to go by before I realized that even that state of defeat was propitious, because there is nothing in the world or the next that is not useful to a writer" (242).

Living to Tell the Tale constitutes the most extensive and eloquent expression of the *refrito*. The "original article" is his lived life; memory is the raw materials of his life; and the "follow-up story" is his "telling the tale." Once again, García Márquez's work demonstrates to what extent the *refrito* constitutes one of the fundamental components of his writing and the crucial role that journalism has played in his development as a writer.

In the life and writing of García Márquez, "good things come in threes," as a proverb says. The epigraph to *Living to Tell the Tale* has a triadic structure that relates directly to García Márquez's life, writing and selves, that is, his life, his memory thereof and how he remembers. Moreover, we see an interrelated tripartite configuration between his life, fiction writing and journalism. He is also recognized as a world famous journalist, short story writer and novelist. García Márquez has said that all human beings have three lives: public, private, and secret. We know that García Márquez had planned three volumes for his memoirs/autobiography, but he only completed one.

Ever since he began to write, García Márquez left numerous references to his personal life in his journalism, novels and short stories. These references lack any chronological order and instead represent a broken-line narrative. Nevertheless, three works in particular correspond to each life/self mentioned by García Márquez and form a triangular relationship: *One Hundred Years of Solitude*-**Secret Life,** *Chronicle of a Death Foretold*-**Private Life** and *Living to Tell the Tale*-**Public Life.** In *One Hundred Years of Solitude*, García Márquez creates a ubiquitous, unlocatable and unidentifiable narrator that does not fit into any recognizable mold. The narrator says a lot but ultimately reveals little or nothing of himself. In *Chronicle of a Death Foretold* this narratorial opacity dissipates somewhat since the first-person unnamed narrator reveals certain personal details establishing that it is García Márquez who, we must bear in mind, did not witness the actual crime in Sucre. These scattered references to his private life in the novel contrast with his "false," self-invented or fictional life inasmuch as the first-person narrator divulges nothing about his past except that associated with the objectified narrated "I" at the time of the crime. Finally, in *Living to Tell the Tale*, García Márquez focuses exclusively on his public life/self and how he came to be a writer to the exclusion of discussing other personal and private facets of his life.

Obviously, the chiaroscuro pattern of his different selves has much to do with the desire to control the narrative of his life and maintain his public life as a writer. Either fame, or a traditional autobiography, or memoirs could all have proved detrimental to this primary goal. One could speculate that García Márquez stopped writing in 2006 because of his distrust in autobiography and memoirs and perhaps he had decided to let Gerald Martin "finish" the story of his life which itself ends in 2006. The most valuable tool to tell his story is the *refrito*, which liberates him from narrating what happened in his life and enables him to concentrate on how one remembers it in order to recount it. Free of chronology, linearity and dates, he can control the flow of information connected to his three selves and concentrate on and reorder the essential "events" within the framework of felt history. He always conceals more than he reveals in the end in his hybridized version of his autobiography. In a sense, *Living to Tell the Tale* is written as a follow-up story of his public and "false," self-invented life in which he merges fiction and reality just as he has done from the beginning.

García Márquez started out as a sort of writer whom Bakhtin describes in the following manner:

> The journalist is above all a contemporary. He is obliged to be one. He lives in a sphere of questions and answers that can be resolved in the present day (or in any case in the near future). He participates in a dialogue that can be ended and finalized, can be translated into action, and can become an empirical force. It is precisely in this sphere that 'one's own word' is possible. Outside this sphere 'one's own word' is not one's own (the individual personality always transcends itself); 'one's own word' cannot be the ultimate word. (Bakhtin 152)

García Márquez did not restrict himself to this type of language and, as Bakhtin says, "the word of the journalist, when introduced into the polyphonic novel, submits to unfinalized and infinite dialogue" (152). Journalism quickly combined with short stories and novels, many of which are found in embryonic form in the many articles and columns he wrote between 1947 and 1960.

The continuous intertwining skeins of journalism, literature, and autobiographical discourses within García Márquez's dialogical universe, in which these discourses combine, separate and rejoin in creative ways, produce hybrid works and selves. García Márquez represents a trigeneric writer and self in which fictionality and factuality play equally important roles. Therefore, it is possible to call the three works in question autobiographical novels and/or novelized autobiographies. García Márquez's work and his selves are always a work in process as Bakhtin expresses it:

> There is neither a first nor a last word and there are no limits to the dialogical context (it extends into the boundless past and the boundless future). At any moment in the development of the dialogue there are immense, boundless masses of forgotten contextual meanings, but at certain moments of the dialogue's subsequent development along the way they are recalled and invigorated in renewed form (in a new context). Nothing is absolutely dead: every meaning will have its homecoming festival. The problem of *great time*. (170)

NOTES

1. "Cuando nos enfrentamos a un texto autobiográfico de inmediato pensamos que vamos a leer la 'verdad total' de la vida de quien escribió pues ésta 'ha sido narrada por la persona más autorizada para hacerlo: quien la vivió (Ramírez, 1995, 189). Al leer una obra en la cual se articula un mundo referencial, en donde se presenta una persona real constituyendo un relato retrospectivo de su propia vida, el crítico literario se enfrenta con problemas como los de género literario, sujeto, memoria, verdad, representación, referencialidad, historia y lenguaje, entre otros."

2. See the following article, "Gabriel García Márquez Left Unpublished Manuscript," at CBS/AP April 22, 2014 at the following link: http://www.cbsnews.com/news/gabriel-garcia-marquez-left-unpublished-manuscript-editor/.

3. A refrito, literally "refried," can be an article or work that combines elements and material from previous work and is often referred to as a "rehash" or revised version. A refrito can also be a follow-up article like those that García Márquez wrote for *El Espectador* in 1954–1955 and would play a major role in the structure and narration of his later works.

4. See Gene H. Bell-Villada, *García Márquez: The Man and His Work*. 2nd ed. Chapel Hill: The University of North Carolina Press, 2010, pages 199–208 for an illuminating study of the novel, a discussion of its more remote setting (the nineteen twenties) and a detailed summary of the real crime's strange history.

5. "*Vivir para contarla* puede confirmarlo, pues allí están todos sus libros formando parte de uno solo, refundiéndose y explicándose mientras se va desgranando su vida. Esta única obra no es más que su realidad literaturizada o bien su mundo literario que se nutre, que debe nutrirse únicamente de realidad. Son innumerables en *Vivir para contarla* los pasajes que pueden ilustrar esta falta de cesura en realidad y ficción."

6. "Esa peculiaridad que Francisco Rico ve en el biógrafo, de poder construirse a medida que se va narrando, esa 'fascinación de objetivar el *yo* y reconocerlo *otro*' (Villanueva 21) se marca en *Vivir para contarla* con especial intensidad."

7. "Acabo de regresar de Aracataca. Sigue siendo una aldea polvorienta, llena de silencio y de muertos."

8. "Había pensado escribir la crónica de este viaje, pero ahora dispuse reservar el material para 'La Casa,' el novelón de setecientas páginas que pienso terminar antes de dos años."

WORKS CITED

Bakhtin, M. M. *Speech Genres & Other Late Essays*. Trans. Vern W. McGee. Eds. Caryl Emerson and Michael Holquist. Austin: University of Texas Press, 1983. Print.

Bell-Villada, Gene H. *García Márquez: The Man and His Work*. 2nd ed. Chapel Hill: The University of North Carolina Press, 2010. Print.

Brockmeier, Jens. "Autobiographical Time." *Narrative Inquiry* 10.1 (2000): 51–73. Print.
Faris, Wendy B. *Ordinary Enchantments. Magical Realism and the Remystification of Narrative.* Nashville: Vanderbilt University Press, 2004. Print.
Foster Jr., John Burt. "Magical Realism, Compensatory Vision, and Felt History: Classical Realism Transformed in *The White Hotel.*" In Lois Parkinson Zamora and Wendy B. Faris (Eds.). *Magical Realism: Theory, History, Community.* Durham: Duke University Press, 1995. 267–283. Print.
García Márquez, Gabriel. "Auto-crítica" (1). In Jacques Gilard (Ed.) *Obra periodística Textos costeños* (Vol. 1) Barcelona: Bruguera, 1981. 724–726. Print.
———. *Chronicle of a Death Foretold.* Trans. Gregory Rabassa. New York: Vintage, 2003. Print.
———. *Living to Tell the Tale.* Trans. Edith Grossman. New York: Vintage, 2004. Print.
Holquist, Michael. *Dialogism.* New York: Routledge, 2002. Print.
Lergo Martín, Inmaculada. "La realidad no se equivoca cuando la literatura es buena: *Vivir para contarla*, la autobiografía-novela de Gabriel García Márquez." In *Gabriel García Márquez, la modernidad de un clásico.* Eds. José Manuel Camacho Delgado y Fernando Díaz Ruiz. Madrid: Verbum, 2009. 255–270. Print.
Martin, Gerald. *Gabriel García Márquez: A Life.* New York: Vintage, 2010. Print.
Morson, Gary Saul. *Narrative and Freedom: The Shadows of Time.* New Haven: Yale University Press, 1994. Print.
Proust, Marcel. *In Search of Lost Time* (Vol. 1). Trans. C. K. Scott Moncrieff and Terence Kilmartin. New York: Random House, 2003. Print.
Segura Bonnett, Camila. "La transfiguración del lugar común: *Vivir para contarla* de Gabriel García Márquez." *Estudios de literatura colombiana* 15 (Julio-Diciembre 2004): 113–133. Print.
Smith, Sidonie and Julia Watson. *Reading Autobiography.* Minneapolis: University Press of Minnesota, 2010. Print.
Tally Jr., Robert T. *Spatiality.* New York: Routledge, 2013. Print.

Chapter 15

Big-Screen Adaptations of Two Gabriel García Márquez Novels

A Reappraisal

Rudyard J. Alcocer and Haley Osborn

This essay explores conceptual issues surrounding Gabriel García Márquez's relationship with the cinema, particularly as concerns cinematic adaptations of his novels. Such a relationship has largely been overshadowed by scholarship on other aspects of García Márquez's massive literary production, despite the fact that cinema informs much of his work: sometimes obliquely but oftentimes quite explicitly. In recent years there has been increased interest in exploring García Márquez's ties to cinema. Relevant studies include those by Álvaro Ramírez Ospina (1996), Claire Taylor (2010), Luciano Castillo (2014), and Alessandro Rocco (2014). The lengthiest of these is Rocco's very useful recent survey, *Gabriel García Márquez and the Cinema: Life and Works*. Rocco, though, is not principally interested in film adaptations of García Márquez's writings; his focus is broader: on García Márquez's entire relationship with the film medium. When Rocco and (especially) other scholars do comment on film adaptations of García Márquez stories, however, their assessments tend to be critical, as if by their very essence the fictions somehow do not lend themselves to cinematic representation. Indeed, it seems fair to ask why film versions of these works have not approximated, let alone equaled, the success of his written narratives. In these pages we will survey García Márquez's relationship with cinema while paying particular attention to film adaptations of his writing: how they fared at the box office and with critics, for example. We then analyze the film adaptations of two García Márquez novels: *Crónica de una muerte anunciada* (1981, film adaptation 1987) and *Del amor y otros demonios* (1994, film adaptation 2009).[1] Ultimately, an analysis of these two adaptations may shed some light on the ways in which narrative works by García Márquez lend themselves (or not) to cinematic representation. Our conclusions are counterintuitive: the more heralded novel has produced a weak film adaptation, while the lesser-known novel has resulted in a more interesting film. The reasons for this contrast, however, may lie more in decisions made by the filmmakers than in any inherent differences in quality between the novels. Indeed, the adaptations help elucidate features of the novels that are otherwise not readily apparent, especially in the case of *Del amor y otros demonios* (*Of Love and Other Demons*).

Let us begin with an overview of García Márquez's relationship with cinema. Despite his tremendous literary success, many of Gabo's admirers are not aware that his love for cinema inspired his desire to write, and thus greatly shaped his technique as a writer. In fact, as a child he experienced the entertainment of film before he had been introduced to books (Rocco 1). Subsequently, his fascination with the medium later moved him to pursue behind-the-scenes involvement in cinema through script writing and other contributions to the production of several films. As a staff writer for *El Espectador* in the 1950s, he first gained experience as a movie critic. According to Rubén Pelayo, García Márquez's weekly film column for *El Espectador* was "the first of its kind in Colombia" (32). Similarly, Rocco adds that this column "introduced serious film criticism into Colombia for the first time" (xiii).

These movie reviews display a keen eye for the visual medium of cinema. In a February 1954 review of the Hollywood picture *Pickup on South Street,* García Márquez writes: "The film is of noticeable merit: it is cinematographic from the first scene to the last. In the first, especially, a skillfully-used camera explains matters without resorting to anything beyond the images themselves."[2] Furthermore, these reviews display a specific awareness of the ties between cinema and the written word, a relationship that is highly variable. In a September 1954 review of the Swiss film *Heidi,* for example, García Márquez writes that the film's director, Luigi Comencini, "has been able to communicate a strong atmosphere of realism and psychological depth, both of which *translated in an extraordinary manner to cinematic language*."[3] Taylor explains that while it may be difficult to extrapolate a unified film theory from these often short and informative reviews, they do reveal a preference for "the close-up; what [García Márquez] calls a 'human cinema'; realism, in particular Italian neo-realism; and films that are critical of the *status quo*" (161).

In 1955 García Márquez was sent by *El Espectador* first to Geneva to cover the "Big Four" Summit of the Cold War Powers, and then to Rome, where he reported on a number of topics, including the thriving Italian film industry. While in Rome he also studied cinema in the sanctuary for neorealist film studies, the Centro Sperimentale di Cinematografia. In 1961, following his stint in Italy and precarious labors as a correspondent in Paris and New York City (among several other locations), García Márquez moved to Mexico City. There he worked as a magazine editor for film producer Gustavo Alatriste while teaching at a cinema school. Collaborating with producers Antonio Matouk and Luis Alcoriza, García Márquez completed three screenplays and many other stories within two years. Soon thereafter, he resumed his collaborations with the Colombian intellectual group, Grupo de Barranquilla, with whom he had previously co-produced *La langosta azul* ("The Blue Lobster," 1954). In addition to this experimental short film, the group produced several others.

Despite the multifaceted expertise he had developed in cinema, García Márquez eventually abandoned writing screenplays due to the artistic limits he felt were inevitable when working with directors; nevertheless, his relationship with the medium was far from over. Perhaps his "most ambitious venture into film" (464), according to official biographer Gerald Martin, was García Márquez's presidency of the Fundación Nuevo Cine Latinoamericano in Havana in 1985 and – in San Antonio de los Baños, a half hour outside the Cuban capital – his establishment in 1986 of the International School for Cinema and Television. As such, it could be argued that not only did film influence the way García Márquez wrote, but that – conversely – his writing contributed to the way Latin American cinema evolved during the second half of the twentieth century. It was, in fact, through film that the author began to understand the aesthetic possibilities of the written word. He explains that through his work in cinema

> not only did I notice what could be done in that medium but rather also what could not be done; it seemed to me that the dominance of the image over other narrative elements was certainly an advantage but also a disadvantage, and all of this for me was a stunning realization because it was only then that I understood that the possibilities of a novel are limitless.[4]

Given his love for film, however, it is no surprise that many of his celebrated novels and short stories, although produced in print form, seem to be written for the mind's "inner cinema" as they possess strong visual elements. In less metaphorical terms, one could surmise that García Márquez's vivid textual descriptions could easily be converted to the vivid, cinematic imagery that has been known to draw masses to the big screen. Over the years, film directors have been drawn to Gabo's stories. In 1988, for instance, the Colombian filmmaker Lisandro Duque Naranjo directed *Milagro en Roma*, a film based on "La santa," a story by García Márquez. At the time, Duque Naranjo observed: "García Márquez's stories are so ingenious and original, with situations that take the reader into a universe full of surprises, all features that make the temptation to transfer them to the cinema practically inevitable" (quoted in Rocco 42). With the notable exception of *One Hundred Years of Solitude*, which in many ways he wrote *against* cinema and whose film adaptation he never allowed (Taylor 164), García Márquez was otherwise generous in allowing many of his stories to be adapted into cinematic form.

In contrast, prior to *One Hundred Years of Solitude*, his written stories strongly resembled film scripts or stage directions for plays on account of their interest in visual details (Taylor 164). Not surprisingly, the first film based on a García Márquez story may be the most successful with respect to critical appraisals: *En este pueblo no hay ladrones* ("No Thieves in this Town," 1964, by Mexican director Alberto Isaac), which has attained almost cult-like status (Rocco 170) and is based on an early García Márquez short story characterized by a linear, realist narrative.

It is after *En este pueblo no hay ladrones* that film adaptations of García Márquez stories become more problematical: in other words, the quality and success of the film adaptations seem to lie in inverse relation to the great success of García Márquez's prose narrative. The author himself argued that the "apparently 'visual' nature of his prose is deceptive" and that visual effects in his prose are created through the "magic of the words" (quoted in Taylor 165). What is more, Rocco argues that a critical stance on film adaptations of García Márquez's stories has become a cottage industry: "It has to be said that a tradition grew up of critics tending to emphasize the difficulty of transposing the author's work to the cinema, to the point where this has become something of a cliché" (168–9). Indeed, it is often held as a truism that formally complex and linguistically rich novels (e.g., those by García Márquez) are more difficult to adapt to cinema than lesser, plot-driven novels. How do we account, however, for adaptations of such uneven quality when they are based on narratives – those by Gabo, for instance – that are similar to each other in their formal complexity and linguistic richness?

Claire Taylor's rigorous overview of criticism of film adaptations of García Márquez novels provides a useful path toward answering this question. She cites, for example, Álvaro Ramírez Ospina, for whom García Márquez's stories "do not succeed in resolving the paradoxes of his works which easily alternate between concrete fact and the resonance of that fact in the collective imagination."[5] She then cites Julián David Correa (and co-authors Lía Master and César Augusto Montoya), who are more systematic in their explanation of why García Márquez's novels fail on the big screen (even if it remains unclear what they mean by "excessive"):

> There are six stumbling blocks which are due precisely to the excessive nature of [García Márquez's] works: the first is the suggestive power of Garciamarquian prose, and linked with this, the difficulty of finding actors capable of portraying the excess; the third is García Márquez's talent for incorporating the fantastic into the most everyday contexts, to which we can add the use he makes of fluctuating timeframes, marked by nostalgia; the fifth difficulty lies in the evident fear of filmmakers – including Gabo himself – of betraying the original written work, and the sixth is that there has yet to be found a cinematic style capable of conveying what his works propose.[6]

In order to begin to understand some of the complexities and potential pitfalls involved with any filmmaker's attempts to adapt a García Márquez novel, let us consider first some features of *Crónica de una muerte anunciada* (*Chronicle of a Death Foretold*), a short novel that is at once simple and deceptively complex. Based on real-life events from during the author's youth, the narrator – Gabo's alter ego – begins by declaring to his readers that a murder will take place: that of Santiago Nasar. The narrator then describes Nasar's activities on the morning of his murder. The novel, then, operates within a curiously unorthodox narrative structure: while its premise could have allowed it to devolve into a simple detective whodunit, *Chronicle* transcends such simplistic categorization. We as readers know from the start, for example, that there was a murder. In addition, we know the identity of the victim and quickly become acquainted with his daily routines. The more pressing questions, however, lie elsewhere: who is planning to murder him? Why? Who else knows about the murder plot? It turns out that nearly the entire town knows, a fact that adds further depth to the narrative and in so doing enables its connection to broader issues characteristic of Hispanic American societies of the early to mid-twentieth century. These issues include – but are not limited to – the pervasive *machismo* in these societies, the importance of fate, the region's subtle ethnic divisions, and so on.

While this is not the place for a lengthier account of the novel's plot and its many interpretive dimensions (others, including Gene Bell-Villada, have already provided rich accounts; see relevant discussion in his *García Márquez: The Man and His Work*), we shall now focus on particular features in the novel that would render a cinematic adaptation problematical. Bell-Villada, for instance, is right in signaling *Chronicle*'s "concentric" elements (200). Indeed, every chapter yields – in Faulknerian manner – new clues and perspectives surrounding the fateful crime that lies at the heart of the narrative. The novel's concentric structure is reminiscent of a very different and less-known novel that was published at around the same time as *Chronicle*: Bruce Chatwin's *The Viceroy of Ouidah* (1980). Although this novel depicts different places and epochs (West Africa during the 1970s, and Brazil and West Africa during the early- to mid-nineteenth century), it is relevant to our discussion on account of its adaptation to film: the famed German director Werner Herzog purchased the rights to Chatwin's novel and shortly thereafter produced a film based on it, *Cobra Verde* (1987). Herzog's comments on adapting Chatwin's novel are revealing:

> The first thing I did was explain to Chatwin that the story in *The Viceroy of Ouidah* was not a film story *per se,* which meant there would be certain technical problems in adapting the book. It is narrated in a series of concentric circles, and I knew a film would have to proceed in a more linear way. (Cronin, *Herzog on Herzog* 212)

We shall see that *Chronicle*'s film adaptation, too, dispenses with the concentricity of Gabo's novel (with undesirable consequences).

While there is, as we learn immediately, a murder that lies at the heart of *Chronicle,* the novel cannot be reduced to this event. Its narrative mode, for example, is conjectural and hypothetical, as opposed to declarative. Rather than opening the novel with "Santiago Nasar died today" or "Santiago Nasar will die today," the narrator begins more subtly: "On the day *they were going to kill him*, Santiago Nasar got up at five-thirty in the morning …" (3, emphasis added). Did they kill him? Maybe. Who is the "they"? Stay tuned. In keeping with its conjectural narrative mode, the novel recounts not only what did happen, but also elegantly surveys all the events that could have happened but did not. Similarly, *Chronicle* reveals the identity of the killers and their tactics, but is merely suggestive about not only their motives but about those who could have prevented the murder yet did not.

To *Chronicle*'s conjectural mode we can add a further enriching component: its epistemological complexity. By epistemological we mean, quite simply, the novel's management of knowledge and ways of knowing, and how – importantly – these matters revolve around the novel's representation of social discourse. Beyond factual questions of the "Who knew what and when?" sort, the novel engages in far more complicated questions such as: who might or might not have known something about the murder? Why might they have known or not known? What might have happened differently had they known? and so on. Furthermore, all these hypothetical questions are imbricated in the ways people speak to one another. As Bell-Villada observes, *Chronicle* "bristles with such indications as 'he said to me,' or 'she admitted,' or 'many agreed that,' and the like" (200). The novel, in short, is *about* many things, including a murder, but also about the types of knowledge that exist or could exist among people and how they, in turn, negotiate, recall, and communicate that knowledge.

Such discursive and epistemological complexities can function successfully in a novel. They certainly did in *Chronicle*. The novel met with wide acclaim when it was published, not coincidentally, perhaps, the year before Gabo received the Nobel Prize in Literature. In its official statement, the Nobel committee described many of his writings including *Chronicle,* of which it stated in terms both broadly relevant to several of his works but also with unequivocal relation to *Chronicle*: "Often his stories revolve around a dead person – someone who has died, is dying or will die" (Nobel). Interestingly, Santiago Nasar – the victim – is all three of these at once in the narrative. Among several admirers, *The New York Times* affirmed in a lengthy review, for example, that "the murder of Santiago Nasar will stand among the innumerable murders of modern literature as one of the best and most powerfully rendered…" (Michaels).

Everything about the 1987 film adaptation of *Chronicle* promised success.[7] While previous adaptations had been limited to García Márquez's short stories, the planned adaptation of *Chronicle* was seen as

> the first major attempt to transfer the author's literary world to the big screen. This project featured one of his greatest successes, *Crónica de una muerte anunciada*, published in 1981, and involved the prestigious Italian director Francesco Rosi and the screenwriter Tonino Guerra. It was a large-scale international production – primarily French and Italian – with a cast of world-famous actors. It may well be on account of the relative lack of success of this film that twelve more years had to pass before another big name director, the Mexican Arturo Ripstein, made an adaptation of a work by García Márquez... (Rocco 168).

Reviews at the time pointed to problems in the adaptation. David Robinson, for example, wrote in a *Times* (of London) review that in the film "Gabriel García Márquez meets Francesco Rosi and the encounter is not altogether easy ... The end seems arbitrary: this is the moment when one feels the rational Rosi's credulity deserts him, and the irreconcilables between director and author are exposed" (Robinson n. pag.). Meanwhile, Iain Johnstone's review of the film for the *Sunday Times* begins with the simple question, "Why is *Chronicle of a Death Foretold* so uninvolving?" His answers include, "The trouble is that Rosi has attempted to forge a love story where the author has written a fable of hate and ridicule," and "... the town never becomes the 'open wound' of the novel ... The poetic conundrum of Márquez's [sic] theme – 'the chain of many chance events that made absurdity possible' – remains tantalisingly over the horizon" (Johnstone n. pag.). Although Rocco does point to additional negative, indeed terrible, reviews of Rosi's film, his own relatively favorable assessment is one of the few in existence: for him, the film has "both a thoughtful tone and a fast pace, creating the effect of suspense in the action and meditation on the outcome and on the responsibility for events which is also characteristic of the novel" (174). With respect to the suspense Rocco identifies in the film, a critic had argued even before Rosi's film appeared that García Márquez's novel owed a debt to Alfred Hitchcock's cinematic strategies for building suspense.[8]

Our own assessment on the film adaptation is in line with the prevailing views, that is, it is far inferior to the novel. This is so, oddly enough, even though Rosi's adaptation is mostly faithful to *Chronicle* in terms of basic features of the plot. There are, of course – as with any adaptation – some deviations in Rosi's narrative. Even these, however, seem ill-advised. This is especially true of the film's romanticized treatment of Angela and Bayardo's reunion, which occurs in the penultimate chapter of the novel. While the novel suggests that the aged and balding Bayardo is now unworthy of the dignified and poised Angela, the film depicts Bayardo as an attractive man who effortlessly wins Angela's affection. Thus, the feminist undertones in García Márquez's ending are completely ignored in the filmic adaptation. Rosi provides, instead, a stylized caricature of Garciamarquian passion.

The adaptation's troubles do not end there, however. Gone from the film is the novel's philosophical and conceptual weight. Rather than begin, for instance, with the suggestive conjectural discourse readily apparent in the novel ("On the day they were going to kill him..."), the film's introduction prioritizes the narrator himself (played by Gian Maria Volonté) who – in his white suit and hat, not to mention the fact that he is on a river boat – resembles the Fitzcarraldo character in Werner Herzog's 1981 film by the same name. The film's already questionable introduction is further problematized given that the narrator, as Robinson explains, disappears mid-film: "By the end the Volonté character is forgotten, as the film climaxes in a bitter-sweet and unrepentantly romantic reconciliation of the middle-aged and mellow Angela and Bayardo ..." (Robinson n. pag.).

While at the level of plot the (linear) film is mostly accurate in its depiction of the events in a (concentric) novel, an additional issue involves basic differences between visual and written expression. The film, for instance, selects from (and in so doing reduces) the various interpretative possibilities suggested by the García Márquez narrative. In the film we *see* Rosi's singular interpretation of the novel's multiple potential paths and ideas. In a sense, then, while the film is seldom inaccurate, it is unable to capture the interpretive richness and depth of García Márquez's novel. Gone from the film are all the things that characters *might* have done or might have said. While we would not go so far as to claim that it would be impossible for any filmmaker to provide a convincing and faithful adaptation of a novel like *Chronicle,* our sense is that many talented filmmakers understand – just as Gabo did – that cinema and prose fiction are distinct provinces with distinct idioms, and that a significant amount of the power wielded by *Chronicle* pertains to its having been written for the printed page. In short, the film is a problematical attempt to tell a concentric tale in a linear way.

Unlike *Chronicle* (the novel), García Márquez's *Of Love and Other Demons* has had an uneven reception. Before surveying the reviews, let us revisit the basic details of the story. Based on the prefatory discovery of the two-hundred-year-old cadaver of a young girl at the Santa Clara Convent in Cartagena (in present-day Colombia), the story then details the life of Sierva María (the young girl) who is bitten by what might be a rabid dog. Believing that rabies and demonic possession are one and the same, the Catholic clergy convinces Sierva María's father, the *marqués*, to leave her in the convent's care where her "demons" would be exorcized. Eventually the priest in charge of her exorcism, Father Cayetano, becomes captivated by her beauty and innocence and devotes many nights to visiting her cell; in its representation of impossible, ardent love, then, *Of Love* is often conveniently categorized as similar to many of García Márquez's other novels, even if it does not approximate them in popular or critical appeal.

On the one hand, *Of Love* has been criticized for many perceived flaws, including what Lon Pearson identifies as (a) a lack of profound character development, (b) an inconsistency of details within the plot, (c) various structural defects, and (d) signs of having rushed to finish the novel for a quick publication. Pearson concludes: "some may feel that the genius that produced his previous masterpieces is just not present in this volume" (182). By the same token, Edward Waters Hood suggests in a review that *Of Love* is less complex and engrossing than many of García Márquez's previous novels (n. pag.). Furthermore, John Bemrose affirms that in the case of *Of Love*, García Márquez's "demon" was "the temptation to keep too tight a grip on his story" and that this demon has consequently "gotten the better of him" (n. pag.). For Bemrose, the novel lacks the suggestive power of good writing and as such, the few positive aspects of the novel do not make up for its rigid and suffocating quality.

On the other hand, there have been favorable assessments of *Of Love*. Bell-Villada, for instance, acknowledges that "unlike most of García Márquez's previous major works, *Of Love and Other Demons* drew relatively little fanfare when it first appeared" (237). He then outlines possible reasons for this modest reception. After a thorough reading of the novel, however, he asserts the novel's place within the García Márquez pantheon: "In countless ways, *Of Love and Other Demons* is among García Márquez's more special books. An impressive range of human experience comes to life in its less than 200 pages" (257). Others (e.g., Julio Ortega 1995) have weighed in with similarly enthusiastic assessments; meanwhile, in the present volume Ignacio López-Calvo makes a surprising but powerful argument for the novel's comic elements.

While our affinities between the two novels may lie in the direction of *Chronicle*, this essay is less about that particular estimation than about a comparison between the two resulting film adaptations. By way of explanation, we shall now turn to *Of Love and Other Demons*, the film.

In contrast to the novel's mixed critical assessment, the 2010 film adaptation by Costa Rican director Hilda Hidalgo (1970–) has received positive reviews in recent, mostly web-based venues. Jennie Kermode, for example, praises Hidalgo's work:

> In adapting the work of Gabriel García Márquez, there can only be one way to go. The spirit is the narrative and only a poetic interpretation can hope to capture its substance. *Of Love And Other Demons* is such a film... It is art and folklore and scripture, a remarkable accomplishment. (n. pag.)

Similarly, Andrew Barker, Editor of *Variety* and *Rotten Tomatoes*, recognizes the film for its "impeccable" acting, "painterly" cinematography, and the "uncanny" sound design (n. pag.). He ultimately labels the film "one of the few screen adaptations worthy of the Colombian novelist's source material" (n. pag.). Surely García Márquez would have agreed with Barker since after leading a workshop where Hidalgo was a participant, it was Gabo himself who gave her the opportunity to adapt *Of Love*. According to María Lourdes Cortés and Odile Bouchet, in 2003 Hidalgo participated in the annual screenplay workshop that García Márquez offered at the International School for Cinema and Television in San Antonio de Los Baños. While there, Hidalgo asked García Márquez why no one had ever adapted *Of Love and Other Demons* to film, a novel that was, in Hidalgo's opinion, "the most adaptable" ("la más adaptable") (Cortés and Bouchet 145). Her instructor, that is, García Márquez, asked her if she might ever attempt to adapt the novel. Hidalgo, of course, replied affirmatively. In Cortés and Bouchet's account, after the initial conversation between Hidalgo and Gabo, the two never spoke again during the workshop about the possibility of bringing *Of Love* to the screen. It was not until Hidalgo returned to Havana in the days following the workshop that Gabo contacted her to map out the details of a possible adaptation (Cortés and Bouchet 145).[9] It stands to reason that he noticed something about Hidalgo and her vision for the film that compelled him to move forward with the project.

The resulting film has been widely praised and, as a result, the faith García Márquez placed in Hidalgo has been justified. Cortés, for example, has gone as far as to laud *Of Love* as "the most ambitious film in Central American cinema" (58).[10] Even so, its positive reception is both surprising and ironic in that it was adapted from one of García Márquez's less heralded novels and also that many other adaptations of Gabo's works were considered failures. What accounts for this surprising outcome?

The less heralded novel, indeed, has yielded the stronger adaptation. Is this so, however, *because* it is the less heralded – and according to some, the weaker – novel? By way of attempting to answer this question it is worth noting that Hidalgo's production offers an alternative interpretation rather than a replica of the original novel's storyline: in direct contrast with Rosi's adaptation of *Chronicle,* Hidalgo dispenses with what is on the whole a linear narrative and develops, instead, a more atmospheric tale centering on feminist issues. Such a loose adaptation may have contributed to the film's success.

There are, it is fair to state, points of continuity between the novel and film versions. Both develop, for instance (albeit to varying degrees) themes like the oppressive force of the church during colonial times, the adversarial relationship between science and superstition, and the idea of all-consuming love. On the other hand, one could argue that in some ways Hidalgo's work is missing much of the verbal charm characteristic of García Márquez's writing: Abrenuncio, for instance, is a "heretical," Jewish physician whose presence and wit are felt powerfully in the novel; in contrast, in the film his role is of a secondary order at most. The film has additional imperfections, not the least of which are a character's anachronistic use of the metric system in describing the length of Sierva María's hair (the metric system would not be introduced in France for nearly another half century). Despite these minor flaws, the power of Hidalgo's film lies in its intense focus on feminist issues. Such issues comprise a theme that is present in the novel but merely as one interesting theme among several others. Hidalgo's interpretation, meanwhile, creates a new space for reexamining the multiple ethnic, sexual, economic, and cultural forces that surround the Latin American female experience.

From the start, the film, on the one hand, prioritizes potentially overlooked female characters in a way that recalls Jean Rhys's reworking in *Wide Sargasso Sea* of Charlotte Brontë's *Jane Eyre*. On the other hand, the film also prioritizes strong female bonds, namely through Sierva María's pivotal friendship with her nanny, Dominga. In the novel, by way of contrast, Dominga is merely a blurry memory from the past, particularly as Sierva María is concerned: Dominga is described, retrospectively, as "a formidable black woman," "tall and bony," with a "clairvoyant intelligence" and a rebellious streak given that she practices both Catholicism and her Yoruba faith "at the same time, and at random" (*Of Love* 11). In other words, the novel's basic sketch of Dominga – that she coexisted with Sierva María before her (i.e., Dominga's) death, that she had a certain authority over the order of the house, and that she represented a hybridity of cultures that influence Sierva María throughout the story – is more important than a detailed rendition of her interactions with characters, which are limited in both texts. The film, by contrast, depicts the two female characters together in the opening scene. In the scene a black screen dissolves into the image of a girl sitting in the front of a canoe with her back toward the camera. The two thick braids of famous red hair falling down her back give her away – it is Sierva María. The identity of the pilot of the canoe, however, is still unknown, as the camera angle inhibits this view. Then a brief sequence of camera angle shifts occurs between Sierva María, who finally turns to face the camera, and the person – Dominga – who is rowing the canoe and leading the girl away from the darkness of the opening black screen. Suggesting a close bond between the two characters, Sierva María notably addresses Dominga as "Do'," an endearing nickname never mentioned in the novel. Subsequently, the camera centers on Dominga as if she were going to respond, but she remains quiet. Finally, Sierva María asks her in a subtitled African language if Dominga will die and asserts that she will die with her. All the while, Dominga never responds or even looks at Sierva María.

Allow us now to draw a textual comparison to the filming technique in this scene. In Isak Dinesen's (Karen Blixen) feminist story, "The Blank Page," for example, the narrator poses the question, "Who then... tells a finer tale than any of us?" Referring to the silent reflection provoked by the absence of explanation, or the "showing" rather than the "telling" of storytelling, the narrator concludes, "silence does" (np). In the same degree, the use of silence as a thought-provoking technique explains the driving force behind the mystery and suspense of the canoe scene. Dominga's lack of speech highlights the importance of her physical actions, specifically, that she paddles the canoe, or guides the voyage, literally and perhaps metaphorically, as well. This silence is the unspoken presence that will shape Sierva María's destiny while also suggesting an interpretive direction for viewers. Meanwhile, and as mentioned previously, García Márquez's text differs greatly in that its preface opens with the discovery of Sierva María's remains. In this way, the opening of the book immediately points to Sierva María's inevitable defeat – she has been conquered by the different *machista* institutions at work in the story, a depiction of their successful dominance over women. Hidalgo's film, on the other hand, commences with characters alive and well on a forward voyage, perhaps even escaping *machismo*. Thus, a contrast between the beginning of the novel and the beginning of the film suggests patriarchal dominance replaced with feminine resistance. As a result, in the film Sierva María's eventual death at the hands of the Catholic Church no longer represents her defeat: that she never gives up her African culture underscores her victory over the Catholic and colonial, male-centered institutions. Ultimately, by having had Dominga as a role model she is able to keep her will and spirit intact.

Dominga in the position of spiritual guide, therefore, not only demonstrates a rejection of *machismo*, but also a related inversion of the master-slave binary in the colonial Caribbean, to which the city of Cartagena – where *Of Love* is set – was crucial. Sierva María's tutelage under Dominga becomes an act of rebellion against the white masters' power systems in that the latter teaches the former to accept the culture of the slaves. As Dominga has control over the canoe's direction in the first scene, she also has control over the way Sierva Maria views and interacts with other cultures. After all, Sierva María represents the next generation and hence the future of the colonization project; if she decides to coexist with slaves as equals, white domination will die. This theme continues throughout the film until the end when Sierva María also rebels against her Catholic captors by refusing to release her "demon," that is, her knowledge of Africanness. In sum, although Dominga only appears at the film's opening scene, her brief presence challenges and reworks the broader theme of social hierarchies in García Márquez's source text.

The film also portrays Bernarda, Sierva María's mother, through a feminist lens. García Márquez's text portrays Bernarda as a moral lowlife who represents the degradation of Hispanic colonial society: She has abandoned herself to her appetites (sexual and otherwise) far too deeply to take much of an interest in her daughter, let alone to intervene on her behalf. The film, however, suggests – particularly in nonverbal ways – a more empathetic version of Bernarda than the novel does. We see this when Bernarda finds out about Sierva María's dog bite. When the maid tells her about the attack in the novel, Bernarda thinks only briefly about the news while bathing for the sixth time that day, but she quickly forgets about it. Moreover, the only reason she thinks about the dog bite again is because she hears the mastiffs barking and fears that they too may have rabies (García Márquez 12). In other words, the novel stresses Bernarda's selfish, profligate nature and her indifference toward her child and husband.

Without doubt, Hidalgo's film also captures many of Bernarda's undesirable characteristics; however, the movie in this particular scene hints at an explanation for Bernarda's hateful attitude. In the film, for example, when Bernarda goes out to the courtyard to look for the dog bite, instead of quickly returning to her room, she pauses as if fascinated with the sleeping image of her daughter. Indeed, it is such a fascination that Hidalgo dedicates a full thirty-six seconds to its unfolding. During this sequence, Bernarda first fixates on Sierva María's face, then approaches her slowly, stretches her hand out toward her, and finally, barely making contact, she caresses the child's hair. In addition, just before she reaches for Sierva María, a foretelling sound that suggests a mystical premonition of an ominous event begins in the background. The filmic Bernarda, then, is in many ways more passive, less developed (and, indeed, less interesting overall) than her counterpart in the novel: She spends much of her time in idleness but lacks the first Bernarda's (and García Márquez's) gift for verbal repartee. Her one redeeming quality lies in the fact that she is noticeably (even if nonverbally) better in tune with her daughter's fate.

Contrary to the novel's description, this moment in the film does not demonstrate the mother's hatred. Instead, it suggests a concern for her child and even, perhaps, her admiration. Sierva María, for example, does not belong to any of the institutional categories that women usually belonged to in colonial times – she is not a prostitute, nun, mother, wife, or a typical child of the white elite. Conversely, despite her white skin, Sierva María represents a cultural *mestizaje*, difference, and female agency, as she lives and behaves according to her own will. Bernarda's emotion toward the girl, then, demonstrates her curiosity and yearning for another way of living that diverges from the male institutions of society. In effect, the scene pardons Bernarda's decadent lifestyle that is detailed in the book. In other words, as opposed to the novel's emphasis on her failings, Hidalgo's version suggests that Bernarda is another victim, to a male-centered social system, but one who has proven incapable of fashioning a productive approach to this system.

Edwin Carvajal Córdoba oversimplifies the intellectual merit of the film by concluding that there are only "two elements that form the movie from start to finish: Sierva María's love with Father Cayetano and the superstitious and exotic elements related to rabies and the marvelous or sublime that takes place in Caribbean Colombia" (51).[11] The theme of amorous love between Father Cayetano and Sierva María remains an important focal point in the film; nevertheless, in the movie this subject has different implications. Rather than being merely a symbol of forbidden love and temptation for the all-too-human priest, Sierva María embodies feminine agency, which captivates even Cayetano, despite the fact that he is a male (and presumably chaste) character. After all, Cayetano learns that he too is imprisoned within a male-centered institution. While love, the exotic, and the marvelous are elements that visually fill many of the scenes, a concern for women's issues lies at the heart of the film: this singular focus that derives from several competing thematic issues in the novel could explain the film's appeal relative to the novel. In contrast, the novel's interests are scattered across several male-centered institutions – the church, science, and all-consuming love felt and chronicled by male thinkers, as the quotations from Garcilaso de la Vega imply. Hidalgo, meanwhile, turns this multiple focus on its head by centering on an exploration of the feminine self on the one hand and female relationships on the other. In interesting ways, then, a film by one of García Márquez's students reworks – and in some ways rebels against (albeit with his approval) – a work by a literary giant. Unlike what occurs in the novel, in the film there is no rupture between Bernarda and Sierva María or, for that matter, between Sierva María and the convent nuns, who figure prominently later in both stories. There is, instead, sympathy if not solidarity between these characters.

To conclude, it is worth pondering an observation by Robert Stam: "A 'faithful' film is seen as uncreative, but an 'unfaithful' film is a shameful betrayal of the original ... The adapter, it seems, can never win" (8). On the one hand, faithful or not, Rosi's film has generally been the recipient of the kind of opprobrium Stam describes. On the other hand, Hidalgo's film seems destined to a more favorable verdict: by avoiding a "faithful" and potentially mechanical adaptation of a novel by the Master of Aracataca, Hidalgo has also avoided falling into the same traps that have plagued other filmic adapters of García Márquez. She has done so by highlighting – and productively so – a potentially overlooked feature of the source text: an original interpretation of the novel that would not have been lost on Gabo. In doing so, Hidalgo reaffirms the social power and significance of adaptations, and interrogates conventional views on adaptations that hold these as necessarily inferior to their source. Ultimately, Hidalgo may have done the Master's text a service, inspiring some (the present authors included) to have a second look at one of his less heralded novels and to better understand the enthusiasm of its champions.

NOTES

1. The title of the English translation of *Crónica de una muerte anunciada* is *Chronicle of a Death Foretold*; we will refer to this novel as *"Chronicle."* Similarly, we will refer to *Del amor y otros demonios* (*Of Love and Other Demons*) as *"Of Love."*
2. "La cinta tiene un mérito apreciable: es cinematográfica desde la primera escena hasta la última. Pero especialmente la primera, donde una cámara muy bien manejada explica sin la ayuda de elementos distintos de las puras imágenes ..." (GGM *Obra periodística* 106; translations are our own unless otherwise indicated).
3. "ha sabido comunicarle una fuerte atmósfera de realismo, una profundidad psicológica, extraordinariamente traducidas al idioma cinematográfico" (GGM *Obra periodística* 286, emphasis added to English translation).
4. Armando Durán, "Conversaciones con Gabriel García Márquez," *Revista Nacional de Cultura,* 1968. Quoted in Vargas Llosa 73.
5. Ramírez Ospina, "García Márquez en el cine," *Kinetoscopio* 1996, pp. 91 and 89; cited in Taylor 165.
6. Julián David Correa, Lía Master, and César Augusto Montoya, "Gabriel García Márquez y el cine: los amores difíciles," *Entreextremos* 1998, pp. 32–33, cited in Taylor 166.
7. Gabo's younger brother Eligio even wrote a memoir on the making of Rosi's film: *La tercera muerte de Santiago Nasar: Crónica de la crónica* ("The Third Death of Santiago Nasar: Chronicle of a Chronicle) Mondadori, 1987.
8. See Matías Montes-Huidobro, "From Hitchcock to García Márquez: The Methodology of Suspense," in *Critical Perspectives on Gabriel García Márquez.* Eds. Bradley Shaw and Nora Vera-Godwin. Lincoln, NE: Society for Spanish and Spanish American Studies, 1986, pp. 105–23.
9. Corrales (2014) also describes Hidalgo's participation in a 2003 cinematography workshop led by García Márquez.
10. The film, in fact, is a Colombian/Costa Rican co-production.
11. "dos elementos que moldean la película de principio a fin: el amor de Sierva María con el padre Cayetano y los elementos supersticiosos y exóticos relacionados con el mal de la rabia y lo maravilloso o insólito que sucede en el caribe colombiano" (51).

WORKS CITED

Barker, Andrew. "*Review: Of Love and Other Demons.*" *Variety.* Web. Accessed Dec. 15, 2015.
Bell-Villada, Gene H. *García Márquez: The Man and His Work,* 2nd edition, revised and expanded. Chapel Hill: The University of North Carolina Press, 2010. Print.
Bemrose, John. "Of Love and Other Demons." *Maclean's* 24 July 1995: 50. *Academic OneFile.* Web. Accessed Nov. 4, 2015.
Carvajal Córdoba, Edwin. "De lo literario y lo fílmico en *Del amor y otros demonios.*" *Acta Literaria* 43 (2011): 45. Web. Accessed Dec. 15, 2015.

Castillo, Luciano. "La escuela de Gabo, un buque insignia del realismo mágico." *Kinetoscopio* 24.107 (2014): 22–26. Print.

Corrales, Gloriana. "*Del amor y otros demonios*, cheque en blanco que firmó García Márquez." *La Nación* (Costa Rica, April 20, 2014). Web. Accessed Feb. 1, 2016.

Cortés, María Lourdes and Odile Bouchet. "La luz en la pantalla: Cine centroamericano reciente / La Lumière Sur L'écran: Cinéma Centre-américain Récent." *Cinémas d'Amérique Latine* 15 (2007): 145–60. Web.

Cortés, María Lourdes. "García Márquez and Cinema: Beyond Adaptations." *ReVista: Harvard Review of Latin America* 8.3 (Fall 2009 / Winter 2010): 58–59. Print.

Cronin, Paul (Editor and interviewer). *Herzog on Herzog*. London: Faber and Faber, 2002. Print.

Dinesen, Isak. "The Blank Page." *Last Tales*. New York: Random House, 1957. 99–105. Print.

García Márquez, Gabriel. *Gabriel García Márquez, Obra periodística Vol. 2: Entre cachacos I.* Edited and with a prologue by Jacques Gilard. Barcelona: Bruguera, 1982. Print.

———. (*Crónica de una muerte anunciada*) *Chronicle of a Death Foretold*. Trans. Gregory Rabassa. New York: Alfred A. Knopf, 1982. Print.

———. (*Del amor y otros demonios*) *Of Love and Other Demons*. Trans. Edith Grossman. New York: Knopf, Distributed by Random House, 1995. Print.

Hidalgo, Hilda (Dir.). *Del amor y otros demonios*. Colombia/Costa Rica: Alicia Films, 2009. DVD.

Hood, Edward Waters. "*Del amor y otros demonios* (Book Review)." *World Literature Today* 69.2 (1995): 327–28. Web. Accessed Dec. 15, 2015.

Johnstone, Iain. "Arts (Film): A Rosi Vision of Absurdity." *Sunday Times* (London, England) June 21, 1987. *Academic OneFile*. Web. Accessed Sep. 30, 2015.

Kermode, Jennie. "Of Love and Other Demons (2009) Film Review." *Eye for Film*. Web. Accessed Dec. 15, 2015.

López-Calvo, Ignacio. "Translation, Unreliable Narrators, and the Comical Use of (Pseudo-)Magical Realism in *Of Love and Other Demons*." In *García Márquez in Retrospect*. Edited by Gene Bell-Villada. Lanham, MD: Lexington Books, 2016. Print.

Martin, Gerald. *Gabriel García Márquez: A Life*. London: Bloomsbury, 2008. Print.

Michaels, Leonard. "Murder Most Foul and Comic." *New York Times*. March 27, 1983, natl. ed.: G1. Print.

Montes-Huidobro, Matías. "From Hitchcock to García Márquez: The Methodology of Suspense," in *Critical Perspectives on Gabriel García Márquez*. Eds. Bradley Shaw and Nora Vera-Godwin. Lincoln, NE: Society for Spanish and Spanish American Studies, 1986. 105–23. Print.

"The Nobel Prize in Literature 1982: Gabriel García Márquez, Press Release." *www.nobelprize.org*. Web. Accessed Sep. 8, 2015.

Ortega, Julio. "Del amor y otras lecturas." *Cuadernos Hispanoamericanos* 539–40 (May–June 1995): 71–78. Print.

Pearson, Lon. "*Del amor y otros demonios* by Gabriel García Márquez." *Chasqui* 23.2 (1994): 180–82. Print.

Pelayo, Rubén. *Gabriel García Márquez: A Biography.* Westport, CT: Greenwood Press, 2009. Print.

Robinson, David. "Arts (Cinema): Colombian Caper." *Times* (London, England) June 18, 1987. *Academic OneFile.* Web. Accessed Sep. 30, 2015.

Rocco, Alessandro. *Gabriel García Márquez and the Cinema: Life and Works.* Tamesis. Woodbridge: 2014. Print.

Rosi, Francesco (Dir.). *Crónica de una muerte anunciada.* Italy/France/Colombia: Italmedia Films, 1987. DVD.

Stam, Robert. "Introduction: The Theory and Practice of Adaptation." *Literature and Film: A Guide to the Theory and Practice of Adaptation.* Eds. Robert Stam and Alessandra Raengo. Malden, MA: Blackwell Publishing, 2005. 1–52. Print.

Taylor, Claire. "García Márquez and Film." In *The Cambridge Companion to Gabriel García Márquez.* Ed. Philip Swanson. New York: Cambridge University Press, 2010. 160–78. Print.

Vargas Llosa, Mario. *García Márquez: Historia de un deicidio.* Barcelona: Barral Editores, 1971. Print.

Chapter 16

Remembering Broadway's *Chronicle of a Death Foretold*

Zhanna Gurvich

In spring of 1994, as I was beginning my career as a set designer in New York City, I was asked to come see a workshop production of a new musical directed and choreographed by the renowned, Argentine-born director and choreographer, Graciela Daniele. It was based on Gabriel Garcia Marquez's short novel, *Chronicle of a Death Foretold*. I had read some of García Marquez's work before, of which I was a big fan, but I had never read this particular text. I decided to let the performance surprise me. What I saw in the Lincoln Center rehearsal studio was a beautiful ballet with a minimal narration that told the haunting story of a group of people unable to escape a fate that they all contribute to but that none of them want. Even in rehearsal clothes and at a bare dance studio, the piece was electric. I went home and immediately read the book.

The story centers around a wedding. A wealthy foreigner, Bayardo San Román, comes to a small village looking for a bride. He settles on a young woman named Ángela Vicario whose family is not terribly affluent. She agrees to marry him to help her family's finances. In the middle of the wedding night, however, Bayardo returns her because, as it turns out, she is not a virgin. Now Ángela's brothers find it imperative to restore their sister's honor by killing the man who has deflowered her. They beat her in order to find out the culprit until she gives them a name. She names Santiago Nasar, her brothers' best friend, even though it is not clear from the book that he is, in fact, the guilty party. The brothers have very little enthusiasm for this killing and try very hard to get caught or somehow be stopped before they can go through with it, but circumstances conspire against them. The authority figures in the village who have the power to stop the pair are all too drunk from the night's festivities or distracted by the bishop's impending visit to notice the brother's efforts. In the end the twins find themselves face to face with

232 Zhanna Gurvich

Santiago with knives in hand and kill him with multiple stabs. The novel is nonlinear and begins with a reference to the final murder. It then proceeds to chronicle the recollections of the various participants and witnesses who can't believe that they did not manage to prevent a tragedy that they all should have seen coming.

Soon after seeing the workshop, I was asked by set designer, Chris Barrecca to work with him as Associate Set Designer to bring the musical to Broadway. The challenge was to bring to the show the imagery of the story and its sense of place, without overloading it with production values that could drain the energy out of what was a very successful, simple performance piece. We focused on what was crucial to the story. There were a wedding, a flurry of preparations, a bishop's visit, a family crisis and a murder. There were also the ever-present narrator and the recollections of the villagers who realize in retrospect how predictable and avoidable the whole situation had been.

We began the show with a white scrim with a black shadow of a man painted on it. A scrim is a type of theatrical drapery that can appear opaque when lit from the front but vanishes entirely as front light is removed and objects behind it are illuminated. This transfer from opacity to transparency is called "bleeding through." It was an excellent device for this narrative of hidden truths and meanings. Readers will see a maquette representation of the scrim in figures 16.1 and 16.2. As the instrumental overture wrapped up, the

Figure 16.1 Scale model set up for top show with the scrim lit from the front.

narrator stepped in front of the scrim and into the giant shadow. He began to explain that there had never been a death more foretold. We bled through the scrim to the scene of the death (starting at the end as the book does), with all the villagers gathered around the covered body lying in front of the oversized front door of the dead man's house. Once the scrim went up, we had rewound to the happy, carefree day before the wedding and the crisis that set off the murder.

We created a surround that was essentially a bare stage so that Graciela Daniele's beautiful choreography could proceed unimpeded, as it had in the workshop. We built a giant wall with various apertures that contained hidden doors and windows to represent the different locations in the story allowing us to move between them fluidly. A quirky, puppet window fluttered and twirled like a cheerful butterfly—a powerful image in the represented story —from one hidden aperture to another to take us into the homes of the characters. Then we populated this world with danceable furniture units so that we could follow the characters' memories into the butcher shop or the cantina without interrupting the narrative of the dance.

One of the central images in García Márquez's novel is that of birds. The victim's mother talks about a dream that Santiago, the doomed protagonist, had told her on the morning of the wedding, of trees and birds. She interprets the birds as a favorable sign and will realize only later that she should have focused on the trees as harbingers of doom. As we began designing the surround for the show, García Márquez's birds pursued us as well. Our original idea for the set was to draw upon Latin American cultural imagery. Brightly colored walls and giant murals came to mind as we researched

Figure 16.2   Scale model after the opening scene has "bled through" the scrim.

the area. In a quick paste-together project to throw a painted wall into the set model, we found that we had, quite by accident, created the shape of the bird with the collaged pieces. We decided to emphasize it and weave the bird symbol into the painting of the set. As seen in figure 16.3, at the center of the back wall and mirrored onto the floor is an impression of a bird. It is painted into the overall abstract design that recalls sky as well as peeling, painted plaster. One does not notice it from the outset but as the mother began to speak of the dream, the bird would come into sharper focus. After that it faded in and out of the audience's consciousness as its relevance waxed and waned throughout the production.

The accident that brought the bird to our attention was a fluke of the technology available to us at the time. Ten years earlier I would have simply painted a back wall image and no surprising bird shape would have emanated from my paint brush. Today, working entirely from digital imagery, I would have smoothed and blended any inconsistencies in the image and the back wall would have been the uniform texture that it was intended to be. It turned out to be truly serendipitous timing. Our first-rate lighting designers, Jules Fisher and Beverly Emmons, helped emphasize the image by creating a pattern that matched the drawing to place in front of the light focused on the center of the wall. When doom loomed largest, the light intensified and the bird glowed brighter.

The other important images from the verbal novel that had to be incorporated into the visual world were the front door, the mother's hammock, the kitchen table, the butcher's shop, the wedding feast, the bishop's parade and the bright, white, bloodless sheet that sets off the trouble. There is also the

Figure 16.3   Scale model of set with bird imagery visible on the back wall and floor.

enigmatic later scene between the middle aged Ángela and Bayardo many years after the main events of the drama, and placed in the penultimate chapter in the book. We chose to end the theatrical production with this scene.

The front door of the Nasar family's luxurious home is where Santiago is brutally murdered as revenge for a dishonor he had not committed and was not aware of. The killers, Pablo and Pedro Vacario, the disgraced bride's twin brothers and Santiago's best friends, don't want to go through with avenging their sister's honor. They keep trying to get out of it in some way. Everywhere they go that night, they loudly announce their plans to kill Santiago in the hopes that someone will stop them, yet nobody takes them seriously. As demonstrated in figure 16.4, we made the door enormous so that it loomed over the hapless duo, the place where they must go to do their duty and also the place that they most want to avoid, if only they could.

The hammock, hung on a giant piece of driftwood, evoked the mother's bedroom where the prescient dream is misinterpreted. Readers can see the model and drawing of the hammock in figures 16.5 and 16.6. This branch gave us the second image in the dream, the favorable one of trees that the mother mistakenly focuses on. Ensconcing her in the luxuriously undulating form of the driftwood limb helped underscore the tragic mistake she makes.

The kitchen of the Vicario home is where the preparations for the wedding feast take place and it was done as a lighthearted, comic number with a cook attempting to cut up rabbits on a literally dancing kitchen table. The scene was a pas de deux between the cook and the mischievous piece of furniture. She chases after it with a butcher's knife, trying to prepare the feast, and it

Figure 16.4 Scale model with enormous door pulled out of the wall and dancing kitchen table.

alternately runs away and charges her like a bull besieging a matador. This is all observed with much amusement by the other members of the household. As the cook chased the uncooperative table off the stage, Ángela and her bridesmaids danced on, stretching between them a long piece of white cloth with a large red rose painted in the center. The bridesmaids jokingly

Figure 16.5   Scale model with branch hammock.

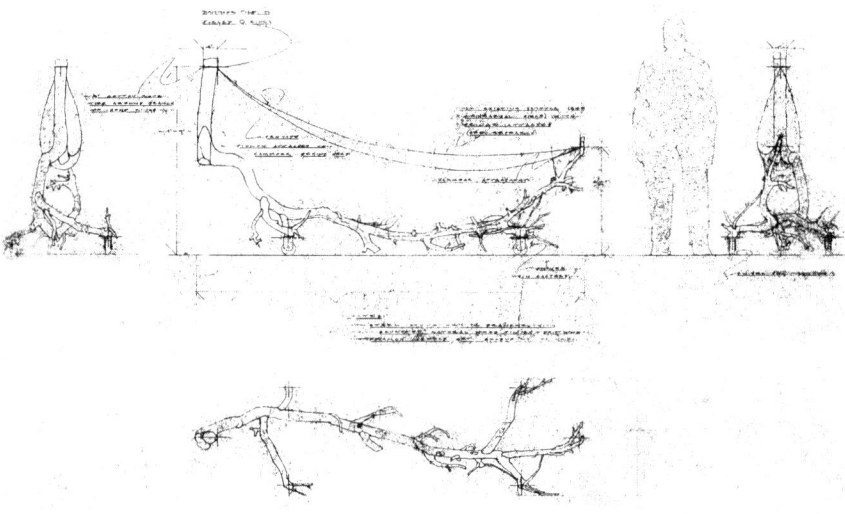

Figure 16.6   Hand drafted drawing of branch hammock.

wrapped Angela, the bride, in the cloth as she danced, bawdily rubbing her bottom against the painted rose that is meant to represent her virginal blood. The wedding feast crowned the celebratory mood. A giant dance number followed that involved the entire village carrying trays full of food and candles that they set along the front of the stage and left flickering as we moved into the fateful wedding night (see figure 16.7). The cheerful anticipation that pervades the village prior to the wedding would serve as a poignant counterpoint to the ensuing tragedy.

For the Vicario family butcher shop we flew down a long row of nasty looking meat hooks hung from strong, chunky chains (see figure 16.8). They swayed ominously above the heads of the twins as the pair sharpened their knives in preparation for the killing. Sparks flew from the pedal-powered whetstone, casting a red glow on the sharp hooks and onto the tortured and determined faces of the unfortunate brothers.

We followed García Márquez's nonlinear approach and jumped around in the narrative, filling the story out. The wedding celebrations faded and the music slowed. As the players were returning to their quiet lives, Bayardo dragged out the miserable Ángela, wrapped in a pure white sheet with no rose in the center. She was left alone in a chair with her livid brothers who proceeded to beat her until she coughed up a name. As the novel states, "… she nailed it to the wall with her well-aimed dart, like a butterfly with no will

Figure 16.7 Scale model set up for wedding celebration with giant banquet table and trays of candles along the stage edge.

Figure 16.8 Scale model set up for Vicar Brothers butcher shop with meathooks and grinding stone.

whose sentence has always been written. 'Santiago Nasar,'" (García Márquez, 47) This revelation sets off the sleepless, tortured night during which Pedro and Pablo unenthusiastically prepare to do their duty. They sharpen their knives and go drinking at the cantina where they proclaim to everyone present that they intend to kill Santiago in order to avenge their sister's honor. Rather than arresting or restraining them, the police officer takes their knives away and sends them home to sleep it off. It does not occur to him, or to any of the other authority figures whose statements we hear speak throughout the novel, that they may have access to many more knives. Father Amador, the village priest, is concerned by the brothers' revelations but is too distracted by the impending visit of the bishop to follow through on his concerns. The narrator reports to us, "'The truth is I didn't know what to do,' [Father Amador] told me. 'My first thought was that it wasn't any business of mine but something for the civil authorities, but then I made up my mind to say something in passing to Plácida Linero.' Yet when he crossed the square, he'd forgotten completely. 'You have to understand,' he told me, 'that the bishop was coming that day.'" (García Márquez, 70)

The bishop's parade presented us with a surprising challenge. We needed a Virgin Mary to be carried across the stage on a litter. Our properties director, Sheri Adler, was sure she could easily find one in New York amongs all of the vendors who cater to the San Gennaro festival parades held in the fall.

However, we soon realized that the Italian version of the Mary, which is the Fatima image, is not appropriate to a Colombian celebration where the Virgin of Guadalupe would be used. That Mary, alas, was not as readily available, and we found that we would need to have one specially made. The fabricator who built our sets, Roger Gray of Centerline studios, had an interesting proposition. He offered to split the cost of the Mary with the production if he could keep it after the show closed and then present it to his wife, who was a fan of the Guadalupe Madonna. The producers happily jumped on that deal as it was no small cost to custom-fabricate a sculpture. However, when the producers asked the artisan, Nino Novellino of Costume Armor, for the bill, he was reluctant to charge for a religious icon. The exquisite Mary that he created became a gift from Nino to the production and then to Roger's wife. It is a story that always serves to remind me what a special production this was.

As the parade passed in front of the Nasar home, we returned to the much-foretold death and the opening image. The carefree Santiago stepped obliviously out of his enormous front door on the morning after his long night of revelry. He cheerfully greeted his good friends. The unbelieving look on his face as they proceeded to disembowel him broadcast to everyone that he had no idea what could have brought on such a fate.

In the novel, in a flash-forward chapter that precedes the actual murder, Ángela discusses the long past events with her cousin, the narrator, who continues to press her about the veracity of her story. She does not explain why she condemned Santiago Nasar to death and, in spite of her continued insistence, we do not know if she was telling the truth when she did so. Instead she tells the chronicler that after Bayardo returned her on their wedding night, she suddenly found that she was in love with him. Meanwhile he, deeply wounded by her betrayal and humiliated by the events, left town immediately after the wedding, so she began writing letters to him. After twenty-three years and thousands of letters, Bayardo returns to her. He has never opened the letters but the sheer volume and longevity of the endeavor is sufficient penance. She has won him back.

For the musical, we refashioned this subplot into the final scene. We used it as an opportunity to get a look into Ángela's mind as, in the musical, we had not really heard her voice up until now. We concluded the play with a pile of letters fluttering down from above over the two aging lovers. This beautiful final image took a great deal of trial and error to achieve. Dropping hundreds of actual letters from a height of a hundred feet would have been a loud, chaotic event. Sealed envelopes would have bounced on the floor with an audible din, flown into the orchestra pit and the audience, and likely caused some minor injury as they made contact with the actors' faces and bodies. On the other hand, envelope-sized pieces of white, rice paper looked more like snow than letters and did not convey the mood we were trying to achieve. At one point we tried using pink, feminine envelopes but they simply looked like rose petals. We needed to create shapes that were, unmistakably, unopened envelopes but that would flutter over the actors and come to rest on the floor in a contained pile rather than drop all over the theater in a noisy jumble. We ran rehearsal after rehearsal with differently weighted, shaped and colored letters until we stumbled upon the right combination. If I recall correctly, we folded cream-colored rice paper into envelopes to give them some heft but still allowed them to float gently down and we dipped them in tea to give them a slightly aged look. The moment was magical.

It was a stunning production. After a prolonged search for just the right theater, we would settle on the Plymouth on 45th Street. The theater hunt was the biggest challenge for me personally. I redrafted the plans five times as we tried the Vivian Beaumont, the Helen Hayes, the Longacre, the Broadhurst and finally the Plymouth. Several times a week I made the two-hour drive to Centerline Studios, in the town of Cornwall, in upstate New York, to hand them new drawings and withdraw any obsolete ones. The theaters varied vastly in size and I was terrified that the wrong set would be delivered and would not fit. In the end all the hard work paid off. The supremely talented and energetic cast starred Tonya Pinkins (Clotilde), Saundra Santiago (Ángela), George de la Peña (Santiago), Alexandre Proia (Bayardo San Román), Gregory Mitchell and Luis Pérez (the Vicario twins). As musical theater performers they were drawn from a variety of backgrounds. George, Alex, Gregory and Luis were best known as dancers on the New York theater scene. Tonya Pinkins did the bulk of the solo singing. Whatever their primary background, all the performers danced, sang and acted their hearts out. They were a pleasure to watch every day of the two-month-long technical rehearsal and preview process. Toni Leslie James's fabulous costumes brought the characters and the period to life while allowing the dancers to move effortlessly through their challenging choreography. Graciela Daniele, a superb choreographer and director who has led numerous Broadway productions, was the driving force behind getting this musical made. She loved the story and had really wanted to bring it to the stage.

García Márquez was not, at first, overly enthusiastic about allowing anyone to adapt his narratives to other media. He had allowed a film adaptation of *Chronicle of a Death Foretold* a few years earlier and it had not gone well. It took Graciela Daniele a long time to convince the author to let her try her hand at adapting her favorite story. He finally agreed to a limited run. Graciela brought in lyricist and writer, Jim Lewis, and went right to work on the script. Bob Telson and Michael John LaChiusa composed the sometimes jubilant, sometimes haunting music that weaved together the events as they unfolded.

As a limited run, the musical version of *Chronicle of a Death Foretold* was not a huge commercial success though it did receive some excellent reviews. Vincent Canby of *The New York Times* wrote that *Chronicle* was "a frequently stunning show that is less a conventional musical adaptation than a performance piece." (Canby, www.nytimes.com) Brad Leithauser of *Time* magazine wrote that the musical was "smart, surrealistic and visually entrancing." (Leithauser, www.time.com) Our *Chronicle of a Death Foretold* was nominated for multiple Tony Awards including Best Musical, Best Book of a Musical, and Best Choreography. It also received six Drama Desk Award nominations. The year 1995 was a highly competitive one on Broadway: Jonathan Larson's wildly popular musical, *Rent*, took most of the top awards that season. Once García Márquez had relented and allowed the adaptation, he was gracious enough to allow the creative team to proceed with the production unimpeded. Seeing him for only a brief moment on opening night, I never got a chance to ask him how he felt about the final product but I am thrilled to have been a part of the creative process.

WORKS CITED

García Márquez, Gabriel. *Chronicle of a Death Foretold*. Trans. Gregory Rabassa. New York: Knopf, 1983.

Canby, Vincent. "Theatre Review: Chronicle of a Death Foretold; A Tale of Fate And Magic, Told Back to Front," *www.nytimes.com*, June 16, 1995.

Leithauser, Brad. "Theatre: Perchance To Dream," *www.time.com*, July 10, 1995.

Permissions

Excerpts from THE GENERAL IN HIS LABYRINTH by Gabriel García Márquez, translation copyright © 1990 by Gabriel García Márquez Used by permission of Alfred A. Knopf, an imprint of the Knopf Doubleday Publishing Group, a division of Penguin Randomhouse LLC. All Rights Reserved.

Excerpts from CHRONICLE OF A DEATH FORETOLD by Gabriel García Márquez, translated by Gregory Rabassa, translation copyright © 1982 by Alfred A. Knopf, an imprint of the Knopf Doubleday Publishing Group, a division of Penguin Randomhouse LLC. All Rights Reserved.

Excerpts from LIVING TO TELL THE TALE by Gabriel García Márquez, translation copyright © 2003 by Gabriel García Márquez Used by permission of Alfred A. Knopf, an imprint of the Knopf Doubleday Publishing Group, a division of Penguin Randomhouse LLC. All Rights Reserved.

Excerpts from STRANGE PILGRIMS: TWELVE STORIES by Gabriel García Márquez, translation copyright © 1993 by Gabriel García Márquez Used by permission of Alfred A. Knopf, an imprint of the Knopf Doubleday Publishing Group, a division of Penguin Randomhouse LLC. All Rights Reserved.

Excerpts from OF LOVE AND OTHER DEMONS by Gabriel García Márquez, translation copyright © 1995 by Gabriel García Márquez Used by permission of Alfred A. Knopf, an imprint of the Knopf Doubleday Publishing Group, a division of Penguin Randomhouse LLC. All Rights Reserved.

Bell-Villada, Gene H. "Names and Narrative Pattern in *One Hundred Years of Solitude*." *Latin American Literary Review* 9, no. 18 (1981): 37–46.

Gabriel García Márquez and the Heirs to the Estate of Gabriel García Márquez. For permission to quote from the following works of the author.

García Márquez, Gabriel. *Cien años de soledad*. Buenos Aires: Editorial Sudamericana, 1967.

———. *Crónica de una muerte anunciada*. Buenos Aires: Editorial Sudamericana, 1981.

———. *Del amor y otros demonios*. Barcelona: Mondadori, 1994.

——. *Doce cuentos peregrinos*. Buenos Aires: Editorial Sudamericana, 1992.
——. *El general en su laberinto*. Buenos Aires: Editorial Sudamericana, 1989.
——. *Chronicle of a Death Foretold*. Trans. Gregory Rabassa. New York: Alfred A. Knopf, 1982.
——. *The General in His Labyrinth*. Trans. Edith Grossman. New York: Alfred A. Knopf, 1990.
——. *Living to Tell the Tale*. Trans. Edith Grossman. New York: Alfred A. Knopf, 2003.
——. *Of Love and Other Demons*. Trans. Edith Grossman. New York: A. Knopf, 1995.
——. *One Hundred Years of Solitude*. Trans. Gregory Rabassa. New Harper & Row, 1970
Numerous ecerpts [totaling 2194 words] from ONE HUNDRED YEARS OF SOLITUDE by GABRIEL GARCIA MARQUEZ, translated by Gregory Rabassa. English translation copyright © 1970 Harper & Row Publishers, Inc. Reprinted by permission of HarperCollins Publishers.
Pantoja, Oscar et al. *Gabo: Memorias de una vida mágica*. Bogotá: R + N (Rey Naranjo Editores). Solamente con "®Rey Naranjo Editores, Colombia." Image reprinted with permission in Héctor Hoyos, "Rediscovering Ice: García Márquez, Aira, and Vallejo on Chilling Memories."
Olivia, Vázquez-Medina. "Reading Illness in Gabriel García Márquez's *Of Love and Other Demons*." *Modern Language Review* 108.1 (2013): 162–179. Reprinted with permission.

Index

Note: Page references for figures are italicized and locators followed by 'n' indicate notes section

Adler, Sheri, 238
The Adventures of Miguel Littín, Clandestine in Chile, 30n29
Aira, César, xxii, 103–10, 112
Alatriste, Gustavo, 214
Alcocer, Rudyard, xxv, 184–85, 213–27
Alcoff, Linda Martín, 165, 166
Alcoriza, Luis, 214
Alencar, José, 14
Allende, Isabel, 4, 6, 8, 22, 130, 186
Allende, Salvador, xix, 22, 30, 31
Amado, Jorge, 17n3
Amaya Uriana, Ángel, 55–56
Amis, Martin, 13
Anaya, Rudolfo, 9
Anderson-Imbert, Enrique, 107
Aracataca, xxvi, 46, 61n4, 206
Araya, Enrique, 184
Arcimboldo, 29
Arellano, Jerónimo, 103
Arenas, Reinaldo, 82
Areta Marigó, Gema, 92
Arguedas, José María, 5
Arlt, Roberto, 8
Asturias, Miguel Ángel, 8, 184

Augé, Marc, xxiii, 149
Austin, Texas, 104
The Autumn of the Patriarch, xiv–xv, 3, 14, 22, 25, 29, 30, 31, 33, 56, 185

Bakhtin, Mikhail, 53, 209
Balcellsm Carmen, 143n8
Baldo (comic strip), xvii–xviii
Baldwin, James, xxi
"Balthazar's Marvelous Afternoon," 131
Balzac, Honoré de, 14
Barker, Andrew, 222
Barnes, Julian, 13
Barranquilla, xvii, 50, 51
"Barranquilla Group," 50, 215
Barrecca, Chris, 232
Barth, John, 11
Barthes, Roland, xxiii, 150–51, 160n33
Batista, Fulgencio, 22, 23
Bayly, Jaime, 184
Bay of Pigs invasion, 23, 35n5
BBC, 142
Beat movement, 36n11
Beatles, 109
Beckett, Samuel, 4

245

Bell-Villada, Gene H., xx–xxi, 11, 67–76, 80, 82, 94, 123, 131, 137, 183, 187, 210n4, 217, 218, 221
Bemrose, John, 221
Bergquist, Charles, 52
Bhaba, Homi, 36n15
"Big Mama's Funeral," 24, 25, 34, 36nn11–12, 49, 56, 57, 107, 129, 131, 133–34, 139
Birdman (film), xvi
Birns, Nicholas, xviii–xix
Birri, Fernando, 139
Black Cat Books, 12
Blanco Aguinaga, Carlos, 68
"The Blank Page," 224
Blixen, Karen, 224
Bloom, Harold, 15
Blue Lobster, The, 144n11, 215
Boccelli, Andrea, 87
Bolaño, Roberto, 6, 106, 184
Boldrewood, Rolf, 14
Bolívar, Simón, xxii–xxiii, 3, 117–26
Bombal, María Luisa, 130
"Bon Voyage, Mr. President," 130, 132, 134, 135, 136, 140–41, 148–49, 150, 151, 152, 155–56, 159n18, 160n25
Boom of the Latin American Novel, The, xviii, 5–6, 129
Borges, Jorge Luis, xxii, 4, 8, 75, 87, 130, 131, 132, 136, 184
Bouchet, Odile, 222
Bowers, Maggie Ann, 183
Boyle, T. Coraghessan, 11
Brennan, Timothy, 14
British Petroleum (BP), xvii
Brockmeier, Jens, 197–98
Brontë, Charlotte, 223
Bryant, Kobe, 12
Bryce Echenique, Alfredo, 184
Bucheli, Marco, 22
Buell, Lawrence, 99, 100
Buendía Tours, xvii
Buñuel, Luis, 23
Burke, Edmund, 30

Burton, Robert, 165, 176
Bush, President George H. W., xvi
Bush, President George W., xvi
Bushnell, David, 35n4

Cabrera Infante, Guillermo, 21, 23, 35n5, 184
Calle, 13, 6
Camacho Delgado, José, 94
Camayd-Freixas, Erik, 183
Camus, Albert, 199
Canby, Vincent, 241
Caraballo, Francisco, 55
Caracci, Annibale, 86
Caravaggio, xxi, 86–87
Carey, Peter, 4, 13
Caribbean region, 17n3, 49, 51–52
carnivalesque, 53
Carpentier, Alejo, 5, 8, 9, 53, 104, 106, 130, 184
Carreras González, Olga, 90
Carrington, Leonora, 23
Cartagena de Indias, 50, 56, 61n4
Carter, Pres. Jimmy, 35n3
Carvajal Córdoba, Edwin, 226
Castellanos, Rosario, 184
Castillo, Luciano, 213
Castillo Armas, Col. Carlos, 22
Castro, Fidel, xxii, 7, 15, 23, 35n7, 121
Centerline Studios, 239, 240
Centro Sperimentale di Cinema, 5, 133, 214
Cepeda Samudio, Álvaro, 50
Cervantes, Miguel de, xix, xx, 42–45, 47, 183
Césaire, Aimé, 144n12
Chabon, Michael, 10
Chapman, Peter, 22
Chatwin, Bruce, 217
Chávez, César, 36n11
Cheever, John, 131
Chekhov, Anton, xviii, 131
Chénétier, Marc, 11
Chicago Bulls, 12
Chile, xix, 7, 15, 22, 30, 31

China, xvii
Chronicle of a Death Foretold (Broadway musical), xxvi, 231–41, *232, 233, 234, 235, 236, 237, 238*
Chronicle of a Death Foretold (film version), xxv, 213, 219–20, 222, 226, 240
Chronicle of a Death Foretold (novel), xv, xix, xx, xxiv–xxv, 4, 6, 22, 30, 31, 57–58, 109, 198, 199, 200–5, 208, 217, 218, 231–35, 238, 239
Cisneros, Sandra, 9
climate change, 37n24
Clinton, President Bill, xvi, 7, 12, 17n3, 110
CNN, 15
Cobra Verde (film), 217
cockfighting, 95–96
Colombia, 49–61
Colosio, Luis Donaldo, 110
Comencini, Luigi, 214
conceptismo, 144n14
Cooper, James Fenimore, 14
Coover, Robert, xvi
Correa, Julián David, 216
Cortázar, Julio, 5, 6, 35n7, 75, 86, 129, 130, 184
Cortés, María Lourdes, 222
Costume Armor, 239
"Crack" Movement, 104
Cuando era feliz e indocumentado, 133
Cuba, xxii, 8, 21, 22, 24, 25, 25, 31, 36n11–12, 38n32, 110, 111–12, 124, 215, 222
Curiel, Rosa, 89

Damas, Léon, 144n12
Daniele, Graciela, xxvi, 231, 232, 240
Dante, 26, 32, 33
Danticat, Edwidge, xviii, 9
Daydí-Tolson, Santiago, 161n36
"Death Constant beyond Love," 29, 130, 139–40

decolonization, xix, 22
De Castro, Juan E., xviii–xix, 3–17
Deep Ecology philosophy, xxi, 90, 93, 95, 97
de la Peña, George, 240
de la Vega, Garcilaso, 177
Devall, Bill, 90
"Dialogue with the Mirror," 138
Diatriba de amor contra un hombre sentado, xxiv, 130
Díaz, Antolín, 52
Díaz, Leandro, 57
Dickens, Charles, xv
Dictionary of Latin American Authors, xxii, 103, 106–10
Dinesen, Isak. *See* "Blixen, Karen"
Disney, Walt, xiii
Doane, Mary Ann, 171
Doctorow, E. L., 7
Dogtology, xvii
Dohman, Barbara, 73
Donoso, José, 184
Don Quixote, 42–45
Dostoevsky, Fyodor, xviii, xix, 42–45
Drama Desk Award, 241
Duffin, Jacalyn, 176
Du Lauren, André, 176
Duque Naranjo, Lisandro, 215
Duvalier dictatorship, 22

Eco, Umberto, 12
Ecocriticism, xxi
Egan, Susanna, 203
Eisenhower, Gen. Dwight, 35n3
Elbow, Gary S., 91
Eliot, T. S., 4
En agosto nos vemos, 197
Eréndira (book), xv, 35n2, 129, 139
"Eréndira" (story), 130, 137, 140
Escobar, Pablo, 106
Escuela Internacional de Cine y Televisión (Cuba), 5, 222
Espectador, El, 199, 201, 210n3, 214
Esquivel, Laura, 9, 130, 186
Europe, 148, 149, 155, 157

"Eva Is Inside Her Cat," 138
Eyes of a Blue Dog (book), xix, 129, 138
"Eyes of a Blue Dog" (story), 130, 138

Fals Borda, Orlando, 51–52
Fanon, Frantz, 171
Faris, Wendy, 183
The Farming of Bones, 9
Faulkner, William, xix–xx, 6, 10, 11, 17n3, 43–48, 138
Feinberg, Leonard, 98, 100n1
Fernández, Gastón J., 32
Fernández, Macedonio, 184
Fernández de Lizardi, Joaquín, 184
Ferré, Rosario, 130, 184
Fielding, Henry, xix, 42
Fischler, Claude, xxiii, 151
Fishburn, Evelyn, 53
Flaubert, Gustave, xix, 42
Fletcher, John, 42
Flores, William, xxi
Fox, Nicols, 97
Fragrance of Guava, 56
France, 22, 35n3, 133, 223
Franco, Gen. Francisco, 30
Franco, Jean, 110
Freud, Sigmund, xxiii, 22, 136, 149
Fuenmayor, Alfonso, 50
Fuentes, Carlos, xvi, xx, 5, 6, 7, 8, 17n3, 47, 129, 130
Fuguet, Alberto, xxii, 6, 15, 104, 110
Fundación Nuevo Cine Lationamericano, 215

Gadamer, Hans-Georg, xxiii, 165, 168, 177–78
Gámbaro, Griselda, 184
gamecocks, 95, 96
García, Cristina, xvi, 9
García, Eligio, 227n7
García, Luisa Santiaga de, 26
García Barcha, Rodrigo, 24
García Márquez, Gabriel, *passim*:
 autobiography in, xxiv–xxv, 141, 142, 197–210;

blacklisted by U.S. immigration, xvi;
death in, xix, xxiii, 21–38, 129, 135–36, 139–41;
death of, xxvi;
early years, 5–6, 23–26, 107, 214–15;
environmentalism in, 89–100;
Faulkner's influence on, xi, xix, 10, 12, 17n3, 23, 41, 43, 46, 47, 48, 107, 139;
film and, 144n11, 213–15;
food in, xxiii, 147–58;
humor of, xiv, xxiv, 53, 183–92;
illness in, 166–80;
journalism of, 199, 201, 206;
legacy of, xv–xviii;
mamagallismo in, 49–51, 53, 56–60;
Nobel Prize, 4, 16, 26, 31, 46, 107;
political views of, xvi, 7, 15, 21–38, 111–12, 124;
presence in United States, xv–xvi, 7, 8, 9–13, 130;
presence in world, xxii, xviii–xix, 6–7, 13–14, 130;
range of, xxiii–xv;
reaction against, 103–13;
romantic love in, xiv–xv;
view of reality of, xiii; women in, 72, 73, 79–82;
work in other fields, xxiv, 197–229
The General in His Labyrinth, xxii–xxiii, 3, 14, 35n9, 46, 110, 117–25, 166
Genette, Gérard, 199–200
Geneva, 214
Gentile Chimento, Cayetano, 31
Ghana, 13
"The Ghosts of August," 132, 135–36, 147, 152, 156
Gilard, Jacques, 50
Gilman, Sander, 168, 171
Ginsburg, Allen, 36n11
Girard, René, 178n2
Gogol, Nikolai, xii
The Golden Cockerel (film), 5

Gómez, Juan Vicente, xiii
Góngora, Luis de, 44
González, Aníbal, 175, 177
González Echevarría, Roberto, 130
González Iñárritu, Alejandro, xvi
Goya, Francisco de, 140
Gramsci, Antonio, 71
Gray, Roger, 239
Great Britain, 13, 22, 35n3
Grossman, Edith, xix–xx, 120, 183, 187, 188, 190
Guajira (telenovela), 55
Guajiros. *See* "Wayúu people"
Guatemala, 22, 31, 35n3
Guerra, Tonino, 219
Guevara, Ernesto "Che," 23
Guillén, Nicolás, 23
Gurvich, Zhanna, xxvi, 231–41

"*había de*" ("was to," verbal phrase), 119–22, 124
Hall, Rodney, 13
Hamsun, Knut, 6
"The Handsomest Drowned Man in the World," 139
Haraway, Donna, 104
Harry Ransom Center, Univ. of Texas, 103
Harss, Luis, 73
Hart, Stephen, 24, 35n2, 36n12
Harvard College, xvi
Hawthorne, Nathaniel, 180n26
Hay Festival of Literature and the Arts, 56, 61n5
Heidi (film), 214
Hemingway, Ernest, 44
Herzog, Werner, 217, 220
Hidalgo, Hilda, xxv–xxvi, 221
Highet, Gilbert, 100n1
Hitchcock, Alfred, 219
Hodgart, Matthew, 100n1
Hodgins, Jack, 13
Homer, 87
Hood, Edward Waters, 221
How I Became a Nun, xxii, 103, 104–5

Hoyos, Héctor, xxi–xxii, 103–14
Hugo, Victor, xv
Hume, David, 22
Husserl, Edmund, 165

India, 14
In Evil Hour, 24, 107
Innocent VIII, Pope, 170
"I Only Came to Use the Phone," 132, 149
Iowa Writers' Workshop, 15
Isaac, Alberto, 216
Isaacs, Jorge, 8
"I Sell My Dreams," 132, 135, 136, 149, 150, 152, 153–54, 158n10, 159n17, 161n34
Iwasaki, Fernando, 184
Israel, 35n3

Jackson, David, 7
Jackson, Phil, xix, 12
James, Toni Leslie, 240
Janes, Regina, xix
Johnson, Dane, 7
Johnstone, Iain, 219
Jordan, Michael, 12
Joset, Jacques, 29, 113n4
Joyce, James, xix, 4, 41, 131

Kafka, Franz, xii, 4, 6, 136, 138
Kakutani, Michiko, 131–32
Kawabata Yasunari, 33, 129
Kennedy, William, xvi, 4, 11
Kermode, Jennie, 221
Kerouac, Jack, 36n11
Khan, Soha Ali, 6
Klein, Melanie, 160n26
Koeppel, Dan, 22
Kurniawan, Eka, 6, 9

LaChiusa, Michael John, 240
Larson, Jonathan, 241
"Last Voyage of the Ghost Ship," 130, 139
Latin America, 47, 140
Latour, Bruno, 103

Leaf Storm, xix, 3–4, 24, 107
Lee Ja-Ram, 142
Legrand, Catherine C., 22
Leithauser, Brad, 241
Lejeune, Philippe, 158n9, 197
Lethem, Jonathan, 11
Lewis, Jim, 240
"Light Is Like Water," 104, 113n3, 132–33, 141
Lincoln Center, 231
Littín, Miguel, 30
Living to Tell the Tale, xvi, xxiv–xxv, 34, 38n30, 41–42, 46, 197, 198, 202, 206–10
Lizardi, Joaquín Fernández de, 184
Lolita, xv
López, Rosa Matilde, 55
López-Calvo, Ignacio, xxiv, 183–94, 221
López-Cabrales, María del Mar, xxi, 77–88
López Pumarejo, Pres. Alfonso, 52
Los Angeles Lakers, 12
Love in the Time of Cholera, xv, xix, 3, 4, 6, 10, 14, 23–24, 32–33, 56–57, 109–10, 141, 166
Lugones, Leopoldo, 6

Macondo, xvii
Magdalena River, 51, 53, 118
magical realism, xii–xii, xxiv, 6, 9–14, 53, 54, 124, 139, 184, 185–87
malleus maleficarum, 170
El Malpensante, 110
mamagallismo, xx, 49–61
Mann, Thomas, 75, 131
Manzoni, Alessandro, 14
Marechal, Leopoldo, 184
"Maria dos Prazeres," 130, 132, 134, 136–37, 149, 150, 152, 156, 158n10
Márquez, Col. Nicolás, 54
Martin, Gerald, 22, 31, 35n9, 36n14, 38n3, 107, 117, 121, 122, 142, 143n31, 199, 207, 209, 215

Masiello, Francine, 105, 106
Matouk, Antonio, 214
McAleer, Paul, 184, 192
McDonald's, 15
McEwan, Ian, 6
McOndo movement, xix, xxii, 15, 104
Melville, Herman, 10
Memories of My Melancholy Whores, xvi, xix, 33–34, 59–60
Mena, Lucila, 22, 27, 35n2
Mendoza, Plinio Apuleio, 56
"The Metamorphosis," xii
Mexico, 110, 214
Ministry of Tourism (Colombia), 6–7
Miracle in Rome (film), 215
"Miss Forbes's Summer of Happiness," 130, 131, 132, 133–34, 136, 141, 150, 152, 154–55, 158n10
Mitchell, Gregory, 240
modernism, 4–5
"Monologue of Isabel Watching It Rain in Macondo," 130, 131, 138–39
Monroe Doctrine, 25
Montaner Ferrer, María Eulalia, 80–81
"Montiel's Widow," 24
Moreiras, Albert, 183
Moreno Blanco, Juan, 53
Morrison, Toni, xvi, xviii, 7, 9, 10, 12, 47, 130
Mo Yan, 9, 130
Murnane, Gerald, 14
Murphy, Patrick, 10
Mutis, Álvaro, 119

"Nabo: The Black Man Who Made the Angels Wait," 26
Nabokov, Vladimir, xxi
Nasser, Gamal Abdel, 35n3
Natali, Marcos P., 35n11, 36n15
Nava, Gregory, xvi
National Front (Colombia), 23, 35n4, 51
negritude, 144n12
Neruda, Pablo, 30, 135, 136, 150, 153–54
Neue Sachlichkeit, 104

New York City, 21, 23, 214, 231
The New York Times, 8, 218, 241
News of a Kidnapping, 106
Nietzsche, Friedrich, 165
Nigeria, 13
Nichols, John, xvi
Nicolitti, Andrea, 170
Novellino, Nino, 239
Nobel Acceptance Speech, 16, 31, 37n24, 46
Nobel Prize, 4, 107
No One Writes to the Colonel, 24, 58–59
"No Thieves in This Town," xxv, 23, 216
El Norte, (film), xvi
Novellino, Nino, 239

Oates, Joyce Carol, xix, 11
Obama, Pres. Barack, 7
Obeso, Candelario, 52
Ochoa, Ana María, 106
Ochoa, Gen. Arnaldo, 121
Odría, Gen. Manuel, 22
Of Love and Other Demons (film version), xxv–xxvi, 213, 221–26
Of Love and Other Demons, xv, xxiii–xxiv, 166–81, 220–21;
  humor in, 183–92;
  illness in, 166–81, 214
Okri, Ben, 9
Olsen, Margaret, 171
One Hundred Years of Solitude, xi, xii–xiii, 3, 4, 8, 9, 10, 12, 15–16, 21, 22, 23, 25, 26–29, 30, 31, 33, 103, 104, 105, 106, 112, 119, 124, 131, 139, 142, 166, 185, 188, 199, 205, 208, 215, 216;
  banana company in, xiv, xvii, xxi, 22, 90, 92;
  death in, 26–29, 33, 37n22, 54;
  ecological consciousness in, 89–100;
  humor of, xiv, 98;
  impact of, xii, xvi–xviii, 4, 8–14, 78;
  magic of, xii, xiii, 5, 188;
  names in, xx–xxi, 67–76;
  origins of, xi–xii;
  range of, xii–xiv;
  publishing history of, xii, 103, 112
  strike scenes in, xiii, 22, 91, 98, 99;
  technology in, 97–98, 99;
  Úrsula (character), 72–73; 78–79, 80, 81, 82–86, 87;
  women in, xxi, 73–75, 78–81
"One of These Days," 35–36n10
Onetti, Juan Carlos, 8
Oprah's Book Club, xvii, 4, 67
Ortega, Julio, 178n3, 221
Ortiz, Fernando, 104
Osborn, Haley, xxv, 213–27
Otero Silva, Miguel, 135
"The Other Side of Death," 23, 24, 131

Padilla, Heberto, 7, 35n7
Pakistan, 14
palabrero institution, 54–56
Palacios, Marco, 35n4
Palencia-Roth, Michael, 172, 180n30
Paley, Grace, 131
Pamuk, Orhan, 14
Panama Canal, 35n3
Pansori music, 142
Pantoja, Oscar, *108*
paratopia, 148, 149–50
Paris, 23, 142, 148, 214
Pearson, Lon, 221
Peden, Margaret Sayers, 79
Pelayo, Rubén, xxiii, 129–44
Perdasdefogu (Sardinia), 142
Pérez, Luis, 240
Pérez, René, 6
Pérez Galdós, Benito, 14
Pérez Jiménez, Gen. Marcos, 22, 23, 56
Perón, Gen. Juan, 22, 23
Piar, Gen. Manuel, 121
Picasso, Pablo, 138
Pickup on South Street, 214
Piñera, Virgilio, 112
Pinkins, Tonya, 240
Pinochet, Gen. Augusto, 7, 30

Plato, 175
Plutarch, 176, 178n1
Plymouth Theater, 240
Polit, Gabriela, 113n2
Polonius, 123
Poniatowska, Elena, 130
Popular Liberation Army (EPL), 55–56
Portugal, 29
Prensa Latina, 21, 23, 142
Prieto, Genaro, 184
Proia, Alexandre, 240
Proust, Marcel, xxv, 104, 118, 207–8
pütchipü'ü institution, xx, 54

Quevedo, Francisco de, 29, 139–40, 183
Quijano, Aníbal, 190
Quintana, María Concepción ("Tachia"), 142
Quiroga, Horacio, 8
Quiroga, Osvaldo, 143n3

Rabelais, François, 139
Ramírez, Victoria, 10
Ramírez Ospina, 213, 216
Real Academia Espanola, 107, 109
lo real maravilloso, 104, 106
Reati, Fernando, 186
refritos, 199, 208, 209, 210n3
Rent (musical), 241
Restrepo, Laura, 6
Rhys, Jean, 223
Rico, Franciso, 203
Rivera, José Eustasio, 104
Roa Bastos, Augusto, 8
Robinson, David, 219
Rocco, Alessandro, 213, 214, 219
Rodó, José Enrique, 122
Rodrigo, Joaquín, 87
Rodrigue, George, 138
Rodríguez Imbriaco, Laura Verónica, 81
Rodríguez-Monegal, Emir, xxii, 67, 75
Rodríguez-Vergara, Isabel, 53, 81
Rojas, Fernando de, 183
Rojas Pinilla, Gen. Gustavo, 22, 23, 50
Rome, 86, 133, 214

Rómulo Gallegos Prize, 113
Roncagliolo, Santiago, 16–17n2
Rosenblatt, Ángel, 49
Roses, Lorraine Elena, 79
Rosi, Francesco, xxv, xxvi, 219, 220, 222, 226
Roth, Philip, 11
Rotten Tomatoes, 222
Rubens, Peter Paul, 140
Rulfo, Juan, 5, 8, 23, 25, 130
Rushdie, Salman, xviii, 4, 9, 14, 42, 130
Russian Formalism, 159n13

Sábato, Ernesto, 184
"Saint, The," 132, 133, 134, 147, 149, 155, 215
Salazar, Pres. António de Oliveira, 29, 30
Saldívar, Dasso, 24, 50, 91, 107
Samper, Ernesto, 49, 53
Sandinistas, 30
San Gennaro festival, 238
Santa Maria del Popolo (church), 86
Santos, President Juan Manuel, 6
Santiago, Saundra, 240
Santos Chocano, José, 6
Saramago, José, xxi, 32, 84, 87
Scahill, Andrew, 179n19
Scorza, Manuel, 9
Scott, Sir Walter, xix, 14
"Sea of Lost Time, The," 27
Segura Bonnett, Camilla, 197
Senghor, Léopold, 144n12
Sepúlveda, Luis, 6
Sessions, George, 90
"Seventeen Poisoned Englishmen," 132, 134, 141, 149
Shadbolt, Maurice, 13
Shakespeare, William, xxi, 42
Shaw, Donald, xxi
Shaw, George Bernard, xxi
Shelton, Thomas, 41
Shklovsky, Viktor, 75
"Short Course in Ideological Orientation for García Márquez," 110–12

Sienkiewicz, Henryk, 14
Sims, Robert L., xxiv–xxv, 197–211
Singleton, Rebecca, 11
Siskind, Mariano, 35n2
Skármeta, Antonio, 184
"Sleeping Beauty and the Airplane," 129, 131, 132, 151–52, 155
Smith, Sidonie, 197, 198
Smollett, Tobias, 42
socialist realism, 5
Socrates, 123
"Someone Has Been Disarranging These Roses," 24
Somoza dictatorship, xiii, 22, 30
Sosa Blanco, Jesús, 24, 36n14
Soviet Union, 32
Spenser, Edmund, 21, 35n1
Stam, Robert, 226
Stavans, Ilan, 36n11, 36n14
Steinbeck, John, 17n3
Sterne, Laurence, xix, 42
Stiles, Kent B., 8
Strange Pilgrims, xxiii, 34, 129, 130–41, 147–62;
"Prologue" to, 147, 149–50, 160n26
Stroessner, Gen. Alfredo, 22
Styron, William, xvi, 17n3
Sucre (Colombian town), 202
Suez Canal crisis, 35n3
Swanson, Philip, 22, 27
Swift, Graham, 13
Swift, Jonathan, 29
Switzerland, 133

Taylor, Claire, 213, 214, 216
Telson, Bob, 240
tenebrismo, 87
Theroux, Paul, 11
"The Third Resignation," 23, 24, 27, 129
Tiananmen Square, xvii
Time magazine, 241
Times (London), 219
Tolkien, J. R. R., xiii
Tolstoy, Leo, xviii
Tony Awards, 241

Torres, Camilo, 24–25, 26
"The Trail of Your Blood in the Snow," 131, 132, 134, 141–42, 158n10, 160n33
"Tramontana," 131, 132, 134
Trujillo, Rafael, xiii, 22
Tsujii Nobuyuki, 87
"Tuesday Siesta," 24, 131, 139
Twain, Mark, xix, 17n3, 42

Ulysses, xix
the uncanny, 149, 159n11
United States, 124
Updike, John, 11

Valenzuela, Luisa, 184
Valerio-Holguín, Fernando, xxiii, 147–63
Vallejo, Fernando, xxii, 103, 110–13, 113n4
vallenato music, 52, 53, 57
Valverde Barrenechea, Leticia, 81
Vanden Berghe, Kristine, 148
Variety, 222
Vargas, Germán, 50
Vargas Llosa, Mario, xx, 5, 7, 8, 16–17n2, 47, 61n4, 129, 184
Vásquez, Juan Gabriel, 6, 15–16, 17n4–5
Vázquez-Medina, Olivia, xxiii–xxiv, 165–82
Vega, Ana Lydia, 184
Velasco, Marcela, xx
Venezuela, xiii, 22, 23, 49, 54, 56
"A Very Old Man with Enormous Wings," 134, 139
The Viceroy of Ouidah, 217
Videla, Gen. Jorge, 7
Villada, Carmen, xvi
la violencia, 22, 50
Viramontes, Helena María, 9
Virgin of Guadalupe, 239
Volkening, Ernesto, 79
Volonté, Gian Maria, 220
Volpi, Jorge, 104, 124

Walcott, Derek, 17n3
Watson, Julia, 197, 198
Wayúu people, xx, 53–56
Weinstein, Harvey, 17n3
Wells, Marion, 178
West Point, 43
Whitehead, Alfred North, 103
Wiedlin, Jane, 12
Wilkinson, Lise, 170
Williams, Raymond L., 89, 91, 183
"The Woman Who Arrived at Six o'Clock," 138–39

Wonder, Stevie, 87
Wood, Michael, xxii–xxiii, 117–26
Wood, Robin, 179n19
Woolf, Virginia, 104, 138
Wright, Richard, xxi

Yúdice, George, xxiii, 151

Zambra, Alejandro, 6
Zamora, Lois Parkinson, 183
Zapata Olivella, Manuel, 50
Zavattini, Cesare, 144n11

About the Contributors

Rudyard Alcocer holds a doctorate in Comparative Literature from the University of Iowa (2002). He is the Forrest & Patsy Shumway Chair of Excellence in Romance Languages and associate professor of Latin American literature and culture in the Department of Modern Foreign Languages and Literatures at the University of Tennessee, Knoxville. The author of *Time Travel in the Latin American & Caribbean Imagination: Re-reading History* (Palgrave Macmillan 2011) and of *Narrative Mutations: Discourses of Heredity and Caribbean Literature* (Routledge 2005), he is currently co-editing a volume about cinema and slavery. Alcocer also directs the University of Tennessee's Humanities Center Faculty Seminar on Latin America & the Caribbean.

Gene H. Bell-Villada, Professor of Romance Languages at Williams College, is the author and editor of twelve books. Among the latter are *Borges and His Fiction: A Guide to His Mind and Art* (1981; 2nd edition, 2000) and *García Márquez: The Man and His Work* (1990; 2nd edition, 2010; translated into Spanish and Turkish). His wide-ranging study, *Art for Art's Sake & Literary Life: How Politics & Markets Helped Shape the Ideology & Culture of Aestheticism, 1790–1990* (1996) was a finalist for the 1997 National Book Critics Circle Award and was translated into Serbian and Chinese. Besides two volumes of fiction, *The Carlos Chadwick Mystery* (1990) and *The Pianist Who Liked Ayn Rand: A Novella & 13 Stories*, he has also published a memoir, *Overseas American: Growing Up Gringo in the Tropics* (2005). His latest book is *On Nabokov, Ayn Rand and the Libertarian Mind: What the Russian-American Odd Pair Can Tell Us about Some Values, Myths and Manias Widely Held Most Dear* (2013).

About the Contributors

Nicholas Birns (Ph.D., English, New York University, 1992) is Associate Professor of English at the College of New Rochelle. He is the author of *Contemporary Australian Literature: A World Not Yet Dead* (University of Sydney Press, 2015), *Barbarian Memory: The Legacy of Early Medieval History in Early Modern Literature* (Palgrave, 2013), and *Theory After Theory: An Intellectual History of Literary Theory from 1950 to the Early Twenty-First Century* (Broadview, 2010).

Juan De Castro received his Ph.D. in Comparative Literature from the University of Southern California in 1998. An Associate Professor at Eugene Lang College, The New School for Liberal Arts, he is the author of *Mestizo Nations: Culture, Race, and Conformity in Latin American Literature* (2002), *The Spaces of Latin American Literature: Tradition, Globalization and Cultural Production* (2008), and *Mario Vargas Llosa: Public Intellectual in Neoliberal Latin America* (2013).

William Flores is Associate Professor of Spanish and Coordinator of the Spanish Program at California Baptist University (CBU). He received his Ph.D. in Spanish from the University of California, Riverside in 2010. His current work includes peer-reviewed publications in *Hispania* and elsewhere, and a book, *Ecocrítica poscolonial y literatura moderna latinoamericana*, recently published by the University Press of the Universidad Nacional de San Marcos and subsequently presented at the Lima International Book Fair (FIL-Lima 2015) and the 2015 Guadalajara Book Fair. In his book, Flores examines the environmental crisis and its impact on the life and literature of Latin America by exploring the ecological consciousness manifested in the thought of authors such as José Vasconcelos, Mario Vargas Llosa, Rómulo Gallegos, Gabriel García Márquez, and Rodrigo Fresán. His fields of scholarly research include twentieth- and twenty-first-century Hispanic literature, theory of satire, narratology, and postcolonial theory, particularly ecocritical approaches to the study of modern Latin American narratives.

Edith Grossman, a translator, critic, and occasional teacher of literature in Spanish, received her PhD in Spanish American Literature from New York University in 1972 and is an Adjunct Professor at Columbia. She has been the recipient of numerous awards and honors including Fulbright, Woodrow Wilson, and Guggenheim Fellowships, the PEN Ralph Manheim Medal for Translation, an Award in Literature from the American Academy of Arts and Letters, the Queen Sofía Translation Prize (Spasin), the Independent Foreign Fiction Prize, and induction into the American Academy of Arts and Sciences. Grossman has made available in English the poetry, fiction, and nonfiction of major Latin American writers, including Gabriel García Márquez, Carlos Fuentes, Mario

Vargas Llosa, Álvaro Mutis, Mayra Montero, and Sor Juana Inés de la Cruz. Peninsular works that she has translated include *Don Quixote*, by Miguel de Cervantes, novels by Julián Ríos, Carmen Laforet, Carlos Rojas, and Antonio Muñoz Molina, poetry of the sixteenth and seventeenth centuries, *The Solitudes* of Luis de Góngora, and the *Exemplary Novels* of Miguel de Cervantes. Among her own scholarly works is *Why Translation Matters* (Yale, 2010). She lives in Manhattan and has two sons, both of whom are musicians.

Zhanna Gurvich is an award-winning designer and painter who has designed for theater, dance, opera, and film at the Brooklyn Academy of Music, the Joyce Theatre, Chautauqua Opera, and the Juilliard Theatre. Ms. Gurvich's favorite designs include *Radiance* for Axial Theatre Co., *Hello and Goodbye* for Rattlestick Theatre, *Ladies in Retirement and Chaos Theory* for Pulse Ensemble Theatre, *The Most Dangerous Room* in *the House* for The Susan Marshall Dance Company, *Tears for Violetta and Tierra de Nadie* for Ballet Hispanico, *The Seagull, Man and Superman*, and *Three Sisters* for Juilliard, *In the Air* and *La Llorona* for Stageplays Theatre, *Hansel and Gretel* for Chautauqua Opera, *Ping Pong Diplomacy*, *Havana Bourgeoisie*, and *Billboard* for Reverie Productions, and *Luck* for Epic Rep. Ms. Gurvich received an HOLA Award for Outstanding Set Design for her work on *La Llorona*. She has painted for Scenic Art Studios, Goodspeed Opera House, Virginia Opera, Dallas Theatre Center, Mannes Opera, and The Mint Theatre Company, including critically acclaimed portraits for *Mary Broome* and a mural for *Black Snow*. Ms Gurvich is a member of United Scenic Artists Local 829 and holds a B.F.A. in Studio Art from Clark University, as well as an M.F.A. in Stage Design from Southern Methodist University, with a concentration in scenery and lighting design.

Héctor Hoyos is Assistant Professor of Latin American literature at Stanford University. He holds a Ph.D. in Romance Studies from Cornell University (2008), and degrees in Philosophy and Literature from Universidad de los Andes in Bogotá. His book, *Beyond Bolaño: The Global Latin American Novel* (Columbia University Press, 2015), examines post-1989 Latin American novels of globalization and their relevance for world literature. He is the co-editor of the special issue "Theories of the Contemporary in South America" for *Revista de Estudios Hispánicos*. His second monograph project, for which he has received an Alexander von Humboldt Fellowship, develops the concept of as well as on the author's representation of traumatic violence and on the politics of his late short stories.

Regina Janes (Ph.D. in English, Harvard) is a Professor of English at Skidmore College. Her various published books and articles include

Gabriel García Márquez: Revolutions in Wonderland (1981) and *One Hundred Years of Solitude: Modes of Reading* (1991). Transculturation as a way of integrating new and historical strands of materialism in the study of narrative. He has published scholarly articles on comparative biographies of García Márquez,

María del Mar López-Cabrales (Ph.D, University of Pittsburgh) teaches Latin American and Spanish culture and literature at Colorado State University. Her research focuses on the intersection of literature and culture in Latin America and Spain. She is particularly interested in women's writing as a "space" in which women create social discourses and communicate with each other. Her publications include numerous scholarly articles and author interviews, as well as six books, among them *Marinera en tierra adentro: Edicion anotada de la obra narrativa de Pilar Paz Pasamar*, (Ediciones Alcor, 2013), and a book of interviews with contemporary Cuban female writers titled *Arenas Calidas en alta mar: Entrevistas a escritoras contemporáneas en Cuba* (Cuarto Propio, Chile, 2006). Professor López-Cabrales served a two-year term as Secretary of the Asociación Internacional de Literatura y Cultura Femenina Hispánica. She has served as a visiting professor at the Universidad de Cadiz, Spain (Summer, 1999) and on the Semester at Sea program (Fall, 2000).

Ignacio López-Calvo is Professor of Latin American literature at the University of California, Merced. He received his Ph.D. in Romance Languages from the University of Georgia in 1997. He is the author of seven books on Latin American and US Latino literature and culture: *Dragons in the Land of the Condor: Tusán Literature and Knowledge in Peru* (Arizona UP, 2014); *The Affinity of the Eye: Writing Nikkei in Peru* (U of Arizona P, 2013); *Latino Los Angeles in Film and Fiction: The Cultural Production of Social Anxiety* (U of Arizona P, 2011); *Imaging the Chinese in Cuban Literature and Culture* (UP of Florida, 2007); *"God and Trujillo:" Literary and Cultural Representations of the Dominican Dictator* (UP of Florida, 2005); *Religión y militarismo en la obra de Marcos Aguinis 1963–2000* (Mellen, 2002); *Written in Exile. Chilean Fiction from 1973-Present* (Routledge, 2001). He has also edited the books *Roberto Bolaño, a Less Distant Star—Critical Essays* (Palgrave, 2015), *Magical Realism* (*Critical Insights*) (Salem Press, 2014), *Peripheral Transmodernities: South-to-South Dialogues between the Luso-Hispanic World and "the Orient"* (Cambridge Scholars Publishing, 2012), *Alternative Orientalisms in Latin America and Beyond* (Cambridge Scholars Publishing, 2007) and *One World Periphery Reads the Other: Knowing the "Oriental" in the Americas and the Iberian Peninsula* (Cambridge Scholars Publishing, 2009), and co-edited *Caminos para la paz: literatura israelí y árabe en castellano* (2008). He is the co-executive director of the academic journal *Transmodernity: Journal of Peripheral Cultural Production of the Luso-Hispanic World*.

Haley Osborn is a doctoral student of the Spanish Program in the Modern Foreign Language and Literature Department at the University of Tennessee, as well as Editor-in-Chief of the department's graduate student e-journal, *Vernacular: New Connections in Language, Literature, & Culture*. She holds a Master's degree from Loyola University in Chicago and a Bachelor's degree from Hanover College. Osborn is also an instructor of undergraduate Spanish courses. Her areas of study include the relationships between written and filmic narratives, and representations of slavery.

Rubén Pelayo (Ph.D. University of California, Riverside, 1993) is a Professor of Spanish and twentieth-century Latin American Literature at Southern Connecticut State University, New Haven, CT. He is the author of two volumes and several essays on the life and works of García Márquez, *Gabriel García Márquez: A Biography* (2009) and *Gabriel García Márquez: A Critical Companion* (2001), both books published by Greenwood Press. In an effort to bring Gabriel García Márquez to a worldwide audience, Professor Pelayo has four mass-media publications through YouTube, one of which is:

"The Myth of *One Hundred Years of Solitude*." http://www.youtube.com/watch?v=OR9GAskpPnE
You Tube. You Tube, LLC, 20 December, 2013.

Robert L. Sims is a Professor of Spanish in the School of World Studies at Virginia Commonwealth University. He was a Fulbright scholar in 1987, 1988 and 1992 in Colombia, where he taught courses in Latin American literature. He served in the Peace Corps between 1968–1970. Dr. Sims received his Ph.D. in French with a minor in Spanish at the University of Wisconsin-Madison in 1973. He wrote his dissertation on "The Use of Myth in Claude Simon and Gabriel García Márquez." He has also published *The First García Márquez: A Study of His Journalistic Writing from 1948 to 1955*. He specializes in the theory and function of myth in modern literature, modern French and Latin American novels; the structuralist study of literary texts; dialogic criticism; reader-response criticism; narratology; deconstruction and the critical writings of Mikhail Bakhtin; the image of Christopher Columbus in modern literature; the New Latin American Historical Novel; and postmodernism/postcolonialism in Latin America.

Fernando Valerio-Holguín (Ph.D., Hispanic Literatures, Tulane, 1994) is a Professor of Spanish at Colorado State University, where he was awarded the

John N. Stern Distinguished Professorship 2013–2014. He has been invited to lecture and read poetry at venues such as the Smithsonian Institution, the University of Newcastle-Upon-Tyne, University of Warsaw, University of Antwerp, and the Library of Congress, among others. He has published sixteen books and more than one hundred articles, poems, and short stories. He teaches courses on Latin American popular music, cinema, gastronomy, literature and culture.

Olivia Vázquez-Medina (D. Phil, Oxford, 2009) a native of Mexico, was a Lecturer in Hispanic Studies at Royal Holloway, University of London, from 2010–2015. She was appointed Associate Professor and Fellow in Spanish at Wadham College, Oxford, in 2015. Her scholarly publications include the volume *Cuerpo, historia y textualidad en Augusto Roa Bastos, Fernando del Paso y Gabriel García Márquez* (Iberoamericana-Vervuert, 2013).

Marcela Velasco received her Ph.D. in Political Science from Boston University in 2007. She teaches Comparative Politics and Latin American politics at Colorado State University. Her most recent researches on Colombian social movements and on ethnic politics have appeared in *Latin American Research Review*, *Local Environment*, *Handbook of Social Movements across Latin America* (the latter an edited book, Springer), *Bulletin of Latin American Research*, and *Journal of Environment and Development*.

Michael Wood (PhD in French, Cambridge, 1961) is Professor Emeritus of English and Comparative Literature at Princeton University. Among his relevant books are *García Márquez: One Hundred Years of Solitude* (Cambridge UP, 1990; reprinted 2008); *Children of Silence: On contemporary fiction* (Columbia UP, 1998, paperback, 1999; Chinese translation, Rye Field Publications, 2001); *The Road to Delphi: the Life and Afterlife of Oracles* (Farrar, Straus, 2003; Chatto & Windus, 2004; Picador paperback, 2004; Pimlico paperback, 2005); and *Literature and the Taste of Knowledge* (Cambridge UP, 2005).